Caesars and Apostles

Emil Bock

Caesars and Apostles

Hellenism, Rome and Judaism

Floris Books

Translated by Maria St Goar

First published in German in 1937 under the title
Cäsaren und Apostel by Verlag Urachhaus
First published in English in 1998 by Floris Books

Revised edition © 1978 Verlag Urachhaus, Stuttgart
This translation © Floris Books, Edinburgh 1998

British Library CIP Data available

ISBN 0-86315-273-2

Printed in Great Britain
by Biddles Ltd, Guildford

Contents

Figures Around Christ

Acknowledgments

Unless otherwise stated, all quotations of the New Testament are from the translation by Jon Madsen (Floris Books), and from the Old Testament are from the Revised Standard Version. Where the context requires it, Bock's own translation has been translated into English. These are marked *B* after the reference.

Preface to the New Edition
1958

Since the first edition of this book was published two decades ago in 1938, a number of upheavals and catastrophes have befallen humanity. Archaeological investigation has made significant discoveries, revealing evidence of decisive historical developments. And part of the discoveries made in this way, namely the discoveries at the Dead Sea, directly concern several chapters in this book. It would therefore seem obvious to take the new developments into account in a new edition and thus bring the book into line with current research.

However, with regard to the discoveries by the Dead Sea, the author finds himself in a unique position. More than twenty years ago, based on extensive descriptions by Rudolf Steiner, I portrayed in this book, particularly in the chapters dealing with the Essene Order and their great teacher and reformer, Jeshu ben Pandira, the very facts and circumstances that sceptical modern science stumbled upon and became seriously interested in only due to the discoveries by the Dead Sea.

In a series of articles that I wrote in the years 1950 to 1957, in which I followed the Dead Sea discoveries step by step, I could repeatedly point out that tangible confirmation had now been found for what I had presented as early as 1937. Furthermore, I indicated that the key for the riddles and questions which had been raised anew could be found in my descriptions. I may therefore count on the reader's understanding if I allow the book to be published again unchanged in its original version despite or rather precisely because of these 'sensational discoveries.' Moreover, the reader will understand if, in addition to the writings of Philo of Alexandria that deal with the Essenes, I include as a second Appendix the main contents of my articles; articles in which I accompanied the ongoing discoveries and brought them into context with my book.*

* See Appendix Two

Preface to the First Edition
1937

The word, *Urchristentum,* ('primal' or 'early' Christianity), expresses more than merely an historical concept. It evokes a loftier sense of home in all those who are inwardly connected with Christianity and arouses in them a loving reverence, a spiritual homesickness.

When Goethe spoke of the *Urpflanze,* the 'primal plant,' he did not refer to an external visible form which once stood at the beginning of all plant evolution. He referred to something spiritual, endowed with being. His vision beheld the presence of this primal plant in each individual plant as a constantly alive, creative element that brings forth from itself the single structures of leaf or blossom.

As the primal plant relates to the individual plants, so early Christianity, even though it is itself a phase of development, relates to the particular historical developments and figures of Christendom. The events referred to in the Gospels and Acts of the Apostles, and even the main episodes of the first three Christian centuries, are more than merely earthly history. In them, super-earthly events enter earthly ones; in them, heaven becomes earth and God, man. More clearly than during any other period of time, the celestial sphere of primal archetypes is discernible behind earthly, visible phenomena. A super-earthly, superhuman essence of spirit and being incarnates. And it is therefore only justifiable to describe the history of early Christianity if at least we attempt to make the one mighty spiritual totality visible through all the particular events. To the extent that this attempt succeeds, the outlines of a countenance begin to take on form within all that happens and we realize that early Christianity is itself a living entity, a divine and human 'genius.' And finally, if we focus our attention on this being's cosmic redeeming act of love, we can even say: early Christianity is a human entity.

Early Christianity is not accorded its due significance in the conventional historical descriptions of Christianity's development. Above all, the books produced by Protestant theology that deal with Christian ecclesiastic history nearly always begin with a description of the post-apostolic age, following brief prefatory remarks about the period of Jesus and the Apostles. These works expand in their rich detail only at the point where early Christianity is already at an end.

The superficial reason for this is the delimitation of theological discipline. The ecclesiastic historian leaves the life of Jesus as well as the destinies and deeds of the Apostles, including those of Paul, to his colleagues whose task is the exploration of the New Testament. To us, on the other hand, it seems that a fundamental defect comes to the fore here due to the institution of theological specialization. The separation of the Gospel teachings from the historical presentation of Christendom leads to the point where the events described in the New Testament are not taken seriously as history, let alone as the very heart and turning point of the whole of humanity's history. Moreover, this leads to ecclesiastic history being deprived of its spiritual foundation and source.

The history of early Christianity and the way in which it unfolded during the first three centuries of our Christian era, particularly the outer and inner course of the first fifty years, offer the basic key for the history of Christendom. It was then that the essential reality of destiny became clearly manifest, a reality which, in later times, became obscured. It should be an innermost motivation for any description of the history of Christendom to lift the spell cast over this reality and cause it to arise again in renewed form. The attempt, the first installment of which is presented with this volume, consciously negates the separation between the theology of the New Testament and that of ecclesiastical history. The events that are reported by the books of the New Testament will be described as an organic and, at the same time, absolutely central part of world history. And we shall dare to depict the historical development of Christendom and of more recent humanity in general by focusing on the essential evolution of early Christianity and, lastly, on the progressing destinies of the Christ being itself.

This attempt at an organic view of history, a view that tries not to move from single facts to the whole but from the whole to details, makes it necessary to relinquish yet another division that is customary in conventional theology. The more the Christ event is recognized as the centre point of all human history, the more impossible it becomes to separate the history of pre-Christian humanity from that of Christendom. We need an inner linkage between what theology separates as study of the Old Testament and religious history on the one side and, on the other, research of the New Testament and ecclesiastical history. The conventional trend of specialization leads to the point where the Old Testament and the history of the remaining pre-Christian religions lose their inner meaning, while Christianity, on the other hand, is reduced to one religion among many. It is not fully understood why Christian theologians should still place such value on the study of the Old Testament. We lose sight of the inner universality and all-inclusive humanness of Christianity. Only when we learn to recognize the pre-Christian history of Christianity and the destinies of the Christ being prior to his human incarnation in Old Testament history as well as in the other religious persuasions of humanity, only then will the pre-Christian era regain its deeper meaning and Christianity its absoluteness. But then it is necessary organically to connect Christian with pre-Christian history and the events described in the New Testament with those in the Old Testament. Early Christianity can either be comprehended based on an all-encompassing, universal totality, or not at all.

This is the reason why the present books concerning early Christianity are so closely related to the three previously published volumes concerning the Old Testament and the spiritual history of humanity.* Care is taken, as far as this is possible, to make the description of early Christianity comprehensible on its own as well. But it must be emphasized that the descriptions are based on the preceding events more than the specific references to the past would lead one to think. The endeavour to place early Christianity as organically as possible into its surroundings,

---

* *Caesars and Apostles; The Childhood of Jesus; The Three Years* and *Saint Paul* as well as *The Apocalypse* concern the New Testament, while *Genesis; Moses* and *Kings and Prophets,* cover the Old Testament period.

surroundings that had come into existence much earlier, and to show how Christianity emerges out of the history of the last pre-Christian centuries, brought about what follows. To begin with, therefore, the more recent preceding history of Greece, Hellenism, Rome and the Jews had to be outlined in the first half of this volume, which continues with the books of the Old Testament and prepares for the presentation of early Christianity.

More than my now completed description of Old Testament history, the attempt to depict early Christianity historically is a risk with regard to method. Here, where so many supersensory facts, so much of inner soul trials and blessings entered earthly events and 'made history' in the fundamental sense of the word, a historical presentation is bound to fail that feels obliged, 'for the sake of being scientific,' to doubt and negate anything that cannot be proved by way of reference to documents and sources. The most essential aspects of early Christianity, above all of the original event described in the Gospel, elude any external tradition and proof. One really has to denote the Christ Event, including what the disciples experienced after Good Friday, as 'the Mystery of Golgotha.' The mysteries of the ancient world, a world about to end, were intentionally kept secret. This Mystery remains secret because it is only disclosed to a human being to the extent of that person's inner sense of delicate comprehension. To speak as a historian of this 'Mystery of Golgotha' and the mystery elements of the environment into which it entered, necessitates reverence as well as daring. The sceptical agnostic way of thinking on the part of the 'scientific view of history' comes to concise expression in the following sentences:

> I must call attention in particular to the fragmentary
> character of all our historical knowledge, even the most
> complete. The wealth of information, the facts of past
> history are in content and extent far beyond the range of
> our knowledge, even if we were to pursue our
> investigations for thousands of years. Of the vast canvas
> of history only a fraction is accessible to the historian,
> only what is transmitted through source material and
> records. Everything else that was not transmitted or could

not be transmitted because it belongs to the inner life of the spirit, to the hidden sphere of the psychic life, to the inner domain of the personal life, cannot be 'known' by the historian; it can only be surmised. And this 'surmise,' however careful and conscientious our investigation, will at all times be marred by defects and subjective factors. When Goethe says: 'No created spirit can penetrate into the heart of nature,' we must add to this dictum, 'And nobody can penetrate into the inner recesses of history.'[1]

Rudolf Steiner, who quotes this passage, emphatically points out how this resignation with regard to the attainment of knowledge by scientific means betrays itself here through misquoting Goethe. The lines:

No created spirit can penetrate into the heart of nature.
Fortunate are those to whom she reveals her external shell alone.

are not by Goethe. Goethe merely quotes them in order to turn angrily against them:

I have heard this refrain now for sixty years and am heartily sick of it. Nature has neither kernel nor shell, she is both at once — a unity. First test yourself and find out whether you yourself are kernel or shell.

Only a description of history that puts courage linked with reverence and thoroughness in the place of obligatory doubt and lame agnosticism can appeal to Goethe. As is nature, so, too, history is 'neither kernel nor husk, but both at once.' And more than any other history, the history of early Christendom is both kernel and husk, primal archetype and phenomenon, super-earthly and earthly history at once. To present it in such a way that, thereby, its inner truth becomes visible and is given its rightful place, is only possible when it is done with much courageous daring.

Particularly in the second half of this book, I had to increasingly distance myself from the methods of conventional theology, even at the risk of being accused of fantasy. Much may appear to the reader as unsubstantiated claims. But it should also be noted how, in instances where it was deemed necessary, the phrasing leaves many things open; moreover, I always endeavour to grasp historical reality as far as possible so that at least a picture arises of how it may have been.

It is characteristic that a large portion of the literature that deals with early Christianity and specifically the life of Jesus, literature that is certainly to be taken seriously, is cloaked in the genre of novels. For it was always felt that one was dealing here with historical realities that are disclosed more readily to artistic fantasy than to critical scientific reason. Following the spiritual view brilliantly opened up by Rudolf Steiner and his trail-blazing historical indications, I dare to make the attempt to include an element of inner artistic imagination in the research and description of early Christianity's history. Based on the experiences of my earlier work on the Gospels and moreover my depiction of Old Testament history in three volumes, I believe I can address myself to a circle of readers who are ready to follow a descriptive style which, first and foremost, has the aim of communicating views of inner relationships and totalities. This is a style that can leave open the details in both the presentation and the reader's acceptance, because it does not proceed from the detail; instead, the single detail is discovered and comprehended out of the whole.

The risk, though taken in confidence, is particularly great in the case of this first volume, because it is of a predominantly preparatory nature and really can do no more than mark off an outline on which, subsequently, to build. If a first overview is to be attained, an overview somewhat like a map, I have to impose on myself a terseness in most instances that is merely in the form of an indication, even at points where the description has to make an initially unfamiliar and strange impression. I regret that I cannot add a whole number of detailed and specialized studies to the first half of this book, for example, in reference to Jeshu ben Pandira. Such studies could substantiate what is here only briefly sketched. But this would imply writing a whole library of books rather than one volume. Though it was even more risky, I could confidently formulate the second half of the volume in this manner since, in later descriptions, the same relationships will be dealt with in detail from different starting points. In order to be able to present really detailed and intimate depictions, I plan to describe the life of Jesus in two volumes, *The Childhood of Jesus* and *The Three Years*. Moreover, a number of Christological elements that are here merely stated or even have to be presupposed will be dealt with in detail after the fact, either in the descriptions of the life of Jesus or in the book about Paul.

May the attempt undertaken in these books be a contribution in our time to the revitalization and strengthening of the original Christian spirit.

Emil Bock

The Cultural Environment

1. Greece:
The Athens of Pericles and Alexander's Expeditions

It was based on profound insight into the innermost evolutionary laws of humanity's history that Paul, in his Letter to the Galatians, could coin the sentence: 'But then, in the fullness of time, God sent his Son' (Gal.4:4).

The point in time when, through the events of Golgotha, Christianity came into this world was not an arbitrary one. The new impulse was not implanted at just any moment in time in a world grown old. First, a new world had to be born out of the womb of the old; a world still upheld by divine powers, but one caught up in decline. Humanity first had to elude the spell of the gods and begin to be culturally creative based purely on human ability. Earlier, the time had not yet been fulfilled. While the Christ impulse formed the basis of a completely new development, it did presuppose the dawn of a new phase, above all in the evolutionary stages of human consciousness. Not until humanity, having emerged out of superhuman evolution, had arrived at the human stage could that being be born on earth who, by becoming man, was to bestow on humankind, now placed in a position of completele self-reliance, the faculty of a new divine ascent.

1.1 Aftermath of the Persian Wars

Night in her maternally creative infinity abounds in miracles. We even sense this when we stand under the starry sky. When, trusting ourselves to supportive divine hands, we enter the sphere of sleep, we would be overwhelmed by the wonders of the nocturnal spiritual realm if clarity of consciousness did not then cease. And when the rising sun gives birth to the day out of the depth of night; when upon awakening we open our eyes to the world of morning's joyous lights and colours, then the portals of a realm of wonders likewise open to us. The wonders of day are those of beautiful distinctness and clear form. The wonders of night are more veiled and they are deeper. Where would all the beauty and magic of day be, if maternal night did not bestow on them her life? Day has no less wonders than night. But night possesses more secrets than day. She dwells in mystery. Once, humanity crossed a threshold that is comparable to the ascent of day out of night's realm of darkness. This was when, out of the ancient world, the stage of which was the primal mother, Asia, the new world was born — young Europe that developed in Greece.

Nowhere in history have the miracles of the young, morning-bright day found a more corresponding and purer cultural realization and incorporation than in the Athens of the age of Pericles. At that time, when the small nation of the Greeks had victoriously repulsed the gigantic, dark Asiatic wave of Persian armies, Athens became adorned with all the rich gifts of light-filled, clear beauty. Looking out far across land and sea, proud white marble temples arose on the Acropolis. Radiantly pure statues of a never previously known symmetry emerged from the work places of sculptors. The statues represented gods in completely human form and thus unveiled the divine nobility of the human body. Everywhere the open-air theatres appeared with their classic tiers that circled round and rose up toward the sky, where an astounded throng listened, mesmerized, to dramas by great poets.

Viewed superficially — and the customary conception remains mostly on this surface — one could assume that it was predominantly the national uprising brought about by the Persian Wars through which the miracles of Periclean Athens were conjured forth out of a primitive, insignificant earlier condition. But it was not as if nothing had formerly existed in Greece and Athens. Even as the young day is not a beginning out of nothing, but owes its life to night, its mother, so, too, the Athens of Pericles did not come into existence without a rich maternal source. But pre-Periclean Greece was of a completely different nature. The era of Pericles was at least as rich in miracles of creative beauty as the earlier period. But the Greece of antiquity was much richer in secrets than the one that in its generous and beauteous brilliance subsequently cast its spell over the world.

The Greece that preceded Pericles was the land of the mysteries, a land whose quiet sources of divine wisdom were nurtured and guarded by just a few initiates: on Samothrace, the island of the gods in the north; in Ephesus, the city of Artemis on the coast of Asia Minor; in Delphi, the Apollo sanctuary, located on a prominent hill; in Eleusis, the mystery site of Demeter and Dionysius on the green shores of the blue sea. The prevailing manner of thinking, extending today even to history, is like that of a person who has no sense organ for the secrets of the night. This form of history knows only what can be seen in 'broad daylight.' Indeed, how can it know anything real about the world of the mysteries if it merely looks at those events which are clearly documented? It was in the nature of the mysteries to do all in their power not to leave behind any evidence that could have fallen into the wrong hands. We cannot understand in isolation events like the Persian Wars or those of the Periclean age which occurred 'in broad daylight' on the openly accessible surface of existence. Behind it we have to behold the darkly concealed silent 'realm of the mothers,' the world of the mysteries. That was the source from which sprang forth all this splendour and beauty. The art and culture of Periclean Athens represents a popularization and transformation of the mysteries on the largest scale. A world of bright daylight was freed from the spell of night.

For some time, a decline had befallen the mysteries that had always nurtured the spiritual and even political life of Greece. The Greek mysteries had not succumbed to the same degree of magical degeneration and decadence as had the mystery centres of Asia, on which not much more than the power struggle of alternating ruling nations fed itself. Nevertheless, a slow exhaustion and diminution of spiritual energies could be felt in leading centres and wellsprings of Greek civilization. It came to the attention of more and more people, even in the general vicinity of the mysteries, how the leaders who emerged from the initiation sites — though they still raised claims of authority — no longer possessed the living wisdom and certainty that are comprehensible and gain hearing on their own merits. Large numbers of educated Greeks were on the verge of developing a self-awareness through which they were eventually to declare that they had come of age and had outgrown the tutelage of the ancient leaders' authority.

Moreover, with the Persian Wars a period of intense trials and tribulations came over the Greek people. It was not just the confrontation of two nations, one of which was small but rich, the other large and hungry for conquest. Two worlds collided: an Asia grown old, that forcibly clung to its divine past and thus had become caught up in demonic magic; and a young Europe that was ridding itself of the ancient spell and had begun to waken to its own potential. The decadent mysteries of ancient times tried by militant means to exert their suggestive influence over that part of humanity that dared enter a completely new realm, the world of bright, clear day. The fact that, along with the Persian armies, the Greeks were successful in repulsing the spell of the Asiatic mysteries helped them — quicker than would have been possible without the Persian Wars — to assume a changed attitude towards their own mysteries and to utilize them in a culturally creative manner.

One of the important consequences of the naval battle at Salamis, which included Aeschylus among the Greek combatants, was not merely that the Greeks were at last left in peace by the Persian attackers but that, above all, the courage grew in Hellas to part from the ancient world and even its holy mysteries. Believing in the human being as much as or more than in the ancient gods, people rose to an unheard-of undertaking: they broke the spell of secrecy and brought the world of the mysteries out of dim darkness into the light of day. The threshold that the Hellenic people crossed when in exuberant joy of creating they adorned the city of Athena with so much new beauty, was the same at which humanity as a whole had by then arrived. Five hundred years earlier, as if they were vanguards and pioneers on the paths of humanity, the same transition had been undertaken by the people of the Old Testament. At that time, the reconstructed, splendid Jerusalem of Solomon had put an end to the mystery darkness that had lasted even until the age of David. The structures on the rock of Moriah above the Kidron Valley were forerunners of the Parthenon — the temple that arose during the

age of Pericles in Athens on the Acropolis and which afforded a
view over the bay of Salamis.

When, four hundred years before Solomon, the young revolutionary future-oriented Egyptian, Pharaoh Amenophis IV,
Akhenaton, constructed his 'city of the horizon' at the banks of
the Nile in the desert, the time had not yet come for the birth of
a culture of daylight. Only too soon, the night-related power of
ancient mystery traditions had once again wiped out any trace of
the work that this premature lover of day had wished to create.
But the Solomonic age with its new courage for artistic form, and
even more the age of Pericles with its lavish faculty and love for
beauty — the first like an actual prophecy, the second like a
human fulfilment — truly represented the birth of day out of the
womb of night. Out of the dim mystery background, the cultural
life emerged into the foreground where everything acquired
clarity of form and colour. Solomon had blazed the trail in the
courage of bidding farewell to the esoteric world of secret
spiritual revelations, of lifting the veil, of publicizing the
mysteries and inaugurating an exoteric public culture accessible
to all human beings. The Greeks of Athens between Pericles and
Alexander the Great were those who, in the purest and most
consistent way and now in the name of all humanity, followed
the impulses that had first appeared on the stage of human
evolution in Solomon.

1.2 The fine arts

In its proud external unfolding, the emergence of the Periclean
culture was like the opening of blossoms that are transformed
over night into a sea of splendid, colourful flowers. What had
ripened in seclusion now emerged openly in astounding, abundant
beauty.

The unassuming, darkly massive, ancient Doric temples of
early Grecian times, sparse in number and size, were mostly
hidden from the sight of the populace. Those who did not belong
to the direct surroundings of the mysteries or oracle centres
sensed more than actually beheld the presence of those dwellings
of the gods. Now, a completely novel attitude of construction and
joy of building arose. Architecture broke its silence; it cast its

spell over all, the artists and the common folk, and enkindled in them an enthusiasm that urged them on to creative activity. It appeared to be a quite new hierarchy of gods that now bid men construct for them dwellings on earth. The ancient, titanic and sombre chthonic sequence of figures of primal cosmic forces, among whom belonged Uranus and Kronos-Saturn, had finally abdicated. The more luminous sons of gods of the Zeus lineage, who were closer to humankind, remained behind. In the abundance of beautiful temples that arose in the Greece of Pericles, the Olympian gods openly and freely entered into the midst of the life of men. Just as the Parthenon overlooked Athens from the Acropolis, so the glistening white temples, tokens of a new world, shone down brightly into populous cities everywhere.

A change of far-reaching consequence occurred when, suddenly, in all areas of culture, there appeared a number of clearly distinguishable personalities, artists and scholars whose names were soon on everyone's lips. Until then, all creative activity had been strictly tied to schools that transcended the personal element. These schools operated in accordance with ancient venerable traditions under the tutelage of the temple priesthood. Their teachers were acknowledged by the common people as servants of the holy mysteries. Now, suddenly, in addition to the progressive master builder, there were the renowned, independent sculptors who not only freed themselves of the priests' guardianship but even from the rule of the archaically severe style. At their head was the great contemporary and friend of Pericles, the Athenian Phidias (500–429), the daring creator of the golden and ivory images of Zeus in Olympia and Athena on the Acropolis. The sculptural art of a Phidias quickly found followers, as did the architecture of Ictinos who constructed the Parthenon. For this was the unheard-of and at the same time fascinating thing: the new art followed a teacher available to anybody, namely nature, and above all the miraculous structure of the human body. Henceforth, the gods were shaped in ideally beautiful human forms.

The customary view of art history is as follows. It assumes that in that age sculptural and artistic styles generally developed from a primitive level upward to astounding perfection. But the change was a much more fundamental one than this view can discern. The severe archaic style, which in sculptures resembled Egyptian works of art, by no means resulted from a primitive, earthly way of seeing things. Rather, it was the expression of what was once experienced in a more supersensory, visionary way, the sacred tradition of which was guarded in the realm of the mysteries. This is why the examples of pre-Periclean Greek art were never without a certain magical element that extended beyond human dimensions. The new element, evident in the sculptures by a Phidias, for instance, was this: the physical earthly senses had so fully awakened and matured in man that, in place of the forces of ancient vision, he could risk becoming creative in artistic and cultural forms. The nocturnal senses of the human being were now entirely replaced by the alert organs of day; the world of the mysteries made way for the realm of the earthly foreground, a foreground rich in splendour but poor in secrets. Along with this was born the sense of beauty, which has since dominated human souls for more than two thousand years. The physical, sensory form, modified to its ideal pure shape and proportion, was considered beautiful.

In painting, which remained a less prominent art in Greece, the same change to a completely new level occurred when the Athenian, Apollodorus, introduced the perspective of three-dimensional space to the pictorial surface and thus brought about such a naturalistic approximation of the picture to the representation of sensory reality that his contemporaries must initially have been shocked and startled. Here, too, the style that had prevailed hitherto, a style devoid of perspective that removed all the figures from their spatial order and, like the Egyptian art forms of painting and relief, consigned them side by side or one above the other onto one surface, was by no means a primitive elementary stage but rather an expression of ancient supersensory vision. With the introduction of perspective in pictures that attempted to represent the three dimensions of space, earthly sense once again pushed aside the ancient mystery view and its magic.

1.3 Aeschylus, Sophocles, Euripides

Nowhere can we discern the emergence of culture from the core of the mysteries more clearly than in the birth of Greek tragedy. The illustrious constellation of the first three Greek dramatists, Aeschylus, Sophocles and Euripides, did not merely lead from the generation of those who still fought against the Persian army over to those who implemented the mighty cultural change after the Persian Wars. They also represented a clear progression that allows us to recognize the emergence of the world of daylight from the still shrouded dawn of early morning.

Ancient Greece had been familiar with drama and dramatic representation. Yet, in regard to both performance as well as enjoyment, these arts had remained confined to the closely guarded esoteric circle of the mystery sites. The primal form of drama is the mystery play which, on high holidays of the gods, brought the secret teachings of initiation wisdom to expression in artistic pictures and words. People of that period must have felt that the appearance of a completely independent form of theatre, drama and acting in which the whole nation was to have a share was something incredibly daring and modern. Indeed, it was the boldest popularization of the mysteries. The first generations of those who were allowed to join in the pleasure of this new source of experience must still have known the special sense of tension with which a spectator in the theatre awaited the play and, along with it, insight into another world.

The magical superhuman greatness of the primal drama that was withheld from the eyes of the masses still found a certain continuation in the dramas of Aeschylus (525–456 BC). He came from Eleusis, one of the most important sites that cultivated the old sacred plays of the gods. Just as in the Eleusinian holy plays that allowed the secret of death and resurrection to become visible in the pictorially displayed destinies of the gods, so, too, the tragedies by Aeschylus were still very far from any earthly realism, let alone naturalism. Nobody expected performances of events that occur on the physical plane. People knew that what was being done and said on the stage made a higher world that eludes sensory perception visible and audible. The tragedies of Aeschylus made use of a seemingly minimal measure of performing means. Only two actors in *cothurni* (buskins) and masks appeared before the audience. But what was beheld were not human figures; what was heard were not human dialogues. These were not human destinies that moved the souls. Gods or demigods had left their otherwise hidden sphere of activity. Here, the essential meaning of dramatic art still signified the revelation of the deepest of world mysteries.

In the case of Euripides (480–406 BC), human beings with all their earthly limitations appeared on stage. The psychological drama was born. Euripides had already far outgrown the realm of silence and censure that prevailed in the mysteries. As a man of the world, he even dared depict the human, all-too-human element in dramatic form by allowing the female, turned completely worldly, to appear on stage and, along with her, the confusions of soul that humans suffer because of the tension between man and woman. Rather than relating to the mystery-philosophy and its devotion to the gods, Euripides consciously associated with the newly-emerging, purely worldly-oriented enlightenment, natural science and rhetoric.

The actual Periclean dramatist was Sophocles (496–406 BC) who occupied a position somewhat between Aeschylus and Euripides. He was the one who bestowed on the Athens of Pericles the poet's dedication to beauty. Here, the mystery-dusk of Aeschylus' tragedy was already brightly filled with light, yet it had not given way to the flat surface light of Euripidean psychology. The lovely balance between divine and human elements that was characteristic of the sculptures of Phidias also prevailed in the dramas of Sophocles. Although the ancient, dark earnestness of the deity resounded through them all, the tragic hero was the human being who passed through the trials and mysteries of destiny. Yet, at the same time, the beginnings of true humanness became discernible everywhere; a humanness destined in the end to remain victorious over all darkness.

The great mystery popularization, to which the Athens of Pericles owed its existence, was not an intentional deed springing from a consistent will. Nor was it as if a mighty cosmic event had simply carried everyone along with it. Many allowed their will to be enkindled by the fire of the new impulse. But there were many, too, who opposed all the new trends, deeming themselves to be empowered as guardians of the sanctuaries. It was therefore not possible, without bold progressive courage, to belong among the great mystery revealers of that age. The hindering forces that caused opposition to and persecution of the creative geniuses in the name of the ancient principles of secrecy and tradition could not so easily be driven from the scene.

Throughout antiquity, the trial conducted against Aeschylus on charges of mystery betrayal was viewed as typical. In the schools of rhetoric of later times, his was the typical example by which the students had to practice their advocate's skills. It is said[2] that once, during a performance of one of his plays, Aeschylus was attacked by a group of furious opponents and almost stoned. By a hair's breadth, he succeeded in escaping to the altar of Dionysius. Subsequently, the Areopagus, the supreme tribunal of the wise men, investigated the charge of mystery betrayal properly by means of a trial. Finally, Aeschylus had to be acquitted. Many different assertions exist concerning the reasons for the acquittal. Heraclitus says it was handed down because of the heroic deeds performed by Aeschylus during the battle of Marathon. Aristotle[3] states it was proven that Aeschylus had not been aware of having expressed in his poetic works mystical matters which were to be kept secret. Several centuries later, the Christian theologian, Clement of Alexandria, put the matter like this: it was ascertained that Aeschylus had not been initiated at all into the mysteries.[4] Now Aeschylus, as a citizen of Eleusis, had doubtless shared in a part of the Eleusinian initiation rites. It is not without reason that, prior to the contest in his comedy, *The Frogs,* Aristophanes has him praying:

> Demeter, thou who hast reared my spirit,
> Grant that I shall be worthy of thy holy rites.

Yet, from this whole trial, we clearly discern how the bounds of mystery affairs became blurred. All attempts to reinforce the realm of secrets had to fail. Irresistibly, the rays of the bright light of day penetrated the veils. People were now awakening and maturing to the point where, regardless of whether they still belonged to the confines of the mysteries or stood quite outside them, they were capable of independently discovering secrets in their thought-illumined soul realm. These were truths that were previously handed down only under the seal of secrecy. The subsequently customary representation by rhetoricians about the trial of Aeschylus therefore proceeded from the following assumption: it may have been possible that the goddess Demeter herself had in a dream communicated to the poet the secrets he was accused of bringing to expression. What was so significant, after all, about lending poetic expression to previously secret wisdom, when the whole existence of the new art of drama and acting was an actual mystery popularization!*

The persecution that Aeschylus experienced on the part of fearful guardians of the mysteries were not directed at him alone. A man like Phidias, for instance, had to suffer much from them. Finally, even Socrates became their victim when, in 399, he was condemned to drink the cup of poison. The accusation of blasphemy that he was charged with was nothing but an altered form of the charge of mystery betrayal. Mystery betrayers were they all, the great men of that age, whether they knew it or not. The new world of day compelled all of them into its service.

Yet it was Aeschylus in particular who, standing between two ages, had to suffer great difficulties from both sides. To the ancient caste of priests and leaders he was an impertinent blasphemer; to the people, on the other hand, to whom access to the spiritual life was now wide open, he by no means went far enough. When, in 468, he returned to Athens from Sicily where success had eluded him, he had to witness how the people did not honour him with the laurels of victory in the poets' contest but preferred the younger Sophocles over him. The tragedies of Aeschylus were still too full of the cloudy gloom of mysteries far removed from earth and man. The common people found the dramas of Sophocles more appealing; they were closer to the human level and directly comprehensible. During this cultural transition, the more modern an art form was, the more popular it

---

* From the beginning, scholarly debate has pursued the question of what were the secrets which Aeschylus stood accused of betraying. A popular view was that it was less a matter of unveiling secret doctrine than the public presentation of facts regarding the ceremonial rituals. See, for example, Nestle: *The World View of Aeschylus.*

became. The people were the actual counterpart of the conservative groups of priests; consistently, they helped advance the new cultural impulse. The departure from the mysteries quickly became ever more complete. The age of the select few was over; the time of the many dawned. After it had diminished in effectiveness, initiation into the mysteries, whereby the select few had been elevated from the ranks of the people, now even lost much of the high esteem and recognition formerly accorded to it. The age of Pericles was at the same time that of democracy.

The scenes that arise in our mind, when we stand on the Pnyx, the rocky plateau on the western edge of the city in front of the steps of the stone-hewed speaker's pulpit, are inseparable from the image of the new Athens. Here, in full view of the whole splendid city with its three hills — the steep Lykabettos, the nearby, central, temple-crowned summit of the Acropolis, and the secluded mystery-enveloped hill of Philopappos, the realm of the Areopagus — stood Pericles, facing the multitudes of the people, attempting with his rhetorical skills to direct the will of the many, a will that now had to have a decisive say in the forming of the nation's destinies.

1.4 Socrates, Plato, Aristotle

The youngest offspring of the mysteries, philosophy, fully emerged into the light of day only when the creative peace of the Periclean age, a peace that lasted a mere thirty years, had given way once again to more restless times filled by the noise of battle. Heraclitus, the 'dark one,' in the environment of the Ephesian sanctuary, and Pythagoras, the world-traveller, whose destiny led him through all the lands of the great civilizations of antiquity, were themselves initiates, messengers of a philosophy that still wholly possessed the character of a secret mystery wisdom. It was not until the appearance of the trinity of Socrates, Plato and Aristotle that the great popularization and farewell to the mysteries occurred in the realm of philosophy. Of these three, the older was always the teacher of the younger one. Socrates was forty years older than Plato, and Plato forty-five years older than Aristotle. Only Socrates (469–399 BC) still belonged to the age when Pericles was alive. Plato (429–347 BC) was not born until the year when Phidias died and Pericles succumbed to the plague.

Conversations that Socrates held with his students no longer dealt with contents of a higher world. The exchange of thoughts was kindled by external earthly relationships, questions of social life among human beings. But the form of teaching that Socrates practised, in that he tried to evoke insight from the student's own soul, resembled the methods utilized during the soul-guidance by the hierophants in mystery and initiation centres. Moreover, we can still see the shadow of mystery practices that fall on the figure of Socrates in the fact that nothing was further from his mind than to write down his teachings.

In Plato, mystery popularization took an important, clearly distinguishable step. He was the first great philosopher-author. The principle of secrecy or mere oral tradition was already quite foreign to him. This was fraught with consequences as, although like Socrates no longer initiated himself, Plato was nevertheless a student of the initiated Egyptian priests of Heliopolis.* Thus, a great number of cosmic and mystical teachings, which until then had been considered secret teachings, appeared openly in the Platonic Dialogues. Texts dealing with the relationship of the human soul and human thought to the spiritual world are found side by side with those meant to contribute to a wisdom-filled understanding of earthly conditions. The logical, thought-imbued impulse, coming as it does from Socrates, and the mystical impulse of Heliopolis intermingled one with the other.

Aristotle (384–322 BC) was the great destroyer of ancient mystery practice. Through him, there occurred a universal popularization of the secrets, a progressive conversion in the broadest possible form of ancient wisdom into the culture of thought. Through summing up the knowledge gathered and cultivated by the ancient world in the circles of initiates, by translating this knowledge into the language of the new world, a language of

---

* In this mystery centre, called On in the Old Testament, Isaac's son, Joseph, and Moses were initiated. See *Genesis,* 'Joseph and his Brothers: The Egyptian Destinies' and *Moses,* 'Education through Egypt.'

logical head-thinking comprehensible to all men, Aristotle became the comprehensive, encyclopedic inaugurator of Occidental logic and science.

The students' circle of Socrates had been kept on a quite personal level. Likewise, the *Academy* of Plato had retained the thoroughly intimate character of a mystery centre school, with personal, oral transmission of knowledge. In the *Lyceum,* so named after the temple of Apollo Lyceios, on the other hand, which Aristotle led during the last thirteen years of his life, something completely new made its appearance. A well organized teaching and research institute of an almost modern scientific appearance came about. Humanity's knowledge and experience were brought together in organized form. Classifying reason was supposed to place the immeasurable wealth of the earthly world under the rule of the human spirit. Before he wrote his science of politics, Aristotle asked 158 Greek towns to record their constitution as well as their history in exact detail. A corresponding effort took place with regard to data relating to the plant and animal kingdoms and likewise all remaining areas of knowledge. Plato's dialogues are consciously created works of art. They raised no claim to exhaustiveness. Here and there, in the far-spread realm of human existence, they allowed the creative genius with its sparks to enkindle a beacon of knowledge. The innumerable works of Aristotle, of which only a small fragment has been preserved, were even then broadly conceived textbooks. By creating such an encyclopedic literature, Aristotle caused the impulse of clear sense perception and a rational world-view to mature to such a degree that it could be bequeathed to the young new world as sustenance for its consciousness.

Even though Aristotle had irrevocably led humanity out of the sphere of the mysteries, his magnificent life accomplishment remains incomprehensible to us if we fail to recognize the essential link he still possessed to the world of the mysteries with their thoughts of gods and divine forces. In and behind his creative activity, such an all-inclusive and progressive spirit and will becomes evident that we can arrive at the idea that it was the genius of the vanishing mystery world itself who, through Aristotle, motivated the great transformation and popularization. Aristotle consciously saw his task as that of a bridge builder from an esoteric to an exoteric wisdom and culture. This can be discerned from the fact that during the existence of his Athenian *Lyceum* and aside from the public teaching activity, he continued esoteric instruction in a smaller circle. In the morning hours, the lessons called *acroamatic* were given. They were limited to a carefully selected and prepared group of students. Then, nearer to evening, the exoteric, more public lectures followed.

Nevertheless, the extent to which Aristotle consistently sought to realize the principle of mystery popularization can be discerned from a brief and yet world-historical exchange of letters between him and his royal disciple, Alexander.[5] Alexander the Great did not share the resolute courage of his teacher to let go of the mystery principle. Something in his nature would have liked to cling to the ancient world's order. He did not wish to give up the advantage that he had over ordinary people as one who was knowledgeable in esoteric teachings. He therefore reproached Aristotle for having surrendered even the contents of the *acroamatic* lectures to the public:

> You did not do right to publish the word spoken in the trusted circle of disciples. For in what way should we distinguish ourselves from the others, if the words of instruction that we have partaken of become accessible in the same manner to all? I would rather distinguish myself from the others through knowledge that relates to the world of ideals than through power.

Aristotle was guided through and through by the courageous confidence that all truths and responsibly presented spiritual facts are inherently protected, inasmuch as they only become evident to the extent that a person is mature enough to grasp them. And so he gave the classic reply:

> You wrote me concerning the text of the special instruction and you felt that it should be kept secret. Know then that these words are publicized as well as unpublicized.
> For only those can understand them who hear us ourselves.

Rudolf Steiner frequently characterized the emergence of Greek cultural life from the mystery traditions and, along with this, the popularization, absorption and adaptation of mystery wisdom which took place. From one of the many descriptions, a few sentences are quoted here as an example:

And so, in face of the grandeur of these unparalleled figures (Homer, Aeschylus) we must conceive that these men did indeed elaborate something that was entirely the product of their own souls, of the weaving of the ego in the ego, but that it had first been laid by higher beings into these souls in the temple-sanctuaries. That is why the poetry of Homer and Aeschylus seems so infinitely profound, so infinitely great ... And because the secrets of the life in supersensory worlds were conveyed in a certain human form to the artists of Greece, they were able in their sculptures to embody in marble or in bronze, what had originally been hidden in the secrecy of the Mysteries. Even what confronts us in Greek philosophy clearly shows that its highest achievements were in truth ancient Mystery-wisdom translated into terms of intellect and reason ... In Aristotle everything appears as though in forms of logic — indeed here one must say that the ancient wisdom has become abstraction, living worlds have been reduced to concepts. But in spite of this — because Aristotle stands at the terminal point of the ancient stream — something of the old wisdom still breathes through his works. In his concepts, in his ideas, however abstract, an echo can still be heard of the harmonies which resounded from the temple-sanctuaries ...[6]

1.5 Alexander the Great

The life of Aristotle fell in an age when, even outwardly, the whole world acquired a new appearance. His conversion of the old wisdom, in fact, was an effective component in this mighty reformation of the world.

In the year 367 BC, the seventeen-year-old Aristotle had joined the disciples of sixty-year-old Plato in Athens. In the remaining twenty years of the teacher's life, during which the disciple could prepare for his life's work, the young nation of the Macedonians made its appearance. Inhabitants of northern Greece, they took advantage of the disunity of the Greeks whose culture they had earlier adopted. Now, they finally gained control over all of Hellas. In 343, three years after Plato's death, Aristotle of Athens was summoned to the court of the victorious Macedonian king to educate the latter's thirteen-year-old son, Alexander, the heir apparent. Thus, one of the most consequential dispensations of destiny in world history was fulfilled.

In the midst of the turbulences of an age of unrest and upheaval, the succession of philosophers' generations that derived from Socrates and Plato entered a completely different sphere of life. One who was to be king, a coming world-ruler, was among the students of philosophy. Twenty-one-year old Alexander ascended to the throne having taken his teacher, Aristotle, along to Athens. From there, the astounding gamble succeeded: in a mere twelve years, a young man with his armies not only moved through the whole civilized world but subjected it to his absolute reign. We must not assume, however, that Alexander became unfaithful to philosophy when he turned into a world conqueror. The opposite was the case. The impulse for Alexander's expeditions was not so much brought about by the desire for power but by this very philosophy, the spark which the spiritual discipleship had kindled in the young king. As a pupil of the spirit that emerged from the darkness of the mysteries into the daylight of thought, Alexander the Great felt motivated to make a powerful impression throughout the whole world with his campaigns. It seemed as if the genius of the new spiritual life were dispatching Alexander as his messenger and missionary. While, through Socrates, Plato and Aristotle, philosophy had amounted to an ongoing popularization of the mysteries, now more than ever the spiritual politics that ensouled Alexander's expeditions signified a further intensification of this externalization. The militant actions of Alexander's armies concealed a spiritual outpouring that embraced all humanity.

The motives for an undertaking like the expeditions of Alexander, which took an almost supernatural course, must always be sought at much deeper levels of existence than those where an individual engages in conscious considerations and resolutions. Profound human destiny-relationships and reminiscences of humanity's distant past play into such motives. Even in antiquity, the strange concurrence of dates was experienced as an illuminating symbol: Alexander the Great was born on the same day that the temple of the ancient Artemis sanctuary, ignited by the torch-brand of Herostratus, went up in flames on the coast of Asia Minor in Ephesus. Europe was a daughter of Asia. Young Greece, the firstborn of Europe, sensed the dusk-enveloped realm of the mother over yonder in Asia. Ephesus, one of the oldest sites of Greek life located in Asia across from Hellas, was a constant reminder to the Greeks never ungratefully to forget the great mother. Was the fiery blaze that flamed up high into the sky — a fire whose glow is reputed to have been visible even across the Aegean Sea on the Attic shores — not a cry for help by the primal mother, Asia, who was falling victim to a dreadful twilight of the gods? And did the birth of the boy, with regard to whom it soon became apparent that an unprecedented destiny awaited him, not have to be viewed as if Europe were making ready to answer the signal from Asia?

When Alexander moved from West to East, it seemed as if ancient human migrations and army expeditions were being reversed, migrations out of the womb of Asia by colonists who once had been dispatched in order to found daughter-cultures in the West, or campaigns by leaders of the declining East, such as Gilgamesh, who had tried to link up with the still older western-Atlantean sources.

Alexander, the pupil of Aristotle, was filled with the vitality and awareness that a new spiritual energy had awakened in young Europe, a force whereby even the ailing ancient world of Asia could recover. Nevertheless, it was far from his intentions simply to force Greek cultural life on the countries he passed through. His expeditions were not ideological propaganda ventures anymore than undertakings that had emerged from a power-hungry lust to conquer. Regardless of where he went, Alexander appeared everywhere as one who knew, understood and revered the local religious traditions and their wisdom. He paid homage in the temples to the gods of the land and offered up sacrifices to them. He did not proclaim and introduce new gods. Serving the old gods, he must have appeared to have been called and sent by these very deities. This was the reason why in almost all places the initiates and priests acknowledged and greeted him like one of their own. They opened their temples to him and in this way passed on to him the most important influence over the political leadership of their nations.

In many locations, the approaching Greek king was welcomed in the first place by those who, due to the decadence and misuse of the local mysteries, had suffered under tyrannical rulers. They believed they were recognizing in him the heaven-sent saviour from great need, the mighty reformer. And by establishing academies in several countries of Asia with the aid of the large number of scholars who accompanied his army, Alexander did in fact introduce a cultural advance that the local inhabitants would no longer have been capable of on their own.

Two centuries before, the young Persian king, Cyrus, had united large parts of Asia into an empire in a similar manner, more through superior spiritual greatness than through mere military might. Like Alexander, aware that he served a higher, all-encompassing spirit, he too could acknowledge the religious cults of the countries he invaded. At the same time, he could lift these cults to a purer and higher level, since he was experienced everywhere by the various people as a saviour summoned to them by their own gods. This was why even the Greek world saw in Cyrus an embodiment of the ideal man and ruler enfolded in godly radiance. The Greek poets and writers glorified him, even though his sons and successors were the ones who had allowed the misery of the Persian Wars to be inflicted on Hellas.

In Alexander the Great, the astounded Greek world now possessed its own realized ideal of humaneness that encompassed all mankind and yet was expressed and lived in a completely personal form. Alexander appeared like the fulfilment of what Cyrus had merely been the prophecy. The new world condition that Alexander was able to conjure up in the twelve years before he died so young at the age of thirty-three was much more remarkable and amazing than the blossoming of Periclean Athens after the Persian conflicts. It did not matter that, following the death of its inaugurator, the grand Alexandrian empire soon fragmented politically. The uniform cultural fibre that had originated through the spirit of Greece and its buoyant joy of thinking remained in existence for many centuries throughout distant places in the Orient.

The world of Hellenism blossomed across many lands, as if it had not been brought to life through a man but from heaven through the Olympian gods themselves. All at once the bright

Greek language became the language of the world and remained so for longer than half a millennium in all of Asia Minor, replacing the dark Aramaic of the Babylonian and Syrian world. The luminescence of thought born in Greece and the brilliance of the Athenian miracle of day was poured out over all humanity — a humanity that had only recently still been asleep in the dusky darkness of ancient divine dreams. Humanity had arrived at the level of man. The world was imbued with a mood that came about because man awoke to himself, began to feel like a personality and grew into the feeling of his own being's maturity and dignity. The spark of personal human pride had been sown everywhere by the royal youth who had subjugated the world under his rule.

We sense that behind the outer sequence of facts that surrounded Alexander's expeditions and the innovations that occurred during this time, profound riddles of spiritual world activities are concealed. For what was it that caused all the nations so quickly to become receptive and submit to the will of the young king? Surely it is impossible to surmise that the almost unbelievable success was purely and solely due to the impression evoked by Alexander and his armies. Alexander's campaigns met with great longing and expectation everywhere, even if in many instances people were only dimly aware of this. All the world was awaiting one who was to come, one who fundamentally would change the life of humanity. And so, when Alexander appeared in such radiant splendour, preceded by reports of all the unheard-of innovations that he had brought about in other countries, was it not almost a foregone conclusion that people welcomed him as the one who had been anxiously awaited?

Over all the nations of the world a twilight of the gods had been descending for several centuries. When the mighty Baldurdirge over the death of the youthful, handsome deity, Osiris, Adonis or Tammuz, resounded in Egypt, Phoenicia and Babylonia, the feeling that man had been abandoned by the gods had emerged for the first time. Soon, like a fast falling night, this sensation had extended to all the corners of the earth. Even at the core of Greek life, a life which at this very moment shone forth in such rich, creative beauty, the tragic undertone was present that was summed up in the lament, 'The great Pan is dead!'[7] The sense of a profound turning point of time emerged, an era in which humanity would be incapable of helping themselves. Thus, their longing for redemption developed. And in many places in the world this longing gave birth to the confidence-inspiring intimation: maybe the radiant divine light in the heights was extinguished only because the deity has embarked on a journey down to earth. The god is on his way to us. If we await him with ardour and moreover with patient hope, maybe we will yet live to see how the god himself will appear in human form in our midst as the mighty helper and provider of salvation and, lo, make everything new!

The great prophets who came forth among the Israelites at the time of that nation's worst degradation were able most clearly and devoutly to express this powerful Messianic longing and hope. Yet it was not merely the people of the Old Testament who possessed Messianic prophecies. In the most diverse ways, all the nations on earth were looking out for the redeeming divine hero.

Alexander was not the awaited Messiah, no more so than Cyrus had been. But did his being really appear only coincidentally in such Messianic radiance to the nations? Was his coming not linked in some way to the coming of the divine being, for whose reception humanity was preparing? Were the expeditions by Alexander perhaps the earthly shadow of events that took place at that time in the spheres of the spiritual world, where the mighty Expected One was just reaching the final steps of his descent?

1.6 Alexander and Jerusalem

Before we dare pursue this question further, we must deal with an episode in Alexander's life that may lead us closer to the Messiah-riddle concealed in the background of the events of that period.

While, as a rule, Alexander showed a positive understanding and tolerant attitude with regard to alien religions and spiritual movements, it appears that, in the case of Judaism, the manner in which he conducted himself indicates a still greater benevolence and sense of reverence. According to the unanimous early Jewish and Greek reports,[8] Alexander's entrance into Jerusalem must have been accompanied by strange and remarkable effects. After the conquest of Tyre, the king approached the holy city. The inhabitants, along with the high priest, were terrified of the conqueror's army. They expected the plundering and destruction of the city since they had recently refused the demand to dispatch troops to aid in the siege of Tyre. But then the high priest was granted a comforting revelation in a dream. In compliance with it, he had the city decorated with wreaths and ordered all the gates to be opened. Together with the whole priesthood and clad in the most formal vestments, he then moved toward the Greek king at the head of his people.

When Alexander caught sight of the solemn procession in white garments, led by the priests attired for the greatest offering, something occurred that annoyed and astounded all his retainers who even then expected the order to commence plundering. The king dismounted from his horse, hurriedly moved forward unaccompanied and knelt down in worship before the Jewish high priest. His royal underlings and generals at first believed that Alexander had lost his senses. They prevailed upon him until he made known to them that, in the solemn procession of the Jews, he had recognized a vision once bestowed on him in a dream. The god, whose high priest had just stepped up to him, had once revealed himself to him. And it was this god, so Alexander explained, who had given him the task and courage in the first place for his expedition into Asia.

Together with the Jewish priests, Alexander then ascended to the Temple on the rock of Moriah and, following the high priest's direction, offered up the sacrifice. And instead of imposing any burdens upon the people, he granted them privileges and liberties far beyond those of all the other nations in his huge empire. It is possible that such reports extend beyond the level of tangible history and factual reality due to the imaginative, legendary element contained in them. Nevertheless, it is a fact that in the Hellenistic world created by Alexander the Great, Jewish culture not only enjoyed great freedom and esteem but moreover found fertile ground for a far-reaching, new unfolding of its philosophical and spiritual gifts. Through its union with the Greek spirit, a portion of late Judaism was able to produce a culture representing a quite essential contribution within the newly established world that was oriented completely on the human being, the very world subsequently encountered by Christianity.

It was really Alexander the Great who liberated the Jewish people from the bondage of the Babylonian exile. When the Persian king, Cyrus, conquered the Babylonian kingdom, a fair number of Jews who lived in exile were able to return to their homeland. Yet, despite a number of liberties granted by Cyrus to the enslaved people, a Persian serfdom actually took the place of the Babylonian one. It was Alexander who, having subjugated the Persian kingdom, did away with this degradation. Henceforth, albeit for a short time, Palestine was an independent member of the Alexandrian empire on equal footing with the other larger kingdoms.

Judaism awaited the coming of the Messiah with greater clarity and fervour than the other nations of that period. It did not succumb to the error of viewing Alexander as the longed-for saviour. Nevertheless, a realization of the preliminary significance due the great Greek king and the spirit that emanated from him passed through the Jewish consciousness like distant flashes of lightning, a consciousness that was preparing for the impending Messianic world-transformation. Large and important parts of the Jewish world experienced a happy spiritual accord between the Judaism marked by the age of the prophets and the Periclean-Alexandrian Greek culture. Innumerable legendary traditions attest to this, though they do not concur with the external set of facts. Instead, they point to an important spiritual relationship. They frequently refer to Aristotle and his relationship to the prophetic Jewish spirit. It is said that Alexander appointed his teacher curator of the precious Solomonic library; for this reason, the Greek philosopher actually owed the wisdom contained in his writings to Jewish literature. At the end of his life, in Egypt, Aristotle supposedly became acquainted with the Old Testament itself, converted to the Jewish faith and renounced his own works. It sounds less fantastic, yet equally odd, when Aristotle was simply listed among the figures of the Jewish prophets.[9]

What were the mysterious points of mutual attraction felt between Judaism and Greece in the Alexandrian age, partly expressed in such fantastic legends and partly actualized in the Hellenic-Jewish culture? The feeling of affinity that ensouled a large portion of Jewry arose from the fact that both cultures embodied a similar stage in the evolution of human consciousness. Though they originated from completely different ethnic lines, they were nevertheless like brothers within humanity with regard to the contribution which they had to make toward the spiritual awakening of humankind at that particular time.

Judaism and Hellenism were both destined to play their part in the mighty popularization and transformation of the mysteries through which the new world, the world of ego-endowed human faculties, was to emerge from the twilight of the ancient world. Early on, when Moses, the one on whose forehead the transformation from the ancient visionary gift of the gods to the ego-like power of human thinking was beginning, led his people out of Egypt's domain of mysteries and temples, the first step was taken in man's monumental emancipation and process of maturing. But until the age of David, the history of Israel still remained in the soul realm of mysteries borne by the gods. Solomon was the one who took the next big step. The new appearance that Jerusalem acquired during the Solomonic era was the sign of a profound leave-taking from the world of the mysteries. A consciously exoteric culture based solely on human faculties was inaugurated. During the age of the prophets, the translation, begun by Solomon, of the ancient wisdom of revelation into language of thought accessible to all human beings continued in an increasingly broader sense, though initially it was illuminated by much divine inspiration. In the Babylonian schools of scribes and scholars, this evolutionary process reached its culmination.

While the miracles of the Periclean period blossomed in Greece, the way in which the thought element was perfected and nurtured in Judaism following the Babylonian exile was unlike the intellectualism that later on pervaded humanity with soulless cold, an intellectualism grown devoid of spirit and lost in the external world. In the thinking practised in the Jewish centers of learning, it was still possible to sense that it was nothing else but the gods' wisdom translated into human language, the mystery made public. A breath of imaginative supersensory perception was still woven into it all like a memory and echo of ancient devout spiritual life; an esoteric quality remained perceptible in it, even though one had become distanced from the principle of secrecy. The secret was no longer guarded by silence but by the manner in which it was expressed. It protected itself, inasmuch as it became disclosed to the cognizing one only to the extent of his or her maturity.

In Alexander's time, the spiritual life of Judaism therefore stood in the middle between the esoteric initiation culture of the mysteries that belonged to the past and a completely exoteric culture of thought yet to be developed in the future. It could be described as an esoteric culture of thought. At the same time, the Greek life of the spirit in the age of Socrates, Plato and Aristotle was first and foremost also an esoteric culture of thought. It maintained a fine balance between the mysteries and a scientific practice that had become completely worldly and imbued with the early radiance of human egohood. Neither Plato's dialogues nor the broadly conceived teachings of Aristotle, which represented the cultural wealth that gave Alexander the impulse for his world-encompassing activities, could deny their origin from out of the mysteries. The reflection of heaven's glory still shone in them clearly; moreover, their imaginative-esoteric element born of vital reverence was never extinguished. This is how it could come about that the Greek and Jewish cultures encountered and recognized one another as spiritually akin and how they blended in the philosophy of a Philo or another of the luminaries of Jewish Hellenism.

1.7 The Michael age

Yet, with what has been outlined above, we have only groped our way from the external facts to what took place spiritually in the days of Alexander. The actual spiritual events of the period, events that hold the key for the great riddles we have encountered, occurred beyond humanity's reach. What happened on earth, namely the mighty range of Alexander's expeditions, was astounding for the very reason that it was the earthly shadow of mighty super-earthly developments. Before the time had been fulfilled and the incarnation of the long-awaited divine being could in fact take place, the sunlike, victoriously radiant arch-angel of Christ, Michael, had assumed time's guidance from within the circle of the lofty archangels who, as spirits of time, take turns to direct the inner destinies of humankind. The era of his rule, the Michaelic age, had started when newly founded Rome experienced its mythical royal period and when, in Israel-Judea, the sequence of the great prophetic proclaimers began with Isaiah (around 700 BC). It lasted approximately until the death of Alexander the Great.*

As the time spirit, the archangel Michael sent impulses into humanity that caused the earth to become the stage of a rich and distinguished gathering of human spirits. This facilitated the ascent of one of the first cultures of reason and faculties of heart and mind borne by the proud forces of egohood and personality, and initiated the birth of the new world. The wondrous concur-rences in the spiritual life of humanity came brightly to the fore in the light of the Michaelic time spirit. One and the same age produced the great artists and philosophers of Greece, from Heraclitus and Pythagoras to Alexander; Israel's prophets, from Isaiah to Ezra; the great Buddha in India; in Persia, the mysteri-ous author of the Gathas of Zarathustra; and finally, in the Far East, the wise teachers, Lao-tzu and Confucius. Rulers, who appeared surrounded by the Messianic radiance of a deity and at the same time as embodiments of the ideal of true manhood, intervened in the earth's destinies with astounding good fortune, as if they were direct instruments of the sunlike time spirit himself, namely Cyrus, the Persian, and Alexander, the Macedo-nian.

In two places in particular, Michael, the lofty sovereign of thought, sowed the seeds of consciousness and freedom: in Israel

---

* Earlier, in the description of Old Testament history, mention was made of this Michael age (see *King and Prophets,* 'Daniel: Michaelic-Apocalyptic Elements' and 'The Book of Esther: Breakthrough of the New Spirit'). As outlined on several occasions by Rudolf Steiner and described earlier by medieval scholars like Trithemius of Sponheim and Agrippa of Nettesheim *(De occulta Philosophia* III.24), the names of the seven archangels who, during a time span of approximately four hundred years, alternate as spirits of time, are: Michael (the archangel of the sun), Oriphiel (Saturn), Anael (Venus), Zachariel (Jupiter), Raphael (Mercury), Samael (Mars) and Gabriel (Moon).

and in Greece. And so originated the twofold stream that was motivated by the courage to take leave of the gods of the past and popularize the mysteries. As bearers of the Michaelically inspired esoteric culture of thought, both these nations spread throughout humanity: the Jewish-Israelite tribes in woeful, degrading slavery; and Greece, though under the leadership of the half-alien Macedonian king for only a short time, as the pivotal nation of the most powerful worldwide empire. Through them, all of humanity was supposed to be imbued by the new force which alone makes the human being truly 'man.'

The spiritual gifts of this last pre-Christian Michael age, above all the cultural life of the Old Testament which began with its inspired prophets, and Greek-born philosophy so closely akin to art, have to be recognized as preparations for the Christ Event. Before the lofty divine being, through whom human beings would receive the power for a new ascent to heaven, was bestowed on humanity, a spiritual life in the sun-archangel's brilliance was given to men. Through this they would come to a self-awareness and be capable at the same time of comprehending the Christ Event, once it was fulfilled.

After his earthward journey during which he had passed through all the spheres of the spiritual world, the Christ being had drawn close to the level of human incarnation. And from the sphere where he now sojourned, the archangel who 'stands before the countenance of Christ' sent into humanity rays and forces of light that were meant to help human beings acquire egohood. Egohood had to be attained by human beings; otherwise, the time would not be fulfilled for God to become man.

Let us try to picture to ourselves the super-earthly events of that age in human images. The archangel sensed that now, when such all-important events were about to happen, the time set for his activity within humanity was running out. His being then surged forth in a mightily urgent will. The anxious question arose: has the spiritual preparation of the way been successful? Have men comprehended the power and light, whereby they will be fortified for the reception of Christ? As if he wished to make sure of the success his activity had attained, the great 'Lord of Thoughts' held a mighty gathering in the soul realm of all humanity. Would an immense battle of the spirits not break out when the lofty divine being entered upon the earthly plane? Would demonic powers of the abyss, fighting for every human being, not contend with him who was to arrive? This is, fundamentally speaking, what constituted the remarkable greatness and irresistibility of Alexander's expeditions, namely that they were an earthly silhouette of the great Michaelic hosts.

In the countless novels on Alexander that have sprung up in all countries and languages, from the Greek narrative by Callisthenes all the way to the Middle High German *Ode to Alexander* by Lamprecht the priest (thirteenth century), something was divined of the spiritual event that made such a stir behind the physical events. What people consider to be fantastic descriptions of unimaginable encounters and events, even to the point where we are told that Alexander reached the portals of paradise, are in reality dimly sensed images of the supersensory event that occurred in the sphere of Michael.* Before he withdrew once more from the guidance of time, the time spirit wished to conduct a profound test in order to find out how much power the impulse of thinking and egohood, which had newly been implanted into humanity, had by then acquired. What came to life in Greece was poured out over the whole world by Alexander. And lo, what the Lord of Thoughts had bestowed on humankind seemed to prevail. The signs were increasing. Soon the time would be fulfilled and the one sent by God could come — He whose coming the whole world awaited.

---

* In reference to the passage in the *Ode to Alexander,* where it is said that Alexander advanced all the way to the gate of paradise, Rudolf Steiner states:
    '... the expeditions of Alexander were not undertaken for the mere sake of making conquests ... still less to reconcile the Barbarians with the Greeks. No, they were permeated by a real and lofty spiritual aim. Their impulse came out of the spirit.' *(World History in the Light of Anthroposophy,* lecture of December 27, 1923, p.67).

2. Hellenism:
The Diadochi and the Maccabees

2.1 Sons of the Titans

The miracle of Alexander's expeditions gave way all too soon to dark chaos. Even while the corpse of the young king still lay in state in Babylon, the bloody feud over his legacy broke out. It was a struggle that led to the breakup of the empire, magically created within the short period of twelve years, into a number of warring territories.

Yet we would be mistaken were we to see nothing else in this but the so often repeated tragedy of the great man whose work is wasted by weak successors. Deep riddles of destiny and providence are revealed in the circle of personalities who had gathered around Alexander the Great. More than is commonly realized, the generals and counsellors who surrounded the king like a circle of paladins were involved in the extremely auspicious successes of Alexander. Fate had caused figures of gigantic life forces, of truly primal world dimensions, to associate with the crowned youth as his supporters. In its tremendous extension, Alexander's kingdom really corresponded more to the nature of these men under his command than to his own nature.

But unlike their king, Alexander's paladins were not progenies of the emerging new world. The bright light of thought that Aristotle, the heir and disciple of Socrates and Plato, had implanted in the king's soul penetrated them only in a broken flickering manner, since they were still possessed of an ancient, more instinctive soul character. As long as Alexander was alive, they served the consciousness embodied in him and made available to him their titanic forces. Yet afterwards it was inevitable that these very forces, without which the worldwide empire could not have been conquered, chaotically turned against each other as if a directional guiding light had suddenly been extinguished.

For once, the destinies of these paladins ought to be traced. Then it becomes apparent that we deal with a generation of giants, men that appear not as sons of mortals but as belated offsprings of demigods and heroes. In marked contrast to Alexander's life, completed already at age thirty-three, many among them continued their almost superhuman achievements far into old age. Even then they would not have retired from the arena of history if they had not died a violent death. The progenitor of the Seleucid dynasty, Seleucus I Nicator, a contemporary of Alexander, was slain aged eighty-four, just at the point when he was about to engage in a new military campaign, after he had waged countless battles and founded even more cities. And the mysterious, feared, one-eyed Antigonus, who appeared for a while to succeed in seizing power over the whole empire, was killed aged eighty-two in the battle of Ipsus that brought his ambitious plans to a sudden end. Composed of so many ancient and new nations and cultures, the empire of Alexander with its colourful, partly tamed, partly wild play of forces, offered fertile ground to the larger-than-life figures of the Diadochian age on which to express their titanic will.

Alexander had drawn the outline of a gigantic structure. Now, a generation of giants arrived to build on this structure. But they changed the plans as they built. A far-extending dome for all humanity was to have arisen. Now, gigantic fortifications rose up that warred one against the other. The miracle of the Diadochian age is this: as ferociously as the emerging dominions fought against each other, the seed of the Greek spirit and the Greek language, sewn by the philosopher's disciple, did nevertheless spring up everywhere and caused a uniform culture to blossom forth. And across all the chasms and segregations of nations, races and continents, this culture awakened a living sense of one humanity.

Three kingdoms in particular soon emerged from the passionate chaos of battles after Alexander's death. A Hellenistic empire came about on the stage of the ancient sacred Egyptian civilization under the lineage of Ptolemy Lagus, one of Alexander's titanic companions-in-arms, whose life the king himself had once saved in battle. The capital of the Ptolemies was the city founded and named after him at the mouth of the Nile delta, Alexandria, which soon grew to be the largest city of the world, populated by the greatest mixture of nationalities. In the East, encompassing even the territories of the ancient kingdoms of the Babylonians, Assyrians and Persians but extending everywhere far out into the land between the Euphrates and Tigris, a kingdom was established under the reign of Seleucus Nicator and the Seleucids who descended from him. In the newly founded Syrian city of Antioch, a city that quickly expanded into a metropolis, the rulers of this empire took their seat. In Asia Minor, right in the middle between the two larger realms of the Diadochi, arose yet another smaller kingdom of the Attalides with its capital city of Pergamum. There, where the ground was being prepared for the domain of the Pauline congregations and also the quiet activity of the visionary of Patmos, the old presbyter and evangelist of Ephesus, Hellenistic life remained closest to its Greek origin. There, the turmoils of the Diadochian period did not surge up so high. But this more tranquil empire of Attalus did not last long; it soon surrendered its independence to the newly arisen Roman empire.

In quicker succession, it appears as if the duality of Egyptian and Syrian-Asian Diadochian rule repeated something of the polar development which even in ancient times existed between the cultures of the Pharaohs on the Nile and those of Babylonia and Mesopotamia. In the age of Gilgamesh, during the third pre-Christian millennium,[10] the more diverse, mixed civilization around the Euphrates and Tigris was falling even then into a certain decadence and superficiality, whereas Egypt was allowed to go on existing for a while longer in its unbroken, static and magical mystery uniformity. Similarly, now, after the departure from the original impulse of the Alexandrian expeditions, a relapse into the magical sphere of forces of the past occurred more quickly in the East under the Seleucids than in the West under the Ptolemies.

2.2 Alexandria and the Ptolemies

Through the founding of Alexandria, Alexander the Great implanted a seed in arid Egyptian life. For some time, its growth and development maintained the enthusiasm of a courageous, modern cultural life. Initially, the city of the great king threatened to become a 'new Babylon,' where immeasurable wealth flowed from all parts of the world into this international harbour of commerce, a place where the dizziness of riches and sensual desire ensnared people in their ecstatic spell. But then Ptolemy Lagus, the only one among Alexander's paladins who was not just a general and autocrat but had shared in his philosophical and scientific interests and endeavours, and likewise his son, Ptolemy Philadelphus, succeeded in turning Alexandria primarily into a 'new Athens.'

This came about through the enlargement of the academy which Alexander had created in Alexandria. Under the first Ptolemies, the *museion* of Alexandria soon became the richest and most famous seedbed of the sciences. Great riches were generously spent for the cultivation of the new institution of knowledge and research. Scholars came together here from all the different countries of the world. Something of the intimate character of a temple or philosophers' school had still clung to the school of Aristotle, even though it had assumed the principle of literary activity in contrast to Plato's school. Now, here in Alexandria, even the last vestiges of such an intimate character were stripped away. In the most generous form possible, a purely worldly, exoteric institution of teaching and research came into being. Auditoriums with seats were available for the teachers who lectured by way of speeches and disputations. The *peripatos,* the large university garden, offered space for those who presented their thoughts while they walked up and down in the old manner with their groups of students. For the researchers of natural science, experimental laboratories were available, likewise botanical gardens and menageries in which plants and animals from all the four corners of the world were collected. A huge library was established with an army of scribes; all of the then existing poetical, philosophical and scientific literature was collected, catalogued and — the first beginning of the book trade — reproduced through copying. Egypt, the land of the papyrus shrub, produced paper for the whole world. It thus brought into humanity's cultural life a similar outward direction as occurred later through the invention of the art of printing.

The unceasing diligence of scholarly work caused the new spiritual development begun in Periclean and Aristotelian Athens to be accelerated with almost impetuous speed. Just as the empire of Alexander appeared to have been suddenly conjured forth, so now, too, all the beginnings of the scientific life of modern humanity were present. Euclid, the inaugurator of geometry whose textbook, *The Elements,* forms the basis of all schoolbooks on this subject to this day, taught at the Academy of Alexandria. Though not present there in person, Archimedes developed his fundamental discoveries in the area of arithmetic and physics. Great geographers appeared on the scene and for the first time publicly offered a complete view of our earth's surface. Eratosthenes instituted cartography by drawing the meridians into the world map, thus making it easy to survey. Astronomers constructed the celestial globe and made the principle of calendars, until then an affair of the mystery centres, accessible to anybody. Aristarchus of Samos even dared develop the heliocentric world picture for the first time in scientific fashion. Great physicians such as Erasistratus paved the way for an up-to-date anatomy by starting to dissect human corpses for scientific purposes. During these first exposures of the human brain, the system of arteries and veins and the human heart, secrets of far-reaching consequence were made public which, for good reason, had remained concealed in the world of antiquity, for example within the practice of Egyptian mummification. Physicists like Ctesibius readily entered the field of discoveries from which a completely new trend for externalization was to penetrate humanity. The first machines appeared in which the pressure of air and steam as the driving force was utilized. It is an almost dizzying experience to see all this originate; all these innovations whose further development we have been tracing for the last two thousand years and whose effects on the relationship of man to the world we have long since experienced on our very own being.

The encounter between Hellenism and Judaism assumed a quite special form in the almost reckless intellectual bustle of Alexandria. Soon after its establishment, the city became the centre for a completely new sort of Judaism and thus not only ranked alongside Athens but also Jerusalem. The spark was struck between Greek and Jewish cultural life. Developing quickly, supported by the privileges granted the Alexandrian Jews by Alexander the Great himself, a high Hellenistic-Jewish academic standard spread from Alexandria over the whole world.

51

The noblest fruit and soon preferred means of dissemination of the new cultural direction was the Septuagint, the Greek translation of the Old Testament. Legend has it that, independently of each other, under the second Ptolemaic ruler, Ptolemy Philadelphus, seventy men (hence the name *septuaginta* = 70) started on the Greek translation of the holy scriptures and miraculously arrived at an identical text. In this pictorial wording, the claim was expressed that this was not merely a matter of a philological translation, but that one dealt with a book that owed its origin to an inspiring cooperation by the spiritual world. And it is a fact that the Septuagint, which signified an important aspect of mystery publication, is a book that has a spiritual charm all of its own and is irradiated by countless sparks of insight. Something quite new came into being — the texts became light-imbued by being lifted out of the dark mystery heaviness of Hebrew into the clear, bright Greek language. The imaginative breath of the Greek element of thought lives in this translation. It becomes directly noticeable that a language of gods which had become human is reaching our ear.

Suddenly, people the world over could share in the Messianically ensouled spiritual treasures of the Old Testament, particularly since numerous editions of the Septuagint were disseminated due to diligent copying. Subsequently, it was this Greek version, as is shown by the Old Testament quotes in the Gospels and Letters of Paul, by which the disciples and Apostles of early Christendom came to know the Old Testament. The Hellenistic faction of Judaism fashioned the paternal religion into a philosophy. By disseminating the holy scriptures together with the works of Plato and Aristotle, this faction played no small part in bringing about the modern, ego-imbued, thought-filled consciousness. After it had seemed for several decades that under the rule of the Ptolemies Egypt would continue to be a worthy stage for the spiritual culture inaugurated by Alexander, a dark counterforce, as if surging up from subterranean chasms, set in. It was as if the sleeping giant of Egypt's former life was beginning to arouse itself. The demons of the old world became aware of the unwelcome arrivals and made ready to do battle.

The leading circles of neo-Egyptian life, above all the house of the Ptolemies themselves, soon succumbed to the tempting lure of the spirits of the past. It was true that the new cultural life, particularly in the way it unfolded in the direct vicinity of Alexandria's royal palaces in the *museion,* produced infinitely interesting results. But were not all these innovations fundamentally all too human? This would finally lead to the point where all men would be equal. Where would the privileges of rulers and noblemen be then? The ancient enchanted world (albeit with its dark, ominous divine forces) — had it not possessed a magic that now threatened to disappear? In former days, the secret initiations had transmitted powers to those who passed through them, powers whereby these persons were exalted above all other men. Were not some of the temples of the gods and colossal statues to the deities, in which the initiated Pharaohs had been depicted as gods, still standing in the sands of the desert? The allure of the pyramids and sphinxes became stronger and stronger.

The Ptolemies wished to emulate the ancient times. A decadence invaded their royal court that soon degenerated in demonic directions. From early on, consanguineous marriage had been customary among the Ptolemies. It had been practised on occasion in ancient Egypt in connection with initiation practices that were turning decadent even then. Such unions now became the source of confusion for all moral and social relationships. Unpredictable power instincts erupted from all sides.

A new will to build on a gigantic scale emerged when, greedy for power, men became jealous and envious of the ancient times of the gods. All of Egypt was dotted with new temple structures that but copied the old. The ancient extinguished mystery sites, or at least those that had become completely degenerate, were to be awakened to new life and placed in the service of a ruler's own lust for power. We need only allow the impressions first of a temple dating from genuine ancient times, say the one in Abydos, and then of a Ptolemaic temple like the one in Denderah to affect us. We shall see that when people began to reawaken the old gods, they in fact conjured forth demons. Benevolent paternal or maternal world forces are symbolized in the shadowy, solemn, pillared halls of Abydos. Ominous forces of illusion seem to stare down on us from the moon caricatures on the capitals of the temple of Hathor in Denderah, forces bearing the same spiritual makeup as the completely abstract, rigid relief images chiselled into all the walls. The old and the new world became involved in strife. It appeared that the powers of the once divinity-filled night, powers turned spectral, were winning out over the young morn of humanity's awakening thinking.

2.3 Seleucids and the beginning of Caesarean cult

The mighty Diadochian empire of the Seleucids underwent a slightly different development. When the culture of Alexandria developed under the protective calm of peaceful times, the East had constantly been filled with the din of wars. And so it came about that the sleeping giant of the ancient world woke more quickly under the progressive steps of those who tried to bring a new spiritual life to that region. The thought-imbued, Hellenistic spirit worked like drops of water that fall on glowing metal. The smouldering primal powers of the depths hissed, boiled and sent up frothing smoke clouds. This made itself felt in the power struggles that threatened to break out in the eastern parts of the empire directly following the great Alexander's death. The house of the Seleucids was unsuccessful in taking over power immediately.

A pair, who symbolically reflected future developments, appeared on the stage of history and held all those in check who contested their power: old, gloomy, one-eyed Antigonus and his reckless intemperate son, Demetrius. Demetrius, a fascinating Luciferic nature like that of Absalom, the son of David, or Alcibiades, the daring, unstable friend of Socrates, was a real forerunner and herald of the demonized Caesarean cult that clearly emerged for the first time under the Seleucid Diadochi. Demetrius not only possessed strange power over people due to his alluring handsomeness and lavish vanity, he also seemed to possess magic means for directing his luck. The twenty-one-year old had already led and won mighty battles that enabled his father and him to proclaim themselves kings. He was called Demetrius Poliorcetes because he conquered towns and fortifications with quite novel machines of war he had personally invented. It quite corresponded with his blazing ambition that when he entered Athens he was proclaimed a god and an altar

2. HELLENISM: THE DIADOCHI AND THE MACCABEES

was dedicated to him. Soon afterwards, he used the lack of a royal palace in Athens as an excuse to take up his abode in the House of the Virgins on the Parthenon, the temple of Athena on the Acropolis. He had himself revered there as the divine brother of the goddess. Following the battle of Ipsus (in 301 BC), in which Antigonus had been killed, Demetrius, a flickering caricature of the god-man expected by humanity, wandered as an adventurer all over the world.

Now the Seleucids stepped into the foreground. Seleucus I Nicator, who had married the beautiful daughter of Demetrius, finally rid himself of his still dangerous antagonist by causing him to become the victim of his own intemperateness. In the gardens of pleasure where he imprisoned Demetrius, the latter drank himself to death on fine wine. Like the first Ptolemies, the first Seleucid rulers continued the work of Alexander the Great. But how differently it all developed here! Only traces existed of the abundant scientific development pursued in Alexandria

From the beginning, everything tended towards titanic dimensions fit for giants. Aroused from their slumber, the dark primal powers of Asia intruded in it all. Amidst the ongoing din of war, Seleucus I Nicator and his successors became world history's mightiest founders of cities. An overwhelming obsession for construction appears to have spurred them on. Seleucus built no less than sixteen cities and named them Antioch after his father, Antiochus. First place among them was taken by the splendid world capital and royal city, Antioch in Syria, the contender of Alexandria, where the first centre of pagan Christian life formed later on and Paul carried on his first Christian activity. But even the Antioch of Asia Minor in Pisidia, which plays an important part in the history of Paul's journeys (Acts 13), was founded by this first Seleucid. Seleucus gave five new towns the name of his mother, Laodicea. Among them is the town to whose Christian congregation the last of the seven letters is addressed in the Apocalypse of John. Finally, nine towns were named Seleucia by Seleucus after himself.

The largest of these was the one he constructed in Babylonia at the shore of the Tigris River, quite near the ancient capital of Babylon. It was to become a new Babel but far surpassed the old one in splendour. The farewell to the old world was brought to expression by having the new city of Seleucus rise on the ruins of ancient Babel. The apocalyptic myth tells us concerning the sun-archangel Michael that every time he ascends to the light-filled guidance of humanity he vanquishes the dragon forces in the spiritual worlds and casts them down onto the earth. Whenever the atmosphere above earth has been cleansed, therefore, and bright spirit light can shine down upon human beings, humanity has to contend with the shadow of this light, the dark dragon forces (Rev.12:9, 12).

When, along with Alexander's expeditions, the brilliant rule of Michael came to an end and was replaced by the darker age in which Oriphiel ruled, the archangel of Saturn, it was as if earthly men had been left alone with the powers of the dragon and the abyss. The shadows threatened to become mightier than the light. The dark counter-images of what had only recently shone forth in the brightly illuminated spiritual sphere grew stronger. Out of the depths, ominous powers rose up like vapours and, as if trying to mock the heavens, formed into distorted images of the upper gods.

Most of the shadows that haunted the world of the Diadochi, especially the Seleucid realm shaken by ancient titanic will forces, were actual caricatures and counter images of the approaching Messiah being. Out of seething, subterranean depths, a magic impatience rose in the souls of those in power. Certainly, the god-man was coming, the world sensed and felt this. Yet, in the chaos of forces in the slowly ebbing Asian life, it was not easy to calmly expect him in devout patience. Passion and greed for power diverted the concept of the Messiah. The ruler himself wished to be the most powerful one. It was quite alien to his thinking to look out for a greater one whom the future was yet to bring! An almost cosmic fear prevented souls from looking into the future. Thus, the shadow of long vanished millennia assumed form anew, millennia in which the kings had truly been initiated envoys of divine forces. Now, also, the rulers wished to be gods. The common people were supposed not merely to obey but to fall on their knees and worship them. Thus it came about that in the end none but parodies of the longed-for god-man sat on the rulers' thrones, creatures of their own impatience and power-greedy egotism.

The successors of Seleucus I all have names that are the clearest expression for the claim of being a god who has become man. The first Antiochus who ascended to the throne after having allied himself with the murderer of his eighty-four-year old father, Seleucus Nicator (281 BC), named himself Soter, meaning 'Saviour.' The second Antiochus (261–246) assumed the surname of Theos or 'God'; and the fourth was named Epiphanes, 'the one appearing from heaven.' Yet the path of these kings, adorned as they were with such resounding Messianic surnames, was marked by murder and spilling of blood. It is not as if the Diadochian rulers had simply capriciously decreed the Caesarean cult and demanded divine adulation. They employed a means through which they could believe they were truly altering their own being from the ground up in the sense of deification, namely through initiation practices of the ancient mysteries.

In far-distant past ages, when mystery centres were still in possession of genuine power and wisdom, certain specially chosen individuals had in fact been elevated as inspired leaders over their nations by means of the stern trials and purifications of initiation. Lusting for such a world order that was based on the spiritually privileged position of one person, the Diadochi, among them particularly the Seleucids, quickly became unfaithful to the impulse of the age of Aristotle and Alexander. This was an age that aimed for the most generous popularization of the mysteries and the establishment of a spiritual life that, in the long run, would be accessible equally to all men. These rulers were understandably not willing to subject themselves to the stern inner discipline to which initiation in the mysteries had once been linked. And thus the foul principle began to evolve which was to appear openly on the historical plane among the Roman Caesars. The rulers misused their power in order to obtain initiation by force in any number of mysteries which by then had turned decadent. Thus, as a dark and harmful counter-image, mystery pillage and mystery abuse confronted the free, future-oriented mystery popularization.* In the Caesarean cult of the Diadochi,

---

* Rudolf Steiner unveiled the secret behind the Caesarean cult in his description of the Roman Caesars. In the chapters dealing with Roman culture, we will refer to this again.

Asia began to revenge herself for the pride with which young Europa had believed she could bring new life to the mighty continent of her mother.

Antiochus IV Epiphanes (175–163 BC) was the one who, among the Seleucid kings, was the most symbolic embodiment of the Caesarean cult in the sense that it was a caricature of the Messiah concept. Because he had provoked the battles with the Maccabees, he was the one who was viewed as the false Messiah and Antichrist incarnate far into times of early Christianity. In him fluctuated changing moods that surpassed human measure, moods that appeared like a reflection of the battle raging in the supersensory realm between the old and new world. The ego-form that holds the soul together must have ruptured in him due to the misuse of initiations acquired by force. Having fallen victim to Caesarean madness, an affliction that was to make history more than once in the early Christian period, Antiochus IV vacillated in moody unaccountability between working himself up to a fury of the most tyrannical cruelty, and being thrown in turn into the strangest fits of self-denigration, a distorted image of the new impulses that made men equal to one another.

The ancient authors Polybius, Diodorus and Livy present us with graphic descriptions of Antiochus Epiphanes' character which went to extremes in all directions. They speak of his exorbitant love of luxury and mania for construction, but above all of the distorted playful urge towards the purely human:

> Eluding his servants in the palace on occasion, he would appear here and there in the city and stroll around in the company of one person or another. Often he could be found in the workshops of silver or goldsmiths, where he chatted with moulders and other workmen to demonstrate his love of art to them. He stooped to confidential intimacy with the first person at hand from among commoners and drank with the lowliest strangers who happened to be present. If he heard that young people were having a revelry somewhere, he would come without prior announcement, excitedly bringing along a horn and bagpipe so that, frightened by this strange sight, most would be off and away. Often, he discarded his

royal attire, put on a toga and went to the forum as a petitioner for some office. He would take some by the hand, put his arms around others and beseech them to give him their vote, at times for the position of an aedile, at other times for that of tribune of the people. When he had attained the office and sat on the ivory chair according to Roman custom, he took notice of the contracts concluded on the forum and dispensed justice conscientiously with great eagerness. Sensible people therefore did not know what to make of him. Some thought he was a simple, unpretentious man. Others believed he was insane, for when handing out gifts he acted in a similar manner. To some he gave dice made of bone, to others, dates and to still others, gold. And frequently he quite unexpectedly gave gifts to people whom he encountered somewhere and had never seen before ...[11]

Even his contemporaries are reputed on occasion to have changed the godly by-name of Antiochus Epiphanes to *Epimanes*, meaning 'the possessed one.' Both the longed-for god-man and the newly awakened 'ego-man' were caricatured. And when, in the course of his attempts at tyrannizing the people of the Old Testament and their form of worship, he had his own statue erected on the ancient rock altar of the Temple in Jerusalem, this was not only experienced as a desecration of the sanctuary but as the symbolization and visualization of a supersensory set of facts. The demonic power which the prophet Daniel called the 'desolating sacrilege,' 'the abomination of isolation,'*[12] (RSV: 'the abomination that makes desolate') appeared to go about on earth in human form, the very counter-image of the egohood that was supposed to live one day in divine perfection and fulfilment in the imminent Messiah, but then also as a new power in every human being.

---

* Note by Translator: Bock translates the Greek term *eremoseos* (isolation) with the German word *Ichsucht* or 'egomania,' hence: 'abomination of egomania.'

2.4 Antiochus Epiphanes and Jerusalem

Palestine played a special role in the increasingly tense, power-mad controversies of the Diadochian kingdoms. When the duality of the Ptolemaic-Egyptian and Seleucid-Asiatic rulerships had fully developed, Palestine as the land in the middle became the object of controversy, for it was the region through which the two warring armies had by necessity to pass. This had been the case for Palestine once before in the middle of the second pre-Christian millennium, when the two mighty empires of ancient Egypt and Babylonia had become embroiled in tension and strife. During the period following immediately after the death of Alexander the Great, Palestine initially was included in the sphere of Ptolemaic rule. The spirit of new eagerness for knowledge and encyclopedic scholarliness shone across from Alexandria to Jerusalem. Greek language and art found peaceful, ready access particularly in the northern parts of Palestine in Galilee and Samaria, but also in Judea and the surroundings of Jerusalem. A time of undisturbed cultural exchange allowed the significant encounter between the Jewish and Hellenistic spirit to become fruitful.

But before long, the Seleucids' quest for power was triggered from north and east. The armies of Antiochus III, who is called the Great (222–187), attained a decisive victory over the Egyptians. Palestine changed from the Ptolemaic to Seleucid domain of power. This battle (in the year 198 BC) was a reverse of the Battle of Megiddo in which, around the middle of the second pre-Christian millennium, the great conqueror, Pharaoh Thutmose III, vanquished the Babylonian armies and even added Palestine to his Egyptian empire.[13] Once again, a battle raged in the green plains of Galilee, this time at the foot of the majestic, snow-covered mountain range of Hermon, where in those days the little town of Panias had been built around the ancient, sacred grotto of Pan at the fountainhead of the River Jordan, a town later called Caesarea Philippi.*

The new ruler of the land still adhered to the intentions that

---

* Today [1937], the small impoverished Arab village, in the neighbourhood of which the ancient Pan grotto of the Jordan fountainhead is still shown, is once again called Baneas (Panias), 'the site of Pan.'

had sprung from Alexander the Great's impulse even though he too was one of the bearers of the titanic Diadochian will, a will oriented back to the ancient world. The Jews' right to free and undisturbed exercise of their religion, explicitly decreed by Alexander, remained untouched. Even under Syrian-Asiatic rule, the Temple in Jerusalem with its ritual life continued in undiminished prominence. This changed completely under the successors of the third Antiochus, above all under Antiochus IV (175–163 BC). Now, prompted by the incorporation of Judea into the Seleucid empire, spiritual tension and antagonism increasingly came to the fore. Two worlds collided; a spiritual battle ensued.

It soon became evident that Antiochus Epiphanes was filled with a deeply rooted hatred against the Jews. Where had the harmony between Hellenism and Judaism gone that had emerged so auspiciously in Alexander's era and that of his first Ptolemaic successors, a harmony seemingly prepared by the powers of providence and the higher intentions of the Spirit of the Age? The customary superficial view of history holds that the ferocious conflict and collision between Antiochus and Maccabean Judaism came about because the Syrian king tried by force to continue with the hitherto peaceful Hellenization of Palestine, but that a stern Judaic movement, which clung to the unbroken Law and pure doctrine, heroically arose and opposed this. But it is wrong simply to see in Antiochus Epiphanes one who promoted Hellenism. He was no longer truly a bearer of Alexander's impulse. A different will had taken possession of him, a will that only created the appearance of being clothed in the cultural forms customary under Alexander. Asia's dark reaction against the penetrating light of the new world turned him, who pretended to be a successor of Alexander, into its instrument. A Hellenism infected by Caesarean elements and thus turned into its opposite, lived in the passionate, moody Seleucid.

The fact that Antiochus first closed and then banned a large number of Greek philosophers' schools in his empire before proceeding against the Jews makes it amply clear that he did not hate the Jews because they objected to a Greek cultural direction introduced by him. Above all, the schools of the Epicureans had to suffer many persecutions because of him. In Antiochus

Epiphanes, the principle of mystery popularization had been replaced by that of mystery plunder. The Caesarean egoism in him could not tolerate it that all people were to partake in the mysteries, mysteries by means of which — if he alone possessed them — he, the god-man, would rule and lord it over all other men. He therefore hated not only Jewish but also Greek culture, even though he owed his ascent and power to the latter. All thought-imbued culture that emerged from the mysteries and yet was still esoterically ensouled aroused in him a most furious antipathy. His desire was to snatch up all that still existed in the way of the mysteries and place it exclusively in the service of his own Caesarean deification.

Thereafter, Antiochus' hatred of the Jews grew to an extreme when he sensed that a secret was held sacred and cultivated in Jerusalem to which he would never be allowed to gain access because the people there actually viewed him as the very antagonist of this secret. The clear, prophetically proclaimed Messiah-concept was the reason why he directed his attention with raging jealousy and greed towards Jerusalem, the more he succumbed to the delusion that he himself was the god incarnate.

If the Temple on the rock of Moriah had merely been a sanctuary like any other, Antiochus would have dealt summarily with it. He would soon have found a way to acquire the traditions of wisdom and power cultivated within it. But now he had to come up against the fact that convictions and institutions existed there which, by their mere presence, disputed and refuted his illusory claims. He realized he had subjects in his kingdom who would never pay the prescribed divine homage to him, because they awaited another in calm assurance. It was not the philo-sophical but the Caesarean Hellenism that Antiochus wished to force on the people of Judea. And this was synonymous with his forcing them to acknowledge him in person as god and Messiah.

Only this explains the moody arbitrariness and tyrannical unpredictability of his increasingly relentless interference in the religious life of Jerusalem. His behaviour did not spring from the rational ideas of the spreading Greek spirit but from the demented idea of the Caesarean cult. On the ancient altar of burnt offerings in the Temple, where the pious of the Old Covenant enkindled the flames of the offering as a sign of their ardent

Messiah longing, Antiochus Epiphanes erected a statue of Zeus that bore his own features. He desecrated the holiest of holies, the unapproachable image of the sphere whence the Messiah was to come, because he wished to coerce from the Jews the confession: 'He whom we await has come; you, oh king, you are the one!'

The behaviour of Antiochus Epiphanes caused a part of Jewry to come forward which, until then, had remained quietly in the background, as if in a mystery context. This group must be clearly distinguished from the one that had felt so familiarly attracted by the philosophy and science of Hellenism. Groups of people lived in Jerusalem and in the close vicinity of Judea who, under the leadership of the Pharisaic Order, tried to maintain a conscientious and consistent segregation (Pharisee = the segregated one) from all foreign influences and were intent on an unbending adherence to the Law. They called themselves Hasidim, 'the Pious.'

We must not think, however, as so often happens, that the Hasidim carried on with their stern obedience to the Law merely for the sake of their own soul's salvation. On the contrary, they viewed this as an all-important aspect in the service of the Messiah-concept that concerned the whole nation, a nation of which they felt they were the very centre. In order to make possible and prepare the world-transforming arrival and birth of the longed-for god among his chosen people, they unceasingly tried to keep not only each and every rule of the Mosaic Law but also the regulations prescribed by the Pharisees. It was a Messianic group which, in Jerusalem and Judea, strove anxiously to maintain absolute purity of race and customs. It goes without saying that the community of the Hasidim rejected and avoided any sort of integration with Greek culture and its language.

Nevertheless, for a while the Hellenization of large portions of the Jewish people progressed peacefully alongside the Hasidim. Both factions in their own way believed they were preparing the way for the Messiah. Those who joined the new cultural world movement did indeed contribute to an understanding of Christ, once he had come. Those who segregated themselves and were faithful to the Law were simply and solely concerned with making it possible for the Messiah to be born. It was only when the spiritual Hellenization from Alexandria was replaced by the Caesarean infection from Antioch that the Hasidic Jews, who until then had been quietly engaged in their efforts, emerged from their seclusion. And while Hellenistic Jewry had proven themselves through their open world-view, the sternly Jewish circles now proved themselves through their determined militant heroism and martyrdom.

2.5 The seven sons of the widow

Events began to unfold when, in addition to Hellenistic and Pharisaic-Messianic groups in Jerusalem, a party of individuals emerged from the circles close to the high priests and the Temple who were susceptible to the Caesarean cult from Antioch and its garish splendour. There were those who wished to be on the side of the men in power in order, thereby, to gain influence and advantage. Others, misled by an impatient Messiah-expectation that was directed towards outward politics, allowed themselves to be blinded by the claim of divinity on the part of Antiochus Epiphanes. They behaved like Hellenists, built gymnasiums and, although they belonged to the priesthood of the Temple, participated in competitive games in the Palaestra and the processions of the Dionysian festival. As long as they let it go at that, nobody actively opposed them, even though they incurred the disgust of the Hasidim. But then this group of people who were the complaisant instruments of Antiochus Epiphanes managed to have him appoint one from their own ranks as high priest, an individual who belonged to the family of the high priest. This was Jason who then deposed his brother, Onias III, who occupied the office of high priest. Later on, he even had him murdered. With this, the battle between the different consciousnesses was unleashed. Those who vied for the favour of the Seleucids made themselves instruments of an invasion by anti-Messianic demons into the realm of the pure Messianic expectation.

Insofar as they fought one another with intrigues, bribery and assassination, they dragged their nation into the vortex of chaotic conflict, and so in this way they gave Antiochus the welcome opportunity to proceed against the hated Jews by force of arms. In the year 170 BC, the Syrian king for the first time triggered a terrible blood bath in Jerusalem and robbed the Temple of its treasures. He took with him to Antioch the three sacred gold objects from the central room in the Temple. They were the altar of the burnt offering, the seven-armed candelabra and the table of the shew-breads. Antiochus believed that by so doing he was placing the power of the Jewish cult in the service of his Caesarean self-deification.

Henceforth, each time he suffered a setback in his military undertakings, Antiochus Epiphanes vented his rage on Jerusalem, as if the great rival who would contest his divinity were already present. The king appointed overseers in Jerusalem, not only to squeeze taxes from the people but, first and foremost, to force on the Jews the Caesarean cult clothed in the forms of the Greek cult of gods. Observance of the Jewish Law was to be suppressed by threatening anybody caught in such observance with the death penalty, for example the keeping of the Sabbath and circumcision. Those suspected of opposition were coerced into breaking the Law, for instance, by eating forbidden foods before all the people. Anybody who resisted such coercion was cruelly tortured to death. The demonic hatred reached an extreme in the desecration of the Temple.

This showed that the antagonists knew only too well where the heart of the true Messianic spirit was beating. The desecration consisted in the erection of the Zeus-Antiochus image in the most holy ancient site (in the year 168). Now the dark opposing power, the Antichrist who in the spiritual realm fought against the coming of the Messiah, was reproduced visibly in human form. The tyrant had produced a cosmic symbol that sent great fear into the Jewish people. Yet, at the same time, it was a symbol that could not but signify for this nation the mightiest arousal and ignition of their soul forces. For although none dared speak of it, the secret was known to all: before Christ comes, the Antichrist has to reveal himself; when the opposing force makes its appearance, the arrival of the Messiah is no longer far off.*

---

* The Greek name, *Christos,* is the exact translation of the Hebrew word, 'Messiah.'

We stand at a point in history where, more than is normally the case, the accent and reality of events does not lie in the sphere of earthly appearance but in the supersensory. Spiritual battles took place in which, even outwardly, only the side that resisted true progress was represented in an impressive and demanding manner. On the surface, those who struggled on the other side were unassuming. Once again, history did not progress due to overbearing wielders of power who could crush any resistance mercilessly, but through the meek silent figures who, not yielding to force, sealed their spirit-devoted strength and faith with sorrow and death. The tyrant's pretentious will was spiritually defeated by the victims whom it assumed it was eliminating by shedding their blood.

The two books of the Maccabees point to a handful of people, most of them not even mentioned by name, as actual bearers of progressive historical development; victorious pioneers of the future in whom the will of the deity was germinating. When the anti-Messianic horrors were at their worst, these individuals suffered the death of martyrdom: a ninety-year-old man and an aged widow with her seven sons.

The mystery drama of this quiet spiritual victory that nevertheless brightly illuminated all the heavens, is described merely in a few sentences as an episode in the Second Book of the Maccabees as if veiling a secret. Only the apocryphal Fourth Book of the Maccabees deals with it exclusively and demonstrates how the example of particularly this group of martyrs had a clear and inspiring effect around the turning point of time and even the period of Christian persecutions.

A secret surrounds the figures who made their heroic confessions, one after the other under the most horrendous tortures, finally sealing them with a most painful death. Only the old man, who preceded the seven men and youths in martyrdom, is mentioned by name. His name, Eleazar, is the Hebrew version of the name, Lazarus, Grecianized by the New Testament. It is said of him that he held a high rank among the sages and scholars of the Jews and that when he appeared before his tormentors his figure shone with dignity. In him, a man suffered death whose soul was filled through and through with the spirit of devout Messianic expectation, not unlike that of old Simeon in the

Temple. The seven sons of the widow are not mentioned by name. We sense that each one had a completely individual character and that together, in a significant way, like the tones of an octave, they formed a totality.

Yet we are unable to discern the outlines of their individual personalities through the veil that is discreetly drawn over them. The whole manner of the description, on the other hand, arouses a feeling in us: are these men really the sons of a widow in a superficial, coincidental sense only, or are we to rediscover the truth of this relationship in the soul-spiritual dimension by means of the external picture? Were they perhaps 'sons of the widow' in the sense of the mysteries where the initiates were thus depicted?[14] Is it possible that, in the seven sons of the widow and their mother, a Messianic stream utterly devoted to the spirit — a stream that existed apart from the Pharisaic circles and normally remained hidden in mystery obscurity — sent forth its noblest representatives into the arena of history where, taking the place of all their people, they then suffered torture and death?

When the books of the Maccabees emphasize that the tormentors tried to force their victims to break the dietary laws, this may be an indication that Eleazar and the widow with her sons belonged to the unassuming social groups of the Essene Order where, like the custom among the Nazarenes, the adherence to certain dietary laws was part of their soul training. An important figure of historical evolution can be deciphered from the story of the seven sons of the widow. An unobtrusive but significant symmetry exists in the events before and after the Christ Event. The martyrs of the apostolic age have their correspondence in the last chapter of Old Testament developments.

The events of the Maccabean age are like a prophetic mirror image of what took place in early Christendom. The Event of Golgotha is the dynamic spiritual centre. The Christ being's approach to earthly incarnation was accompanied by signs of the times similar to those that accompanied this being's first worldwide activity following his passing through earthly death. The thought of the imminent coming of the longed-for Saviour gave the martyrs at the end of the Old Testament the strength to face death courageously and gladly. What harm could death do them if it led them into the world whence Christ was just making ready to depart, but where they could still encounter him in his actual being? Did the cruel tormentors not help the devout souls to go and meet the Messiah and receive him as messengers sent forth by humanity? The martyrs of the Maccabean period died for the Christ who was in the process of coming; those of early Christendom died for the one who was once again growing beyond the human form in which he had been incarnated.

2.6 Judas Maccabeus and his brothers

On the level of earthly appearance, the soul victory of the martyrs created no deliverance from travail. The Caesarean tyranny only became the more fanatical and demonic, the more it shed the blood of its victims. But then it appeared as if, through the martyred witnesses, a spark of courage had been drawn down from the power-enfilled heavens to drive the people on from the heroism of enduring to that of fighting.

One year after the Temple desecration in Jerusalem, the spark was kindled. The flame flared up free and tall in Modin, a small Judean town in the foothills above Lydda (then Diospolis) with a view far across the Mediterranean Sea. When the agents of the Syrian king appeared there to coerce the population to offer up sacrifices to the gods and Caesar, the priest, Mattathias, stepped forth. Incensed by divine wrath, he not only cut down Antiochus' overseer but also a Jew who had been willing to submit to alien coercion. Once again, a group of brothers turned into vessels and bearers of the fire-kindling enthusiasm of courage that struck down from heaven like lightning. The seven sons of the widow were now followed by the five sons of Mattathias. They did not wish to remain in obscurity like the former but tried to actively intervene in the prominent events of their time; for this reason, their names are mentioned: John, Simon, Judas, Eleazar and Jonathan. They stand in history like the very core of a nation of soldiers of God.

Following the first blazing eruption of militant will, it seemed as if the people had been thrown back to the more inward heroism of martyrdom due to the sternness of the paternal Law. Along with a large number of the Messianically pious, Mattathias and his five sons fled into the mountainous desert of Judea, to the hiding places where, nine hundred years earlier, David had sought protection from Saul's persecution. A whole army gathered, heroically determined to repulse the enemy. Then the Syrian troops advanced. But something dreadful occurred. The attack took place on a Sabbath. Did the deity itself wish to snatch away the weapons of its faithful followers? Abiding by the Law that prohibited nothing more sternly than use of arms on a Sabbath, Jews without number allowed themselves to be cut down without resistance. But a new and powerful impulse of courage flamed through Mattathias and his sons. Was it the Law that was at stake or was it not rather the great Messiah-secret itself, in the service of which the Law could merely be a means of education and preparation? Now was not the time to prepare by means of the Law's discipline for him who was to come. Something more difficult was required. The coming of the Messiah itself was at stake.

The dire situation caused a dawning light of future freedom from the Law to flash through the people's souls. Mattathias and his sons now proclaimed a battle, for the sake of which even the stern Sabbath command had to yield. Jerusalem's congregation of Hasidim* determinedly intervened in the course of events by approving and supporting the daring step of the priest from Modin. It was as if the spirit of the age of the judges had returned, an age when the courage of leadership in battle had descended like a fiery flame on one or another chosen medium who was readily acknowledged and followed by the nation as the spiritually designated leader.

Mattathias and his sons travelled throughout the land. They gathered the faithful willing to fight and condemned those who had cowardly submitted to Caesarean pressure. They destroyed the altars forced on the people, circumcised male youths and bore the kindling torch of courage from place to place, from city to city. In the midst of the furious preparation for battle, the priest, Mattathias, died. Now the constellation of his five sons truly appeared like the instrument of a warrior angel from heaven.

---

* 1Macc.2:42 does not merely refer to a 'company of pious ones [Hasidim].' What is meant is the community of Hasidim, formed like a religious Order (in Greek: *synagoge Asidaion*).

Judas assumed the leadership, a man whose second name, Maccabeus, soon became not only the designation for the whole family of leaders but, beyond that, of a whole era.

Judas Maccabeus was a mysterious, larger-than-life figure. It was as if he consisted of pure fiery will, a will sustained not only by human but superhuman sources. The Messianic image of the 'Lion from the house of Judah' seemed to have taken on form already in Judas Maccabeus: 'He was like a lion in his deeds, like a lion's cub roaring for prey' (1Macc.3f). The customary interpretation is that the term 'Maccabee' means 'hammer,' and it certainly fits in substance, for it evokes a picture of the great Maccabean's inexorable and irresistible will element. But the tradition that traces the name back to the letters, M K B J, said to have blazed on the battle flag of Judas, is at least equally valid. In Hebrew, these are the first letters of the words for the Michaelic name of the deity, 'Who among the mighty is like you, oh God?'* If this latter interpretation is correct, the name Maccabee was a rune for invoking the warring victorious sun-archangel. He had once been Israel's folk spirit, then the time spirit between the ages of the prophets and Alexander. Now, as the spiritual herald preparing his way, Michael stood exclusively before the countenance of Christ. The Michaelic-Messianic character of the Maccabean battles would in this case be contained even in the name.

The miracle happened: Judas Maccabeus led the small army of those faithful to the Messiah from victory to victory against the troops of the mighty kingdom of the Seleucids. The smallest land within his kingdom set a boundary against the Caesarian madness of Antiochus Epiphanes, a boundary that all his rage and efforts were unable to surmount. As in the days of Joshua, armies of gods appeared to be fighting on the side of a small number of heroically battling humans. The spiritual struggle above the heads of men flashed into earthly events. The Michaelic hosts who were paving the way for the Christ being's access to the earthly plane were mightier than the demonic dragon forces of an ancient world, forces that were unwilling to allow anyone to contest their power. In the year 165, three years after the desecration of the

* Translated, the simple archangelic name Michael means, 'Who is like God?'

70

Temple, Judas Maccabeus, having made himself ruler over the city of Jerusalem, was able to provide the Temple with new altars and once again to dedicate them to the service of the offering. Each year from then on, the day on which this took place was celebrated as Hanuka, the Feast of Dedication of the Temple.

Judas turned Judea into an independent state. From the northern provinces of Samaria and Galilee, he brought into this state those Jews who were devoted to the Law. Henceforth, only a Hellenistic Judaism imbued with the Greek spirit could be encountered north of Judea. An unbroken unity was to be prepared as a pure vessel for the approaching Messiah. Moreover, it appeared that destiny was coming to the aid of the Maccabeans in a special way: Antiochus Epiphanes perished in a Persian campaign (163 BC) during an attack on the sun temple of Elymais, where Antiochus III, too, had earlier met his death, lusting also for the mysteries present there. Yet it was reminiscent of Heracles' battle against the Hydra. When one head of the serpent was cut off, many others grew forth in the same spot. Having been disturbed in their sleep and turned demonic, Asia's primal world spirits only found more numerous instruments. Even though the new rulers fought amongst themselves, the Seleucid kingdom resembled a dragon of ominous unpredictability. Judas sensed this, although he did lead his army once more to a decisive victory and subdued and killed the feared commander, Nicanor. He decided on a step fraught with consequences. He called for help from the Romans. And the delegates whom he sent to Rome were indeed successful in bringing about a treaty of friendship and alliance between Rome and Judea.

In those days, Rome was still far from being the worldwide empire it would later become by the time of Christ. After the destruction of Carthage during the Punic Wars, Rome was just on the verge of expanding the spheres of its influence. Rome's emergence was supported by a quite novel attitude of life that developed in its citizens and was Rome's contribution to the new world, a world born earlier in Greece. For Romans were ensouled by a basic consciousness of personality. The ego impulse emerged in Rome, too, but here it was not nourished by the rich life of thought and art as developed by the Greeks in transforming their mysteries. Instead, it was brought about by the proud awareness that, as Romans, they were predisposed to personal competence and the civic virtue of justice. The discovery of the ideal of practical humaneness passed like a roar through the Roman world and even motivated the first larger military undertakings with which Rome began its ascent to a worldwide empire. Initially, Romans saw themselves less as conquerors than as pioneers of a humanitarian culture that contrasted with the old world's tyrannical civilizations.

When the delegates of Judas Maccabeus arrived, Rome had been observing for some time the Caesarean course pursued by the realm of the Seleucid kings with watchful distrust. For, after all, when hard pressed by Rome, Hannibal, their mighty Carthaginian opponent, had not escaped to Antiochus the Great in Antioch by coincidence. Judas Maccabeus must have been in a strange frame of mind when he concluded the treaty with Rome. What was it that induced him who stood at the zenith of his heroic successes to seek foreign support? Why was it that the unpredictability of the Seleucid power structure frightened him so much? For even though it emerged anew after the death of Antiochus Epiphanes, would it not shatter in the face of a clear and alert will as it had before? Had the support of the inspiring will of God diminished and did uncertainty befall the victor and hero because he felt thrown back on his own resources and power?

The power of the opponent suddenly appeared to him to have grown to gigantic proportions. But was he now inclined to overrate all foreign elements? He had heard of the deeds of the Romans (1Macc.8:1–6), their stand regarding Caesarean ambitions (8:14f) and their willingness to protect unjustly threatened nations (8:1). But were the high expectations he now entertained of Rome not born of an overestimation of what Rome currently represented? Perhaps it was a presentiment of the greatness and might to which Rome would ascend in the next few decades that at this point flashed through Judas' troubled soul.

Yet precisely because of this, tragedy resulted from Judas' decision. Rome would eventually become powerful and succumb to the same lure of Caesarean madness that presently dominated the Syrian enemies and oppressors of Jerusalem. The Romans did not come immediately when Judas Maccabeus called for their assistance. And when they finally arrived, the Caesarean hunger for power had already begun to drive away their former love of justice and humanitarianism. Soon, the original allies and helpers turned into wielders of power who exercised an increasingly oppressive alien rule. By the time of the Event on Golgotha, Rome's hand weighed heavily on Judea and Jerusalem. It had been Judas Maccabeus who, without intending to do so, had summoned the foreign rulers into the country.

The delegates had not returned from Rome when great misfortune befell the Jews. Did Judas have a foreboding of the calamity or did he bring it about because of his uncertainty? Hardly two months had passed since his great victory over Nicanor, when in the spring of 161 a Syrian army of such overwhelmingly superior force approached that panic and fear drove the Jews to flight even before the battle. The contingent that remained steadfast fought with desperate superhuman courage but was mowed down mercilessly. Among the fallen was Judas Maccabeus himself. For seven years, Judea now had to submit to the will of the victor.

His brother Jonathan stepped into the place of Judas Maccabeus as leader of those who gathered together for the final Messiah-preparation. While Judas had protected and directed the destinies of Judea through the force of his iron will, Jonathan now accomplished the same by circumspection and astuteness. After he had utilized the seven-year interim period to bolster people's spirits, he successfully took advantage of the strife between the parties who were competing for Seleucid power. They viewed Judea as holding the balance of power and alternately tried to gain the ascendancy by drawing the Maccabean nation to their side with promises and privileges.

Strange scenes occurred. When the usurper, Alexander Balas, who passed himself off as the son of Antiochus Epiphanes, celebrated his wedding with an Egyptian princess, Jonathan sat by his side as his guest of honour in a splendid purple robe. High Syrian titles and honours were bestowed on the Maccabeans. At one point, Simon was even named the 'strategist' or military governor of all the lands between Tyre and Egypt. Yet, eighteen years after the death of Judas, Jonathan fell victim to the game in which luck had favoured him for so long. Under the pretense of wishing to engage in special negotiations with him, one of those about to usurp power lured him into the enemy camp. He walked into the trap and was treacherously slain along with his companions.

The only task that remained for the by then aged Maccabean, Simon, was to conserve what his brothers had built up, Judas through strength, Jonathan through astuteness. And it was indeed the faculty of wise conservation that he could avail himself of. With much circumspection, he bestowed a social order on the people. They in turn assigned the office of high priest, an office that included the political leadership over Judea, as a hereditary honour on his descendants. Thus originated the Maccabean-Hasmonean dynasty.

The occasionally reoccurring attempts to attack and tyrannize Judea from Antioch were repulsed by Simon and his sons. But then (135 BC), along with his sons, Mattathias and Judas, Simon fell victim to a cowardly murderous plot that his son-in-law, Ptolemy, vying for the favour of those in power, staged against him at Jericho when Simon was in the midst of visiting all the communities of the pious in the land. Along with the office of high priest, John Hyrcanus, Simon's surviving son, continued to lead the people. But it was not long before the uniformity and strength of the Maccabean will was at an end. Political tensions and one-sidedness came to the fore. It is as if the history of the Jewish people had to be steered to just a certain point by the superior power of the five Maccabean sons; as if, until that moment in time, the spiritual battle and approaching Messianic activity above the sphere of humanity had required a spiritually strong, unified nation as its vessel. But then, the approaching future impulse appeared to be sufficiently safeguarded and guaranteed. The people's history diminished to an irrelevant disorder of equal and opposing forces. Independently of external events, ever more clearly, the spiritual element went its own way.

Simon was the last of the five Maccabean sons. All his brothers had lost their lives before him. The first had been Eleazar who had fallen in the battle led by Judas Maccabeus against the Syrian army after the death of Antiochus Epiphanes. In the belief that he was confronting the mount of the young king, Eleazar stabbed a huge elephant but then was trampled to death by the colossal beast. Judas Maccabeus was the second to die the death of a warrior. Soon afterwards, now that the Syrians possessed all the power in Jerusalem, John lost his life when he tried to carry the Temple treasures to safety in the Sinai region. Hordes of Arabs, who sought to curry favour with the Syrian rulers, killed him. Simon and Jonathan only managed by a hair's breadth to retrieve the precious objects from the robbers and escape with them. Finally, at the end of the period during which they had been leaders of the people, Jonathan and Simon met their deaths at the hand of assassins. All five sons of the priest, Mattathias, thus died violent deaths. They became martyrs in active service for the future of their nation, even as the seven sons of the widow had become martyrs in purely inward heroism. As they had done through their deeds, the five Maccabean brothers also revealed the markedly individual element of their personalities through their death. Their being and destiny had fully emerged from behind the mystery veil — a veil behind which the seven sons of the widow had remained concealed.

2.7 Judith

The inner and outer battles and heroic deeds of the age of the Maccabees represent a significant contribution to bringing about the new world. An importance is due them that is similar and yet again greater than the Persian Wars conducted so courageously by the Greeks. Along with the armies of Persians, the young nation of Greeks repulsed the demons of the past from Europe. It thus prepared the stage for itself on which to produce the miracles of the Athens of Pericles and Plato, first gifts of a new spirit of humanity.

Similarly, under the Maccabees, the small and ancient Jewish nation was aroused to an heroic accomplishment by which the spirits of antiquity were similarly fended off, spirits that had turned darkly demonic and were poised for a mighty counter-attack. Yet, in Palestine, the stage was set for more than merely a new epoch of human cultural accomplishments. Here, above all, a vessel threatened by greatest danger was saved, one that was to serve the human incarnation of the highest divine being. More was at stake during the battles of the Maccabees than in the

Persian Wars. Not only the future of Europe but the future of all humanity, insofar as the latter required the redeeming divine impulse that could only be brought about by the Christ being.

The importance due the battles and heroism of the Maccabean age, an importance extending far beyond the physical plane, found expression in a classic manner in the mythical imagery of the story of Judith. It appears that a single heroic scene from the times of tribulation is being related. In reality, we are supposed to see through the earthly image into the process that compresses all the single battles into one mighty spiritual battle. Not merely an earthly city was beleaguered by the cruel enemies; the mythical name, Bethulia, points to a higher level. Not only did individuals courageously resist duress and danger but the soul of the nation became visible in the figure of Judith, who struggled against the tyrant intent only on violation.

In the Old Testament's succession of female figures — Ruth, Esther, and Judith — the highest intensification of militant tension was reached. The Bethlehem peace personified in Ruth and her maternal devotion to the Messianic future of the people appear as if far removed. And yet the act of desperation courageously carried out by Judith, when she cut off the head of the drunkenly sleeping Holofernes, had only one meaning: to hold open the space for the one who was to come. A demonic Caesarean will tried to claim the nation's soul for its own pleasure, a soul that only wished to surrender herself to the one divine being that would soon be born from her womb as a human being. Like the shepherd boy David who long ago lifted up the cut-off head of the giant as a frightening Medusa countenance, so Judith now carried the horrible trophy of the Holofernes-head through the ranks of her already discouraged, despairing people. Its sight rekindled the flame of courage; the superior power of the enemy was overcome. The path was open: the divine being who sought its nation could make its entrance.

2.8 Secrets of destiny

Insofar as it is through the fulcrum of the Christ Event that everything in the books of the Bible as well as the history depicted in them is given its order and meaning, they abound in figures that conceal secrets of providence and destiny. The most obvious example of the symmetry of destiny reflected in the Bible is the correspondence between the twelve sons of Jacob at the beginning of the Old Testament and the twelve Apostles at the beginning of the New Testament. As we move forward from the one group of twelve to the other, we move from a human order based on blood ties of family and folk to one where the various individual personalities are brought together through kinship of the spirit. Between these two groups of twelve, history as well as the Old Testament places an additional group of twelve, albeit in veiled, barely visible form, if we include the apocryphal books of the Maccabees. They are the figures of the martyrs and heroes of the Maccabean age, the seven sons of the widow and the five sons of Mattathias. The course of the Old Testament begins and ends with a group of twelve. Once again, at the beginning of Christ's earthly journey, a group of twelve indicates the universal radius of events. A quite special mystery prevails between the last two groups of twelve, separated as they are in time by a mere century and a half.

Rudolf Steiner has illuminated this secret through the light of spiritual research, and has thus made visible a bridge of destiny between the Old and New Testament, a miracle of providence that fills us with reverent amazement. In his lecture cycle on the Gospel of Mark, Rudolf Steiner unveils the fact that the same individualities who lived in the age of the Maccabees as the seven sons of the widow and the five sons of Mattathias then incarnated after an unusually short period of time as the twelve Apostles of Christ. We thus behold a group of twelve souls who, representing a quintessence of all humanity, crossed over the mightiest threshold of historical evolution. The last from among pre-Christian humanity — a humanity filled with a mood of anticipation — turned into the first who gathered around the Saviour-become-man. During the Maccabean age, these twelve were still fully entrenched in purely nationalistic endeavours and emotions within close blood-related groups. Nevertheless, they were brought quite close to grasping their immortal individual essence through their exalted power of faith. In the following life, incarnated independently from each other and grown up in greatly differing individual circumstances, they were allowed once again to become a community, this time by pursuing only the spiritual direction of a common spiritual conviction and devotion. And their utter dedication and surrender to the nation's destiny during the times of the great Messianic tensions and dangers now allowed them to become the intimate circle of disciples of him whose coming they had once longed for so ardently and actively.

Rudolf Steiner describes this significant destiny relationship in the following way:

All the progress that has been made consists in this: souls are becoming individualized. They are connected with the supersensory world not only indirectly through their group-soul nature, but they are also connected with it through the element of the individual soul. He who so stands before humanity that He is recognized by the beings of earth and is also recognized by supersensory beings needs the best element of human nature to enable Him to sink something of the supersensory into the souls of those who are to serve Him. He requires such men as have themselves made the furthest progress in their souls according to the old way. It is extremely interesting to follow the soul-development of those whom Christ Jesus gathered around Him; the Twelve whom He particularly called to be His own who, in all their simplicity, as we might say, passed in the grandest way through the development which, as I tried to show you ... is gained by human souls in widely varied incarnations.

A man must first become accustomed to being a specific individuality. This he cannot easily do when he is transferred from the element of the nation in which his soul has taken root into a condition of being dependent upon himself alone. The Twelve were deeply rooted in a nationality which had constituted itself in the grandest from. They stood there as if they were naked souls,

simple souls, when Christ found them again. There had
been a quite abnormal interval between their incarnations.
The gaze of Christ Jesus could rest upon the Twelve, the
reincarnated souls of those who had been the seven sons
of the Maccabean* and the five sons of Matthathias,
Judas and his brothers; it was of these that the apostolate
was formed. They were thrown into the element of
fishermen and simple folk. But at a time when the Jewish
element had reached its culminating point they had been
permeated by the consciousness that this element was
then at the peak of its strength, but strength only —
whereas, when the group formed itself around Christ, this
element appeared in individualized form.

We might conceive that someone who was a complete
unbeliever might look upon the appearance of the seven
and the five at the end of the Old Testament, and their
reappearance at the beginning of the New Testament, as
nothing but an artistic progression. If we take it as a
purely artistic composition, we may be moved by its
simplicity and the artistic greatness of the Bible, quite
apart from the fact that the Twelve are the five sons of
Matthathias and the seven sons of the Maccabean
mother ...[15]

The same remarkable destiny relationship that spiritual
research reveals to us here was also caught by the deeply poetic
soul mirror of Grimms' fairy tales. There, the fairy tale of 'The
Twelve Apostles' can speak for itself:

Three hundred years before the birth of the Lord Christ,
there lived a mother who had twelve sons, but she was so
poor and needy that she no longer knew how she was to
keep them all alive. She prayed to God daily that he
would grant that all her sons might be on the earth with
the Redeemer who was promised. When her need became
still greater she sent one after the other out into the world
to seek bread for her. The eldest was called Peter, and he
went out and had already walked a long way, a whole
day's journey, when he came into a great forest. He

---

* This refers to the seven brothers in 2Macc.7.

sought for a way out, but could find none, and went farther and farther astray. At the same time he felt such great hunger that he could scarcely stand. At length he became so weak that he was forced to lie down, and he believed death to be at hand. Suddenly there stood beside him a small boy who shone with brightness, and was as beautiful and kind as an angel. The child clapped his little hands together, until Peter was forced to look up and saw him. Then the child said: 'Why art thou sitting there in such trouble?' 'Alas!' answered Peter, 'I am going about the world seeking bread, that I may yet see the dear Saviour who is promised, that is my greatest desire.' The child said, 'Come with me, and thy wish shall be fulfilled.' He took poor Peter by the hand, and led him between some cliffs to a great cavern. When they entered it, everything was shining with gold, silver, and crystal, and in the midst of it twelve cradles were standing side by side. Then the little angel said, 'Lie down in the first, and sleep a while, I will rock thee.' Peter did so, and the angel sang to him and rocked him until he was asleep. And when he was asleep, the second brother came also, guided thither by his guardian angel, and he was rocked to sleep like the first, and the others came, one after the other, until all twelve lay there sleeping in the golden cradles. They slept, however, three hundred years, until the night when the Saviour of the world was born. Then they awoke, and were with him on earth, and were called the twelve Apostles.

3. Romanism:
Caesar — Cleopatra — Herod

3.1 Ancient, pre-Caesarean Rome

When we visit Rome today, a city so rich in history, two periods with their imposing monuments are offered to our view: the Rome of the Caesars and of the Popes. The secular impact of the thermal springs of Caracalla, the Colosseum and the emperors' forums, the ecclesiastic pomp of the innumerable baroque structures, above all the Dome of St Peter, obscure anything else. Are traces of pre-Caesarean and pre-Christian Rome extinguished or do they merely elude us? The Rome of early Christendom can indeed be discovered if one knows how to pursue less prominent leads. First, the many Romanesque campaniles that rise in pregnant silence over the din of the city can point the way for us. Moreover, anywhere at the edge of the city we can enter the subterranean world of the Catacombs and allow a hint of early Christian life to touch us. We look in vain, however, for pre-Caesarean Rome. Apart from a few insignificant exceptions, nearly all the old edifices that surround us originated no earlier than about the turning point of time. And yet, for centuries prior to this, Rome had had a very significant history and exhibited most characteristic cultural features.

We cannot conceive of a greater difference than the one between pre-Caesarean and Caesarean Rome. All too easily, when trying to form an idea of the older Rome, we remain under the spell of the impressions of imperial Rome that are forced on us with such intensity. Perhaps it is easier to make contact with ancient pre-Caesarean Rome when we venture southward out to the Roman campagna on the old Via Appia. Isolated ruins of tomb structures, dark stone-pines and cypress trees line the ancient roadway. But it is mainly an atmospheric element that imbues the pleasant scenery and directly conjures forth the spirit of times long ago. A touch of simplicity can be felt, of something forthright and genuine, a quite introspective pride in human competence. It tells us something of Rome's soul before the consciousness of the Caesarean age of power placed the mark of its nature on it all. And when the south-bound traveller looks up to the blue outlines of the Albanensian mountains to which the ancient road leads, he might even be able to re-evoke the devout emotion that filled Romans of earlier times when they looked up to the site where once the priest state of Alba Longa flourished, the mother of the great daughter city, Rome.

As the younger brother of Greece, its older sister, ancient Rome was a significant part of the new world. Yet, from the very beginning, the features of Roman life differed greatly from those of Greek life. Hellas was still linked to the abundant wisdom of the mysteries of antiquity because its history reached farther back and its location was closer to the world of Asia Minor. It could produce its culture by transforming and publizing the world of the mysteries.

Rome, on the other hand, had never possessed mysteries of its own. As a young stream of humanity, Rome had always had to rely on producing a culture based on purely human forces. While it was surrounded by neighbouring folk who, like the ancient Etruscans, were still in possession of ancient Atlantean faculties and traditions of magic, Rome could only learn from them by isolating itself from them. Only by fighting them could Rome become aware of its own strength. Those from whom Rome did receive cultural impulses were the Greeks who had founded and cultivated their rich colonies in southern Italy and Sicily. But even then, the culture they brought contained the awakening element of the new world, having been liberated from the dusky darkness of the mysteries. A new bright spirit emanated from the Greek colonies towards the initially unpretentious surroundings of Roman life.

The cultural will of early Rome, unlike that of Greece, did not aim at a development of philosophy, science or art. It turned singularly and solely to the development of man's own character and personality and the structure and balance of social forces of the state which holds individual human beings together. Here, the first signs of life of the ego epoch were not discerned in the sphere of thinking or feeling but of will. In the exercise of personal capabilities and the virtues of bravery, duty and allegiance to the whole nation, Romans learned to experience themselves as ego-imbued, single personalities. More than any communications of ideal teachings and wisdom, it had an educational effect on the minds of the young to be confronted with moral role models. There was the example of a Mucius Scaevola, who burned his right hand because he had not achieved what he had meant to despite his heroic action in battle. There was Cincinnatus who received news of his appointment to be dictator and chief of the troops while tilling his field and, having led the people to victory, returned to his plow as if nothing had happened. There was Lucretia who, having been dishonoured by a ruler, ended her life and thus motivated the whole nation to shake off tyrannical rule. And there was a Virginia who was slain by her father because her honour was endangered, whose death likewise became the signal of a battle for freedom.

A sense for the value of the human personality that strives for virtue, an inborn love of justice and the social well-being among men led the Romans, once their early period of the seven mythical kings was over, to develop and perfect their state into a balanced work of art. Roman law was Rome's essential contribution to the configuration of the new world. The proud feeling of being a personality was nourished in each person through the proud awareness of being a Roman. This was why the thought of the whole national body, to which each individual relates only as the single limb does to the human body, had so much power that it was possible to bestow equal rights to all without impeding stern discipline. Egohood marked by the will matured along with the ideal of the virtues of citizens.

Thus, although it still exhibited a quite humble appearance, Rome, the yet unassuming republican city-state, developed the democratic principle and had arrived at a certain completion of this in the age when Alexander the Great disseminated Greek cultural life through the whole world. Around the year 300, the development had advanced to a point where, for example, not only patricians but also plebeians were admitted to the office of priest and augur. Even those who owned no real estate could be registered as citizens with full rights in the regional lists of the *tribus*.* The social balance of such a democratic structure remained in existence without any major disturbance for about two hundred years and made room for the organic development of the ego impulse.

The military struggles Rome had to conduct until about the year 300 BC, hence into the period directly following the death of Alexander the Great, can be compared with the battles the Israelites had to wage against the neighbouring nations of Phoenicia and Canaan in the era of Joshua and the Judges. As the Israelites struggled against the Philistines and Ammonites, so the Romans fought against the Samnites and Etruscans in order to maintain their own identity against older magical cultures. The wars which then followed and soon turned Rome into a military state, causing it to emerge into the historical foreground as a power factor, were connected with the development involving the split of Alexander's empire into the Diadochian kingdoms.

It was not long before democratic Rome felt that, as the nation fighting in the vanguard of the new impulse in humanity, it had to confront the demons of the past that arose among the Diadochi. The wars then waged by Rome were not yet wars of conquest. Even when their legions finally fought battles in all parts of the world, the Romans could still believe that they were serving the spirit of justice and order against dark, inhuman, tyrannical forces. This even applies to the Punic Wars that finally ended with the destruction of Carthage, and even more so to the armed expeditions against the Seleucid power, which the Romans felt compelled to undertake when Hannibal sought refuge with Antiochus III. And when Judas Maccabeus turned to the Romans for help in his struggle for freedom because he had heard that they protected unjustly attacked nations and 'possessed such high virtue that not one among them had made himself king' (1Macc. 8:14*B*), this was really based on a sense of kinship and rapport in the spiritual mission of both nations.

---

* *Tribus* refers to one of the three original tribes of the Roman people.

3.2 *Marius and Sulla*

On the one side, military life offered Romans the opportunity for a perfect development of male virtues and the establishment of ideals of lawfulness and humanitarianism. On the other, it amounted to a temptation for them. Rome was not spared the old world's revenge, a world whose spirits had so quickly cast their spell over the Hellenistic people. While any form of imperialism was originally foreign to the Romans, in the end they would have had to remain less successful in their wars in order to remain protected from the temptation to seek power. The ambition of military leaders; the delight, which eventually turned to greed, in the riches amassed by means of the victorious wars, had to disrupt the social balance of the democratic system. The attempts at social reform under the Gracchus around the middle of the second pre-Christian century are a symptom of the fading of ancient Roman democratic life and an ominous rumbling of a threatening undercurrent.

The subsequent development took its course dramatically and became evident in a characteristic group of figures. In Marius (156–86 BC) and Sulla (138–78 BC), a representative of the ancient Roman spirit and the firstborn of a completely different attitude of soul and will — a consciousness that henceforth would increasingly come to the fore — confronted each other around the year 100 BC.[16] Marius, not an urban Roman but a descendant from peasant stock, confessed extreme loyalty to the original simplicity and straightforward decency that he saw as the nature of a true Roman. He was not favourably inclined towards modern education and a culture that tended even then to luxury, even where it brought the spirit of Greece to Rome along with the Greek language. He held that these new ways emasculated men physically and morally. He possessed an inborn share of the folk spirit's healthy instinct; believed firmly in the mental sovereignty of the people and was a man quite after their hearts. They therefore elected him consul time and time again. A proper swordsman with a short thickset body and a square head, he felt most at ease among his legions. Military Rome had taken on form in him. He was the creator of the mercenary troops; Rome eventually conquered the world with them. The memory of successfully fought wars, above all the repulsion of the advancing Germanic tribes of Cimberi and Teutons, remained foremost in his mind throughout his life.

Sulla, a native of the city of Rome, far surpassed the peasant-like Marius in education. Because of his great ambition, his sensation-seeking vanity and restlessness, he was susceptible to the temptations to which the ruling houses of the Diadochi had long since succumbed. In his youth, he had enjoyed roaming around with rioutous groups of actors and even liked to show off as a mime. When, for the first time, he had to assume a command of his own in Asia Minor while serving in the military under Marius, he immediately fell under the spell of the Orient. Before long, Sulla set himself sharply against Marius. He knew how to crowd out the old soldier, who was becoming somewhat embittered and peculiar, and to discredit him in the eyes of the people. By limiting people's rights and through force, he held down their free expression of opinion. Once, he placed himself at the head of the troops who were ordered to suppress an uprising of the people in favour of Marius, who by then lived in retirement. When Sulla faced personal danger, he had no better recourse than to escape to the home of Marius. The latter followed the sentiments of ancient Roman virtue and to his own detriment saved his enemy's life,

Bitter over the end of good old Roman freedom, Marius became more and more reclusive. Finally, having become addicted to drink, he died a miserable death. Sulla rose in callous egoism on the ladder to fame. He managed to be given the command over the military invasion against the Persian king, Mithridates. Intoxicated with power, Sulla moved through the towns that once had been sites of the beautiful blossoming of Greek life. An objective interest in what the Greek spirit had produced was far from his mind. He viewed the ancient treasures of the gods and their wisdom solely in the light of how he could increase his power through them. Wherever he encountered traces of the ancient mystery practices, he was only too eager to acquire the faculties connected with them. He looted the temple treasures of Olympia and Delphi in order to lead the expedition against Mithridates with the currency coined from this treasure. Henceforth, as an amulet, he always carried an old consecrated image

of Apollo with him. He sent the handwritten documents of
Aristotle to Rome as special spoils of the war.

The conclusion of the war was surrounded by strange riddles.
Sulla had completely vanquished his opponent. Yet Mithridates
remained in complete possession of his kingdom. Why was it that
Sulla did not take advantage of the victory for which, for so
many years, Rome had made the greatest sacrifices? A strange
scene is described to us. The final negotiations were conducted
by the two rulers personally. In the end, Sulla approached the
defeated king and hugged and kissed him. What did this signify?
It has always been noted that Sulla then returned from Asia to
Rome a completely changed man. He had hardly made himself
master over Rome again when, as if possessed by bloodthirsti-
ness, he unleashed a carnage of terrible magnitude. For the first
time, Rome experienced the horror of proscriptions which would
be repeated under the first Caesars. Long lists of names were
made public and a high reward paid to anybody who brought in
the head of one who had been outlawed. It surely touches upon
an important historical truth to have connected the transformation
in Sulla's character with that strange kiss he gave Mithridates
instead of taking his kingdom from him:

> Whence came the sudden, exceedingly grotesque cruelty
> of the man? Was it merely revenge for what Marius had
> done? Sulla came back from the Orient. The Sultan's
> spirit of Mithridates had passed over into him since that
> kiss which Sulla had given Mithridates. Who can deny
> this? The actor Sulla now played the Sultan. And it was
> then that Mithridates butchered Rome in Sulla's form.[17]

Some scenes possess great historical value. This kiss by Sulla
doubtless belongs among them. Perhaps more is concealed behind
it than merely the personal suggestive influence of an Oriental
potentate on a European army leader. Sulla was the one who first
brought the poison of the Caesarean cult from the realms of an
East grown old and demonic into the world of the Occident. Is
it not also possible that he embarked on the Caesarean principle
of mystery plunder in place of mystery popularization, due to
which the new world became unfaithful to its true nature and
mission? Maybe Mithridates provided Sulla, who was addicted to

magic, with initiations into decadent mysteries. Sulla in turn did not insist on the ceding of territory. It may well be that these initiations completely transformed his soul and filled it with unbounded satanic hatred against Rome's contribution to the creation of a new purely human culture, namely democracy. Sulla's proscriptions were no more the means of party strife and greed for money than were those of the Caesars. They were the passionate expression of hatred against a world-view. In them, the old world defended itself against the new.

3.3 Pompey and Caesar

A generation later, two personalities again stand out from the increasingly tumultuous play of forces, a pair in whom the tension between the original and a new kind of Romanism becomes evident: Gnaeus Pompeius, Pompey (106–48 BC) and Julius Caesar (100–44 BC).

Pompey, a soldier in body and soul, who had even grown up in an army camp, did not possess a brilliant, agile mind; rather, he was slow and ill at ease. It is said of him that when he had to address more than one person he blushed, even in old age. From his youth onwards, a sovereign and at the same time benevolently radiant humaneness won him the hearts of everybody and later the enthusiastic loyalty of his legions. His unconditional warm-hearted devotion and decency were a most beautiful personification of the ancient Roman ideal. The love of his troops brought him his successes and made him — who was averse to all power politics — a factor that even a Sulla had to take into consideration.

Because of his deeply genuine instinct and attitude towards life, Pompey was an unerring devotee of the still delicate, germinal traces of the new ego-epoch. He sought and loved noble Greek erudition, not because his talents would have called him to a creative participation in it but because, like a flower to the sun, he simply felt drawn to it. He sensed that his innermost human essence was sustained by it. Once, when one of his slaves escaped in order to satisfy his craving for learning in Athens, Pompey did not punish him. Instead, he gave the slave his freedom and made him the scholar of his home. After the death of his first wife, Julia, the daughter of Julius Caesar, he took as his wife a young student who occupied herself with philosophy, geometry and music so that, through her, he could receive a reflection of modern cultural life. Pompey was the first who, following the Greek model, constructed a theatre in Rome built of stone and made the stipulation that only Greek plays could be presented in it. At the opening he prohibited the gladiator matches because it was abhorrent to him to see human blood spilled to satisfy curiosity. Instead, he requested lion hunts.

By comparison, Julius Caesar had a political consciousness through and through. His keen agile intelligence, given wings by his ambition, enabled him to attach success and fame to his person in a more planned and lasting manner than was possible for Pompey. Caesar possessed a politically acute sense for the possibilities in any given situation. When it was a matter of increasing fame and power, he did not allow himself to be obstructed in his plans by any human consideration. The ideal of loyalty and fairness came second to the goals his brilliant ambition envisioned. We are used to seeing in Julius Caesar one of the greatest Romans. And this he was. But Pompey was the more genuine Roman. Caesar brought about the Rome that finally ruled the whole world. It is often forgotten, however, that Rome became great only through a tragic, though historically necessary disloyalty to itself, through a betrayal of its original ideals, ideals still alive in one like Pompey.* Though very different in character from Sulla due to his stern self-discipline and earnestness, Caesar was susceptible to the same historical temptation. And although he cannot be described as the first Roman Caesar, it is no coincidence that his name finally became the denotation for all those ruthless men of power.

The most important wars waged by Pompey were still those in the service of the new ideal of humanitarianism and culture. He conquered the pirates who were more a danger to the spirit and culture of Europe than to the personal safety and possessions of a few voyagers. They plundered mystery sites in order — together with the aged fiend, Mithridates — to alienate Europe

---

* A view of history predominantly motivated by political thinking will always lean towards favouring Caesar over Pompey. An example of this is Mommsen's *Römische Geschichte* where Pompey merely appears as the humble politician, Caesar on the other hand as the brilliant genius.

from herself and to infect her with the magical spiritual life of Asia's decadent mysteries. Above all, the ancient mystery island of Samothrace with its temples was looted by the pirates. Even though Pompey was able to repulse them, the Persian mystery cult of Mithras came to Europe through the pirates. In the end, it was Pompey who once and for all crushed the decaying kingdom of the Seleucids, against whom the Maccabees had so heroically defended themselves. He turned it into a Roman province and thus destroyed one breeding ground of Asian demons.

By comparison, Julius Caesar's wars were waged mainly in the service of an imperialism that made its appearance in Rome. World domination and power now became goals in themselves. From this, it naturally followed that Caesar had to get rid of his personal rivals, even in Rome. Initially, Caesar, who liked to stress that he was Marius' nephew, had tried to ally himself with the democrats, the party of the people. Moreover, he had thrown in his lot with Pompey, the favourite of the nation and army. But eventually, when he felt powerful enough, he knew how to manipulate matters so that the contrast, which had basically existed all along, became evident and was settled by military means.

Forced to fight against Roman troops, Pompey was helpless and soon driven into a corner. Defeated on land and at sea, he ultimately fled with a handful of companions to Egypt and asked for protection and asylum. But the Egyptians knew that victorious Caesar was hot on the heels of the fugitive. In order to curry favour with the powerful one, they killed Pompey even before he had stepped on Egyptian soil. They then carried the cut-off head of the one who had once been Caesar's friend towards the pursuer, whose ships were just arriving. And now something surprising happened. Even though the gruesome sight sealed his triumph, tears flowed from Caesar's eyes. As in the case of Sulla's kiss, here, too, with Caesar's tears, we are witnesses of a historic moment of the greatest significance. Secrets of human history were concentrated in a picture.

What about Caesar's tears? Were they merely an expression of human distress? Or was a traditional Roman feeling aroused in the victor and the insight that, with Pompey's death, a part of ancient, genuine Rome itself had ended? Or did Caesar even sense the symbolic nature of the moment, the tension between the old and the new world in regard to the history and evolution of human consciousness? For when Perseus lifted up the shocking head of Medusa, when David held up the cut-off head of the giant and Judith the cruel head of Holofernes, this gesture expressed a triumph of the new over the old world. The dark mask — a mask become diabolic — of a world in which the human head had not yet become the seat of thought-illumined, ego-imbued free consciousness, had been overcome. Now the picture had been reversed. Egypt, the decadent world of ancient magic, tried to cast its spell over the ego-sphere that shone upon the forehead of the human being. And thus, before him whom they wished to lead astray, the Egyptians raised up the head of one whose shining forehead they could only extinguish by means of assassination, one whose free and selfless humaneness would never have succumbed to their seduction.

3.4 Caesar and Cleopatra

Profound misfortunes of destiny were evoked because it was Egypt of all places where Pompey's flight had led Caesar's steps. The republican, Pompey, thus steered the most eminent man of his nation to the country from which the spirits of the old world were to make a forceful entry into Rome. Since the days when the first Ptolemies in Alexandria had laid the foundation for such a rich and far-reaching cultural life with their *museion,* Egypt and its ruling family had long since succumbed to complete spiritual and political decadence. Having been awakened from their slumber, the subterranean forces of magic had gained power over the new spirit that had invaded their realm.

At this time, two siblings happened to be engaged in controversy over the throne. In accordance with the sinister tradition that always prevailed under the Ptolemies, they were married to each other: Cleopatra and her brother who was still only a boy. For some time, Egypt had been courting favour with Rome. Cleopatra's father, the Pharaoh Ptolemy Auletes, had resided in Rome for a while; with huge sums of money he had tried to gain recognition and assurance of Egypt's independence. Finally, in the year 55, Roman cavalry troops had taken the unprincipled king back to his country. The fourteen-year-old Cleopatra had been fascinated by the sight of the Roman soldiers and found herself in ecstatic giddiness, especially over the handsome tall figure of the riders' leader, Mark Antony, in whose life she was later destined to play a significant part. It seemed as if this last daughter of the Pharaohs carried within herself the whole Luciferic soul of decadent Egypt, an Egypt that, prior to its demise, tried to rise up once again. From out of subconscious depths, with a force even overpowering to herself, a seductive will rose in her that she now always let loose when an important Roman came near her. Did the spirits of Egypt look through her for a new dwelling place and vessel? For a brief time, a son of the great Pompey had been her lover, but he had soon withdrawn from her spell. Now twenty-one, fate passed to the most powerful first man in Rome.

Cleopatra's brother was in possession of the royal Alexandrian palaces. His ministers had been the men who had killed Pompey and prepared Caesar's dramatic reception. Cleopatra's troops were camped at the edge of the city, separated from the royal castle by several arms of the Nile. Cleopatra thought up a ruse to appear before Caesar. She had herself sewn into a sack and rowed across the river by a slave at night. At daylight — Caesar had just gathered his generals around him for consultation in a luxurious hall of the palace — a slave suddenly lugged in a sack, opened it before Caesar, and from it Cleopatra emerged. To the amazement of all the witnesses, something occurred that had never before happened in the life of the fifty-two-year old disciplined man of duty. At first sight, Caesar was spellbound by the seductive suggestion of this woman's soul. A passionate feeling of love henceforth bound him to her.

There were reasons why Caesar did not immediately return to Rome. He had to fight several battles for the purpose of establishing order in Egypt. In the course of these conflicts he had to decide at one point to burn a number of ships to prevent them falling into the hands of his enemies. Was it mere coincidence that the fire spread to the buildings of the famous academy and consumed the huge library in which all the literature of that age had been gathered? Or did fate try to proclaim through a gigantic fiery sign that a danger threatened the new world of culture?

Even after the conclusion of the Egyptian War, Caesar delayed his return to Rome where he was awaited with impatience and consternation. For almost a year, Julius Caesar remained in Egypt. He had no political reasons for doing so, yet neither were Cleopatra's amorous skills the only reason that held him. Through Cleopatra, he was affected by the magic spell of ancient Egypt with its temples and mysteries: 'The secrets and the age of the land, the secrets and the youth of Cleopatra — both cast their spell over Caesar in Egypt.'[18]

Caesar exhibited a strange thirst for knowledge. From distant temple sites, priests were brought to him who had to answer about the mysteries of their region. A long voyage on the Nile that he undertook with Cleopatra led him to the locations of the temples and wisdom of the ancient world. Obviously, his power and the office of high priestess traditionally occupied by Cleopatra must have gained Caesar entry to any number of long since decadent mysteries. He broke faith with young Europe and courted the seductive goddess of antiquity.

Finally Caesar returned to Rome. But to the amazement of all proper Romans, not only did the Egyptian queen accompany him into Rome; he himself had become a different person. Those who formerly had been his friends sensed in him a different spirit. A will now ensouled him that they experienced as anti-democratic and therefore anti-Roman. They clearly saw danger arising for the democratic culture that Rome had created. These men, who preferred the noble human character to the degenerate magic element of divinity inherent in the old methods of rulers, must have felt the greatest consternation to see that Caesar was taking a number of steps that amounted to a cult of his own person. He suddenly placed increased emphasis on his descent from Aeneas and the priest-kings of Alba Longa; he had coins made that depicted him as the *Pontifex Maximus,* the highest of all priests. In his human behaviour, too, any number of odd traits surfaced. The question forces itself on us whether the attacks resembling epilepsy that so frequently overcame him now were caused by a physical disposition or a decadent Egyptian mystery initiation.

Inspired by ancient Roman ideals and devoted to the bright light of Greek philosophy, a group of idealistic young men like Cicero and Cato the Younger gathered round representatives of

the new ego-directed intellectual life and finally formed a con-
spiracy against the omnipotent ruler. And when Brutus, together
with his friends, pointed the dagger at Julius Caesar in the year
44 BC, he believed he was repelling Egypt's spirits from Rome.
When she heard of Caesar's death, Cleopatra fled Rome. But was
it still possible to protect Rome against the magic spectres of the
past — spectres seeking to cross over to Europe from dying
Egypt?

3.5 Antony and Cleopatra

Once again, a contrasting pair of figures appeared on the stage of
history, the later Augustus (63 BC – AD 14) and Mark Antony
(82–31 BC). Would a Roman of the old type, like Marius and
Pompey, pit himself once more against Rome's threatening
degeneration? Following the murder of his uncle, Octavian,
Caesar's nineteen-year-old great-nephew, immediately rushed
back from Greece where he had been the disciple of a philosophers' and mystery school. With manly determination and
prudence, the youth intervened in the chaotic situation then
prevailing. First he confronted Mark Antony who in his fanciful
passionate ambition believed he could assume Caesar's legacy. It
still seemed possible to put a stop to Rome turning completely
Luciferic. But soon it became evident that Octavian, specifically
nominated by Julius Caesar as his heir and the one to continue
his work, confronted a situation that coerced him in a definite
direction. The dead Caesar forced his will upon his successor.

The issue was to curb Caesar's killers who had the support of
all idealists and defenders of democratic Rome. For this reason,
Octavian allied himself with his former competitor, Mark Antony,
and united various political factions in a triumvirate, just as Caesar had once done. Near Philippi, the former Macedonian capital,
the democrats were beaten. Now Rome experienced a gruesome
blood bath of proscriptions, a blood bath of horrible dimensions
far surpassing the one under Sulla. Endless were the lists of the
outlawed on whose heads large sums of money were placed: the
cut-off heads, brought forward in brutal greed, were stacked up
in ghastly pyramids. Since the property of all those on the lists
was confiscated by the state, one might assume that the proscrip-

tions were only promulgated to fill the state treasuries for the far-flung plans of Octavian. But the actual motive for this large scale slaughter was the annihilation of a quite definite way of thinking. Victory was thus assured to the decadent Egyptian-Diadochian trend that infiltrated Roman history, insofar as those who were eliminated were bearers of the new ego-imbued humanity.

Once again, scenes stand out from the general events that appear to us like symbols of world history. Urged on by his fanatical, spiteful wife, Fulvia, Mark Antony ordered Cicero's cut-off head to be brought to him. With cynical jokes he made fun of the appalling sight. Was it not the laughter of demons who had felt uneasy because of the birth of the new world and who now triumphed because the blood of even the last true Romans had been shed? Three images move next to one another: The world of Cleopatra holds up the head of Pompey to Julius Caesar; Antony mocks the head of Cicero; Herodias gloats triumphantly over the bloody platter bearing the head of John the Baptist. The spirits of intemperance and lust for power, who were nothing but spectres of a world come to an end, hated the free human being — hated above all the ego's light arising like a star on the forehead of man.

Following their gruesome retributions, Caesar's heirs partitioned the empire. Octavian took over the European, Antony the Oriental part of the by then enormous territory. More than had Sulla, Antony succumbed to Asia's suggestion from the beginning. His soul felt akin to the old magical East. His intemperance, ostentation and sensuousness, even the suggestive element inherent in his nature which, as a student of eastern schools of oratory, he knew how to employ in masterly fashion,* allowed him to be in his element. Though he had a fine education, the spirit of liberal mystery popularization that proceeded from Greece was completely foreign to his nature. Where he knew of or came across initiation centres or mystery sites, his sensation-seeking consciousness and lust for power were aroused. We are told that he forced the priests of Eleusis to initiate him into the

---

* The classic description given of him by Shakespeare in *Julius Caesar* and *Antony and Cleopatra* comes to mind.

Eleusinian mysteries. In a brilliantly playful manner he exercised the Caesarean principle of mystery appropriation and began to behave as if he were a god.

Cleopatra realized that her hour had come. Had Antony and she not been charmed by each other once before? She now came to Mark Antony in a different manner from the way she had approached Julius Caesar. In a luxurious ship of splendour, dressed as Venus, she sailed into the pompous camp of Antony in the harbour town of Tarsus on the coast of Asia Minor where, four decades later, Paul would be born. The goddess came to the god. Sumptuous celebrations sealed their union. Antony slavishly fell under the love spell of the Egyptian queen, who henceforth was the one who actually ruled the eastern part of the Roman empire. Frequently, the two resided in Antioch, the city of the Seleucids, playground of all cultures. In the role that Cleopatra played in Roman history, it was as if deeply concealed levels of destiny were trying to come to the fore. All the decisive events occurred at the seven-year turning points of this enigmatic woman's life. When Cleopatra was fourteen years old, she encountered Antony for the first time. The twenty-one-year old appeared before Julius Caesar in her fantastic, magic-filled manner. Now that she was sailing to Tarsus to meet Antony, she was twenty-eight years old.

In Rome, people followed the directions in which Mark Antony was heading with suspicion and displeasure. Octavian made many an attempt to free his co-ruler from the spell of the female Pharaoh. But even marrying him to his sister Octavia kept Antony away from Cleopatra for barely three years. Finally, in the year 34, after a victoriously concluded campaign, Antony moved the triumphant celebration not to Rome but to Alexandria and, to top it all, this was followed by a coronation ceremony which surpassed in its opulence all previous occasions. During this ceremony, Cleopatra had the crowns of kingdoms belonging to Rome designated to herself and her children by Julius Caesar and Antony. This caused Octavian to decide to procede against Antony by force. The naval battle at Actium (31 BC) sealed his victory. Antony and Cleopatra fled to Alexandria after the destruction of the Egyptian fleet. Yet even now the great seductress did not throw in the towel. She drove Antony to suicide by having her death announced to him and then immediately tried to cast her spell over Octavian who had followed the escaping opponents. For the first time, her magic skills failed her and she killed herself through the bite of a viper.

Cleopatra stands in history like a larger counter-image of Judith. In Judith, it was as if the common soul had taken on form of all those who under the Maccabees had repulsed the powerful spectres of the past. Cleopatra, on the other hand, was the embodiment of the ancient world itself that advanced to the magic counterattack against the new spirit. Even as Asia had been victorious over Greece under the Seleucid Diadochi, so, through the last female Ptolemy, Egypt was victorious over Rome. Rome succumbed to the temptation of power when Caesar and Antony gave in to Cleopatra's seduction. She no longer had to seduce Octavian, the later Caesar Augustus. Although he resisted her, he was already conquered by and filled with the spirit of Egypt.

3.6 Augustus, the Pantheon and Caesarean cult

Fortune favoured Caesar Octavian Augustus, the world ruler at the turning point of time. Since he was merely nineteen at the time of Julius Caesar's death and reached the age of seventy-seven, the period during which he ruled the fate of Rome lasted almost six decades. Throughout the forty-five years of the peaceful cultural development that now occurred, he was in sole possession of power over the world-encompassing *Imperium Romanum*.

Under Augustus' gifted, farsighted genius, Rome appeared to experienced something akin to the brilliant emergence of Jerusalem under Solomon and of Athens in the Periclean age. Earlier simplicity gave way to unlimited ostentatious splendour. Augustus could boast that he had turned an impoverished city of clay into a radiant one of marble. In reality, however, what Augustus conjured forth with his ceaseless desire for building — which everywhere reached grandiose dimensions — cannot really be placed side by side with Solomonic Jerusalem and Periclean Athens. Unlike those two, Augustan Rome was not a pure child of the new world. This was a matter of competing with the immoderate establishment of cities that originated under the Diadochian counter-strike against Alexander's impulse. In outer appearance, Rome was not to take second place to the Ptolemaic and Seleucid metropolitan cities of Alexandria and Antioch. While in a certain way Julius Caesar had still Romanized Egypt, what Augustus brought about was actually an Egyptianizing of Rome.

In all his creations, Augustus had in mind the magic dimensions of the ancient world that had given rise to the age of the Diadochi. Whatever could be obtained in the way of artefacts found its way to Rome. The time began when it was fashionable to bring Egypt's obelisks across to Europe and erect them there. By the side of Augustus stood men like Maecenas, who made available their riches and with true collector's passion gathered together the remnants of a world long since ended — remnants that one really wished to preserve. Augustus knew that initiations and mysteries had existed and did so still. After all, in his youth, he had been a disciple of ancient wisdom in Greece. And he would have liked to bring back those days when, through initiation secrets known only to them, the rulers possessed a magic superiority over those they ruled. He loved the old world more than the new. His amazing pioneering accomplishments notwithstanding, his was a backward-oriented consciousness. And the new metropolis of Rome, the indisputable centre of the whole world with its mixtures of races and peoples, was less a realization than a caricature of the newly acquired humaneness of the human spirit.

The political acumen which had helped Julius Caesar attain such great success was even more pronounced in Caesar Augustus. After the victory over Antony and Cleopatra, he liked to represent himself as the one who had saved the republic from Oriental despotism. And he knew until the very end how to maintain the appearance that he was merely restoring the balance of the democratic state and not appropriating for himself any mandatory powers and authority, except for those stipulated in the republican constitution. But it is clearly recognizable that, more than to the semblance of democracy, his true nature was closely connected with the nature of his offices, something that had necessarily resulted in the inner suspension of any form of democracy. In the year 12 BC, amid extraordinary splendour and in the presence of immense numbers of people who had been brought from all over Italy especially for the occasion, Augustus had himself appointed to the office of 'highest priest,' of Pontifex Maximus.

For some time, with diligent but clandestine efforts, Octavian Augustus had been at pains to revivify this ancient office. This was linked to his profoundly egotistical love of mysteries and cults of the ancient world. His final and highest goal was for Rome to become the seat of an actual Pantheon. The gods from all over the world were to have their temples and rituals here. What advantage was it to the Romans to be masters over nations without having any influence over their gods? Outwardly, it only seemed that images and statues of gods were brought together in Rome by eager collectors. But in reality it was not only the images but the power of these gods that were of concern.

This was why the effort was made, with the aid of initiates and priests from all accessible mystery sites and temples, to establish branches in Rome in which, just as in their countries of origin, all cultic ceremonies and initiation rites were to be conducted. The organization of such a Pantheon was an undertaking of unprecedented daring and significance. But the most unheard-of thing was to broaden the ancient office of Pontifex Maximus, which until then had been limited to a cult of the city-gods, to the point where it became a centralizing pinnacle of all cults and mysteries, a universal religious centre, as it were, that ruled supreme. For this, it was first necessary that the bearer of this office attain in some way to all priestly ordinations and initiations. The brilliant and daring idea of a Pantheon amounted to the creation of a quintessence of all religious powers and magical possibilities that had existed in the past.

It is clear that the lovely cupola structure of the Pantheon in Rome, which in its present form dates from a later age, that of Trajan, cannot have been anything but an externalized symbol for the immense but covert activity of the actual Pantheon. Julius Caesar had assumed the office of Pontifex Maximus in the year 63. In the last part of his life, he had begun to base on it the demand for divine veneration even though, in his day, this office still possessed only its original content. Octavian Augustus was in no hurry to inherit this office of Caesar's. He knew why. Through the unprecedented reconstitution of this office, he wished to prepare the moment when he would pronounce himself the highest priest, but then not just of Rome but of the whole world. And so he calmly awaited the death of the one who had held the position after Julius Caesar. Finally, along with the great moment of his nomination, Rome's Caesarean cult with all its ominous implications and chaotic consequences was constituted.

The establishment of the Pantheon and Rome's Caesarean cult fitted in with the mighty Messianic premonition that vibrated through all the nations. Had the one for whom humanity longed for so ardently not become clearly recognizable? Had a god not actually become man here? Had he not begun to establish a kingdom of God on earth in Rome and the far reaches of the *Imperium Romanum*? In fact, people soon began to venerate Augustus not only in the manner in which the ancient world had in many instances been want to do, but to glorify him as the One, the God-sent Messiah. Everywhere, temples were erected in his honour with inscriptions like those, for example, that were preserved on Halicarnassus and Priene: 'To the divine Augustus. God has sent you, the Redeemer. Sea and land enjoy peace. There will be none who is greater than you. The gospel of the birth of the god has been fulfilled.'

In his *Eclogues,* Virgil had spoken in inspired, prophetic verses of the impending birth of the child in whom a god would take on human form for the sake and redemption of humanity. And later on, when, joining Horace and other poets of Augustan Rome, he praised Augustus as the founder and benefactor of the Golden Age, it is quite obvious that he saw in the great Caesar the fulfilment of his poetic prophecy.

Destiny developed a particularly archetypal formative power in the world's centre around the great turning point of time. Partly due to this and partly because of the deliberate intentions of Augustus, a grandiose counter-image developed to what acquired earthly reality in outward humility in a remote corner of the empire. While in a little Palestinian town the child was even then growing up that would actually become the human bearer of the redemption-bestowing divine being, a world ruler in Rome had himself proclaimed and revered as saviour, the human incarnation of a god. The spiritual significance of Christ's human incarnation for all humanity had its solid counter-reflection in the power that Augustus wielded over the whole globe. The Christ being, who was making ready to incarnate in that humble contemporary of Augustus, had been involved in a great journey during the preceding evolutionary phases of humanity. From the highest levels of existence through sphere after sphere, he had descended to earth. On each stage of his path he had sent down different revelations of light that were placed in different divine figures before the souls of human beings.[19] All the genuine religious movements of the past had once their source in the Christ being and his celestial destinies. The concentration, centre and quintessence of the host of gods was present in Christ. He was the fulfilment, compared to which all ancient world-religions were only prophecies.

The one who ruled the world from Rome as the counterpart of the god-become-man, founded a hard, earthly, Ahrimanic counter-image to this through the Pantheon in which he eventually positioned himself in first place. The god-man shadow on the Caesarean throne was in control of the specially collected powers and secrets of all the gods of the world. Due to the past's suggestive power in his soul, Augustus did not realize that by gathering the religious cults of the ancient world he had brought together vessels that were now either empty or corrupted. All religions and cults had had their time when they had been stations of passage on the path of the god journeying toward the earth. Now he, who had once been their soul and their reality, had long since moved on and had to be looked for elsewhere.

The Pantheon of Augustus could only be a gathering of false spirits and cosmic powers that had turned demonic. It should not be assumed that Augustus simply thought up the idea of a Pantheon. He could arrive at it only because he had participated in certain decadent mystery initiations. He did have insights and impressions of the real spiritual background of his age. But since the sources which he availed himself of were not pure and clear, what he perceived could not but show itself to him in distorted form. Rays of the imminent Christ mystery tried to reach him, but his soul could grasp them only in materialistic and egotistical misinterpretation. The contemporaneity of the Christ Event and the proclamation of Rome's Caesarean cult was not coincidental. A deep fundamental link prevailed. Even here, the shadow owed its origin directly to the light. The outwardly grandiose counter-image arose next to the outwardly insignificant central event like its shadow.

With Augustus' proclamation to the rank of Pontifex Maximus over the Roman Pantheon, the stream of decadent mysteries and the rule of the ghosts of the past finally merged into Roman history. Ancient, pre-Caesarean, genuine Rome had now made way to the colossus of the *Imperium Romanum*. The counter-strike by the ancient world, which had already made itself felt in the kingdoms of the Diadochi and had been announced in figures such as Sulla, Caesar and Antony, now emerged fully incarnated on the stage of history. The last spark of the Diadochian principle was kindled in Rome. But this very spark set fire to the whole world. The blaze of the Caesarean cult, which began to burn not merely against the new world but moreover against the Christ impulse, flared up under the successors of Augustus with ever more consuming flames.

With the support of the Pantheon, the Caesars, from Tiberius, Caligula and Nero to Constantine the Great, tried to cling to the mysteries of the ancient world, because they saw in them the foremost means of power. Now these were mysteries from which Solomonic Judea, Periclean Greece and old, democratic Rome, all of them the firstborn of a new humanity, had decidedly taken leave. All mystery popularization evoked fear and abhorrence in the Caesars. Taking advantage of their power — for were they not all bearers of the most glorious office of highest priest of all the world? — they were addicted to mystery misuse and thus completed the decadence and demonization of the ancient sanctuaries. The spectral, superstitious and hallucinatory spiritual life of the Roman Caesars makes it possible for us to discern the extent of frenzied chaos to which divine clarity had given way. The profoundly soul-invasive execution of initiation practices had to rob the unprepared souls of the Caesars, souls filled with impure drives and instincts, of any ego form and consistent reasoning ability. The Caesarean delusion, through the horrible effects of which the period of early Christianity received its outward characteristic, was more than delusion of grandeur. This delusion made evident a complete confusion of all soul forces, an unavoidable consequence of initiation attained by force.

Augustus, who not only had a brilliant but also a strong mind and never permitted himself to stray ecstatically from the path of common sense and reason, remained unaffected by the mental illness that accompanied the Caesarean cult. But with few exceptions, his successors succumbed to unrestrained passion. How could it not be otherwise that the spiritual tension and contrast that existed between Caesareanism and Christendom should not be dramatically vented in the persecutions of the Christians that now occurred? Rudolf Steiner unveiled the spiritual set of facts that underlie the Roman cult of the Caesars:

> At a time when the Mystery of Golgotha was drawing
> near it was no longer possible to keep secret the Mystery
> teachings as in former times. The hierophants were in no
> way responsible for this ... It was Imperial Rome that,
> without warrant, unveiled the secrets of the Mysteries.
> The time was approaching when the initiate-priests could
> no longer resist the commands of the Caesars. And the
> violation of the spiritual life by the Roman emperors is
> reflected in the events of the time ... In due course the
> Roman emperors, by Imperial edict, demanded to be
> initiated into the Mysteries and this became the accepted
> practice. Augustus was the first to be initiated, but he did
> not abuse the privilege of initiation ...[20]

3.7 Antipater and Herod

The antagonistic shadow of the approaching Christ Event, which took on form in such an impressive and central manner in Augustus and his religious institutions, darkened life in Palestine as well and increasingly assumed tangible shape. After the death of the last of the five Maccabean brothers, it was as if the spirits of the Diadochi, repulsed with so much initiative and success, were finding a way to surreptitiously enter into the Jewish people after all. When John Hyrcanus, the son of Simon Maccabeus (high priest from 135 to 104 BC), broke into the sacred subterranean rooms of David's tomb on Mount Zion in order to buy the favour of the Seleucid rulers with the stolen treasures, this was a first sign that the leaders of the people were on the verge of becoming unfaithful to the spirit of the Maccabean age.

The number of those continued to decrease who wished under all circumstances to remain protectors and guardians of the Messianic future. Only the lesser known groups of the pious were left for this task. In the course of the internal confusion and strife that now began, there was even a bloody persecution of pious ones under Alexander Jannaeus (grandson of Simon Maccabeus; 'King of Judah,' 103–76 BC), in which thousands perished, particularly many members of the Order of the Pharisees. Finally, a fratricidal war broke out between the sons of Alexander Jannaeus (Hyrcanus and Aristobulus II) that ominously gave alien spiritual movements and power factors the possibility of intervening in a dominant way in Jewish life.

The house of the Herodians took the stage. They passed through the New Testament like will-o'-the-wisp caricatures of the true light; human incarnations of diabolic counter-forces. The Herodian figures made their appearance in Antipater, a personality of glittering, serpent-like cleverness and flexibility. Antipater was more Arab than Jew. He came from the desert region of the Bedouin south of Palestine, the region through which the forty-year-long journey of the people had once led. His father, the son of a priest of Apollo, of whom it was said that he had been abducted to Arabia from the ancient Philistine town of Ashkelon, had been nominated by Alexander Jannaeus to be governor of Idumaea. Fascinated by anything possessing or promising splendour and power on earth, Antipater began his machinations. He knew how to turn himself into a confidante and indispensable advisor of one of the two battling Hasmoneans. Before long, he had induced an army of the neighbouring Arabian chiefs, whom he had earlier brought under his influence, to intervene in the fratricidal strife. By so doing, he set in motion a whole avalanche of events. We do not know whether it was calculation or fate, but henceforth the *Imperium Romanum* that was only just coming into being was involved in Palestine's history and that of the Jewish people. The Romans now finally arrived. Judas the Maccabee had asked them for assistance when they were still guardians of justice. But now they were on the verge of themselves becoming bearers of the Caesarean will. And the Herodians, trapped and blinded by the lure of power, turned into their always accommodating but also cleverly calculating go-betweens.

At first it was not Caesarean Rome that took hold of Judea's destinies. Not Julius Caesar but Pompey arrived. He was about to bring Roman order to the vanquished remains of the Seleucid kingdom. Moreover, he wished to bring concord and peace to Palestine. He drove out the army of the Arabs and marched towards Jerusalem. Because of the countless religious traditions linked to it, this town was a puzzle to him. He suspected the presence of hidden mysteries here. As an exotericist, the mysteries had always caused him unease, for he was devoted to ancient Roman sincerity and concise Greek learning and disdained any darkly superstitious secret.

After the capture of the city (61 BC), he entered the holiest of holies in the Temple, but with a very different attitude of mind from that of Antiochus Epiphanes. Surprised and placated to discover nothing but an empty dark room, he expressly protected the Temple and its treasures against any foreign access and granted the Jews religious and ritual freedom, once again renewing the privileges granted them by Alexander the Great.

Pompey organized the Roman province of Syria. While this was being accomplished, cunning Antipater knew how to make his influence felt. Rome was no longer an ally but ruler over Judea, yet still left the Jewish people part of their freedom. And in the very sphere Rome had omitted, Antipater positioned himself, still remaining cleverly in the background. Strange coincidences of destiny worked to his advantage. When the troops of the Syrian governor, who had been installed by Pompey, had to intervene again in Judea so as to maintain calm and order, a cavalry colonel was among them. Antipater was attracted to him in an unusual kinship of character and fate. The latter immediately formed a friendship with Antipater and became his drinking companion. He was Mark Antony, who in the same year (55 BC) saw the fourteen-year-old Cleopatra in Egypt for the first time and felt an equally unusual attraction to her. Personalities flocked together who appeared like exponents of the Luciferic spirit of the age.

After the downfall and death of Pompey (48 BC), the anxious question was: what will Caesar do? The assumption had to be that as he had done elsewhere so, too, in Palestine he would annul the directives promulgated by Pompey and replace them with his own. Antipater's plans were threatened. But like a fox, the cunning man immediately discovered an opportunity to realize his goal more effectively. With an army, he rushed to support Caesar who was embroiled in the Egyptian War and, in alliance with the Jews of Alexandria, extricated him from a precarious situation. It goes without saying that the policy Caesar now pursued for Palestine included an important influential office for Antipater. As a precaution, he had the latter's privileges confirmed by the Roman Senate. Antipater had reached the point where, through guile, he could pass power to his sons born to him by a noble Arabian woman.

Immediately, the figure of the barely twenty-five-year-old Herod stood out. In him, a wild, passionate temperament combined with calculating cleverness. He expressed blazing ambition in all he did. From the beginning, it was possible to see that he would soon outdo his father, Antipater. He, too, was spellbound by all things Roman — a Roman spirit that was just beginning to be adorned with Caesarean splendour and power. Like his father, Herod curried favour with the Romans. As commander-in-chief of Galilee and aware that the Roman governor was a fanatic for civil order, he set out to suppress the zealously Messianic and nationalistic Jewish groups. Like the apocalyptically aroused peasants fifteen hundred years later during the time of the Reformation, these groups were causing unrest in the land. It did not matter to Herod that the Jews in Jerusalem were furious with him. With his execution of a Messianic leader and his followers, he appropriated for himself the power of life and death that rightfully belonged exclusively to the high priest. His only concern was to remain on good terms with the Romans. And it was not long before they placed him into influential positions and aided him in the ascent he so impatiently tried to achieve.

3.8 Herod and Cleopatra

Following Caesar's death, the devout Jewish factions in Jerusalem tried to shake off the tutelage of the foreign-born hirelings of Rome by placing their hope on Rome's republican party. Antipater was poisoned during a banquet. Herod feigned friendship with the murderers of his father and even managed to befriend the party of Caesar's slayers. After the battle of Philippi, the factions in Jerusalem believed they could discredit Herod with Mark Antony because of Antony's connection to the republicans. But they did not consider that Antony would extend protection to the son of his friend. Herod gained Antony's friendship more completely than his father, for he was more like the Roman in character than Antipater had been. Angrily and brutally, the new potentate of the East turned away the delegations of the Jews.

Given over completely to the dizzying intoxication of his union with Cleopatra, Antony overlooked the great danger that was approaching in the form of huge Parthian armies. Antigonus, a Maccabean descendent, had asked the Parthians to assist him against Herod and the Romans. Soon, they had reached Jerusalem on their westward march. Herod had to escape. The neighbouring Arabian rulers refused to support him. He hurried on to Alexandria. In turn, Antony had been summoned to Rome, for he had allowed the Parthian threat to get out of hand.

Octavian tried to take advantage of this opportunity to separate Antony from Cleopatra and arranged for him to marry his sister, Octavia. Cleopatra received Herod with pomp and great honours but could not conceal from him that Egypt was not prepared for war. Overcoming all obstacles, Herod continued on to Rome. In an attitude of accommodation because of the threat from the Parthians, Octavian and Antony acknowledged Herod as an allied monarch and, together with him, offered up solemn sacrifices in the temple of Jupiter Capitolinus.

After Rome had vanquished the Parthian armies, Antony aided Herod in recapturing Judea and Jerusalem and, as a favour to him, even had Antigonus, the last of the Hasmonean kings, executed by beheading — the first time that Rome dealt in this fashion with a defeated ruler.

Herod had learned much from a Rome that was acquiring Caesarean pretensions. This became shockingly evident in the proscriptions through which he now took his revenge in Jerusalem and decimated the ranks of those who differed from him in thought. Due to his involvement with Roman destinies, an increasingly financial character was imposed on his bloodthirsty rampage. His friend and protector, Antony, who himself was in strained circumstances due to Cleopatra's insatiable greed, demanded innumerable tributes from him; funds that Herod could only acquire by violent means since the land itself was utterly depleted from decades of unrest. Following John Hyrcanus' example, Herod, too, ventured into David's tomb on Mount Zion, but found no more gold treasures. Instead, he was frightened by eerie flames from the earth's interior. Herod's character changed and the first symptoms of unease bordering on paranoia appeared. The more chaotic and unbridled Herod's consciousness became, the more knotty the threads of destiny that entangled him.

Under pressure from Cleopatra, Antony turned into his tormentor. The Egyptian queen was filled, indeed obsessed, by her idea of becoming mistress over Palestine. For her, this country in particular possessed a quite mysterious fascination. Did she have a premonition of the significant events about to take place there, traces of which were even then affecting the atmosphere of the landscape? On the other hand, Herod, too, clung with almost absurd jealousy to every part of this land and was profoundly disturbed by the intentions of this woman who was accustomed to realize all her desires. As moths and bats are want to do, did it not seem as if numerous nocturnal creatures were fluttering towards a light yet to come?

In order to gain influence over the ruling Jewish circles, Herod had taken as his wife, Mariamne, the great-granddaughter of the Maccabees. He achieved the opposite. For Alexandra, Mariamne's mother, a fanatical, domineering individual, now took the stage as the most dangerous antagonist of Herod whom she passionately hated as an intruder and false king. She was aware of the weaknesses in Herod's nature. She knew of the deeply rooted fear, hidden behind the power-crazed appearance, and of the hellish tortures of jealousy that arose in him as a result. She knew how to evoke the spectres that could torment him. Once, a

Maccabee had asked democratic Rome to aid him against Diadochian, tyrannical Syria. Now a Maccabean woman, with an even surer aim to harass Herod, turned to the quintessence of the Diadochian spirit in Egypt, to Cleopatra. With the help of the last Ptolemy, who herself was plotting to acquire as much as possible of Herod's country, Alexandra manipulated Antony to nominate her son, Aristobulus, the brother of Mariamne, to the office of high priest. Erupting in diabolic anger that frequently provoked him to unfounded rages of jealousy against Mariamne, Herod killed Aristobulus, not taking into consideration that he would thereby lose favour with Antony.

Antony now gave in to his tyrannical female partner and bestowed on her all the lands bordering on Palestine, above all the rich Mediterranean coast between Tyre and Egypt. Finally, he even intruded upon Herod's own realm. The luxurious Gardens of Jericho north of the Dead Sea, which in their oppressive beauty and opulence were a last vestige of the world of Sodom and Gomorrah, fell into Cleopatra's hands. Herod had to accompany the queen there in person. He could not get over this loss. He in turn leased from this enchantress the very land he had just ceded to her. Yet he was unsuccessful in making her depart. For weeks and months, Cleopatra remained in these magic gardens deep within the bowels of Palestine and unleashed her arts of seduction on Herod. He sought counsel with his companions as to whether he should allow himself to be seduced or strangle Cleopatra during their first encounter. Fear of Antony kept him from either step. Soon afterwards (in the year 34), Cleopatra organized the exuberant apotheosis of her power with the crowning of her children as kings in Alexandria. She thus provoked Octavian into open opposition and brought about the decline of her own fortunes and those of Antony.

3.9 Herod and Augustus

At Actium, the naval forces of Antony and Cleopatra were destroyed. The escaped couple stupefied themselves with frenzied orgies in Alexandria. Herod heard of Octavian's pursuit and immediately was ready to go over to him. Why should he remain loyal to Antony to whom power was more important than loyalty? A powerful earthquake shook Palestine; ten thousand lives were lost and apocalyptic visions were evoked. Had the end of time come and was the long expected god making his entrance into humanity as a stern judge? Confused presentiments may have flashed like hallucinations through Herod's already restless soul. He prepared a pompous reception for victorious Octavian, as if the latter were the deity incarnate. Wasting huge sums of money, Herod accompanied him and his army southward through the whole country on the way to Egypt. Octavian saw in him a support for his own power, returned to him all the territories that Cleopatra had seized for herself and appointed him his counsellor in all Asian matters.

Meanwhile, Herod's apparition-beholding fear and restlessness reached a climax. In a passionate fit of jealousy, he had his wife, Mariamne, the last Maccabean, executed. But this act engulfed him in fear even more. He felt as if he had robbed himself of his sight. He believed he was being pursued by vengeful demons. He was shaken by delirious states of fever. Nocturnal ghosts of madness took hold of his soul. It seemed as if the mental derangement that overcame him was the result of forcefully acquired and misused initiations, as had been the case earlier in a number of Seleucid rulers and later on in successors of Augustus.

When Herod thought he had escaped from the feverish illness, his confusion of soul assumed the form of Caesarean madness. First he raged like a raving madman against friend and foe. Then he was gripped by an unrestrained passion for construction. He tried to emulate Octavian who meanwhile had been named Augustus. Like the latter in Rome, Herod in Jerusalem wanted to create a kingdom of God on earth in all its splendour. But he was far more uncontrollable and passionate than Augustus. It was as if the Diadochian spirit of an Antiochus Epiphanes had reawakened in him. Herod could not do enough in the building of new cities, splendid avenues and mighty aqueducts throughout the land. Jerusalem's appearance was changed from the ground up. How paltry Solomon's Jerusalem had been compared to Herod's — a Jerusalem that appeared to consist of nothing but marble palaces! Was it the dim and distorted presentiment that the true Messiah mystery was about to be realized in Palestine that drove Herod on? And did he now attempt to usurp for Jerusalem something of the grandiose shadow and counter-image even then arising in Rome?

The Messiah-idea played a significant role in Herod's confused soul. He was one of those who most eagerly proclaimed the message that Caesar Augustus was the great, long-awaited god-man from heaven. A large number of temples to Augustus, on which Messianic inscriptions were decoratively displayed, date back to Herod or were built upon his instigation. At the foot of Mount Hermon next to the primeval grotto of Pan by the spring of the Jordan, Herod constructed such a temple out of white marble which, later on, was turned into the centre of the town, Caesarea Philippi, by one of his sons. At the site of the old marine fortification, Strato's Tower, by the Mediterranean Sea, he ordered the building of a harbour town of mighty dimensions, named it Caesarea in honour of Augustus and crowned it with a temple, visible far across the sea, and a colossal statue of Augustus. Ahab's town of Samaria was likewise reconstructed by Herod, given a temple dedicated to Augustus and named Sebaste, the Greek translation of the name Augustus.

To the dismay of the devout, the wild, ecstatic spectacles continued endlessly in Jerusalem's newly constructed amphitheatres. Bloody gladiator matches alternated with animal contests. Henceforth, every five years, in the Actian games conducted for the celebration of the victory at Actium, the whole nation was to pay homage to Caesar, the god. Often, it is hard to tell whether Herod really referred to Augustus or to himself with all these ebullient Messianic rites. Did he perhaps erect this world of earthly glory in the name of Augustus in order to appear in divine light himself?

In Jerusalem, the prophecy was maintained that, once he arrived, the Messiah would renew the Temple. The way he viewed things, could Herod leave this task to one who would come later? Next to the Herodian palaces and ostentatious structures, the Temple built by the Jews after the return from the Babylonian exile looked embarrassingly shabby. It disrupted the new city's appearance too much. Herod knew how to overcome any protest by the people. He even heeded the command that none who were not consecrated were allowed to touch the sanctuary. Specifically for the construction of the Temple, he had two thousand priests trained in the builders' guilds. He ignored the resolute protest of the pious who were quietly awaiting the true Messiah. Thus, fashioned of white marble, the Temple rose on the rock of Moriah in completely new form and considerably larger in size and proportions. Where had the stern simplicity of the sanctuary gone that Solomon had once erected on this spot? And whom did the new structure glorify more, the deity or its builder who in his mentally-deranged thinking sometimes considered himself, sometimes Augustus, to be the promised Messiah?* Herod must have felt completely enveloped in divine glory when, on the anniversary of his ascension to the throne, on the Day of Herod in the year 14, the Temple was dedicated in the most pompous celebration in all of Jewish history.

Many world histories have been written that lack any true consideration of the Christ Event, the central event of all. Nevertheless, it is understandable because this event took place in utmost insignificance outwardly and therefore eludes historians who typically direct their attention only to the external aspect of events. It is hard to understand, however, that, while examining the destinies of Augustus and Herod, attention was not ultimately drawn to the Christ Event and its central significance. The history of the Augustan and Herodian age really defies understanding without the unassuming archetypal image of which this history contains all the counter-images. For once, the shadow must be proof of the light. The time will come when, through the world as viewed and shaped by Augustus and Herod, people will learn with wonder to behold the light of which those in power during that time could only catch distorted and falsified rays.

---

* Early Christian theologians, like Tertullian and Epiphanius report that the Herodians referred to in the New Testament really considered Herod to be the Christ. Tertullian, for instance, states: *Herodiani ... Christum Herodem esse dixerunt.* 'The Herodians have said that Herod was Christ.' (*Praescripta* XLV).

3.10 The infanticide

Viewed from a certain aspect, the imposing accummulation of cultural edifices, of which Herod could not have enough, was nothing but an attempt at escape. The outwardly directed activity became the more urgent and innovative, the more relentlessly the demons of fear, mistrust and confusion intruded in his personal feelings and even the relationships with his closest blood relatives. In the end, the discrepancy, the gap between outer and inner, between cultural accomplishment and personal life, became unbearable. It ruptured the last cohesion of his soul forces and lead to a complete mental breakdown.

Mariamne, the Maccabean, had born Herod two sons, Alexander and Aristobulus. He loved them as idolatrously and jealously as he had loved their unfortunate mother. When they were approximately twelve years of age, he took them to Rome to be educated. Augustus looked after them personally and saw to it that they were lodged within the domain of his palaces. Grown to be young men and having returned to Jerusalem, they soon won the affection of the people with their noble, upright comeliness. In contrast to Herod himself and his Idumaean relatives whose deceptive, untruthful nature was despised, they were experienced by one and all as a living reminder of the heroic age of the first five Maccabean brothers. But even the slightest indication of sympathy enjoyed by the sons of Mariamne sufficed to plunge Herod into depths of suspicion and jealously. His bad conscience made itself felt, for his sons had a more legitimate claim to the royal throne than he.

In order not to allow these sons to gain too much standing, Herod summoned Antipater, a son from a former marriage, to his court. He, however, was a true demon, a sinister soul forever bent on evil, an intensification of the abysmal nature that infested Herod as well. Antipater insinuated himself into his father's favour. Soon the latter was obviously treating him as his favorite son. Thus, it was easy for the fiend to incite the father's suspicion and jealous mistrust against the two detested stepbrothers. Antipater set a number of intrigues and defamations into motion until Herod became firmly convinced that Alexander and Aristobulus were plotting his fall and death in union with the Jews who were sympathetic to the Maccabees. Herod travelled to Rome with his sons to call on Augustus in person to judge them.

Augustus discerned indications of mental illness in Herod. Following attempts to intervene positively between father and sons, he began to withdraw from Herod. When, later on, the hoary despot demanded the death penalty against his own sons from Augustus, the emperor's judgment of Herod was conclusive. Alluding to the fact that Jews are prohibited from the consumption of pork, Augustus coined the drastic saying: 'It is better to be the Jewish king's swine than his son.' He gave Herod discretionary powers over his family relationships but dropped him completely politically. Seventy-year-old Herod raved like a madman, had Alexander and Aristobulus strangled and instigated a brutal carnage among the presumed conspirators. The paranoia, the shadow of Caesarean megalomania, haunted and drove the old man with ever increasing demonic intensity.

In addition, a horrible disease afflicted him. His body became covered all over with open sores. To no avail, Herod sought healing in the hot springs on the eastern shore of the Dead Sea. Antipater, in whose devotion and faithfulness Herod still believed, now sowed the poison of mistrust between his father and younger brothers* who, like him, were studying in Rome. At the same time, he himself plotted an attempt on Herod's life. The latter, almost tormented to death even then by his illness and the spirits of chaos in his soul, still had to experience how the devilish scheme of his favorite son was discovered. A man, on arrival from Rome, had managed to push his way rather obviously into the presence of the king when he suddenly collapsed. It was discovered that he had fallen victim to the same poison Antipater had entrusted to him for the purpose of doing away with Herod. Antipater was lured to Jerusalem and his father had to order his execution, thus burdening himself with the third murder of his own sons. In the Gardens of Jericho, where the ailing old man was searching in vain to alleviate his sufferings, he had an apple and knife brought to him, intending to end his life. He was prevented from suicide but soon afterwards succumbed to his torments. Meanwhile, turbulent unrest was break-

---

* Herod had ten wives altogether.

ing out in Jerusalem. Orthodox Jews proceeded iconoclastically against Herod's ostentatious creations.

The Gospel of Matthew describes how the diabolic, nocturnal spectres of the Herodian destiny form the historic background for the birth of the Jesus child, a child that had descended from the genuine succession of generations of the kings of Judah. We see how the three lofty priest-kings, led by their star wisdom, arrived from the East to pay homage to the babe as the true king of humankind. But before they found the one they were seeking, they encountered his irrationally distorted counter-image, the false king, who was driven by the fear that somebody might cause his powerfully built-up structure of illusion to collapse. And so, the horrors of the Herodian infanticide passed over the locality where, in the paradisal vestiges of this very place, the cradle of the babe was embedded. The Bible thus ranks Herod among the antagonists who, as demonic advocates of an ancient world order, battled against a new, young element of humanity. As did Nimrod at the birth of Abraham and the Egyptian Pharaoh at the birth of Moses, Herod now ordered the infanticide. But as was the case in bygone times, now, too, the child was delivered from the threatening peril. The bloody spectres of horror from the past could not block the path to the future.*

---

* We face extremely difficult challenges if we try to reconcile the report of the Gospel with traditions outside the Bible concerning the life of Herod the Great (for example those by Josephus). The thematic similarity between the historically verified murder by Herod of his own offspring and the infanticide of Bethlehem reported by the Gospel of Matthew as his deed is unmistakable. The two complexes of misdeeds certainly do not exclude one another; they may well have occurred as monstrous products of the same Caesarean madness. A significant difficulty arises, however, from the fact that, according to conventional chronology, Herod died four years prior to the point in time fixed by tradition as the 'birth of Christ.' Since it goes without saying that today's historians ascribe greater scientific validity to 'historical' documents than to the Gospels, they have no choice but to declare Matthew's narrative of the Herodian infanticide to be a 'legend.' Yet it is possible to show that, even in regard to the outward set of facts, the Gospels are no less reliable historically than texts outside the Bible. Aside from the fact that the difference between the Nativity stories as related by Matthew and Luke cannot simply be ignored, a number of centuries-old errors in reckoning time and thinking have to be corrected so as to clarify the apparently insoluble contradictions.

[A detailed study of the Herodian chronology can be found in Ormond Edwards, *The Time of Christ,* published in 1986, long after Bock's books. Editor]

Clothed in imaginative pictures, the Gospel's report allows us to gain insight into the decadent, obscene mystery background of Herod's deeds — deeds dictated by fear and lust for power. As little as in the Abraham-sagas and the biblical story of the childhood of Moses, so here, too, we do not deal merely with a suddenly decreed mass slaying of newborn children.[21] The veil lifts a little from the black-magical secret cults in which brutal horrors, perpetrated on pregnant women and newborn infants, played a part because in that way a diabolical megalomania attempted to force into its service the pure, higher nature forces of mother and child. An inkling of profound secrets of providence can be evoked in us by the local tradition that exists in Bethlehem since ancient times. According to legend, the black-magical cults of Herod the Great performed their rituals in a chamber of the same ancient grotto sanctuary in which, a short time later, the stable of Luke's Nativity story was located.

When Herod was gripped by jealous rage — regardless of whether it was directed against his Maccabean spouse, his sons or some other person — this was, fundamentally speaking, only the surface expression of another greater jealousy, one scarcely concealed behind the unsatiable utterances of homage directed towards Augustus. They were broken rays of the approaching true Messiah Event that kindled the hidden inferno in his soul. Herod was jealous of Christ himself. He, the false king and god, sensed the approach of the true spirit-king and god-man. This was what haunted him. And it was this that caused him to resort to means of horror in the grotto-darkness.

Finally, it was this that elicited in him the monstrous restlessness of building and destroying. And when he had his own offspring slain in devilishly possessed madness and desperation, he basically aimed at the killing of yet another child. The child had to be prevented from being born or was to lose its life shortly after birth, the child that would return to earth-existence the truth, innocence and power of heaven. But it was an impotent performance and struggle that the spectres of nocturnal darkness presented in order to annihilate the light of day. All their rushing and flickering was itself nothing but the effect of the sun that was just then rising above the horizon.

We have traced the destinies of the new world that sprang up in Greece and Rome, the two firstborn of Europe. The bright wisdom of Greek spiritual life, the older sister; the virtuous humaneness of Rome, the younger brother — whatever wonders of beauty and capability blossomed forth from them, they were only too soon obscured and distorted by the gigantic counter-offensive of the powers from the past. A new world of egohood had come into being, but alone it was not strong enough to prevail. It was not able to reject and overcome the spirits of the ancient world that fought against it. Before long, the new faced the greatest danger of being smothered by the strangling hand of the dark giant. Was there no power on earth that could come to its aid? The Christ Event was the mighty divine help for the threatened young world of the ego.

4. Judaism:
Pharisees — Sadducees — Essenes

4.1 Esoteric streams in Judaism

The *Zohar,* the 'Book of Radiance,' one of the most important
parts of the Cabbala, relates that after the destruction of Jerusalem and the Temple by the Romans (in AD 70), Rabbi Simeon
ben Yochai summoned together the wisest teachers of the people
for a sacred and mysterious gathering:

In silence, the companions have taken their seats. Then,
Rabbi Simeon breaks into tears and calls out: 'Woe to me
if I unveil the mysteries! Yet woe to me, too, if I do not
unveil them now!'

Then he seats the companions in a certain order. He
places two on each side of him and says: 'Now we are
the portal of the Temple and its two pillars. We now
represent the triangle, the sum and primal image of all.'

Rabbi Simeon stops speaking and everybody remains
silent. Then, a voice reaches their ears that is like a
murmuring. What sort of sounds are they? It is the
whispering of the lofty celestial gathering that has
convened to listen to the words of the teacher. The
companions are shaking, but Rabbi Simeon says: 'Fear
not, rejoice instead. It is written: "Lord, I have heard the
roaring of your presence and trembled." Once, fear
behooved men; now we should be filled with love. Does
it not say: "Thou shalt love the Lord thy God?" And did
He Himself not say: "I love thee?"' Then Rabbi Simeon
began to teach: 'He who in his soul is without balance
and falters back and forth becomes a traitor of the secrets.
Only he who has achieved inner firmness and composure
can inwardly nurture and preserve the mystery entrusted
to him. Moreover, he who is without inner firmness does

not possess the organ of the spirit with which to
comprehend the meaning of the mysteries; all that he
hears turns in his head like a wheel in water. In the end,
he spills all that he has taken in. The whole world rests
on the secret. And if he has need of reticence even in
earthly matters, how much more necessary will be the
silence in regard to the mystery of mysteries that God
does not even reveal to His highest angels? Heaven bends
down to listen to us, yet even in its presence I hesitate to
speak. And the earth moves better to hear us, yet before
it, too, I would like to remain silent. In truth, we are now
the portal and pillars of the world.'

In the book of the *Mysterium magnum,* it says that when Rabbi
Simeon finally opened his mouth to unveil the mysteries, the
earth shook under his feet and his companions felt this quaking
with trembling soul.*

Such a narrative may well exhibit the mark of later times when
the Cabbala was written down. But it allows us to gain important
insight into the spiritual life that existed in Palestinian Judaism
directly before and after the turning point of time.

Almost without exception, the most inappropriate conceptions
prevail concerning this spiritual life. The reason is that no written
documents and sources exist that would impart any insight into
the spiritual and religious life of Palestinian Jewry from the time
before and after the Maccabean battles until the destruction of
Jerusalem. Direct reports only exist concerning external political
and military events of this period. We do know that the canonic
as well as apocryphal Old Testament scriptures played a significant role in the Judaism of Palestine in those days. For, beginning with Ezra, the development of the canon and the written
recording of the Scriptures, until then often handed down merely

---

* Rendered literally in accordance with the original text, this passage is
contained in the chapter, *Idra Rabba,* 'The great gathering.' Another chapter
is called *Idra Suta,* 'The small gathering.' The word *idra* is identical to the one
used in the Old Testament for 'threshing floor.' This usage of the Cabbala
therefore is also an indication that the Old Testament actually refers to cultic
locations or learning centres when it speaks of 'threshing floors.' This should
be compared with what is said in the volumes, *Moses* and *Kings and Prophets,*
concerning the threshing floor at Ophrah, of Boaz and of Araunah.

in oral form, had been actively pursued. Yet, based on external traditions, we know nothing about what sort of theological, religious and ethical culture developed in connection with biblical literature. Since prevailing historical research and also historical theology rely in all cases solely on written sources, a great error was made. The conceptions formed of Palestine's spiritual Judaism at the turn of time were acquired from the late Talmudic scriptures that originated only after the destruction of Jerusalem (AD 70) and the Bar-Kochba revolt under Hadrian (around AD 130).

If nothing else, the fact that written traditions are silent prior to the destruction of Jerusalem proves that the spiritual life was of a completely different nature than during the time when Talmudic literature originated. The absence of source materials is by no means due to external or coincidental reasons. Spiritual reasons prevented the creation of written documentation. In those days, Jewish religious life was illiterate as a matter of principle since it was still filled with the breath of mystery. To put into writing what was known and passed on in oral teachings would have been considered by the teachers of that age as a profanation and betrayal of secrets. The cabbalistic tale of the 'great gathering' points to the transition that had to occur with tragic necessity when, following the destruction of the Temple, the possibility of quiet, discrete cultivation and transmission of wisdom came to an end. Now the teachers of Jerusalem were forced to reveal the mysteries of the doctrine. Talmudic literature came into being. Everything became different when the sacred veil of silence had been torn asunder. By necessity, it had to become shallow and externalized.

An additional factor was that only one specific stream from among a rich variety and abundance of spiritual life produced the Talmudic texts, for it alone survived the destruction of Jerusalem and the Temple — namely, Pharisaism. When one tries, based on the Talmud, to form some ideas about the spiritual nature of Judaism during the last pre-Christian and first Christian century, one arrives at the completely erroneous one-sided notion that, even then, the Pharisaic stream was the only leading and dominant one. Until the year 70, a strong esoteric stream existed in Judaism. Dating back to the age of the mysteries and cultivated in various branches in the manner of the mysteries, this spiritual stream remained alive and influential. When the legions of Vespasian under Titus caused Jerusalem and the Temple to go up in flames, not only the outward splendour built up by Herod the Great perished but a whole world of esoteric spiritual life. As is demonstrated in the story of the 'great gathering,' the tears of the teachers, who had to bid farewell to the secrets of that time under a roaring heaven and on a trembling earth, mixed with the lamentations over the ruins of the external sanctuary.

Rudolf Steiner once pointed to the esoteric character exhibited by Jewish spiritual life prior to the year 70 by attributing to it the peaceful coexistence that still prevailed between Judaism and Christendom during the first few decades after the Christ Event:

> Now this relatively easy harmony between Christian and Jew peculiar to earlier times came to an end towards the close of the first century. From that time even enlightened Jews became implacable enemies of everything Christian. The Jewish texts which are held to be of importance today date from the second century and testify to a growing discord between Christian and Jew. As we follow the deterioration of this relationship we see how a hatred of Christianity first emerged in Judaism and was associated with a progressive transformation within Judaism itself ... We must realize that in the first century the learned Jewish Rabbis gave a totally different interpretation of the Old Testament from that which is given today ... the further back we go the more we find that at the time of the Mystery of Golgotha there existed in Judaism, in addition to the exoteric Scriptures of the Old Testament, a genuine esoteric doctrine. It is to this esoteric doctrine that must be attributed in large measure the possibility of interpreting the Old Testament in the right way ... Now there existed in Palestine certain Mystery teachings which were a preparation for the Mystery of Golgotha and in respect of which the Mystery of Golgotha was seemingly a fulfilment.[22]

Now is it not true that it was in the departure from the world of the mysteries, in the courage to publicize them, that the progressive trend of the new age was expressed? If the assertion is correct that Judaism preserved its esoteric character beyond the turning point of time, would it not have to be counted among the cultures of the ancient world instead of being considered a pioneer of humanity's future, an older brother of Greece and Rome?

As far as the history of the evolution of consciousness is concerned, Israel's spiritual life as a whole had already gone through the transition from the capacities of ancient clairvoyance, cultivated in the mystery temples, to the free clear power of thought. And this had been at a time when Greece was still enveloped in the misty dawn of its mythical early period; when Rome as yet slumbered far below the horizon of history. But aside from the historical evolution of consciousness, the Jewish people primarily had an existential mission in history, something their spiritual leaders were well aware of. Out of their hereditary stream and blood line, they were to eventually give birth to that human physical form which would be capable of serving as an earthly sheath and dwelling for the Messiah, the god who was becoming man. The sacred Messianic task could be advanced only in quiet instructive work which, guided by hidden wisdom, kept a core of the people in a pure state spiritually and physically and prepared them to be a vessel for the approaching content of heaven. This was the reason why, in Judaism, even though it shared fully in the advancing stream of mystery popularization and transformation, cultivation sites had to be maintained for an esoteric life that resembled that of the mystery centres.

It was because of the duality of the inner mission which the people of the Old Testament had to fulfil that Jewish cultural life moved so obviously in two different directions in and outside Palestine during the time following Alexander's campaigns. World Jewry outside the Holy Land absorbed Greek language and learning with great enthusiasm. The Greek and Jewish spirit came together as if two related souls were meeting. Within a short time Jewish Hellenism and Hellenistic Judaism could become a uniform, creative, cultural factor of the first magnitude, an important member within the new culture of thought based on human capability alone. By comparison the appearance of Jewish life remained quite different around Jerusalem, the people's ancient, sacred centre. The further the Judaism of the Diaspora went in mixing and mingling with Greek culture — for instance, in Alexandria — the more sternly the leaders of the people in Jerusalem and Judea were intent upon segregating themselves from all things foreign. It did not matter that the circle of people uncompromisingly obedient to the Law of Moses declined. Somehow, at all costs, that pure Messianic core of the people had to be preserved. The sacrificial, heroic deeds of the Maccabean age were devoted to this goal and so were the intense efforts of the groups that, for the sake of the Messianic future, remained representatives and caretakers of the mysteries.

Josephus, who wrote his detailed description of Jewish history at the time of Jerusalem's destruction, repeatedly classifies three groups — the Pharisees, Sadducees and Essenes — as the main representatives of Jewish cultural life of that age. We must not make the mistake so frequently made by historians who are misled by the consistently superficial depictions of Josephus and view these three groups as religious parties the people could simply choose to join. We are dealing with strict, segregated Orders, as is clear even from the writings of Josephus. An ordinary citizen could be a follower but not easily a member of one of these exclusive leading groups. Only a detailed consideration of the sternly esoteric character of these communities makes it possible to understand the historical role they played at the approach of the turning point of time.

One error, for example, that circulates in regard to the spiritual Judaism of that time is that the origin of the three leading groups, especially of the Pharisees and Essenes — to the extent that the latter's existence is accepted at all — is supposed to have been in the age of the Maccabees. The reason is that they are then mentioned for the first time in the historical documents that have come down to us. It really will not do to judge the presence and nature of religious Orders — Orders that were carefully surrounded by a veil of secrecy and silence — based solely on public references and descriptions. When written records start to refer to such esoteric groups, this is by no means an indication of when they originated. It is far more a sign that the group in question had relaxed its original conditions of membership. Thus, the atmosphere of tact and silence, once valued so highly by this very group, could be breeched. It therefore goes without saying that the three esoteric streams, mentioned indiscriminately as early as Josephus, date back to far older times in Judaism's history. The age of the Maccabees was simply the cause that none of them henceforth could continue in quiet isolation. About that time, the leading religious groups had to intervene directly in the power politics of the nation's outer destinies which increasingly seemed to turn chaotic.

4.2 The Pharisees and Jewish Hellenism

We can assume, as pointed out earlier in the portrayal of Old Testament history,[23] that following the end of the Babylonian exile (around 450 BC) the Pharisaic Order was established by Ezra as an esoteric core group of the scribes' profession in connection with the Korahites' wing of the ancient prophet schools. As the name Pharisee (the segregated one) indicates, from its inception the Order's mission was to keep the Jewish blood line and spiritual stream pure from any foreign influences. Initially, due to its origin in Babylonia and contact with indigenous schools of wisdom,* the work of the Jewish scribes probably had a tendency towards a certain broad-mindedness. Ezra and the Pharisaic Order then brought about a conscious concentration and limitation on the specific mission of the Jewish people. Nevertheless, when synagogues or houses of prayer were founded wherever Jews lived, an active generous cultural life developed through the scriptural reading and interpretation on every Sabbath. This was concurrent with the dawn of the new world in Periclean Greece. Life in the synagogues had a powerfully democratic impulse. It furthered the spiritual independence of the individual because the contrast between priests and laymen played no part in it. While the theologians, versed in scripture and later called *Rabbunim* or Rabbis, occupied a leading position, many men from among the common people were able to play an active part in the readings and interpretations, so long as they had completed certain teaching courses in their youth.

---

* The Jewish scribes were called by the same name as the Babylonian scribes: in Babylonian, *sapiri,* in Hebrew, *sopherim (Kings and Prophets,* p. 308)

Due to their strict exercises, the Pharisees were the occultly trained core group among the scribes.[24] The more relentlessly and watchfully they guarded the precinct of stern segregation and Messianic preparation in the centre, in Jerusalem, the more they could grant unconcerned free reign to the generous culture of thought found in the synagogues.

Pharisaism confronted a completely new condition and task, however, when the mighty impulse evoked by Alexander's campaigns took hold even of the essence of Jewish scriptural activity. Over the heads of the Pharisees in Jerusalem, the synagogues brought about the great blending between the Jewish and Greek spirit, not just outside Palestine but even in Samaria and Galilee. The Greek language not only penetrated everyday life but also the ritual life of wide Jewish circles once the Septuagint, the Greek Old Testament, came into existence. Worldly Jewish theology, which had spread far beyond the specific profession of the scribes, could believe it had found its culmination through the encounter with Greek philosophy, particularly with the teaching of the Logos, the creative Word of Worlds. The afterglow of the mysteries in this Jewish theology, which gave it an imaginative pictorial tendency, was marvellously illuminated by the brighter Greek language and thought. A clairvoyant radiance became perceptible in it once more and called to mind the fact that human thought, as it appeared in the Jewish and Greek stream, was nothing else but a metamorphosis and paler reflection of ancient clairvoyant vision. The allegorical interpretation of the Scriptures, which Philo for example knew how to employ prolifically and skilfully, blossomed above all on Hellenistic ground.

The electrifying encounter with the Greek spirit gave spiritual Judaism an extraordinary urge to broaden and expand within the briefest possible time. Freely following the trend of the time, Hellenistic Jewry quickly developed a far-reaching spiritual propaganda. It was not so much a matter of converting members of other nations to Judaism. But could the wisdom-filled scriptures of the Old Testament and the exegetic art linked to them not confidently be placed alongside the literature that the late Greek schools of philosophy — above all those of the Stoics — used in their endeavours to spread ideal and moral enlightenment everywhere? The Jewish religion assumed the character of a philosophical and moral world-view and, now that it was no longer so utterly Jewish, it harmonized in every way with Greek philosophy that was no longer so utterly Greek. Thus, the synagogues became in many instances the meeting places for those men from among all the nations who were striving for noble learning.

The rise of Jewish Hellenism brought it about that the centrifugal tendencies, which were directed outward to the far reaches of the world and connected Judaism with the new impulse, suddenly assumed significant predominance over the centripetal tasks of Messianic concentration nurtured in the more isolated circles. How should the Pharisaic Order, the trustee and guardian of the Messianic mysteries, react to the overwhelming drive for dissemination, that powerful tendency of the age which aimed for complete popularization of the mysteries? The Pharisaic Order could not really oppose philosophical Hellenism and simply prevent it from spreading to Judaism. To go against the tide like this would have been completely senseless. The Pharisees could not even desist from lending their guidance and support to the liberal spiritual life of the synagogues.

Nevertheless, if the balance was not to be lost, something had to be done to protect and strengthen the pious Law-abiding Messianic core of the people. The Pharisaic Order was now required to emerge from obscurity and develop an intense education of the people. But such efforts could hardly have begun when the rapid course of events forced a further step. Things did not stop with philosophical Hellenism which was mainly nurtured by way of Alexandria. From Antioch, the Caesarean Hellenism of the Seleucid rulers soon made its appearance. Since it contained a directly anti-Messianic tendency due to the beginnings of the Caesarean cult, it even forced the Pharisees to become involved in the nation's political leadership.

Subsequently, they were the ones who saw to it that the pious in Jerusalem and Judea joined the ranks of Judas Maccabeus and his brothers and were ready to take up arms against the danger. The educational system for the people, increasingly elaborated by the Pharisaic Order, was linked with Mosaic Law. By adding countless, subtle, separate decrees, which gradually became so great that people almost designated them as a 'second Law,' the Law was almost given the character of a system of mental exercises. Even on its own, the Mosaic Law with its thousand strict rules regarding life, rules surrounding the tablet of the Ten Commandments, must not be taken as a moral and social institution in the ordinary sense. The Law owed its magic to the fact that, for any given issue in life, it prescribed to a person a certain behaviour. This amounted to an exclusion of certain specific forces of nature and an inclusion of quite different, initially more remote, super-earthly streams. For example, the command of keeping the Sabbath, always depicted as particularly important, by no means aimed just at the cessation of activity, much less at relaxation from physical work. Rather, it induced a person to submit to a dark, sweepingly melancholic spell. The pious who observed the Sabbath became immersed in an other-worldly sphere far beyond all living things, where the dark abyss of existence prevails; the foundation of the world whence all things originate but to which moreover all things return. They meditated on death and thus became filled with a Saturnian earnestness, in contrast to which all earthly joy and cheer withered and died.*

Through the 'second Law' of the Pharisees, the magic of the Law acquired an unbroken effect on people. Human life was covered by a finely meshed net. In order to serve God, any natural, spontaneous experience was sacrificed to that ceaseless attention and awareness required to select the most appropriate commandment in any given circumstance. The Hasidim, the 'Pious,' who complied with the Pharisaic discipline of the Law, effected a soul transformation that was extraordinarily impressive.

Nevertheless, the result was a one-sidedness of soul. This conforming to the system of the Law not only affected the avoidance of sin but complete detachment from all natural spontaneity. The last remaining forces that bound people to the natural cosmos, forces that had kindled in them the light of instinctive clairvoyance in earlier times, were extinguished in human beings. The final impoverishment of soul necessarily came about. In view of the Messiah's coming, this could be understood to mean that a vessel was being prepared for his incarnation, a

---

* The Sabbath is Saturn's day. Sabbath, 'the seventh,' is at the same time the Hebrew name for the Planet Saturn.

vessel totally cleansed and emptied of any other contents. No old natural forces would stand in the way of the divine forces he would bring. Nevertheless, having been purified of the ferment not only of sin, but of all natural elements, a person who then appeared faultless and just became at the same time quite weak mentally through this negative discipline. A deep, all-pervasive timidity developed in such a person. It entered consciousness as the fear of God. In the end a man's fear of sin and divine wrath had to turn into a fear of life and nature in general.

4.3 Apocalyptic teaching of the Pharisees

The fact that the Pharisees, as stern taskmasters, led those who allowed themselves to be guided by them along such a path was connected with the supersensory conceptions cultivated in their circle. A secret Messianic teaching existed in the Pharisaic Order that was probably limited to members of the higher degrees of holiness. Certain elements of this teaching can still be found in the Talmud, the writings of a later, decadent Pharisaism. The *Minim,* the bearers of this secret teaching, were degraded in the Talmud as the worst heretics. Anybody who came across their books, held to be books of magic, had to burn them. Nobody was allowed to consult one of the *Minim* as a physician. Nevertheless, in some passages of the Talmud rules from earlier times have survived. On one occasion, mention is made of the main two Minaic teachings:

> The *Ma'asse Bereshit* (the teaching of the world's creation) may not be presented in the presence of two listeners; and the *Ma'asse Merkaba* (the teaching of the 'celestial vehicle,' the forms of God) may not be presented even in the presence of one single listener, except if he is a sage and an initiate (*Mishnah, Haggia* 11b).

As follows from the Talmudic indications, the subject of these secret teachings was the reference to the Messiah-Christ, a divine being to be distinguished in the manner of a Son from the Father God. Like the Logos-teaching of the Greek mystery and philosophers' schools, these teachings were searching for the cosmic power and being that should be designated as the World Creator *(Ma'asse Bereshit)* and the solar World Mover and Giver of Life

(Ma'asse Merkaba). The prophetic scriptures referred to this being when they proclaimed the coming of the Messiah. Another aspect of the teachings, nurtured by the Pharisees, becomes visible to us in the apocalyptic literature. Exemplified in the prophets' books of an Ezekiel or Daniel, it emerged abundantly — proceeding from the Fourth Book of Ezra, the apocalypse of late Judaism — in the age following Ezra. The Pharisees looked back to Ezra, the towering inaugurator, as a personality who like the great prophets of past centuries had been able to behold divine images and hear the spiritual word. And they surrendered to the stern soul discipline of their Order in the conviction that in this way they, too, would advance to apocalyptic perception and insight. Josephus says of the Pharisees: 'Due to their affiliation with God, it was thought that they were entrusted with precognition of the future.'

During the initial and still genuinely spiritual period of the Pharisaic community, there may have been persons who on occasion were able to transmit revelations. All in all, however, the secret exercises of the Order probably led only to an increased acquisition of traditionally existing apocalyptic images, contained as they are in the books of a Baruch, Daniel and Ezra.

It goes without saying that the essential core of the apocalyptic images and traditions always related to the arrival of the Messiah. Everything revolved around the coming of the Son of Man out of the clouds of heaven (Dan.7:13), or from behind and above the clouds on the *Merkaba* with the fiery wheels, the celestial vehicle. Yet it was this very image that, for the Pharisees, grew into a tremendously frightening world vision. True to the ancient Jewish saying, 'He who sees God must die,' they could picture the mighty appearance of the Messiah being only by imagining that, thereby, the catastrophic end of the world would be brought about. The coming of him whom all the world was awaiting as the Redeemer had to signify, so they believed, the end of this aeon that would be destroyed amid thunder, lightning flashes and the sounding of trumpets. As they saw it, only then, along with those who, as the just ones, would have survived the cosmic judgment, would the Messiah establish the new aeon, the redeemed world. The Pharisees are the initiators of eschatology, the teaching of 'the final things' and the 'Last Day.' What they taught was artistically depicted by medieval artists in their paintings of 'Judgment Day.' The Pharisaic concept of the Messiah was one that to the highest degree instilled fear as well as hope, yet fear predominated. And when the Pharisees were forced to come more into the open in their efforts at public education, it is possible that, besides their eschatological-apocalyptic views, they may have made known some of the previously closely guarded apocalyptic literature to a wider circle of the 'Pious' who were under their guidance. They did this in order to increase the motivating force of fear in obeying the Law.*

The Pharisaic view of the creation of the *aion erchomenos,* the 'coming aeon,' by the Messiah was identical with their teaching concerning the resurrection of the dead, designated everywhere in literature, for instance in the writings of Josephus but equally in the New Testament (for example, in Acts 23:6f), as being characteristic of Pharisaism. The Pharisees did not teach the resurrection of the dead theoretically as a universal law, valid everywhere and at all times. They taught it dramatically as one act within the mighty Messianic world catastrophe. Their belief in Messianic redemption and world renewal was the most extreme belief in miracles the world has ever known. Over-whelmingly intense apprehension and fear must have filled those souls who were anticipating the coming of the Messiah as an event close at hand. The Pharisees made use of this apprehension in their instruction of the common folk. They never tired of proclaiming that only those who meticulously obeyed the Law and all additional directives would prepare themselves to be included on that 'Last Day' in the mighty resurrection of the world.

---

* Because their existence cannot be documented historically until this point in time, conventional theory holds that the apocalyptic scriptures, along with the Book of Daniel, did not originate until the age of the Maccabees. The correct part of this view may be that these books were put into writing at that time. Their origin, on the other hand, doubtless dates back much further. Customary theology gives far too little credence to the oral tradition of sacred texts. It does not occur to such a theology that the principle of secrecy or the prohibition to put them into writing could have existed with regard to books of genuine revelations.

4.4 Degeneration of Pharisaism

It is difficult to give the Pharisaic Order a positive valuation, even if one's view is directed solely to its pure original form. In almost all historical descriptions the Order does not play a very praiseworthy role. The reason was that, as the very exponent of the great transition experienced by humanity at that time, it was filled with tensions from the very beginning, tensions that soon brought the Order into the dangers of decline. These dangers were magnified by the chaos of war and politics that increasingly forced the Order to emerge from its spiritual isolation. The more sternly the Pharisees had to make known their educational requirements for the populace under the pressing difficulties of the Maccabean age, the less were they still in a position to maintain any tolerance towards even the noblest representatives of Jewish Hellenism.

In the end, so as not to put the absolute validity of their doctrine of Law in question themselves, they had to become virtual proponents of the religious arrogance of their followers. Was a person who obeyed and followed all the rules — rules linked to the promise of Messianic resurrection and redemption — not forced to consider any other person, who took the Law less seriously, as one condemned to eternal death? If, due to the system of the Law, a calculable path to salvation existed, it was of course even easier to figure out and determine whether a given individual was on the path to perdition. In this way, those who originally had been the patrons of the liberal democratic spirit of life in the synagogues soon became religious tyrants and fanatics who judged those who did not submit to their discipline and laws. The designation of those who did not belong to the Hasidic and Pharisaic devotees, the claimants of the new aeon, namely the *Am-ha'aretz,* 'the people of this world,' became an abusive word.

A hidden but all the more tragic stumbling block for Pharisaism was that, from the very beginning, the way the Pharisees experienced the apocalyptic images of the Messianic world future contained the seed of a materialistic misinterpretation. The imaginative-intuitive visions announcing the great, imminent, spiritual world reversal had already yielded to a coarsening process when people pictured their realization in the form of an outward catastrophe that signified the end of the world. And this misunderstanding could only rapidly increase when the Pharisaic scribes intentionally took advantage of people's anxiety and, as preachers of penitence, placed before their souls the images of Judgment Day as a means to evoke fear. The actual spiritual meaning of the images that pointed to the necessity of inward decisions was obscured. In the end, nothing but a passionate wave of religious egotism and pride could be attained in this direction.

Insofar as its nature was concerned, the deepest and most dangerous root of degeneration, however, lay in the hybrid position occupied by the Order between the two tasks of Judaism, namely, between the popularization of the ancient mysteries of wisdom and the conservation of the Messiah mysteries. Being themselves in possession of a secret teaching and an occult discipline that was meant to lead to supersensory and apocalyptic experiences, the Pharisees were forced to appear to the people as leaders of a purely exoteric culture of thought, a culture cleansed of all vestiges of supersensory content. Through the extended Mosaic Law, they even had to subjugate their followers to an education and discipline, the result of which was a complete extirpation of the ancient clairvoyant soul forces. The great prophets, to whom the world of spirits was still open as a source of revelations, had had to fulfil a similarly contradictory task. In a lofty supersensory vision, had Isaiah not been given the mission to contribute to the extinction of supersensory sight, to the hardening of the people's hearts by the sternness of his proclamation?[25]

In the case of the Pharisees, any loss of spiritual standing however slight, any entanglement in the power struggles of the age, any externalization of their spiritual system of teaching, had to turn their activity into a form of double-dealing and duplicity because of the duality of their task. Most of all, an element of untruth had to take hold of the Order to the extent that the occult soul discipline no longer raised the souls up to an actual experience and perception of the spirit. Instead of the original true spiritual authority, only pretensions were imperiously brought to bear. The seed of fearfulness that had been sown in the souls of the people finally proliferated in the members of the Order. The ability to approach the threshold of the spiritual world decreased and the fear of the spirit was obscured by high-handed fanaticism. This is how it came about that, when the human incarnation of the awaited divine being had actually taken place in obscurity, the forbidding exclamations of woe against the Order resounded from the lips of this very being, the Order whose mission it would have been to guard the mystery of His coming and to prepare his way:

Woe to you, you scribes and Pharisees, you hypocrites! You shut the kingdom of the heavens against men. You cannot find entrance yourselves, and so you want to bar the entrance to those who can find it. (Matt.23:13, compare Luke 11:52).

One should not minimize the devastating words that Christ hurled against the Pharisees by misunderstanding them. They neither signify that the Order of the 'segregated ones' could no longer avail itself of any spiritual faculties at that time, nor were they meant to accuse the individual members of the Order of personal transgression and malice. The words: 'Beware of the leaven of the Pharisees which is nothing but hypocrisy.' (Luke 12:1) were not meant merely in a moral sense. They hit at the very foundation, the spiritual principle that had developed in Pharisaism. *Hypokrisis* or 'hypocrisy' was not meant to indicate the untruthfulness of individual persons; it referred to the untruthful double-dealing of the whole movement that consisted in leading human beings away from the mysteries of the spiritual world while yet claiming them for itself. At that time, the degeneration of Pharisaism had become complete. Due to the materialistic misinterpretation of their revelations and their blindness of soul obscured by false claims, the Pharisees did not recognize him, the preparation of whose paths had been the sole meaning of their Order.

It is an exact historical comparison fitting in all details if the Pharisees are called the Jesuits of the turning point of time.[26] Following a short period of purely spiritual activity, the Jesuit Order likewise succumbed to rapid degeneration when it was turned into the fanatical tool of political power struggles and allowed the fatal element of duplicity to enter its ranks. For even though the Order had at its disposal secret doctrines and occult means of discipline, this element motivated it to proclaim: Christians should believe; they should not strive for any knowledge of the spiritual world. It is therefore no coincidence that it was the Jesuits who, on a Christian foundation, preached with particular emphasis the fear-arousing Pharisaic teaching of the chasm between this world and the one beyond; the teaching of Judgment Day and the eternal torments of hell.

4.5 Origin of the Sadducees

In principle, any Jew who was obedient to the prescribed preparations and conditions could become a member of the Pharisaic Order despite the strict cohesion pursued in it. The unifying, integrating element consisted in a common effort and activity. Nobody could become a Sadducee, however, who was not one from birth. The unifying bond within this community was simply and solely a close familial blood relationship. The Sadducees were a branch of the Levite tribe, a tribe that since the age of the first kings was held to be especially noble and of pure blood. Starting with their ancestor, Zadok,* the first high priest of the newly erected Temple of Solomon, only one member of their family had been allowed to assume the office of high priest.

Within this noble temple family that, from out of its ranks, regulated the religious, political and social leadership in accordance with dynastic principles, a particularly aristocratic, exclusive pride of nobility had prevailed for some time. Early on, a chasm came about between Temple and synagogue, because the Sadducees could only look down with contempt on the democratic activity that developed in the institutions of learning under the leadership of the Pharisees and scribes. The foundation occupied by the Sadducees was that of ancient established traditions and rights. Their noble lineage that went back far into the distant past and the privileges linked to it in the religious and national life gave them a sense of superiority and power over all others. When the prophet Ezekiel was describing the new temple he envisioned in exile, he had said:

---

* Sadducee is a Grecianized form derived from the Hebrew name, Zadok.

... and the chamber which faces north is for the priests
who have charge of the altar; these are the sons of Zadok,
who alone among the sons of Levi may come near to the
Lord to minister to him (Ezek.40:46).

Their past-oriented view and their insistence upon lineage, in-
herited privilege and tradition evoked a strong sense of worldliness among the Sadducees. Around the turning point of time
aspirations for earthly influence and riches had become pre-
dominant among the clan of the high priests. We know, for instance, that the fanatical old man, Annas, had accummulated
tremendous riches and was possessed by almost pathological
avarice.

Yet we must not presume that spiritual insights were not cultivated at all within the circle of the Sadducees; that the
ceremonial ritual for which they were responsible had simply
fallen victim over the course of time to superficiality and
secularism. On the contrary, what established the power of this
Temple clan was that, just like the Order of the Pharisees, it, too,
availed itself of occult means and faculties, although in a totally
different manner.

In order to comprehend Sadducean 'spiritual life,' we have to
refer back to Zadok, the first Sadducee. Under David, when the
unassuming sanctuary containing the ark of the Covenant still
stood on peaceful Mount Zion, the priesthood that carried out the
sacred service was still led by two high priests of equal rank. By
Zadok's side stood Abiathar. Zadok was the highest bearer of
Levite tradition. Abiathar was the only survivor of the priests
from the mysterious oracle centre of Nob in the Judean Desert.
This was the place that had offered sanctuary and help to David
during his flight from Saul, but then had betrayed him and been
cruelly destroyed by David (1Sam.21–22).[27] The then still young
son of Nob's high priest had been successful in saving the sacred
oracle implements from the fury of destruction and had brought
them to David. David then added the mystery cult of the
destroyed oracle centre to the ritual of the ark of the Covenant
and had entrusted Abiathar as second high priest with its
management.

From then on, the juxtaposition of a more exoteric and a more
esoteric cultic practice was expressed in the duality of the high

135

priests. Zadok continued the stream of the outward sacrificial rite dating from Moses and Aaron. The more esoteric, mystery-like service at the sanctuary can perhaps be pictured as a kind of mediumistic questioning of an oracle; priests with special supersensory faculties directed it, for instance, by shaking and tossing certain stones like lots or dice. From their position the priests then read the reply of the gods. When David broke the law of the right of the firstborn and named Solomon his successor, Abiathar was among those who protested most strongly. Did the custodian of the esoteric oracle service realize that Solomon, the powerful exotericist and abolisher of secrets,[28] would also become his opponent? When Solomon took power, he banished Abiathar to Anathoth,* and Zadok was sole high priest in the new temple on the rock of Moriah. It was then that the oracle service, originating from Nob, must have passed on to the completely exoterically-oriented priesthood. These priests could only make far more superficial use of it. Nevertheless, in this way, they did obtain occult magical powers. What had earlier been a means of acquiring genuine revelations now, misunderstood and no longer handled in accordance with the spirit, turned into an anxiously guarded source of power under the Sadducees. The worldly attitude of the Zadok descendants could never have increased to such intensity and lack of consideration had it not been nourished by the magical misuse of supersensory faculties.

As the degeneration of Pharisaism can be compared to that of Jesuitism, so can the degeneration of the Sadducees be likened to that of the men who, beginning in the early Middle Ages, seized upon the Pontificate and Vatican. What has been said of the Popes applies also to the Jewish high priests. They tried to bolster their reflections and decisions by means of spiritualistic oracle methods. Because of this unspiritual and political use, the results of oracle questioning inevitably became subject to increasingly materialistic misinterpretation. At an important point of the Christ drama, the Gospel of John shows us the Sadducean spiritualism in action: after the resurrection of Lazarus, the Sadducee Caiaphas made the following pronouncement before the

---

* Later, the prophet Jeremiah, a descendent of Abiathar, was born there *(Kings and Prophets,* p.288f).

Sanhedrin: 'it is better for you that one man dies for the people, than that the whole people perishes' (John 11:50). Pregnant with meaning, the Gospel adds that Caiaphas owed this statement, which was nothing but a contemptuously political and short-sighted distortion of a lofty sacred truth, not to his own thinking but to the use of the oracle workings that, as high priest, he had at his disposal:

> He did not say this out of himself, but, being the High Priest of that year, he foresaw prophetically that Jesus would die for the people (John 11:51*B*).

4.6 Sadducean world-view

The secular, materialistic outlook of the Sadducees found expression in a certain view of the world and humanity. Josephus as well as the scriptures of the New Testament repeatedly emphasize that the Sadducees disputed the immortality of the human soul and were therefore the most outspoken opponents of the Pharisaic, apocalyptic belief in the resurrection. According to the Gospel's report, they even approached Jesus of Nazareth so as to embarrass him with a question. They spoke of seven brothers who died, one after the other, without leaving behind any children, even though, in accordance with the Law and following the death of one of the brothers, the wife of the eldest one always became the wife of the next-eldest brother. And they posed the question, whose wife the woman might become in the world of resurrection? (Matt.22:23f; Mark 12:18f; Luke 20:27f).

Here, too, it would be wrong to view the Sadducees simply as people who denied the spirit. Everywhere, their materialism had its covert reasons. Particularly this sly question reported by the Gospels makes it clear that a quite unique conception of immortality was cultivated in the circle of the Zadokites. Here we encounter the belief, a belief still found among native Americans and Africans, that the soul of man lives on in his descendants and that one who has no children forsakes immortality. A methodical description of late Jewish spiritual life leads us again and again to points where we have to realize how much of an unchanged Judaism was absorbed into the conceptions and feelings of all shades of traditional ecumenical Christianity. The reader will

have noticed this in the description of Pharisaism. The Sadducees' view of immortality is likewise such an element of the
Jewish spirit to which people of recent times are frequently
directed — albeit in this case often outside the dominion of
Christian Churches — because of the inadequacy and spiritual
helplessness of modern world conceptions.

David Friedrich Strauss, who can be called the exponent of
nineteenth-century Protestant theology, finally retained nothing
but the thought that the human being lives on in his or her children. Towards the end of his life he wrote a disconsolate letter of
condolence to a friend:

> To my dismay, this morning I came across the news that
> you have lost your dear, beloved wife ... You have the
> best, living consolation in the children she gave to you,
> the children whom she helped you raise. To seek in them
> the traces of her being; from the daughters, increasingly
> to watch the mother ... develop; to find in the sons her
> example, her heart and mind ... continuing on, ever
> blessing — this in time must be uplifting to you. This is
> the immortality in which we believe and we must prove
> that it contains no less consolation than that of the
> Church's faith.[29]

This view had its valid basis in distant Lemurian and Atlantean
ages when the human being, totally embedded in the group-soul
element, was as yet far from developing individual egohood.
Carried into eras of nascent egoity, such a concept had to obscure
their true nature to human beings. This element of primordial,
outdated spirituality suited the Sadducees' claims of nobility and
power splendidly, for thereby they conjured forth something
almost approaching a cult of deification of ancestry in Judaism.
In this view, any high priest elevated himself when, as happened
in a form of ancestor ritual, he looked up to Zadok, the tribal
patriarch of this lineage and back even further to Levi and
Abraham.

It is obvious that Messianic thought occupied far less room in
the occult foundations of the Sadducees' worldliness than it could
in the Pharisaic eschatological belief of the beyond. If the
promise did in fact rest on one lineage of the tribe of Judah, was
not the lineage of Zadok from the tribe of Levi basically of much

nobler blood and destined for something far greater? It was furthermore quite impossible within the Sadducean manner of thinking to picture the Messiah other than as a man endowed with special magical powers who — naturally only as the political advisor of a Zadokean hereditary ruler — would accomplish the miracle of establishing an earthly kingdom of God. The magical-political, worldly misinterpretation among the Sadducees contrasted with the eschatological other-worldly misunderstanding that the Pharisees entertained towards the Messianic prophecy.

4.7 Sadducean politics

So long as the Jewish people were under the alien rule of Babylonia and Persia during the time of the exile and the following two centuries, the office of high priest had to be limited to its cultic duties. But after Alexander the Great had restored Judea's political independence up to a point, the Sadducees quickly succumbed to the danger of becoming entangled in power politics. Having become, through their own ominous occultism, adversaries of all those spiritual streams that fostered the inner freedom and egohood of human beings by popularizing and transforming the mysteries, they soon began to sympathize with the Diadochian spirit of the Seleucids. Were the omnipotent Syrian kings and autocrats not men, too, who hated freedom and abused the mysteries? And if the aim was power, was it not expedient to side with those in power?

Through the Sadducees, a Diadochian infection entered Judaism. The beginning of the Caesarean cult, the demonic Messiah caricature slowly appearing on the horizon, could thus extend its effects even into the Messianic nation. Sadducees and their followers were the ones who obsequiously prostrated themselves in homage before the likes of Antiochus Epiphanes; double-crossed and deposed their own family members and, in order to acquire power of their own, brought the pagan Caesarean cults to Judea. Finally, supported in the background by the Pharisees who were concerned that the nation remain pure, the Maccabees took the stage against them.

The success of the Maccabean liberation wars at last led to the fall of the Sadducean dynasty. We clearly see in this the involvement of the Pharisees who increasingly intervened in politics. The Maccabees assumed the office of high priest themselves and founded the Hasmonean dynasty. For the first time in Jewish history, the Zadokian succession was broken. For a while, another priestly lineage took on the leadership of the people. It goes without saying, however, that the Sadducees, born politicians and men ambitious for power, did not give up easily. Through unscrupulous employment of whatever means were at their disposal, they succeeded in gaining influence over the Maccabees soon after the death of Simon Maccabeus, the last of the sons of Mattathias. They won John Hyrcanus (high priest 135–104 BC), the son of Simon, over to their side by setting him at variance with the Pharisees. They knew that a person who had broken into the sacred tomb of David on account of the gold treasure it contained would not be able to resist the lure of their riches either. The sons of John Hyrcanus continued with anti-Pharisaic politics under their influence: Aristobulus (104–103 BC) assumed the title of king and Alexander Jannaeus (104–76 BC) vented the Sadducean hatred against the mysteries in a bloody persecution through which he proceeded against the Pharisees and other guardians of the Messiah mysteries.

Only for a short time (under Alexandra, the wife of Alexander Jannaeus, 76–67 BC), did the Pharisees gain influence once more over the political leadership of the nation. But then the Sadducees joined forces with Antipater and Herod. These two for their part were currying favour with Rome, a Rome fast becoming Caesarean. The Idumaean courtiers of Herod, borrowing from the Diadochian and Roman emperor cults, developed their schemes for power in Judea and Jerusalem. And the Sadducees knew that there was no more fertile ground for their objectives than the chaos of splendour and opulence in which Herod's Caesarean madness indulged. They were far from giving any thought to a spiritual obligation with regard to the approaching Messiah future. By the time the Messianic prophecies were fulfilled in quiet seclusion, they had once again succeeded, by means of huge bribes and toadying to the functionaries of the Roman Caesars, to gain possession of the office of high priest. Annas, Caiaphas and their clan had made the great world-historical compromise. It was they who, in front of the palace of Pilate, wanted to be better Romans and Caesarean servants than even the Roman procurator. They shouted: 'If you release him, you are no longer a friend of Caesar ... We have no king but Caesar' (John 19:12, 15). It was not long before educated Jews, among them the historian Josephus, who inwardly were Roman underlings as were the Sadducees, believed that Vespasian, the Roman Caesar whose troops were on the point of destroying Jerusalem and the Temple, was himself the promised Messiah. Josephus wrote of this in no uncertain terms in his *Jewish War*:

> But now, what did most elevate them (the Jews) in
> undertaking this war, was an ambiguous oracle that was
> also found in their sacred writings, how 'about that time,
> one from their country should become governor of the
> habitable earth.' The Jews took this prediction to belong
> to themselves in particular; and many of the wise men
> were thereby deceived in their determination. Now, this
> oracle certainly denoted the government of Vespasian,
> who was appointed emperor in Judea.[30]

In the same connection in which Rudolf Steiner spoke of the ongoing existence of mystery views in Judaism until the year 70 (see p.121), he plainly characterized the historic role of the Sadducees and their inner relationship to Caesarean Rome:

> At the time of the Mystery of Golgotha it was Romanism
> that was most averse to this particular aspect of the
> Jewish Mysteries. There has hardly ever been perhaps in
> the history of the world a more deep-seated antagonism
> than between the spirit of Rome and the Mystery tradition
> preserved by the initiates of Palestine ... we can only
> comprehend the ferment within Christianity when we see
> it against the historical background of the Mystery
> teachings of Palestine. This Mystery teaching was full of
> hidden knowledge about the 'spiritual man' ...
> Ramifications of this Mystery teaching were also to be
> found to some extent in the Greek Mysteries ... The
> essence of the Palestinian Mysteries found no place in
> Romanism, for Rome had evolved a special form of
> community or social life which was only possible if the
> spiritual man was ignored ... why did Romanism develop
> such a strong antipathy to Christianity? ... At the trial

before the Sanhedrin, which condemned Jesus Christ, the
Sadducees played a leading part ... They were a sect
which wished to eradicate, to suppress everything that
proceeded from the ancient Mysteries. They had a fear, a
horror of every form of Mystery cult. The courts and the
administration were in their hands. They were completely
under the influence of the Roman State ... There is
unmistakable evidence that they purchased preferment for
large sums of money and then recouped themselves by
dunning the Jewish population of Palestine. It was they
who realized — and thanks to their Ahrimanic,
materialistic outlook they were quick to perceive this —
that Rome was threatened if it should come to be
accepted in any way that the drama of Christ was related
to the fundamental teachings of the Mysteries. They had
an instinctive feeling that Christianity would give birth to
something that would gradually overthrow the authority
of Rome. And this accounts for those fierce wars of
extermination which Rome waged against Judaism in
Palestine during the first century and in later centuries.
These wars of extermination were prosecuted with the
avowed object of exterminating not only the Jews but all
those who knew anything of the reality and traditions of
the ancient Mysteries ...[31]

4.8 The nature of the Essene Order

We enter a completely different world when, penetrating through
the veil of secrecy, we turn to the life of the Essenes. Here, the
sombre fanaticism of the Pharisees, the egotistic materialism of
the Sadducees, has receded far into the distance. The air of
soulful and at the same time spirit-irradiated, meditative piety
surrounds us. We see humble human beings who not only keep
their distance from power politics but, in addition, through stern
ascetic discipline avoid anything that could tie them too strongly
to earthly affairs. Despite their tendency to remain close to the
spirit by denying the material dimension, we realize with
astonishment that this movement had a worldwide radius in the
last pre-Christian era. In various forms, it spread out over all the

lands that surrounded the eastern Mediterranean Sea, following the traces of Hellenism as if it had formed an alliance with the spirit and language of Grecian culture, even though only Jews were members.

Deeply imbued with the consciousness that the spirit-word is profaned and turned into an earthly matter if put into writing, the Essenes avoided leaving behind any written records about their teachings and practices. Even the carefully guarded scrolls were of course destroyed by the Essenes before they would have allowed them to fall into the hands of strangers; scrolls which contained pearls of wisdom handed down from ancient times which were read within the confines of the Order in support of the predominantly oral tradition.*

For a long time, modern historical research had doubted the existence in history of the Essenes due to the lack of written evidence. Historians did not realize that, because of their faith in documentation, they were excluding from their descriptions the most important spiritual streams. And yet, though written by outsiders, we did have some descriptions in existence that gave us a number of important insights into the life of the Essene communities and clearly demonstrated why a more direct and conclusive documentation could not exist. In the text *Every Virtuous Man is Free* by the highly educated Hellenistic-Jewish philosopher Philo of Alexandria, we have a brief representation of the Essenes, and in his text *On the Contemplative Life* we find a quite detailed picture of the life of the Egyptian Therapeutics who were closely related to the Essenes.† Furthermore, Josephus, who in his youth had been a disciple of an Essene hermit and was a novice later on in the Order, divulged what he had been able to find out in his descriptions of *The Antiquities of the Jews* and *The Jewish War,* thus violating their secrets after he was not accepted into the actual brotherhood. Moreover, it was Josephus who reported that anyone who wished to be accepted into the Order first had to undergo a strict ascetic year of probation as a novice; then, along with the baptism by water, he was admitted

---

* The scrolls discovered in the caves by the Dead Sea were secret Essene texts and were believed to be in a safe hiding place.

† The two texts by Philo are reproduced in their entirety in the Appendix.

to the daily sacred washing. After two more years of probation
and following stern vows and a 'dreadful oath of silence,' a man
was allowed to attend the sacred meals.[32]

Even as the Pharisaic Order was directed to the urban life of
Jerusalem because of its active efforts at educating the people, so
the Essenes and Therapeutae with their initially completely
inward-directed meditative work were trying to seek seclusion far
from human habitation. Their hermits dwelt in the sandy desert
of Egypt and in the gorges of the Judean wilderness; there, those
who lived together in groups built their cloister-like settlements.
Similar to the monasteries of Eastern Christian monks that we
find today like pigeon nests on the steep slopes in the canyon-
like recesses of the Judean Desert, we must picture the cloisters
of the Essenes, occasionally even in the identical locations. The
widespread communities of the Order were given cohesion and
a uniform character by larger central monasteries. According to
Philo, the centre of the Therapeutae was located on the Mariotic
Sea in the Nile Delta near Alexandria:

> This community can be encountered at many locations in
> the world ... They live in Egypt in large numbers ... and
> are most numerous in the surroundings of Alexandria.
> From everywhere, the most outstanding people are sent as
> into a common homeland to the site of the Therapeutae
> by the shore of the Mariotic Sea, a location particularly
> suitable as far as safety as well as the balmy warmth of
> the air are concerned.[33]

The centre of the Palestinian Essenes was located by the valley
of En Gedi. As the only area of fertile life, it comes from the
region of Hebron down to the subterranean depth of the Dead
Sea. In typically Roman fashion, the elder Pliny reports:

> The Essenes live west of the Dead Sea but avoid the
> shore beyond which the unhealthy fumes cease. They are
> a reclusive community, strange beyond any people the
> whole world over. They are without women, abstain from
> sexual love and live only in the company of palms. Many
> gather there daily, tired of life and thrown up by the
> swells of destiny, to share in the Essenes' life. Thus,
> since time immemorial, exist an eternal people, though

none is ever born among them. This is how other men's
weariness of life is fruitful for them. The city of En Gedi
is located there; once second in fertility ... to Jericho, now
it, too, is a ruin.[34]

The discipline pursued in Essene and Therapeutic monasteries
and hermitages was one of body and soul. Austere exercises in
fasting and purification alternated with meditative contemplation.
Essenism was an intensified continuation of the Naziritism inaugurated by Moses and later practised in the Nazirite wing of
the prophets' schools. What the Nazirite rule for a thousand years
had aimed for and still achieved in those who dedicated themselves to it, the Essenes and Therapeutae tried to bring to realization in enhanced form. This was the singling out of a noble group
of men who, like an eternal lamp, kept alive the light of ancient
clairvoyant spiritual knowledge, while the nation as a whole
underwent the development of consciousness that lead to earthly
knowledge. Thus, through stern obedience to a whole system of
monastic rules, men tried to avoid all that was earthly and material in their conduct of life, in diet and even the cultivation of the
inner life. What was more, the effort was made to undo the processes of earthly hardening and darkening that had already
invaded human nature; to extract and eliminate them, as it were.
Once again, the physical and soul nature of a man was to be led
as closely as possible to the light-filled spiritual permeability and
purity it had possessed in paradisal primordial times prior to the
Fall.[35]

Rudolf Steiner says concerning Essene and Therapeutic
asceticism:

The Therapeutae were endeavouring by inner paths to
purify and develop their souls, to expel any elements
corrupted by outer concerns and external knowledge, in
order thereby to rise into the sphere of pure Spirit. An
offshoot of the sect of the Therapeutae, where this
subsidiary stream underwent still further development,
was the community of the Essenes in Asia [Minor][36]

The Essenes were men who had isolated themselves
from the rest of humanity and were leading a particular
mode of life of body and soul in orde to re-attain the
primal revelation of the Spirit that was now lost to

mankind. By dint of strenuous exercises and austerity of life, these souls aspired to reach a stage where they would again come into touch with those spiritual regions whence the primal revelations had flowed ...[37]

The system employed by the Essenes for the purification of the soul was, in effect, a continuation of the ancient Nazarite discipline. This form of occult training had existed in Judaism from times immemorial ... First and foremost, the Nazarites subjected themselves to a diet that in a certain respect is still useful today if anyone desires to make more rapid progress in soul development than is otherwise possible. They abstained altogether from eating flesh and drinking wine ... [by so doing] it is possible to develop greater inner resistance to obstacles, greater strength for the overcoming of hindrances arising from the physical and etheric bodies, and a greater power of endurance ... These practices of the Nazarites were continued, but in a much stricter form, by the Essenes who also resorted to quite other usages ...[38]

When a novice was admitted to the first probational year, in addition to the white gown he had to wear he received an apron and a little shovel, to be worn on the belt of the apron, symbols and means of the most extreme bodily and mental purity. Particularly by covering all human waste with earth, an Essene pupil again and again was made aware of his duty to return to the world of earthly matter as much as possible of what in the human organism had become part of the earth.

Foremost among the vows that had to be taken during acceptance into the Order were the oaths of a single life and chastity. Moreover, an Essene was obliged to divest himself of any worldly goods. Anyone who entered the Order turned his back on the world; gave away all his possessions to the poor or surrendered them into the keeping of the Order which exercised the principle of communal ownership of property. As impossible as it would have been among Essenes, the 'servants of peace,' for someone to produce a weapon or participate in any strife or battle, so, too, members of the Order shunned money as an especially dangerous sign of earthly attitudes and involvement. Any trading and purchasing activities were disdained among them. Essenes even embarked on the longest journeys 'without money in their belts,' certain that wherever they went they would enjoy the hospitality of their supporters. The principle of poverty was typically defined by pointing to the brotherliness that the Order tried to achieve. It was because of possessions, so they said, that disparity and thereby strife had arisen among men. Particularly this consequence of the Fall had to be undone and therefore neither slaves nor even servants could be part of the Essene life style. The privilege of the noblest among the Essenes and Therapeutae was to serve the brothers during the sacred washings and at meals.[39]

4.9 Spiritual view of the Essenes

As if he were describing the inner aspirations of the Pythagorean and Platonic mystery schools to which he gave spirited homage as well, Philo could not do enough in detailing the effects of the Essene path on the soul:

> The community of the Therapeutae unceasingly advances
> on the path of vision and aspires to the perception of
> True Being. It tries to transcend beyond the visible sun
> and never strays from this well-ordered path that leads to
> perfect blessedness. Those who aim for the goal of
> salvation receive their incentive neither through tradition
> nor the calling or admonition by a human being. They are
> carried away by heavenly love and are filled with ardour
> like the Bacchants and Corybants. They do not cease until
> they behold what they long for.[40]

Even Josephus was aware that in the four stages which had to be gone through after final admittance into the Order,[41] there always were those:

> who undertake to foretell things to come, by reading the
> holy books, and using several sorts of purifications, and
> being perpetually conversant in the discourses of the pro-
> phets; and it is but seldom that they miss in their
> predictions.[42]

Furthermore, the development of clairvoyant vision signified an actual process of growing into the secrets of the teaching cultivated in the Order, even where it did not lead to a full breakthrough. The indications by Josephus, as meagre and based on rumour as they are, still allow us to recognize that among the Essenes a knowledge prevailed concerning spiritual man, the immortal, soul-spiritual essence of the human being and its relationship to the physical bodily sheath. What would have been the sense of all the efforts at purification from the rigid darkness of the earthly element, if pious attention would not have been directed exclusively and unceasingly towards that part of one's own being which had come from heaven and had originally been fashioned out of pure spirit? In the Essene view of life after death, Josephus stressed a subtle tendency of unworldly longing for heaven, and in this he was probably not mistaken, insofar as he contrasted it to the materialistic denial of personal immortality common among the Sadducees, and the eschatological teaching of resurrection by the Pharisees:

> For their doctrine is this: That bodies are corruptible, and
> that the matter they are made of is not permanent; but
> that the souls are immortal, and continue for ever; and
> that they come out of the most subtle air, and are united
> to their bodies as in prisons, into which they are drawn
> by a certain natural enticement; but that when they are set
> free from the bonds of the flesh, they then, as released
> from a long bondage, rejoice and mount upward.

Moreover, we hear that, like the Greeks, the Essenes held to a conception of a paradisal island of the blessed departed where the good dwell, and of a black cave of Hades where the evildoers are confined after death. Finally, Josephus had to admit:

> These are the divine doctrines of the Essenes about the
> soul, which lay an unavoidable bait for such as have once
> had a taste for their philosophy.[43]

When recounting the oath that had to be sworn by those entering the Order after the three preparatory years, Josephus referred especially to the obligation to keep the names of the angels strictly secret.[44] We realize from this that the Essene teaching of spiritual man continued on in a teaching of the hierarchies. Thus, Man not only appears as the highest member of the kingdoms of nature but furthermore as the lowest member in the sequence of higher beings, beginning with the angels and archangels all the way to the Cherubim and Seraphim. And when a man brought his soul through purification and prayer into the proper frame of mind, he had the means, in certain 'names of angels,' to come into contact with the world above him.

Yet, the very core of the Essene teaching dealt with the coming of the Messiah who, on his way down to earth on the heavenly ladder of hierarchical steps of being, would soon arrive at the lowest hierarchy, that of man. If popular traditions tell us nothing about the Messianic character of Essene teachings and life, this only proves that the Messiah idea, which basically predominated over everything, was for the Essenes the most sacred and secret centre of the mystery, one to which neither Josephus nor Philo found access and about which they too would have kept silent, if indeed they had come in contact with it.

Early on, Naziritism had been established so that despite the nation's evolution of consciousness towards earthly thinking, the visionary comprehension for the Messiah mystery would remain alive somewhere. Here, as quoted earlier in the description of the Nazirite, Samson (in *Moses),* the words by Rudolf Steiner are repeated:

> In point of fact, right through Hebrew history, some
> individuals were ... prepared to be able to understand the
> Christ Event ... Those men who were prepared so as to be
> able to recognize and understand, by clairvoyance, the
> significance of the Christ, were called Nazirites. These
> men were able to perceive clairvoyantly all that had been
> prepared from the earliest days of the Hebrews, in order
> that, out of and through this people, the Christ might be
> born and understood.[45]

The whole motivation for the intense efforts at soul discipline and piety in the Orders of the Essenes and Therapeutae was due to the awareness that a setting of purity had to be prepared on earth for the Messiah. Out of the prophetic vision that was the fruit of this effort, all inner and outer endeavours received new sustenance and strength. Again and again, seers must have existed among the Essenes who not only foresaw and predicted outward events, as Josephus mentions several times, but beyond this could direct their glance at the approaching Christ-being, thus proclaiming to the brothers in the Order where the hand of the spiritual clock of the world was standing at a given time.

4.10   Social activities of the Essenes

The outward-directed practical activities of Essenes and Therapeutae were also pervaded by a Messianic trend. Even though an
attitude of religiously selfish and antisocial alienation from the
world and prevailing culture arose in the hermitages and cloisters,
nevertheless the Order did not remain without far-reaching social
effects. In a way completely differing from that of the Pharisaic
Order, the attempt was made to do justice to the tasks which the
rise of Hellenism posed to Messianic Judaism. Far above the
narrow Jewish nationalism promoted by Pharisaism, the Essenes
and Therapeutae, trusting in the spiritual energy they were foster-
ing, joined in Hellenism's universal outreach. And like a leaven,
they in fact succeeded before long in infusing their own spiritual-
religious influences into all the regions where Greek was spoken
and where Jewish communities existed.

A large number of travelling brothers made use of the freedom
of the synagogues in the countries all around and, in a heart-
warming manner that harmonized beautifully with the Greek
spirit's brightness of thought, taught the people to await the arrival of the Messiah with ardent piety. It was due to their efforts
that, when the Christ Event actually approached, there were 'quiet
ones in the land' everywhere whose hearts were open to the
Christ's message. The sphere of influence attained by the Order
had such scope because friends and supporters of the Essene
brothers appeared from all social levels and professions as well
as from among the scribes of the Diaspora. We encounter one of
the most important and beautiful traces of this in the Whitsun
story of the New Testament which refers to the large number of
devout men 'from every nation under heaven' (Acts 2:5).

The soulful wisdom of the Therapeutae and Essenes related not
only to the higher spiritual spheres of existence. An intimate
familiarity with the beings and forces of stones and plants
endured among them as well. It is said of them that the knowledge of nature they cultivated turned them into masters of
farming and horticulture. Above all, it enabled them to exercise
the art of healing for which the Therapeutae were named.
Josephus wrote:

> They also take great pains in studying the writings of the
> ancients, and choose out of them what is most for the
> advantage of their soul and body; and they inquire after
> such roots and medicinal stones as may cure their
> distempers.[46]

According to Philo, they called themselves 'male and female
healers' because:

> They consider their art of healing to be superior to the
> one practised in the cities. The latter supposedly serves
> only to heal the bodies, whereas theirs cures the soul as
> well from severe and incurable illnesses caused by desires
> and passions; sorrow and fears; selfishness, folly and
> uncountable other weaknesses and afflictions.[47]

When we picture the Essene-Therapeutic envoys, without
money in their belt and in humble dress, moving through the
lands teaching the people and healing the sick, we almost believe
we are watching the Apostles of early Christendom wandering
about. And we recognize how important the quiet leaven-like
activity of these men was for the preparation of Christianity.
Through them, not just an abstract doctrinal but a soulful, living
foretaste of the Messianic sunrise was brought about.

Insight into a particular branch of Essene activity can be
gained through the following indication by Josephus. Although
the members of the Order did not marry:

> they ... choose out other persons' children, while they are
> pliable, and fit for learning; and esteem them to be of
> their kindred, and form them according to their own
> manners.[48]

This probably fits with his other report that, aside from the
strict monastic observance, there were groups of married Essenes.[49] An image comes to mind of village-like settlements and
colonies which, though under the guidance of ordained monks of
the Order, were mainly composed of families who followed a
considerably more lenient rule. In a sense, they must have been
Essenes of lower rank, resembling the lay-organizations of
Tertiaries connected to the Franciscans and other Catholic Orders.
The application of a therapeutic attitude in the realm of child
education must have lent these social structures special attraction
and harmonious compatibility.

Yet even here the social practices were not self-serving. The brotherliness of this communal education and pedagogical art flowed out of wise, quietly nurtured Messianic insights and intentions. For it was not merely a matter of proclaiming the human incarnation of the Messiah and to prepare the hearts of the pious for this event. In a quite practical sense, a family-structure had to be created, a joining of lineages; a wise, eugenic and social activity had to ensue so that, out of the right stream of destiny and heredity, the pure childlike corporeality could be developed.

Nazareth, where the Jesus child thereafter grew up, was in fact such a quiet Essene colony. If outside the Gospels and until the time of early Christianity, there were no traces of this little Galilean town in the traditions so that historians did in all seriousness doubt its existence, the reason is that it was not a public worldly settlement but a community of the Essene Order. The name Nazareth makes it possible to look from yet another side at the Messianic society of the Essenes. The sight of the Essene seers, directed as it was on the Messiah secret, viewed the longed-for event of salvation in the image of a budding shoot that grows in a living way out of the tree of humanity and a certain lineage. The prophetic utterance by Isaiah was a Messianic guideline for the Essenes: 'A shoot shall blossom forth from the house of Jesse, and a branch from out of its roots shall bear fruit' (Isa.11:1*B*). The Hebrew word for shoot is *nezer*. And since the Essenes not only wished to be a living *nezer* on the tree of humankind but the true servants of that one highest divine *nezer,* they named the branch of their Order that was meant to exert particular influence on the sequence of generations in the Messianic lineage, Nazirites.

The most drawn-out scientific discussions concerning the name 'Nazirite' have taken place. It is a name that in the Gospel (Matt.2:23) and in early Christendom was applied to Jesus of Nazareth and moreover, for a long time, to Christians. Again and again, the attempt was made to trace this name back to the town of Nazareth. In so doing, great difficulties were encountered, for it was not known whether this little town was even in existence then and whether it had not received its name much later. All the problems are solved at once if the concept *nezer,* coined by Isaiah and the Essenes, is taken as the basis for consideration. We shall see later (and this will be done in detail in the contents of the next volume, *The Childhood of Jesus)* that the solution to the problem goes back to the descriptions of Essenism that we owe to Rudolf Steiner. Nazareth is the 'town of Nezer,' the 'town of the Nazirites.' The picture of the Tree of Life growing out of Jesse's root, an image that returns countless times in medieval paintings and sculptures, is a symbolic condensation of an important branch of the Essene teaching and activity.* It does not sound unbelievable to us when Katharina Emmerich, the visionary nun from the beginning of the nineteenth century, relates how the Essene seers, upon whose advice the Essene laymen — among them the ancestors of the mother of Jesus — solemnized their marriages, deciphered their answers from the growth of sacred plants, which they called 'root of Jesse.'[50]

4.11   The ritual life of the Essenes

The significant, although quiet effects that the Therapeutae and Essenes exercised upon their surroundings far and wide; the reverent esteem they enjoyed everywhere because of their integrity and genuine religious attitude and zeal, go back last but not least to the rituals they practised in their circle. But they did not simply remain in their secluded monastic settlements. Instead, in the course of time, in all larger and smaller towns, they established hospice-like houses. In these, under the management of a visitors' steward[51] hired especially for this purpose, generous hospitality was offered to all brothers and friends of the Order who happened to be passing through. Their ritual practices therefore were also widely disseminated.

In all the houses of the Order, regardless of whether they were monasteries in the desert or fraternal houses in towns, there was one room which, as a sacramental sanctuary, bestowed temple-like sacredness on the whole building. This was the cenacle, the room of the meal, because the holiest communal rituals of the Essenes were identical with their simple meals. As

* We learn from the texts by Epiphanius (fourth century) that the Nazirites originally called themselves Jesseists after Jesse, the father of David *(Panarion Haereticorum* xxix).

if to symbolize the elevation of soul experienced in this room, the cenacle in the houses of the Order was not designed on level ground but as an upper room. The Essenes were as good as excluded from the ritual carried out at the Temple in Jerusalem because, being opposed to bloody sacrifice, they were uncompromising proponents of the bloodless, inner, sacrificial service.[52] On the other hand, even though reading and instruction from the Scriptures took place at the beginning of the holy meal in their cenacles, these rooms could not be equated with synagogues. They really were the Essenes' temple facilities. Josephus, who did not advance anywhere near the level where he would have been admitted to the holy meals of the Essenes, quite clearly sensed the mood of the mystery surrounding the rooms where the brothers dined. He reports:

> After this purification [ceremonies of washing] is over, they every one meet together in an apartment of their own, into which it is not permitted to any of another sect to enter; while they go, after a pure manner, into the dining-room as into a certain holy temple ... Nor is there ever any clamour or disturbance to pollute their house ... which silence thus kept in their house, appears to foreigners like some tremendous mystery ...[53]

Like nothing else, the ritual observances of the Essenes demonstrate the will for an all-pervading sanctification of the whole of life. What life in uninterrupted meditation was to the Therapeutic hermits and ascetics as described to us by Philo, to the Essenes involved in some kind of social activity was the daily repeated sacred custom of worship and communal divine service.

Every time a new day was born from the womb of night, Essenes greeted the rising sun with the prayer for enlightenment through the sun of the spirit. Josephus said about this:

> Before sun-rising they speak not a word about profane matters, but put up certain prayers which they have received from their forefathers, as if they made a supplication for its rising.[54]

And Philo says concerning this:

> When the sun comes up, they pray for a good day, but a good day in the true sense of the word, a day on which the heavenly light fills their thoughts.[55]

Around the hour of sunset, all the brothers of the Order who were present at one locality gathered with unfailing regularity for the holy washings, calling to mind day after day the memory of the baptism through which they had initially been admitted to the circle of the ordained. Then they put on their formal white garments, crossed over the threshold of the holy room and, in firmly established sequence that depended on the length of time they had been members in the Order, took their seat at the table. Now they could feel they were in the innermost circle of men to whom the holiest mysteries of the community were entrusted and revealed. The partaking of food and drink was preceded by spiritual nourishment through words of scripture and the teaching presented by one of the oldest brothers and received by all in pious silence and attention. Then followed the simple meal, always experienced as communion, as a gift from the hand of the deity — a meal which, when it was most sacred, consisted of nothing but bread, salt and fresh spring water. No day passed without these holy acts; there was no drinking and eating that was not a celebration of communion. All their doings between the sacred meals were sustained and illumined by the consecration and strength received through them.

This sacramental life always reached a culmination point when the seventh day began. This was far removed from the Sabbath magic of the Pharisees. It was as if the sun's gentle radiance was trying to penetrate the day of Saturn, since the members of the Order remained on that day even more unceasingly and insistently in the bountiful sphere of the spirit. And the Sabbath of all Sabbaths, the ancient sacred festival of Pentecost that was celebrated when, following the celebration of Passover, seven times seven days had passed, brought the greatest exultation of joy. Then, the evening meal continued on in the holy night celebration, until the morning prayer to the sun reached its highest intensification in the inspiring communal hymn. This was a hymn in which the brothers and sisters of the Order greeted the fiftieth day, the day of Pentecost.[56] A presentiment of a new creation imbued all hearts and souls; out of evening and morning, the new day was born.

4.12   Jeshu ben Pandira

The picture we tried to form of the life of the Essenes and
Therapeutae probably fits the last pre-Christian century most
accurately. Earlier, in connection with the Nazirites and the Nazirite prophets' schools, a large variety of Order-like groups may
have existed that featured ascetic Messianic traditions and aspirations. Around the turning point of time, on the other hand, a certain decadence had taken hold of the Essenes, especially of those
who were unable to make the transition to Christianity.

The Therapeutae and Essenes received their actual cohesion,
spiritually defined form and fulfilment during the last century BC
through the towering figure of a leader known to Talmudic scriptures as Jeshu ben Pandira. The clarification of the role and
importance of this figure is one of the most significant acts of
historical insight of Rudolf Steiner. Light is finally shed on errors
and confusion that are nearly two thousand years old.

From the very first periods of Christianity, as if an ill fate had
been involved, Jeshu ben Pandira, who lived one hundred years
earlier, has been confused with Jesus of Nazareth. Features from
the earlier figure were used to denigrate the later one. The result
was that Jeshu ben Pandira was hardly ever viewed, much less
taken seriously as a figure of historical existence and significance
in his own right. In the text by the Greek philosopher Celsus on
The True Logos (around AD 180), which is familiar to us from
Origen's refutation, this confusion emerged for the first time in
literature. Celsus claims it is a mis-statement to speak of the
virgin birth of Jesus of Nazareth. In actual fact, he had been the
son of a charwoman who, cast out by her husband, a carpenter,
as an adulteress, conceived him by a Roman soldier named
Pandira or Panthera. This same mix-up has been repeated even in
our own time. For example, in the Theosophy of H.P. Blavatsky
and Annie Besant, where it became one of the main reasons for
the utter misjudgment and contempt of Christianity. In many
theosophical books, for example in *Esoteric Christianity* by
Annie Besant, we read that Jesus did not live at the time of
Augustus, Tiberius and Pilate, as reported by the Gospels, but a
hundred years earlier, and that he was not crucified but stoned.

It is quite obvious that the confusion between Jeshu ben Pandira and Jesus of Nazareth did not originate because of a conscious intent at falsification or a mistaken tradition. This is something mentioned a number of times by Rudolf Steiner, who had to separate from the theosophical movement precisely because of its incorrect view of Christ and Christianity. The confusion has an occult basis and for just this reason had such ill-fated consequences. The figure of Jesus of Nazareth, the human bearer of the Christ being, eluded the historical retrospection of an atavistically undisciplined and therefore superficial and misdirected clairvoyance. In its place, images of that figure turned up who lived on earth a hundred years earlier. The central event of humanity's history was thus literally overlooked. At the same time, the significant personality of Jeshu ben Pandira was lost to historical view.

This mix-up intrudes into Jewish and Christian theology because of the opinion that passages in the Talmud that mention Jeshu ben Pandira refer to Jesus of Nazareth. These passages should therefore be viewed as evidence of hatred by Rabbinical Judaism against Christianity. Volumes upon volumes have been written on the theme, 'Jesus in the Talmud.' If the confusion is discerned, we realize that the Talmud contains practically no references, much less aspersions against Christendom. To our surprise, a comprehensive, clear biographical picture of Jeshu ben Pandira arises instead from those passages, sparse and confused as they are, where mention is made of this personality. And because of the concreteness of the individual biographical features, we can only be surprised again and again that it was even possible to relate these references to the one of whom the Gospels speak.

It may have been towards the end of the reign of John Hyrcanus (135–104 BC) when Jeshu ben Pandira was born in Palestine. He was also called Ben Stada, 'Son of the Harlot,' because his mother, Miriam, whose profession it was to curl the hair of noble ladies, gave birth to him out of wedlock.[57] A few ancient narrators seem to know that as punishment for her adultery Miriam had to die a cruel death; she was hung by her breasts.

As a young man, Jeshu ben Pandira became the disciple of a famous teacher in the Pharisaic Order, Rabbi Joshua ben Parachya. At that time, King Alexander Jannaeus, the son of John

Hyrcanus, ruled supreme. Owing to Sadducean machinations, he allowed himself to be lured to the great bloody persecution of the Pharisees and other Jewish mystery communities. Rabbi Joshua ben Perachya belonged among those who left the country. He fled to Egypt with his pupil, Jeshu ben Pandira, and finally chose Alexandria as his domicile. It must have been of the greatest significance for the younger man to become immersed in what still survived as the atmosphere of the Egyptian mysteries.

After a while, the paths of teacher and student parted. As a result of decisive encounters and insights, Jeshu ben Pandira must have arrived at the point where he recognized and took up his own mission. This came about when news of the end of the persecution arrived from Jerusalem. Joshua ben Perachya received a letter from Rabbi Simeon ben Shetach, the brother of Queen Salome Alexandra, who, contrary to her husband Alexander Jannaeus, sided with the party of the Pharisees. He interpreted the letter as a summons to return to Jerusalem and was ready to embark on his journey. Jeshu ben Pandira then refused to accompany him. By then, a far-reaching difference of spiritual views and convictions divided them. The Talmudic text recounts this in hieroglyphic imagery. It says that teacher and disciple found themselves in an inn where great honour was paid the teacher. Joshua ben Perachya was full of praise over this place. The pupil did not join in the praise and instead uttered the puzzling words: 'Rabbi, it has small eyes.' Enraged, Joshua ben Perachya laid him under a ban. This has to mean that the spiritual dissension became evident because of the differing evaluation of a mystery location and teaching centre, a place the teacher embraced fully but one that the disciple criticized because of its lack of spiritual vision and insight. The text is as follows:

When King Jannai ordered our rabbis slain, Rabbi Joshua ben Perachya [and Jeshu] went to Alexandria in Egypt. When peace was reestablished, Simeon ben Shetach sent him a message: 'From me, [Jerusalem], the holy city, to you, Alexandria, in Egypt [my sister]! My husband sojourns in your midst, but I sit by myself.' Then he [Rabbi Joshua] departed and came to a certain hospice where great honour was done unto him. He said: 'How beautiful this inn is!' He [Jeshu] said to him: 'Rabbi, it has small eyes.' He said: 'You scoundrel, do you occupy yourself with something like this?' He had four hundred men go out with trumpets and put him under a ban. Frequently, he came before him and beseeched him to accept him again. But he paid no attention ... *(Babylonian Sanhedrin* 107b).

Jeshu ben Pandira remained for a while longer in Egypt. It must have been then, surrounded by the colourful diversity of Hellenistic life and in the domain of the Therapeutae and Essenes, that he assumed his mission. Soon he turned into the great spiritual reformer of these Messianic communities.

The Talmud contains only scattered indirect references to the far-reaching spiritual activity that Jeshu ben Pandira engaged in in Egypt and, following his return, in Palestine also. The indication that he had five pupils, Matthai, Naki, Nezer, Buni and Toda, shows that a solidly founded, well-organized spiritual structure had been established. In veiled form, the names of these disciples contain a subtle Messianic theology. They signify: 'When?'; 'the Innocent'; 'the Shoot'; 'my Son'; and 'the Thanks.' The Talmudic text really indicates this by bringing together scriptural sayings relating to the Messiah which contain these names, and at the same time evokes the secret of the martyrs' death suffered, along with their teacher, by the five disciples. It says in the *Babylonian Sanhedrin* (43a):

Our rabbis have taught: Jeshu had five disciples: Matthai, Naki, Nezer, Buni and Toda.

When they brought Matthai, he said to them: 'Should Matthai be slain? For it is written (Ps.42:2): I, Matthai (= when?) shall come and behold the face of God.' They replied: 'Yes, Matthai shall be slain, for it is written (Ps.41:5): Matthai (= when?) shall die, and his name perish.'

They brought Naki. He said to them: 'Should Naki be slain? For it is written (Exod.23:7): Do not slay Naki (= the innocent) and the righteous.' 'Yes,' was the reply, 'Naki shall be slain, for it is written (Ps.10:8): Secretly, Naki shall be slain.'

They brought Nezer. He said: 'Should Nezer be slain? For it is written (Isa.11:1): And Nezer (= a shoot) shall come forth from the stump of Jesse.' They said: 'Yes, Nezer shall be slain, for it is written (Isa.14:19): You shall be cast out of your tomb like a loathed Nezer.'

They brought Buni. He said: 'Should Buni be slain? It is written (Exod.4:22): Buni (= my son), my firstborn, Israel.' They said: 'Yes, Buni shall be slain, for it is written (Exod.4:23): ... behold, I will slay your Buni (= son), your firstborn.'

They brought Toda. He said: 'Should Toda die? For it is written (Ps.100:1): A Psalm for Toda (= to thank for the Eucharist).' They said: 'He shall be slain, for it is written (Ps.50:23): He who offers up Toda (thanks), praises me.'*

It is significant that one of the five disciples bears the Essene name 'Nezer.' He must have been given the specific task of reforming and leading that branch of Essenism which had to prepare the incarnation of the Messiah through its eugenic-pedagogical activity, the branch from which emerged the colony of Nazareth.† The names of the other disciples likewise direct us to branches of Essene spiritual life newly established and organized by Jeshu ben Pandira. Thus, the name of the fifth disciple, 'Toda' or 'thanks,' which corresponds exactly to the

---

* The Old Testament verses are rendered into English from Emil Bock's German translation. The RSV equivalents are:
'When shall I come and behold the face of God?' (Ps.42:2).
'When will he die, and his name perish?' (Ps.41:5).
'... do not slay the innocent and righteous.' (Exod.23:7).
'... in hiding places he murders the innocent.' (Ps.10:8).
'There shall come forth a shoot from the stump of Jesse ...' (Isa.11:1).
'... but you are cast out, away from your sepulchre, like a loathed untimely birth ...' (Isa.14:19).
'Israel is my firstborn son ...' (Exod.4:22).
'... behold, I will slay your firstborn son.' (Exod.4:23).
'A Psalm for the thank offering.' (Ps.100:1).
'He who brings thanksgiving as his sacrifice honours me ...' (Ps.50:23).

† In the Talmud, Jeshu ben Pandira is occasionally called 'Jesus, the Nazirite.' This title significantly added to the confusion, discussed earlier, in which historians remained entangled. The reference to Jeshu ben Pandira, however, is obvious everywhere. Once again, we have an indication that the term 'Nazirite' is of older Essene origin.

Greek term, *eucharistia,* is the designation of the sacred cultic act. It evokes in us an inkling of the great teacher's restructuring of sacramental life.

Apart from mentioning the disciples, the Talmud furthermore contains a valuable indirect testimony to Jeshu ben Pandira's innovative activity. Insofar as we see how the Talmudic rabbis fulminate against this 'heretic,' we discover that, even during the first Christian periods, there existed men who performed healings in the name of Jeshu ben Pandira. Does the great reformer thus not stand before us as the one who imbued Essenism with an advanced therapeutic wisdom and art?*

Following his return from Egypt, Jeshu ben Pandira was soon opposed by the Pharisees who meanwhile had regained power and were even then beginning to proceed with the fanaticism of an inquisition against all dissidents. They saw in him the apostate and teacher of heretical doctrine and accused him of having brought along any number of abstruse magic tricks from Egypt. In reality, they probably sensed that rich results would begin to emerge all across the land from his different Messianic work.

His enemies finally trapped him by means of a ruse. One listened in on a confidential conversation in which others engaged him. They brought him to the point of divulging some of his secrets. He was put on trial for blasphemy and condemned to death. But he evidently had supporters at the court of Queen Alexandra who followed her husband Alexander Jannaeus in ruling the nation (76–67). His enemies therefore could not simply do away with him. For forty days, they led the condemned man through the town. A herald called out the accusation raised against him, the judgment imposed on him, and invited anybody who might have proof of his innocence to step forward. Finally, on the eve before the Passover festival, Jeshu ben Pandira, who was probably no older than thirty to thirty-five, was first stoned and then hung on a cross in Lydda near the Mediterranean coast,

---

* Frequently, reference is made to the fact that followers of Jeshu Ben Pandira had healed those who had been bitten by snakes or were in danger of suffocating (for example, *Kohelet rabba* 10:5). Then, it always says that it would have been better for the sick to have died than to be cured by the heretics.

a town where the legend of St George, the conqueror of the dragon, first appeared in early Christendom. Jeshu ben Pandira's spirit, on the other hand, lived on powerfully in the piety and Messianic zeal of Essenism and the Therapeutae.

Of the trial and martyr's death of Jeshu ben Pandira, it says in the Talmud:

> Concerning all other mortal sins in the Torah, one does not waylay a person, except for one who corrupts others to idol worship. How does one proceed against him? One lights the lamp for him in the inner room and places witnesses in the outer room who can see and hear him whereas he does not see them. Then one says to him: 'Tell me once more in confidence what you said earlier.' When he has said it, one says: 'How could we leave our god in heaven and serve strange gods?' If he repents, fine. But if he says: 'It is proper and fitting for us,' then the witnesses who listen outside take him to the house of judgment and stone him. Thus did they proceed against Ben Stada [Ben Pandira] in Lydda and subsequently hanged him on the eve of Passover. *(Babylonia Sanhedrin* 67a).

> On the eve before Passover, they hung Jeshu, and the herald went before him for forty days and called out: 'Jeshu, the Nazirite goes to be stoned, because he indulged in magic and tempted and seduced Israel. Anyone who knows of a reason to exonerate him should come forward and communicate the same.' But they found no reason to exonerate him and so hanged him on the eve before Passover. Ulla has stated: 'Can he even be counted among those for whom a vindication could have been expected? For he was a seducer ... But it was a different matter in the case of Jeshu, inasmuch as he was close to the leadership' *(Babyl. Sanhedrin* 43a).

When we view Jeshu ben Pandira's figure in the light of Rudolf Steiner's spiritual research; when we recognize in this man one of the last great inspired teachers of the pre-Christian era who imbued Essenism and the Therapeutic movement with their wholehearted Messianic wisdom and devotion, we are close to the central event of world history. We sense that before long 'in the fullness of time, God send his Son' (Gal.4:4). But once more, as a final link between the prophets of the Old Covenant and John the Baptist, a messenger had come to prepare the way. Through the light that he brought, lights were enkindled far and wide; lights with which the 'quiet in the land' would be able to receive him who was to come.

A few of the references by Rudolf Steiner concerning the mission of Jeshu ben Pandira can serve to conclude our considerations regarding the environment that surrounded the Mystery of Golgotha. In them, our glance is directed to the lofty teachers of wisdom who affect humanity from out of spiritual worlds; individuals whom the Orient designated as Bodhisattvas. In each of the large epochs of historical evolution, a Bodhisattva is active as the one who supplies humanity with the necessary spiritual insights required during that particular period. He continues until he himself ascends to the rank of a Buddha and is replaced by another Bodhisattva. Succeeding the historical Gautama Buddha in whom the last Bodhisattva withdrew from the role of world teacher, another being now sends his inspiration down to the earth, one whose task, above all, it is to help humankind acquire a comprehension of the Christ who passed through his earthly incarnation.

Rudolf Steiner describes the personality of Jeshu ben Pandira as having been inspired by the Bodhisattva of our present world epoch:

> Thus since that time the Bodhisattva who then became Gautama Buddha has been succeeded by the new Bodhisattva who had a particular mission to fulfil in the history of mankind. The task allotted to him was the spiritual guidance of the movement represented in the doctrines of the Therapeutae and Essenes and it was in these communities that his influence worked. During the reign of King Alexander Jannaeus, a certain individuality was sent by this Bodhisattva into the communities of the Essenes to be their guide and leader. This individuality — he is well-known in occultism and also in exoteric Talmudic literature — was the leader of the Essenes about a hundred years before the appearance of Christ Jesus on the Earth

... He is known in Talmudist literature under the name of Jesus, the son of Pandira, Jeshu ben Pandira. He was a great and noble personality, about whom inferior Jewish literature has woven all kinds of fables ... and he must not be confused ... with Jesus of Nazareth ... This herald of Christianity among the Essenes ... was accused of blasphemy and heresy by those to whom the teachings of the Essenes were anathema, and after being stoned was hanged on a tree, in order to add to the punishment the stigma of infamy ...

In Jeshu ben Pandira we have to see a personality standing under the guardianship of the present Bodhisattva ... A stream, as it were accessory to the main Christian stream, originated from the Buddha's successor, from the present Bodhisattva ... who sent his emissary into the Essene communities ...

As bearers of the deeper teachings, the Essene communities disappeared comparatively soon after the Christ Event ... It will therefore certainly not seem incredible when I say that fundamentally and essentially the communities of Therapeutae and Essenes were instituted in order that they might be instrumental in bringing down from the spiritual realms, from the spheres of the Boddhisatvas, what was needed to enable men to comprehend the momentous event of the appearance of Christ. The most important teachings given to mankind with the object of promoting understanding of the Christ Event stemmed from the communities of the Therapeutae and Essenes. Thus Jesus, the son of Pandira, inspired as it were by the Boddhisatva ... was chosen to give teachings whereby ... the Mystery of Christ could be brought within reach of man's understanding ...

[Through the strict practices of these Essene communities some] became what may be called a 'sprout' or a 'shoot' on a branch, on a tree, or on a plant — a sprout that endured through many generations. They were not detached from the tree of humanity but were conscious of the branches uniting them with it ... The name given to [such] individuals in the communities of

the Essenes was a word meaning 'a living branch' ...
'Nezer' ... Jeshu ben Pandira had five pupils or disciples,
each of whom took over a special branch of his general
teaching and continued to develop it. The names of these
five pupils were: Mathai, Nakai, the third was given the
name Nezer because he came especially from that class,
then Boni and Thona [= Thoda] ... The teaching
concerning the inner qualities and nature of the soul — a
teaching connected with the old Nazarite but also with
Nezerism in its later form — was continued by Nezer, the
great pupil of Jeshu ben Pandira. Nezer was specially
chosen to be the founder of a little colony. There were
many such colonies in Palestine, a particular branch of
Essenism being cultivated in each of them. The
cultivation of Nezerism ... was to be the primary aim in
the colony which led a secluded existence and which
then, in the Bible, received the name 'Nazareth' ... Those
whose lives were dedicated to the ancient Nazarite order
lived there in fairly strict seclusion. Hence ... after the
flight to Egypt and the return, nothing was more natural
than that the Jesus of St Matthew's Gospel should be
brought into the atmosphere of Nezerism. This is
indicated in St Matthew's Gospel where it is said that
after the return from Egypt, Jesus was taken to the little
town of Nazareth, 'that it might be fulfilled which was
spoken by the prophets: He shall be called a Nazarene.'[58]

Figures around Christ

5. John the Baptist

5.1 The background

When the Apostles proclaimed Christ's gospel to the first congregations, they indulged neither in scholarly lectures nor in edifying sermons. They merely had to relate the events they themselves had lived through. Yet a marvellous, powerful force imbued their simple narratives. Their speech referred to outwardly unassuming events. But, as if they were a higher form of spirit evocation, their words called forth a tangible spiritual force and presence into their small intimate gatherings. Unaffected and overlooked by the world's hustle and bustle, these meetings took place somewhere in a private home or villa in Rome or Alexandria. The relating of outer events elicited from the devoutly listening souls images that extended far beyond the physical plane and were saturated by the light of a wide-open world of the spirit.

What the Apostles narrated was not history in the ordinary sense. More than any other earthly history, it was at the same time heavenly history. For heaven had descended to the earth; the Word of Worlds had become flesh. If an outer happening was mentioned, the Apostles were at the same time referring to the earthly destinies of a sublime spiritual event. Celestial matters were summoned before the souls of the listeners by those who related earthly matters.

The Gospels have picked up much of the rich harmonies of the secret sounds that vibrated between the simple words of the Apostles. Thus, the rich super-earthly veil of early Christian spiritual presence is woven into them; a veil that covers the outer events of the earthly life of Jesus and those who walked by his side. Much greater courage and more thorough discernment than was thought necessary by the theology of the past centuries is required if a person wishes to penetrate through the veil of secrets and look upon what occurred at the beginning of the turn of time in Palestine and what the first Apostles related to the congregations. The events that implanted the seed of salvation in humanity did not occur at a time of calm peace. Storms and conflagrations swept over the earth. The constantly threatening danger of persecution and death at the hands of the Caesars' bailiffs meant that hardly anybody could hear the message of light without sensing the approach of the surging, demonic darkness. The antagonistic din of the Antichrist rang in the souls of those to whom Christ's word of peace was proclaimed.

In the Revelation to John, which before long found its place among the Holy Scriptures, early Christendom recognized both a description of the raging spiritual battles of the age and a lofty interpretation that gave them meaning. For us, too, the intense spiritual drama of this book has to be a reference to the world that represented the historical background of the Gospels. As we try to look through the veil of the Gospel at the earthly and historical stage, we simultaneously encounter an apocalyptic level. Quiet figures, illumined in celestial radiance, rise above the tumultuous revolts of opposing forces of the depths. They are bearers and harbingers of a peace originating in another world; yet they do intervene militantly in the chaotic strife with the light-weapons of the spirit blazing in them.

Many conceptions have been developed in the Christian era up to the present concerning how the figure of Christ fits into the totality of humanity's evolution and what sort of change it signified for the course of world progress. As yet, hardly any clear concrete concepts and feelings exist in regard to how the man, Jesus of Nazareth, fits historically into his particular time; how he was seen and experienced by his contemporaries. He who was the greatest among them was not noticed at all by his age, let alone recognized as great. He was not counted among the 'great men' who, so it was thought, advanced humanity in their historical development. John the Baptist received incomparably greater public notice and higher esteem by his age than was allotted to Jesus of Nazareth.

Nothing allows us to decipher the relationship of his contemporaries to Jesus of Nazareth more clearly than through the juxtaposition of the two figures, Jesus and John. We do have vivid reports about the great and immediate effects evoked by the appearance of the Baptist, and about the strong popular movement he initiated. Yet the one whose herald John meant to be was overlooked in silence by the world of those days. Outside the Gospels, we have no genuine testimony whatsoever about him from those living at the same time and it is therefore not so incomprehensible that doubt could be cast again and again on his historical existence. The earthly destinies of the very greatest individual, the god who had become man, occurred far from outward success and fame in completely inconspicuous obscurity. Unknown and unrecognized, Christ went his way. Seen from outside, the archetype of the 'great man' and the figure of one whom success eluded stand side by side in John the Baptist and Jesus.

We know that the relationship between the two figures appears to us in a completely different light when we penetrate the superficial appearance. Yet, in reality, even this facade on the surface of history has to be an indication of a deep intrinsic secret. Early Christian pictorial depictions of the Baptism in the Jordan, from paintings in the catacombs to sculptures of the Romanesque domes, retain the same proportion: John, the size of a giant, engaged in baptizing, stands next to Jesus who, in child-like smallness, does not even reach up to John's hips.* How could the artists of early Christianity, imbued as they were by the divine greatness of Christ and knowing full well that John only wished to be and was indeed his ministering forerunner, picture the smaller one so large and the very greatest one so small? What is shown to a superficial historical view seems to conform with what was seen by a certain imaginative soul view. What kind of riddle is here being unveiled to us?

---

* See the first illustration. *John the Baptist and Jesus during the Baptism in the Jordan.*

5.2 John's youth

The first two chapters of Luke's Gospel, forming as they do a wondrously poetic whole all of their own, chapters that one could call 'Luke's Preface Gospel,' place John and Jesus side by side at the very beginning of their earthly path, inasmuch as they join the differing annunciation and nativity stories together. A full calendar year comes together before our eyes since the pictures that the painter Luke draws for us are assigned to the four seasons: spring, summer, autumn and winter. The nativity stories fall on the two dates of the solstice. John is the child of the summer solstice; exactly six months later Jesus is born at the time of the winter solstice. The spiritual annunciations running parallel with conception are in each case experienced nine months earlier, at the time of the equinox. The angel appears to the soul of the priest Zechariah at the beginning of autumn at Michaelmas; Mary is granted the angelic address in spring, at Easter time.

With this, from the very beginning, a diametrical difference is indicated between John and Jesus. The baby, John, grows in the womb of aged Elizabeth and prepares for his birth during those months of the year when, toward the heights of summer, the earth breathes out her soul increasingly towards the heavens. And young Mary bears her little babe mainly during that half of the year when the earth's soul returns from heavenly heights more and more deeply into the earth's womb until the darkest of winter. It is as if the sons of these two mothers had received something into their being of the directional force that indwells the soul of the earth while they grew and developed towards earthly life in the maternal sheath. John's soul seems to be pervaded by a primal impulse for body-free existence, even as is our earth's soul when the summer solstice is approaching. Jesus, on the other hand, is the prototype of the human being who with all his soul-spiritual being moves towards incorporation and is prepared to drink to the last dreg the cup of earthly bodily existence fated for death.

To begin with, we follow the paths taken by John. Whereas the youth of Jesus in Nazareth was irradiated by Galilee's cosmic

John the Baptist and Jesus during the Baptism in the Jordan. Sculpture on an early Christian sarcophagus in S. Maria Antiqua at the Forum Romanum in Rome.

173

magic of childhood, the shadow of profound earnestness fell on John's life from the beginning. From the start, life with such aged parents, with a father who brought home a touch of the sombre sternness of the Temple whenever he returned home from weeks of service as a priest, did not allow a cheerful, childlike atmosphere to arise. The history-laden Judaic scenery of Ein Karem near Jerusalem, dwelling place of Zechariah, fitted the mood that surrounded John as he grew up. His parents, who no longer expected the birth of a child because of their advanced years, viewed the boy as a special miraculous gift of God. Obedient to the angel's direction who had appeared to the father in the Temple during the sacrificial offering, they dedicated him to the stern Nazirite Order. Now, child's play and gaiety had to be permanently forgotten. Along with the many ascetic and atoning exercises a pupil of Naziritism had to carry out, a mental attitude directed more to heaven than to earth replaced unrestrained love for earthly nature and beauty.

His soul blazing in fiery zeal, John must have surrendered to the Nazirite spiritual life, ardently struggling for visionary sight and words of prophetic revelation. The longing one day to appear before his contemporaries as a messenger of the spirit became greater and more urgent in him. But the more the fervent efforts of his soul lifted him out of the dimension of everyday life and consciousness and bore him aloft to the sphere where he sensed the presence of the spirit, the more frighteningly clear it became to him in what a hopeless chaotic poverty of soul humanity was even then enmeshed. Fallen from the supportive hand of God, the world of men seemed to be heading unawares towards a horrible chasm, abandoned to the flaming wrath of an unforgiving world's end and judgment. Only the expectant conviction of the Messiah's imminent arrival, which was always maintained among the Nazirites, gave John the strength to penetrate through the flickering flames of frightening visions that appeared before his soul.

At last, radiant spiritual imaginations and spiritual words of consolation may have responded to the light of Nazirite Messianic hope burning in him, through which he beheld something of the approaching being and force that would bring relief. John pursued his inner path far from human beings in the cosmically intensified desolation of the rugged mountainous wilderness of

Judea, a wasteland estranged from nature and life. Looking down on the subterranean world of the Dead Sea, he felt accepted by a sphere in which only a person who has parted from earthly life can remain. On occasion, he may have encountered other hermits, Nazirites or Essenes who, like him, were keeping a visionary vigil for the longed-for divine being. Most likely, through such encounters he also came to the colonies of the Essenes, colonies that existed in the Judean Desert and by the Dead Sea. Yet, even though he found many among the Essenes who listened to his words, he was always driven back into utter isolation. The souls he encountered seemed to him much too lame and lukewarm; to him, they did not burn ardently enough with the fire of Messianic will.

The rocky cave he turned into his monastic cell was located in a steep gorge in the wilderness surrounded by reminiscences of ancient times. There, by the Cherith Brook, eight hundred years earlier, the prophet Elijah had stayed. Sunk in lonely contemplation, he had taken the suffering of humanity deeply to heart and had received signs of future redemption from the spiritual realm.[59] At the same location, John may well have felt overshadowed by the genius of Elijah when he was struggling to receive revelations. The images of the imminent cosmic Judgment Day then appeared to him like a continuation and intensification of humanity's suffering, images that once arose in Elijah's consciousness in the picture of the mighty drought and famine. And the presentiment of the Messiah's light sphere, a sphere drawing ever closer, imbued John with bliss as if he were given nourishment, as was Elijah who was fed divine bread by the ravens.

When John approached his thirtieth year, the tension and urgency of his spiritual experiences became so great that he could no longer remain in seclusion. A mighty tidal wave of spiritual events appeared to wash him with breathtaking impetuosity onto the shore of earthly humanity. He became aware of a direct summons and mission, a divine calling for a public prophetic appearance. It was no longer proper to keep the overabundance of insights and energy locked away in his own soul, an overabundance that had matured in isolation. And thus John began to speak to the people.

He did not venture forth into the crowds of Jerusalem. He

chose a quite special scenery for his activity. Deep down at the foot of the mountainous wilderness in the Jordan Valley, not in the sphere of the lush gardens of Jericho but where the Dead Sea meets the waters of the Jordan with its ominous effects of death, John raised his voice. Standing at the lowest point of the earth's surface, it seemed that he had chosen for his proclamation a landscape which, as such, was a picture of the inner condition of humankind: a landscape of the Fall, the abyss and universal dying. When he then tore away the veils from the approaching Day of Judgment; when he demonstrated to the people that the axe was even then lying at the root of the tree of humanity, ready to fell it, he merely expressed once more in words what the scenery of Sodom and Gomorrah, where he stood, was silently expressing. But in this very condition of extreme danger, in the world at the edge of the abyss, he had to call out the prophetic words as a challenge to change the minds of men: 'The kingdom of heaven is at hand!'

5.3 John's character

It was not long before the eerie location at the mouth of the Jordan, normally shunned by people, was filled with huge crowds who had come from everywhere to hear John. Josephus specifically reports to us the great and far-reaching effect caused by the appearance of the Baptist: 'Now, ... others came to crowd about him, for they were greatly moved by hearing his words.'[60] The news that a great prophet had appeared in the world must have spread like wildfire throughout the land. A popular movement kept growing that aroused everybody to intense excitement.

What caused the powerful provocative effect that went out from John? On the one hand, the reasons could be found in the age itself. The high Messianic tension; the feverish sense for the great change being prepared in the atmosphere; the nightmarish oppression brought on through the more and more noticeable abandonment by the deity; and the ardent hope for the redeeming miracle had reached a fever pitch in people's souls. The vestiges of atavistic faculties of sensibility brought it about that these feelings became condensed to visionary experiences among growing portions of the populace. All the reports that reached Palestine concerning the development of the Caesarean cult in Rome caused the flames of the Messiah-longing to blaze up. Surely, amid all the excitement, efforts were made on the part of the Essene circles of the 'quiet ones in the land' to maintain devout, subdued patience. But the sole meaning and purpose even of these circles was to await the Messiah with fervent expectation. It is obvious that, once it had reached the people, John's message was like a fiery spark that fell on parched ground. Listening to John's words that the kingdom was close at hand, did not everyone realize that Christ, the longed-for Messiah, was very near?

The reasons for the rapidly unleashed storm could be found in John's nature as well. When he spoke, there stood before those who heard him not a man but a pillar of fire that grew beyond all human measure. The terse, formulaic words John called out, as if he were a herald, were effective not merely because of their content but above all because of their elemental power resembling a force of nature. By no means did he address the people in a reasoning manner, the way a Plato or Aristotle had perhaps spoken to his pupils. In him, a form of being and consciousness seemed to come to life once more that had existed in ancient times of human evolution when the gods still wandered about among men.

When he spoke, John's soul-spiritual being was outside in the surroundings more than within the body. It resembled a cloud that emits lightning flashes and seemed directly connected to the spirituality of higher beings and forces whose word-power vibrated in John's own speaking. He was a man of 'translation,' of body-free states of consciousness. To the soul-vision of those who listened to his words with a receptive state of mind, he seemed to grow to divine, gigantic dimensions when he spoke. This was how people had always pictured Elijah's superhuman quality. The Baptist did in fact resemble that prototype of the prophetic state, and not only because of his elemental manner. The genius of Elijah himself worked once again in and through him. The number of those who believed they recognized the returned Elijah in John may not at all have been small. Had the prophets not noted the divine promise that the arrival of the Messiah would be preceded by the return of Elijah? More angel than man, would Elijah not prepare the way for Christ? 'Behold,

I will send my angel to prepare the way before me ... Behold, I will send you Elijah the prophet before the great and overwhelming day of the Lord comes.' (Mal.3:1, 4:5B).

John represented an end; in him, humanity bid farewell to a principle of spiritual activity still linked completely to a certain form of bodily human nature. Due to a specific kind of heredity and the Nazirite discipline carried out by him with particularly fervent devotion, John availed himself of a bodily constitution that, to a large extent, had remained free of the rigid hardening that otherwise had taken hold of human bodily nature generally as a result of the Fall. This had important consequences for his soul nature. His etheric body, not obliged to shrink down to the contours of the hardened physical body, could instead carry the soul-spiritual being into the environs of body-free existence and consciousness. As if the nature of high summer had become human, so did John appear. If the impression and appearance is considered that John's supersensory being made on receptive souls, it can be said in an exact sense that he was experienced as the archetype of a 'great man.' His superhuman dimension was directly visible to imaginative vision. What passed into early pictorial representations are actual perceptions — whether we behold the Baptist in the early Christian pictures of the Baptism in the Jordan as a giant or whether he confronts us on icons and iconostases of eastern Christendom as a cosmic nature force with wings, whose rushing would unleash a roaring storm. And it was John's all-surpassing greatness of soul to which we are referred even by Christ's words: 'Among all who were born of earthly mothers, none is greater than John the Baptist' (Matt.11:11).

Ultimately, the secret of John's activity rested on the fact that through his words John carried human souls aloft to body-free heights. And on those who were not only his listeners but placed themselves completely under his spiritual leadership, he sealed this transformation of being with the baptism. When he immersed them in the waters of the Jordan, their souls were loosened from bodily bonds. In vision, they beheld the black abyss that threatened sinful human nature. But they also entered the consoling bright radiance of light that allowed them to sense the approach of the Christ being. When those who had been baptized then returned to their ordinary state of consciousness, they brought

John the Baptist, Russian Icon.

along a vivid feeling of the nearby spiritual sphere where the ardently awaited Saviour had arrived. Through the Baptist's power of guidance, they had been allowed in their souls to go and meet Christ. Henceforth, their sacred goal had to be to sustain the transformed state of mind into which the baptism had lifted them and to arrange their life accordingly.

The significance of the experiences conveyed by the Baptist cannot be overestimated, for they were influenced moreover by the unusual cosmic-scenic milieu. Deep down at the site of the conflagration that once had consumed Sodom and Gomorrah, the herald of a new world-judgment and turning point of time raised his voice. The constant glowing heat, surpassing ordinary summer's heat, that rises out of the earth's chasms here and glistens over the Dead Sea was like a memory of the one-time world conflagration and yet helped the souls to soar up to body-free heights. In John's fiery soul and flaming word, the conflagration of cosmic judgment seemed to take on human form and yet it was possible to entrust oneself to him. The souls who gathered round him sensed that they were moving towards a new world.

5.4 The Baptism of Jesus

It must have been about a year after the emergence of John the Baptist that a scene took place down at the Jordan River which, though outwardly unassuming, signified the beginning of a new age of humanity. During the first days of the year 31, a quiet figure walked down to the Jordan Valley along with those who, from far and wide, had made a pilgrimage to see John. Nobody paid attention to him. Their hearts and minds felt drawn with the greatest anticipation to the man who appeared to rouse all the world from its sleep. The quietly moving thirty-year-old had nothing in his demeanour that could have attracted people's attention to him. Only if one had turned to him with great sensitivity of soul could one have become aware of the quite extraordinary process that was taking place in the young man. One would have realized with consternation and concern: this man must have undergone infinite pain; the soul misery of all humanity appears to be concentrated in him as in a focal point; never could anyone feel the world's burden and destitution more powerfully and take it more deeply to heart than did this man. What he suffered inwardly — has it not surpassed all his strength? Does his eye, shining with such an other-worldly will, even behold the things of this world? Whence does he still have the energy to make it all the way to the Jordan and John?

There was one who felt touched to his innermost core by the sight of this man; one out of whose soul an overpowering stream of devotion and love suddenly streamed forth: John the Baptist himself. He, the great one, who was well aware what mighty effects went out from him, felt: this one, who is consumed by humanity's suffering, is infinitely greater than I, even though none notice him. The feeling that overcame John poured forth out of primal depths of destiny. Without being able clearly to recognize, much less put into words, what it was about this man, he would have much preferred to throw himself on the ground before him. How was he henceforth to appear before the people with his admonishing message, when only one wish and desire ensouled him now: to serve this other and pay him loving and adoring homage?

Yet the other man surprised John by asking him to be accepted among his disciples and receive the baptism. Perhaps the sparse words of the Gospel of Matthew point us to a nocturnal intimate conversation that took place between the two. John said: 'It is I who need to be baptized by you — and you come to me?' Yet the other insisted on his request and John complied, though with questioning soul. When John baptized Jesus, the great miracle was fulfilled that the world had awaited with such longing: the lofty divine being who had been on his way to earth from the heights of the gods finally truly arrived in the realm of men. He entered the soul of Jesus of Nazareth, a soul opened wide through infinite pain and self-sacrifice. Christ became man in the most humble form. Nobody noticed what was happening. Most simply thought that, as usual, somebody was being baptized. Only the Baptist's soul was imbued with a wondrous heavenly light while he baptized Jesus. In vision, he observed how living spirit descended out of the wide-open heavens upon the one being baptized, a spiritual element that far surpassed the spiritual experiences that normally were bestowed on people during a baptism. Again, it was not that John arrived at a clear certainty concerning what was happening. Perhaps the overwhelming sense of unbounded love and devotion did not let him arrive at an insight he could have put in definite words. This is why it was possible, several months later, when he was already languishing in prison, that John through messengers directed the question to Jesus: 'Are you the Christ, or must we await yet another?'

Hereafter, John the Baptist no longer possessed the former flawless certainty and convincing power in his activity. A strange Messianic uncertainty filled his mind. In the midst of those who saw and revered him as the mighty prophet, he was of two minds. How could he simply go on as usual since the other one was now here, too, one whom infinite secrets surrounded and to whom he felt drawn by all his emotions and thoughts? He never tired of pointing out the other man to his disciples, particularly those who were part of his closest, most intimate circle of followers. Above all, John would have liked to withdraw completely to make room for the other. And he succeeded in opening the hearts of some of his disciples to the secret of Jesus. But oddly enough, Jesus himself saw to it that they would all continue to see John as their leader. He was concerned that John would not give up his work. He did so by clearly demonstrating that he too wished only to be John's faithful disciple and helper. Jesus did not seek recognition of his own. He did not wish to play any role. He willingly joined in with the Baptist's activity. The Gospels show us that now that he also began to speak to people, he proclaimed nothing original but simply made himself an instrument of John's proclamation: 'Change you hearts and minds. The realm of the heavens have come close' (Matt.4:17 and Mark 1:15). And the Gospel of John even reports to us that Jesus performed the baptism of John on those who desired it (3:22).

The more obviously the Baptist believed that he saw the light of the Christ being shine forth from the other man, the more strongly the wish and will burned in him — He must grow, I must wane — the more the question of how matters would now proceed must have unsettled him. The last and greatest of the prophets of the Old Covenant had to continue his prophetic proclamation, although the proclaimed one was even then walking by his side.

5.5 *The Baptist and Herod Antipas*

At Easter time of the same year, an event took place that quickly had quite unexpected consequences. Once again, a man was among those who had come to hear John who was different from all the others. But this time, it was not a covert difference that distinguished him. All the world knew him and it aroused the greatest attention far and wide that he deigned mingle with the audience of this Nazirite clothed in the garment of a penitent. He was Herod Antipas, the most powerful man in the land, the one among the sons of Herod the Great to whom belonged Galilee and the whole land east of the Jordan including the locality where John was baptizing. Herod Antipas was not imbued with that unsatiable ambition and lust for power which had borne his father up to the proud heights of splendour, only to cast him down again into chasms of fear. Yet, nevertheless, Luciferic will-o'-the-wisp elements flickered through his nature, elements that appeared when inner weakness was masked behind Caesarean demeanour. With clever cunning, he who was called 'the Fox' in the Gospel knew how to guard his advantage and to make his wishes come true. The supernatural world attracted him with suggestive magical power. He lacked the inner strength and perseverance to make any serious spiritual efforts. He therefore turned in playful curiosity and covetousness to any outwardly appearing occultism. Astrological and spiritualistic charlatanism blossomed in his surroundings as in those of the Roman Caesars. When he heard of a psychic or magician, he did not rest until he had been able to pose his questions and concerns to such a one.

Similar sensation-seeking curiosity may have led him to John the Baptist, the prophet whose name was on everybody's lips. He too wished to experience the shock of being out of the body which, so it was reputed, proceeded from the words of this spiritually powerful man. When the crowd that was gathered around John saw the powerful Tetrarch approach with his ostentatious royal household, everybody waited tensely to see how the Baptist would react. Would he not have to experience this moment, when the honour of such an elevated visit was bestowed on him, as a final affirmation of his great success and the powerful effect he was having on his age?

Something completely surprising happened: John had hardly caught sight of Herod Antipas when superhuman rage blazed forth from him. Unrelenting words of accusation were flung by him like lightning flashes and thunder against the one attired in royal purple. The people all around froze in horror at the prophet's unheard-of courage. None doubted that John had forfeited his life.

What was it that had caused him to explode in such rage? The Gospel relates that John reproached Herod on account of his marriage to Herodias, his brother's wife. The conventional view holds that this preacher of penitence had tried publicly to denounce the sovereign's adultery. In reality, the wrath of the Baptist was not merely directed against any infraction of the moral code. His behaviour was more than a moral protest. We see how the sword of sacred wrath flashed in the greatest and most important spiritual battle of the age. For behind Herod Antipas and Herodias arose the world of Rome's Caesarean cult, a cult which at that very moment in time had entered a new disturbing phase.

Even as his father, Herod the Great, had been able to boast of the friendship and favour of Augustus, so Herod Antipas too could describe himself as the friend of Caesar Tiberius who, sixteen years earlier, had succeeded Augustus to the throne of the Roman empire. But he left no stone unturned to hold on to the favour and friendship of the world ruler. As his father had done with Augustus, so he acclaimed Tiberius the Messiah and Saviour of humanity and paid homage to him by constructing temples and cities. Sparing no expense, he had had a whole city built on the western shore of the Lake of Galilee and had called it Tiberias in honour of his imperial friend. He frequently spent time in Rome so as to draw his mighty benefactor's attention to himself and attain at least a reflection of the latter's power for his own purposes.

The bond between himself and Herodias must have come about during one of his visits to Rome. It seems obvious that this could not primarily have been an adulterous, passionate love affair, for Herod Antipas, who celebrated the thirty-eighth anniversary of his rule during the year of his encounter with John the Baptist, was then nearly seventy years old. Herodias was a woman who knew no bounds. In all that she did she passionately aimed beyond the limitations of ordinary human nature. The Caesarean fever of Herod the Great burned more fiercely in her than in Herod Antipas; indeed, perhaps more ferociously than it had in the latter's father. Power over human beings was her ever present desire. It must have been she who induced her first husband to make his home in Rome for such long periods of time.* Rome, after all, was the splendidly adorned centre of the world, the seat of power. Now Herod Antipas, the friend of Tiberius, appeared to the feverishly ambitious woman as a much more suitable tool for attaining her goals than her own husband. For he was one who devoted himself to the distractions and luxurious life of the metropolis but did not share in the burning desire for honour and power. Her marriage to the brother-in-law, probably instigated by her, was an obvious symptom of the epidemic infection of the spreading Luciferic fever of Caesarism in that age. John therefore really turned against the spirit of Caesarism when he raised his objections to the union between Herod Antipas and Herodias. The Christ messenger fought against the feverish spirit of the Antichrist.

It is important to realize that the spiritual world condition had come to a quite specific point, that a particularly acute stage of the already unleashed spiritual battle became visible in the Baptist's holy rage. On the strength of his superior, sober-minded intelligence, Augustus had still been able to personally master the institutions of the Pantheon and Caesarean cult — along with their soul-spiritual consequences — which he had created with brilliant daring. This soon changed under Tiberius, his successor. From the beginning, the gifted aspects of his nature were linked with much impetuousness and indulgence. It became

---

* Josephus states that her husband was Herod Boethos, a younger brother of Antipas, who lived in Rome most of the time. The Gospel, on the other hand, describes Herodias as the wife of Philip. Josephus also mentions a Philip and reports that he later wed Salome, the daughter of Herodias. In accordance with the Gospel, the Slavic versions of the Josephus books call Herodias' husband Philip. Yet, oddly enough, they relate that this Philip was no longer alive when Antipas married Herodias. We need not investigate the exact historical facts in all detail, but feel that it is wrong simply to say that Josephus has the correct indications and the Gospel wrong ones. Apparently, we are here dealing with quite complicated factors.

unavoidable that the morally ill-prepared participation in all sorts of occult relationships and mystery initiations, which Tiberius received through the office of Pontifex Maximus, placed his passionate soul into even more agitated emotional states. Imagining himself to be in possession of divine powers, he wished for the world around him to be more splendid and intoxicating.

In the long run, even Rome became too unremarkable and monotonous. He kept extending the periods he spent on the fantastic, theatrically structured Isle of Capri, the island of the gods that faced Vesuvius. Only here was the fitting stage setting for his superhuman nature. From the year 26 onward, he hardly ever left Capri. But then a change came over his nature that caused those around him great fear. Even earlier, in all his immoderate actions, he had often given the impression of being more animal than man. Now he actually appeared as if transformed into a demon. As a diversion, he arranged the most senseless cruelties. From a certain spot on the island, steeply rising out of the ocean near his palace located 300 metres above sea level, he began the atrocious game of having people thrown into the depths and enjoyed watching the surging waves and how they washed the shattered limbs away from the cliffs. This was the unmistakable outbreak of Caesarean madness, the mental illness that from then on so strongly influenced the destinies of early Christianity.

The deeply shocking thing is that this demonization of the Caesar occurred at the same time that John the Baptist baptized Jesus of Nazareth. The two events belong together like light and shadow: The divine Christ being entered the soul of Jesus at the same time that a satanic, antichristian spirit possessed the soul of the old man on Capri. And at the same point in time when humanity's soul realm was stirred by such spiritual events, even though few people were aware of it, the wedding between Herod Antipas and Herodias took place. Through this event, the demonic shadow from Rome and Capri reached all the way to Palestine. It was not surprising that the Baptist erupted in holy anger.

Even as Elijah had battled against Queen Jezebel more than against Ahab and called down the fire of heaven against her and her priests of Baal, so John the Baptist actually confronted Herodias as the bearer of opposing spiritual powers, insofar as he flung his admonitions against Herod.

5.6 The tragedy on Machaerus: Herodias

The opponent immediately responded to the battle-cry with a ruthless manoeuvre. John was dragged away in chains. A dramatic struggle ensued. Two antagonists confronted each other who reached far beyond human dimensions: a power-obsessed queen and her prisoner. The struggle found a stage which in its eerie splendour was a physically visible symbol of the spheres to which the shackled Baptist pressed forward with the weapon of his genius.

Machaerus, the mountain-stronghold built by Herod the Great, was located on the rugged heights of the Moabite mountain range near the mystery-enveloped summit of Nebo where, at the sacred hidden tomb of the Old Testament forerunner and herald, the archangel Michael had contended with Satan over the body of Moses (Jude 9). On a narrow rocky ridge, from which the whole gleaming scenery of the Dead Sea could be surveyed, the sombre castle stood, ruins of which can be viewed to this day. Four corner-turrets more than fifty metres high and literally built over the abyss made one's sight reel.

When you walk southward today along the eastern shore of the Dead Sea from the mouth of the Jordan, you arrive after a while at Zerka Ma'in where rushing mountain streams, some carrying hot, others cold water, tumble down through steep ravines and pour into the salt lake. These rocky streams have their sources directly below the spot where the castle of Machaerus rose. In antiquity, grottos with fountains are supposed to have existed there in which, out of rocks formed like breasts and adjacent to each other, cold and hot water gushed forth. The strange nature of this place was talked about everywhere. Up there, even today, around steaming hot springs, the rock walls are covered by deposits of sulphur and other minerals contained in the water. It is as if one still encountered traces of the subterranean fire here that long ago destroyed the lush world of Sodom and Gomorrah.

Josephus recorded some of the eerie rumours concerning

Machaerus that circulated among the populace, rumors that made of it a site of black magic and sorcery. Plants supposedly grew there, for example an unnaturally tall rue in the courtyard of the castle; with its roots or fruits, one could heal as well as cast spells over people. The most forbidding place was a dark gorge north of the castle. The blood-red root, Baaras, grew there. Phosphorescent at night, this was a root of which it was said that it brought death to anybody who, without knowing its properties, tore it out of the ground, but bestowed on a knowledgeable person great power over men and spirits.[61]

Herod Antipas had his palace on the hills above Tiberias, the town he had founded by the Lake of Galilee. Following his marriage to Herodias, he appears to have changed his residence to the foreboding castle of Machaerus and stayed there for longer periods of time. And the wars he had to wage in the southern part of his realm against the Arabs were not the only reasons for this move. Machaerus was the proper site of activity for the sorceress Herodias. There she could pursue her craving for magic powers. And she had John the Baptist brought there, whom she hated all the more since she had to acknowledge his mighty spiritual power. John lay in chains in a dark cell of the tower in the demonically imposing castle.

Herod Antipas was struck to the core by the personality of John and his admonitions. When it was possible to do so without the knowledge of Herodias, he visited the prisoner in the dungeon and listened to his words. And as weak-willed as he otherwise was, for a long time he found ways to resist the demands of Herodias to have John executed. But then — tradition fixes the event in August of the year 31 — during a wanton orgiastic celebration, the sorceress succeeded in so duping her husband with the ecstatic dances of her daughter Salome that he acquiesced to the murderous command. The horrendous image now arises before us: in the magic castle of Machaerus, during a night of debauchery, Herodias triumphantly holds in her hands the bloody plate with the cut-off head of the Baptist. Had the demon triumphed over the angel in the spiritual battle?

Herodias is the embodiment of the period; the most symbolic incarnation of the Luciferic lust for power, a lust that the 'ruler of this world' poured into human hearts in order to pull humanity away from the one who was descending from heaven. Yet it was specifically through Herodias that this age paid its most intense and dramatic tribute to the greatness of John the Baptist. Would Herodias have taken up her battle against the man in animal garments if she had not recognized the lofty spiritual power incarnated in him? Even as Jezebel resorted to her demonic trickery against Naboth-Elijah only because she had recognized the profound mystery of his being, so too the motivation for Herodias' antagonism was due to the fact that she knew whom she was facing. Insofar as she did not rest until she had brought about his death and then delighted in holding up the dreadful trophy, she admitted that John was one of the greatest among men.

In contrast, Herod's judgment and that of the age concerning the one of whom the Baptist had said: 'After me comes he who is mightier than I, the thong of whose sandals I am not worthy to stoop down and untie!' differed completely from this admission. Two years later, at the early dawn of Good Friday, Pilate ordered Jesus brought to Herod Antipas, the ruler of Galilee. On that occasion Herodias, too, laid eyes on him for the first time. Herod, who might have heard John speak of Jesus on Machaerus, was filled with tense curiosity. He was hoping to become acquainted with yet another seer, one who would be able to give him fascinating answers from the beyond and could present him with tantalizing magic tricks. 'When Herod saw Jesus, he was very glad, for he had long desired to see him, because he had heard about him, and he was hoping to see some sign done by him. So he questioned him at some length; but he made no answer.' Herod was disappointed. A man stood before him who could do nothing, who was 'merely a human being.' The Gospel of Luke states: 'Then Herod began to despise him. He and all his soldiers mocked him, and he robed him in a cloak of shining white and he sent him back like that to Pilate' (Luke 23:8–12B). The reference to the court points to Herodias. The mocking contempt must chiefly have projected from her. It was she who, with the white garment, the sign of innocence, wished to give expression to the absolute insignificance, the merely ludicrous harmlessness of this man.

When Pilate washed his hands before the crowd and said: 'I find no fault in him,' this was at least an honest expression of

189

human endeavour. But when with the white garment Herodias denoted Jesus as an 'innocent little lamb,' this was nothing but demonic cynicism. By killing John the Baptist, the exponent of the age, she had acknowledged him as great. But she deemed it unnecessary to kill Jesus, for she had nothing but cynical scorn for him. The garment in which Jesus was returned to Pilate signified that the age declared him to be a nobody. The spiritual battle between John and Herodias was not at an end when the hate-filled queen held the bloody plate in her hands. Outwardly, she whose burning will said, 'I must grow to immeasurable dimensions; all men must serve me,' held the field. But in reality, her historical role was even then over, while the spirit of the one whom she had slain and who had said, 'He must increase but I must decrease,' was called upon to work on and contribute to the future of humanity.

5.7 The genius of John and the circle of Apostles

In order to be able to follow the paths pursued by the genius of John after the tragedy on Machaerus, we have to consider a brief outline of the human destinies of Jesus after the Baptism in the Jordan. As a disciple and helper of the Baptist among the people, Jesus must soon have had experiences that caused him to withdraw into seclusion. A fundamental change had taken place in his whole inner being. In rich abundance, insights and powers became accessible to him that did not originate from his human condition. Rather, as a divine celestial content, they streamed into his soul as into a chalice. More and more when he confronted human beings, he had to realize that possibilities were aroused in him and effects went out from him that far surpassed human measure. Unlike John the Baptist, who also had a powerful influence on people, Jesus felt that the superhuman effects he was about to exercise were not caused by an ascendancy of his soul to body-free heights but by an overpowering instreaming of cosmic forces into his humanity. He may have been shocked to discover that he could have wrought miracles. But to be a miracle worker was not inherent in his will and attitude. And so he withdrew into isolation and avoided all human contact.

For forty days, in the same wilderness of gorges where John

had spent his Nazirite youth, Jesus struggled for clarity by devoting himself to stern inner trials and exercises. Then, the three visions of the Temptation arose before his soul. He clearly saw what he would be capable of doing if only he willed to do it. Yet he wished to be only a man among men. He wanted to have no advantage at all over his fellow human beings. He withstood the Temptation and carried out the inward renunciation concerning which Paul coined the classic words: 'Have this mind among yourselves, which you have in Christ Jesus, who, though he was in the form of God, did not count equality with God a thing to be grasped, but emptied himself, taking the form of a servant, being born in the likeness of men' (Phil.2:5–7). The outcome of the forty days was that Jesus incorporated and concealed the divine-cosmic stream of power so deeply within his own being that, once he reappeared among human beings, the miracle-working lightning flash no longer shone forth from him, only pure human humility.

News of John's imprisonment may have induced him to emerge from his seclusion. Did the crowds who had followed John not resemble a herd of sheep who no longer had a shepherd? Nevertheless, Jesus did not do what many surely expected of him. He did not simply continue with John's activity. With a few faithful followers, he started moving quietly around Galilee, here and there giving aid to one ailing on the roadside, now and then replying to a question in the presence of a small gathering of people with the remarkable allegories recorded by the Gospel.

Then came the terrible report of the Baptist's beheading. What would Jesus do now? Would he not take up the banner of the one who had been slain by the enemy's hatred and carry it with determined steps at the head of those who had absorbed something of John's spirit? A surprising thing happened: Jesus sent away the disciples who had recently flocked around him. He dispatched them two at a time. He dissolved the community, which had been the most important support for them all, and made them depend solely on themselves. He himself withdrew again into seclusion. For more than half a year, he disappeared.

Now something remarkable ensued. The disciples who travelled through the land in pairs resembled the unassuming messengers of the Essene Order and yet, quite differently, they realized that they were torchbearers of a fire that sent down its rays from another world. They were able to carry out effects which, until then, they had not even dreamed of performing. Supernaturally strong, helping powers overshadowed them and accompanied their journeys. They sensed how the genius of the great prophet, whose disciples they had been and who had died a martyr's death at the hand of Herodias, continued to be effective in their actions when they now healed the sick, drove out demons or addressed people with the sovereignty of the spirit.

Rumours of the signs that accompanied their travels spread throughout the land. And the Gospel of Mark relates that when Herod heard of the disciples' deeds, he said repeatedly: 'He whom I beheaded, John, has risen. ... that is why such world-powers work through him.' (6:16, 14). A vivid connection opens up before us. Herod had been impressed by the nature of the Baptist. He had had to tell himself: Herodias believes she can rid herself of this opponent if she kills him. But she will be wrong! And after John had been beheaded, he waited anxiously for the genius of the slain one to show itself in all its lofty power. Herod was certain that he would not have to wait for long. Even as the spirit of Naboth-Elijah had mightily confronted Ahab's soul after his earthly death, the stoning through Jezebel,[62] so, too, this powerful spirit would soon appear as the avenger. And when reports of the miraculous deeds of the disciples reached him, Herod knew right away: this is he, whom Herodias thought she could destroy; now he is present again more than before!

The Gospel unveils an important secret here through one of the antagonists, a secret that modern-day spiritual research also reveals. From the very beginning, the powerful and unified power of the Apostles' circle that gathered around Christ was due to the fact that the genius of John the Baptist continued to be active in this circle as its protective, inspiring spirit. John's angel-like entity chose the circle of the disciples as its earthly corporeality and thus contributed to its becoming 'one body and one soul,' a true community from out of the spiritual realm. Herodias had tried to destroy John. In actuality she had helped him join as the mighty helper in the service of Christ, whose coming he had proclaimed beforehand and during whose human incarnation he had been the closest witness by carrying out the Baptism.

During the period before Easter of the year 32, Jesus called the disciples back from their missions. And when he had gathered them around him on a hillside at the Lake of Galilee, it came to pass that the portals of the future opened before their souls. They beheld a mighty stream of generously flowing power that would pass from them to humanity. Like administering priests, they beheld themselves in the midst of innumerable crowds. At the same time, they experienced the great and solemn vision in which, for the first time, they became aware of their universal apostolic mission[63] — the Gospels indicate this vision in the story of the Feeding of the Five Thousand — as the spiritual foundation and consecration of their community. They no longer felt themselves as individuals who were being supported and borne from above; it was as if they were in a quite new way linked to each other as a spiritual family. They recognized the genius of the Baptist in the angelic being that now became the spirit of their community in such an intimate ensouling form. And they felt as if a temple of humanity were vaulting above them, a temple in which, in divinely ordained order, they were allowed to be the pillars, while from the cupola above the out-spread wings of the Johannine spirit were overshadowing them.

But then, in the nocturnal after-effect of the blessed experience, they became aware in holy wonder and consternation who it really was whom they were following: when they sailed over the storm-tossed waves, the spirit-form of Christ appeared before them in the glory of radiant light. It was only then that they quite clearly and consciously made the transition from John the Baptist to Jesus in whom they were beginning to sense the bearer of Christ. The ministering genius of John who hovered above them himself referred them to the one whose herald he had been and had remained.

Here, a passage is quoted from the lectures in which Rudolf Steiner spoke about these relationships:

> This Elijah-soul is at the same time the soul of the Old Testament people, as it enters the Baptist and lives in him. When he was imprisoned and then beheaded by Herod, what happened then to his soul? ... His soul left the body and worked on as an aura; and into the domain of this aura Christ Jesus entered. Where then is the soul

of Elijah, the soul of John the Baptist? The Mark Gospel indicates this clearly enough. The soul of John the Baptist, of Elijah, becomes the group soul of the Twelve; it lives, and continues to live in the Twelve.[64]

5.8 The castle of the Grail and Klingsor's castle

It was in the spirit-event of the wondrous Feeding that the inner sequence of images and stages in the Baptist's drama came to perfect culmination. There, the temple was built and completed that could hold the balance and attain the victory over its demonic counter-image, the magic castle of Machaerus. Even as the radiant, spirit-built castle of the Grail and the dark earthly-abyssmal castle of Klingsor confronted each other in the Middle Ages, so, in the environs of the Gospel, embodying the same archetypal imagery, the spiritual temple of the Apostle-community and the ominous castle of Herodias faced each another. The Klingsor-fortification of the early Christian era on the grandiosely lifeless Gomorrah mountains above the Dead Sea has a scenic surrounding similar to the castle of the sorcerer Klingsor in Caltabellota (called 'Kalot Bobot' by Wolfram von Eschenbach) in the mountainous region of Sicily's interior not far from the southern coastline. And the realm of sunlight and life ether surrounding the Sea of Galilee, where the spiritual structure of the apostolic circle's grail castle rose up high, can appear as the source and fountainhead for the breath of spiritual presence that was felt everywhere where the Grail-mystery was being guarded and cultivated.

Rudolf Steiner revealed the exact counter-imagery that prevails between the Grail-castle and that of Klingsor, insofar as he spoke of the 'Anti-Grail,' the hideous symbol which at all times represented the central point of the Klingsor mysteries.[65] The pure chalice of the Grail with the ruby-red radiant wine, the blood of Christ, is perverted there into a vessel with still warm human blood. Instead of the shining host of bread in the chalice, the cut-off head of a man lies in the bloody dish. The servants of the Grail humbly opened their hearts to the heaven-bestowed gift of grace, while the followers of the sorcerer Klingsor endeavoured to force the powers of those whom they had murdered into their service. Herodias with the head of John appears to us as the first ruler of the Anti-Grail, the early Christian embodiment of the black Klingsor-magic. Yet the Anti-Grail cannot bar the way of the Grail. He whom Herodias had believed vanquished and subjugated under her own power, now worked out of the spiritual realm so that the first circle of the Grail's knights could find each other, a community which subsequently would be fortified and sent out into the world by the Mystery of Golgotha to bestow the means of salvation on humanity.

We find the continuing development of both streams in the Middle Ages. The Grail-castle with its kings, Titurel, Amfortas, Perceval and Lohengrin, rises on the spiritual foundation of the circle that, overshadowed by the genius of John at the Sea of Galilee, began the ministry of Christ. The Machaerus-Herodias destinies continue in the surroundings of the Klingsor-castle. Herodias and Herod Antipas did not achieve their dreamed-of summit of power. Among the successors of Tiberius, they fell into disgrace and as exiles roamed through the world until they died a miserable death in Spain. But even as the secret of John the Baptist is only unveiled to us when we follow the directions of his genius beyond earthly death, we only understand the Herodias-fate when we see how it continues in the larger stream of Christian human history.

It was Richard Wagner who had a special sense for this and expressed what he had recognized in his formulation of the Perceval myth. We see how, in the second act of his *Parsifal,* the sorcerer Klingsor summons the troubled and restless female Ahasuerus-figure, Kundry. He places her in a somnambulistic sleep and evokes the images of past earthly lives from her soul. Finally he exclaims: 'You were Herodias and who else?' Is it true that the unsatiable pride and hatred of Herodias now was avenged in the Ahasuerus-like degradation of Kundry? It is as if the magician had exposed a layer in Kundry's soul which now can rise into her own consciousness as well. In Klingsor's magic garden, carrying out the will of the sorcerer, Kundry tries to seduce Parsifal, the innocent fool. She makes use of the same magic dances with which Salome long ago broke Herod's will. But Parsifal resists the temptation and a frightening awakening and recognition passes through Kundry's soul. An inner flash of lightning shows her an image from a former life: she had mocked the one who was the Saviour of the world. A shrill scream is wrenched from her breast: 'I saw him and I laughed! Then he glanced my way!' And she realizes why she ceaselessly has to roam throughout the world, never resting. The look by Christ whom she had then derided has continued its effects in her nature and destiny. The scene on Good Friday morning once again arises before us. When Herod received no answers to his questions, was it not Herodias who gave expression to her biting derision? And yet, it was then that the soul of Herodias received the indelible mark of the Christ encounter within the deeper levels of her being: the thorn of Ahasuerus' restlessness.

Here Richard Wagner touches on significant secrets and truths of historical development. Explaining the artistic intuition of the Wagnerian Parsifal-poetry, Rudolf Steiner designated[66] Herodias as the historical personality to whom the Christian legend of Ahasuerus, the wandering Jew, does in fact refer. Behind the figure of the one of whom it was said that he laughed at Christ when the latter collapsed while carrying the Cross and therefore has to roam about the world, eternally troubled without being able to die, the image from the Gospel of Luke arises once more. The laughter of Ahasuerus resounds to us from the early Good Friday scene, where Herodias mockingly has Christ dressed in the white garment of innocence. And once again we find an answer to the question of how Christ appeared as a man within his age and how he was experienced by his contemporaries: if Herodias was the representative of her time, then the laughter of Ahasuerus was indeed the only expression that this age had for Christ. Yet it only seemed as though Herodias won out over John, and Caiaphas over Jesus. The victors of that time paled to restlessly roaming shadows, cut to the quick by the being of the ones whom they beheaded and nailed to the Cross.

5.9 *The nature of the great man*

During the one year between the miracle of the Feeding of the Five Thousand by the lake and the event on Golgotha which still remained for the disciples in their life together with Christ, they were confronted with many a puzzling question and trial. Those among them who awaited the great Messianic miracle, the world-shaking and transforming event, were disappointed. Until the end, the earthly life of the one whom humanity had awaited for thousands of years with ardent longing took place in much greater seclusion and obscurity, in smaller and unassuming groups, than had the activity of John the Baptist. Christ had not come to be great and successful but to become human to the very core and to suffer death, which is man's lot and very essence. He left behind no impressive accomplishment; instead, he left behind his own being, inasmuch as he gave himself to the earth and humanity as the permanently present power of salvation.

Between John the Baptist and Jesus a change occurred in the nature and concept of the 'great man.' The great men of ancient times, the leaders, up until the time of John the Baptist had been great on account of being gripped by the spirit and growing beyond their own dimension to a body-free, ecstatic union with God. Through becoming divine, human greatness existed among a few men in historical evolution. Then God became man in Jesus of Nazareth and the secret of incorporation replaced the principle of deification. When early Christian art in pictures of the Baptism in the Jordan depicted John as tall and Jesus, the greater one, as short, it too expressed the fact that from henceforth true greatness is perceived neither with physical eyes nor with imaginative vision, but manifests in a quite unpretentious and ego-endowed form.

Since Christ became man, greatness is revealed only as incorporation of the divine spark in the human soul, as inner beauty and living love — a love that, desiring no success, shines forth from a person. The power of ecstasy is replaced by the quiet radiance of true humaneness. No longer are the successful people the only great ones; henceforth, those are truly great who are selfless enough to make room in themselves for the secret of incorporation, regardless of whether they have a name in the world or go their way in complete modesty. This great transition can be deciphered in no more moving a manner than in the sequence of the pre-Christian and Christian incarnations of the individuality of John the Baptist. Spiritual research reveals to us[67] that the same being who lived in the prophet-figures of Elijah and John the Baptist was later incarnated in Raphael and Novalis. Prophetic ecstasy turned into brilliant inward artistry through the Christ impulse. What, in Elijah and John, was deeply earnest superhuman strength and intensity, frightening and shocking, was then transformed after the inner connection with the Christ Event into quietly emanating radiance of beauty and poetry. Seemingly, Elijah and John are greater than Raphael and Novalis. In reality, the essential greatness of manhood has merely moved within. In place of the ancient overpowering greatness, a new greatness has appeared, one that warms and transforms the world from within.

6. Judas Iscariot

6.1 The Judas question

The figures in the *Last Supper* by Leonardo da Vinci are dominated by a significant polarity of light. A radiance flows around the head of Christ that cannot be explained by the natural illumination of the scene anymore than the shadow that darkens the area around the head of Judas Iscariot. An inner sun appears to be circling through those seated at the table while the sacred meal is celebrated. The light of this sun causes Christ's countenance to shine, host-like. Its shadow lies like an inwardly justified darkness upon Judas who ducks his head sideways from Peter and John. Christ and Judas: it is one of the most profound riddles of man's being and life.

How could Christ accept among his disciples the one who would betray him? And how could one who for three years had experienced the direct presence and guidance of Christ become his betrayer? Despite and perhaps even because of this question, Judas is the Apostle in whom, in all ages of Christian development, struggling souls thought they recognized themselves as in a mirror. As if they viewed themselves in this image, serious-minded Christians were especially struck by the picture of the disciple who, although he too had clung with love and devotion to his Lord, finally stood before the Cross on Golgotha and blamed himself for the unimaginable horror of this death. For two thousand years, the riddle of the Judas figure, the universality and reproachfulness of his destiny, has bothered Christian souls. Will something of this difficult question be solved if we try to understand Judas' consciousness and attempt to follow the historical and biographical traces of his life?

It was no coincidence that, as he moved about on earth, Christ linked himself in a special way with a circle of twelve men. Even the Gospels make it evident that the number of those connected with him as followers or disciples was in reality much greater. The Twelve were an especially composed, chosen group. A cosmic order found human reflection in their circle. It is quite inappropriate to believe that the Twelve were simply men who understood Christ particularly well or were especially true and close to him. As long as we cling to such ideas, we simply view the Twelve as like-minded followers of a great, revered man. The riddle of the number twelve remains unsolved.

The Twelve are representatives of humanity. Each one is an embodiment of a spiritual human species. An inner, twelve-sided configuration inherent in humanity assumes form in the Twelve. The circle is closed; among the disciples of Christ, there is no human soul-nature that does not have its representative in one of the twelve Apostles. As the sun moves through the starry heaven that is surrounded by the twelve constellations of the zodiac, so does Christ move through humanity, a humanity represented by the twelve Apostles.

The Gospel itself at one point mentions the star-name of one of the disciples by designating Thomas as the 'Twin.' If it were to mention the star-name of Judas Iscariot, it would name him 'Scorpion.' Even as there has to be a scorpion among the constellations of the heavens, so there had to be a Judas among the disciples. To be surprised that Judas was accepted by Christ among the disciples is the same as being surprised that there is the constellation of Scorpio or that November is one of the twelve months of the year. What would the course of the year be without the death-shivers of the month of November? What would the circle of the Apostles be without the figure of Judas? Should those among human souls who tragically have no light and peace not have their emissary, too, within Christ's circle? Yet it would be a mistake to believe that it was through Judas that human iniquity and falseness found its place in this circle; that it was merely a criminal nature that was present. The reasons for the betrayal of Judas do not lie so plainly on the surface of morality. The more we try to trace these reasons, the more deeply will chasms of general human distress of soul and tragedy of consciousness be revealed to us.

6.2 Judas and Judea

From the very beginning, Judas Iscariot must have assumed a unique position in the apostolic circle. The majority of the Twelve were simple fishermen from Galilee. Judas, on the other hand, was from Judea and probably belonged to those social groups that were in possession of a predominantly intellectual education and culture. As far as its composition is concerned, the apostolic circle was a repetition of the twelve divisions into which the people of Israel were grouped at the beginning of their history. The larger part of the twelve tribes, which later separated as the kingdom of the ten tribes, dwelt in the northern regions of the land, in Galilee and Samaria. These people were attuned in heart and mind to the cosmic forces of the world. Only two tribes that finally remained as the kingdom of Judah lived in Judea and formed the specifically Jewish element, one that was more attuned to an abstract inner soul nature. The minority of the Jewish tribes in the composite of the Israelite nation corresponded to the minority of the Judean disciples within the circle of the Twelve. While each of the twelve Apostles differed from the others in a characteristic manner, inasmuch as he embodied one of the twelve nuances of humanity, profound disparity existed between the two regionally distinguished groups, the numerous 'men from Galilee' and the Judeans, mainly represented by Judas.

In Galilee and especially around the Sea of Galilee — where nature has remained rich in cosmic-paradisal reminiscences, in forces that envelop and support the human being (something that can be sensed even today) — ancient faculties of mind and soul survived for long periods of time. Vestiges of a natural, atavistic clairvoyance, more recently superficially designated as 'second sight,' remained alive there and must have been particularly active in the souls of the Galilean disciples. By contrast, the consciousness of people in Judea had become altogether earthly, for popular education of the Jewish wing of Israelite culture had deliberately worked towards the elimination of ancient, visionary soul forces. Judeans were characterized by the quite one-sided development of a purely intellectual consciousness. Rather than carry them aloft to the supersensory, their inward motivation thus drove them to fanaticism. The images that arose in the soul of a

Judean when he tried to reach beyond the actual world that surrounded him also related purely to the earthly realm of the senses.

While Galileans inclined toward atavism, Judeans therefore leaned toward utopian ideas. They felt a fervent urgency for a social and political reform of worldly conditions that corresponded to their ideals. We have to picture those who formed the core group of Jesus' disciples as being ensouled by a notable fiery ego-intensity. After all, in them, the individualities lived on in whom had blazed the heroic and sacrificial will of the Maccabean age.[68] Having passed through a martyr's or a warrior's death such a short time ago, and having been torn out of a life full of passionate devotion, it was as though they could simply link up again to the inner forces they had previously been unable to live out to the fullest. All the fervour, once focused in warding off the anti-Messianic Diadochian demonism in the defense of the nation's fight for survival, was now free to be transformed into completely personal reverence and devotion toward the one whose coming the past had so ardently awaited.

In the individual disciples, the great destiny-induced soul intensity led to an increase of all inner faculties, even of those tied to the character of the topography, be it that of Galilee or Judea. We therefore must picture Judas Iscariot in particular as a fervent soul in whom the will, directed towards certain expectations of the future, was passionately enkindled again and again.

It was often thought that the disciples generally were imbued with a purely national and political Messiah-expectation and therefore pictured the one to come only as one who, in the manner of the Maccabees, would place himself at the head of the Jewish people, overthrow the foreign Roman rule and restore the kingdom of David in its ancient splendour and greatness. But this is actually true only of Judas Iscariot. The 'men from Galilee' by no means felt themselves to be Jews in such a pronounced sense that they could have gone along with Jewish nationalism. In fact, the Messianic expectation and idea had a different nuance in each of the Twelve.

Spiritual research reveals to us[69] that, in Judas Iscariot, the soul of Judas Maccabeus, a soul that worked out of such a fiery element of will a century and a half ago, continued its earthly destinies. It was as if he were still under the powerful spell of past endeavours and exertions of will. The extreme predisposition stemming from both Judaism and the powerful unconscious reminiscence of the previous incarnation were the reasons why Judas Iscariot's ideals and conceptions of the future, pouring forth as they did from his fervent soul, related to political and social conditions as if they were caught up in the sphere of the purely earthly realm. The image of the Messiah whom he sought with such ardour really arose in his soul only like a glorified version of Judas Maccabeus. Judas Iscariot imagined that the Messiah would emerge one day and miraculously establish a glorious, all-encompassing kingdom of God on earth, in which, as its king and high priest, he would be enthroned in Jerusalem.

Along with such ideas and expectations, a strange relationship to Romanism must have prevailed in the soul of Judas. The Romans were the ones who ruled in Judea through their procurator, although they had never conquered the land, having been summoned instead as allies to lend support during the age of the Maccabean conflicts. The establishment of a new Davidian Messianic-Jewish kingdom would therefore be possible only by defeating Roman rule. Therefore Judas, too, viewed the Romans as annoying intruders and enemies. On the other hand, at that moment the Roman empire represented the most glorious realization of what Judas dreamed of as the Messianic future of his people. Once King Messiah would establish his kingdom on earth, he would have to do so after the example and pattern of the *Imperium Romanum.* With a part of his soul, therefore, Judas admired and envied Rome and its culture. A Rome-complex, a suggestive attraction for Rome, inhabited his soul in unresolved conflict against the feelings of enmity that he also experienced, though more superficially.

The fascination Judas Iscariot felt for Romanism must have been a continuation of the esteem that Judas Maccabeus had experienced with regard to the Roman state — a state that at that time had emerged in the foreground of history and had induced him to ask Rome to be his ally. The same Romans whom Judas Iscariot in his former life on earth had personally invited to his country, had turned into world rulers and now stood in the way of the Messianic national ascent of Judaism as he envisioned it.

Yet nothing more was really required than to turn Jerusalem instead of Rome into the capital city of the already existing worldwide empire. Judas felt certain the Messiah would emit such irresistible royal dignity that the world would fall at his feet.

However, Judas Iscariot failed to recognize one fact when, half with envious admiration, half with enmity, he turned his glance to Rome. Judas Maccabeus had still been able to call on the Romans as patrons of humanitarian justice against the demonic principle of the Caesarean cult which was then coming into vogue in Antioch. In the meantime Rome itself, and with it the civilized world, had been subjected to the reign of this principle. The Caesarean trend, against which Maccabean Judaism had once fought in league with pre-Caesarean Rome, had become the general rule. The only way to counter it was through an infinitely potent spiritual impulse that no longer originated on the level of political power struggles. Only the evocation of a completely different unearthly world of divine forces could now help. What sort of fortification against the Caesarean spirit of evil would have been erected through a yet greater Jewish national state? Rome had to encounter not a competitor but a spiritual opposite, a cosmic power not of this world. The great tragedy into which Judas Iscariot was led by his inner destiny was to confront Christ with expectations which, the more ardent and passionate they were, the more they had to turn into disappointments. In the end, the betrayal was the last desperate attempt to urge Christ on to the great miracle which Judas so impatiently awaited as the revelation of the Messiah-sovereignty.

6.3 Judas and Oedipus

The profound human and biographical secrets concealed behind the few brief Judas-scenes of the Gospel found moving expression in ancient Christian legends. In the form of an imagination, we are told the following: Once upon a time, in Jerusalem, there lived a Jew named Rubens with his wife, Ciborea. When she was with child, she foresaw in a dream that the babe she was carrying in her womb would cause the greatest disaster ever perpetrated by a human being. When he was born, wishing to divert the misfortune, the parents placed the infant in a small box and entrusted him to the waves of the sea, as the mother of Moses had done with her little boy. In time, the ocean carried the little box to the shores of an island named Scariot. The queen of that land found it at the beach. And since, to her great sorrow, she had been denied children, she claimed the strange little boy as her own and raised him.

Some time later, the queen did give birth to a boy and devoted all her love to him. In young Judas, hatred arose against his brother. Again and again, by quarrels and mistreatment, he made the younger one suffer for having alienated his mother's affections. Finally the queen had no other recourse but to reveal to the older boy his foundling's origin. In a fit of rage, thinking that he had to seek revenge, Judas slew his foster-brother and fled far away. After many an odyssey, he arrived in Jerusalem. He was assigned the office of a steward in the palace of Pilate, the Roman governor. One day, Pilate stood in the courtyard of his palace and looked across into the garden of his neighbour, desiring the apples that adorned the trees there. Judas, ever the faithful servant, hurried to obtain what his master desired. He entered the neighbouring garden, but soon became embroiled in an argument with the owner who tried to deny him his request. Judas struck the man down in sudden anger. He did not know that he had killed his own father. As a reward for his loyalty, Pilate presented him with the neighbour's house and gave him as his wedded wife the man's spouse: Ciborea, Judas' own mother.

One day, when Ciborea gave vent to her feelings and told of the little boy she had once entrusted to the waves of the sea, Judas became aware of his abysmal fate. Desperation gripped him. Who would lift up the heart-broken man again? Ciborea, who was a devout woman and one of the 'quiet in the land,' had kept track of the activites of the Nazarene with great love and veneration. She brought her son, who was also her husband, to Jesus who in compassionate kindness accepted him among the circle of his disciples. Finally, as if driven by tragic mischance, Judas committed the third and worst evil deed — the betrayal of Christ.

It is strange that particularly with regard to the Judas-destiny, the ancient Christian legend rose to the heights of mythology, the momentum of tragedy. Was it not as if the Greek saga of

Oedipus, the murderer of his father and husband of his mother —
a basic theme of classic tragedy formulated by Aeschylus and
Sophocles — had been transplanted to the dimension of early
Christian destinies? Moreover, not just the pictures of the
Oedipus-saga lived once again in the Judas-legend. Even the
mystery of the childhood of Moses and Joshua is repeated here.
Once more, as in the stories of Moses and in the Joshua-legend,[70]
the picture of the closed little basket stands before us, a container
in which, in order to avoid misfortune, a little boy is entrusted to
the waves of the seas.

Nothing allows us to sense the human universality of the
destiny-mysteries that surround the Judas figure more than this
confluence of mythical motifs from such divergent cultures.
When we try, in the images of the legend, not to recognize outer
events but the course of an inner soul destiny, Judas, like Oedipus, appears before us as the archetype of the human being who
has arrived at a quite specific turning point of evolution. Judas is
the Oedipus of early Christendom; Oedipus is the human being
of the new world, the world in which egohood comes to birth.
Before the prophecy of the oracle is fulfilled by him that he will
slay his father and wed his mother, Oedipus solves the riddle
posed by the sphinx in front of the gates of Thebes, the riddle to
which the answer is: Man.

Oedipus-Judas was the human being at the moment of
evolution when man had become 'purely' human. Earlier, in
childlike-divine manner, humanity had been an integral part of
the world, the paternal heavens and the maternal earth. But eventually they separated from the protective union with the all.
Neither knowing nor willing it, human beings tore themselves
away from heaven, took hold of their individual being and
became entangled in the earthly realm. Heaven ceased to be
man's spiritual home; he forgot the 'Father in the heavens.'
Henceforth, heaven was populated for humankind merely by lifeless celestial bodies, worlds that move on their course like the
soulless mechanism of a clock. The father was slain by the son,
without the son intending to do so. Earth, once the sacred mother,
became the stage and object of lust and instinct, of greed for
power and selfishness. Earth turned into the whore for man, without his clearly being aware of it.

Man was now in possession of a new faculty that bestowed on him an awareness of self. The intellect awakened in him; with its help he found the answer to the sphinx's riddle. But was the ego-imbued intellect of the head not the very weapon with which the son, having become ignorant of the deeper riddles of existence, slew the father? Abstract sense-bound and therefore death-imbued thoughts supplanted the living spirit. In each and every thought of the head is a murder not perpetrated on the paternal spirit out of whom we are all born? Is the intellect that alienates us from our spiritual origin not at the same time the forerunner of our state of being lost in the earthly realm, our impure union with earth, our mother? As a prize for the solution to the riddle of the sphinx, the mother gives herself as wife to the son through whose dark deed she has become a widow.

What is the consequence of this twofold fate to which the ego-endowed human being falls victim? When, suddenly, Oedipus became aware of the horrors, he blinded himself and henceforth, as the blind king, moved about on his lamentable journeys. As ego-endowed human beings, we believe we have sight because of our intellect; but we have turned blind to the true world. While we do awaken in the Oedipus-destiny to self-awareness, this is at the same time an awakening to blindness, to the tragic loss of the actual world light. In the Judas-destiny, we see the Oedipus-tragedy magnified beyond the personal level; the act of blinding himself was replaced by the betrayal of him who could say of himself: 'I am the light of the world.' Insofar as Judas caused Christ's death on the Cross due to inner delusion, he blinded the eye of the world. And if it then says: 'And [he] went and hanged himself' (Matt.27:5), the progressive element of the Judas-tragedy over against that of Oedipus comes to expression once more.[71]

One can only guess at the form in which the twofold Oedipus-offence was present as a state of mind in the soul-nature of Judas. The combination of cold head-bound thinking and ardent passion, a passion ultimately directed to earthly goals, only points us in the direction of the deeply concealed recesses of mind out of which erupted so much fateful tragedy. Outwardly, this inner misfortune was projected the most clearly in Judas' strange ambivalence between Judea and Rome. Judea was the site of unequivocal intellectualism. The Jewish people's history of consciousness had been a systematic eradication of those soul forces that long ago had linked human beings in their perception and action with the world of the supersensory. In Judea, man slew his father. Only dead thoughts remained as corpses of the paternal spirit. The routine of the Law's skeletal structure turned human beings into lifeless shadows who bore the mark of patricide on their countenance.

On the other side, Caesarean Rome with its inordinate thirst for power and sensory pleasure was dominated by the principle of marriage to the mother, something that actually became symptomatically apparent, for example, in the dubious relationship of Caesar Nero to his mother, Agrippina. It was not merely human lust for power when the Caesars tried to become world rulers. An obscure cosmic instinct to grasp Mother Earth with all one's might played a part in all their intemperance. The Caesarean cult with its murky, demonic occult background was indeed spiritual incest and fornication. As a genuine and typical Judean, Judas shared in the guilt of the universally human Oedipus-offence of patricide. And inasmuch as on a deeper level of his nature he had an affinity for Rome's splendour and greatness, Judas shared in the guilt of the universal Oedipus-offence of incest. Judas was torn between the Ahrimanic danger of dead thinking and the Luciferic temptation of addicted willing.

Now he of whom it was said, 'Behold, the Man!' was born in the same historical human situation in which Judas had to live and experience the misfortune of an ego-endowed human being in mythical archetypal form. And it was he, Christ, who in the victory over Ahriman and Lucifer redeemed ego-endowed humanity from their tragic destiny, implanting in human beings the power to make amends for the Oedipus-offence.

6.4 The thirty pieces of silver

In the few scenes where the Gospel shows us Judas in action, laws of humanity's inner destiny can be precisely deciphered. A sequence of archetypal pictures that have always existed in the realm of the spirit as expressions of certain possibilities and necessities of human evolution seemed to condense and become reality in physical-earthly form. Especially beginning with that ominous moment when Judas left the circle partaking of the Last Supper and went out into the night, his fate progressed in symbols turned to reality and soul-images become physical and tangible: Judas with the high priest as he received the thirty pieces of silver; Judas in Gethsemane where he kissed the Lord; Judas in breathless tension during the trial of Jesus before Caiaphas and Pilate — until all his illusions were dispelled. Finally, we read how Judas returned the thirty pieces of silver by throwing them into the Temple and then met his horrible end.

Once before, there had been a grim Judas who had betrayed another, a radiant being, for a sum of silver pieces, also in a circle of twelve. He was Judah who, among the twelve sons of Jacob, was instrumental in selling his brother Joseph for twenty silver pieces to the Ishmaelite traders going to Egypt (Gen.37).[72] Is the resemblance between the Old and the New Testament events coincidental? Or are we dealing with two legends that were made to resemble each other? No, the history of both the people of Israel and the life of Jesus is an actualization, a divine dramatization of inner facts. And where similar inner mysteries become history, outer events assume similar form as well.

In the Old Testament, we find a prematurely cast shadow of the drama about the thirty pieces of silver first of all in the book of the prophet Zechariah. Down to details, this text refers to the circumstances that surrounded Judas on the night of Maundy Thursday:

> Then I said to them: 'If it seems right to you, bring to me what I am worth; but if not, let it be charged.' And they took the scale and weighed out how much I was worth: thirty shekels of silver. And the Lord said to me, 'Throw it down that it may be given to the potter!' Verily, a lordly sum they deem me worth! And I took the thirty shekels of silver and cast them into the Temple of the Lord, to be given to the potter (Zech.11:12fB).

Were the thirty pieces of silver thrown back by Judas into the Temple not in fact given to a potter as payment for his field of clay which thereafter was turned into a burial ground? It would mean taking a narrow view of the Bible if we simply tried to explain the relationship existing between the words of the prophet and the details of the Judas-story as one being the prediction of the other. Archetypes of the human condition became apparent to the visionary sight of the prophet and assumed earthly form later on in the events most closely surrounding Christ.

The imagery of the thirty pieces of silver appeared to the seer in connection with a vision that showed to him man's tragic yet necessary separation from the divine-spiritual world. Human beings were to ask heaven for new revelations, because the once abundant bright stream of spiritual light was becoming clouded and increasingly faint: 'Ask for late rain from the Lord, then He will cause clouds to appear and give rain for all the vegetation that grows on your fields. For the gods utter ominous oracles, the seers behold illusionary forms and tell of sense-bereft dream visions; no more consolation goes out from them.' (Zech.10:1fB).

The extinction of the celestial gifts of light corresponded on earth to the isolation and loneliness of men. Ancient communities broke apart. The priestly pastoral attitude that prevailed among human beings from the times of primal revelation began to lose its effectiveness. Completely on their own, ego-endowed human beings had to undergo all the misery and agony of abandonment. And so the prophet continued: 'Therefore the people wander like sheep; they are afflicted for want of a shepherd' (10:2).

The decline and end of the shepherd-mystery in humanity never became more clearly evident nor did it occur in a more archetypal manner than in Israel's history. At the very beginning stood the mighty royal figures of shepherds — Abraham, Jacob, Moses: bearers not merely of a lofty personal soul but of a spirit who ensouled, led and carried the community. Yet in the course of evolution the circle of community-building, pastoral power shrank increasingly. Out of the communal folk relationships, the ego nature of the single person became ever more clearly detached. And due to Israel's specific task of cleansing human nature completely of the vestiges of atavistic clairvoyance, the cast of the ego here assumed particular solidity and sharpness. The herd of the great primal shepherd turned into the 'lost sheep of the House of Israel.' Judas was the person in whom the isolation of the ego had become complete. The decline of the ancient God-given pastoral state goes from Abraham all the way to Judas. No more community-building power issued from Judas. The forces of the scorpion prevailed in his nature, forces that separate and scatter rather than draw together. It is not for nothing that for 'scatter,' the Greek New Testament uses the term that gave the scorpion its name, *scorpizein*.

The drama of sorrow and decline speaks out of the turbulently arising pictures of prophetic vision: 'Hark, the wail of the shepherds' (Zech.11:3) in the midst of the raging world-tempest, in the birth-pangs of which the ego is born. Man who is suffering the trial of isolation receives the mission to be himself the shepherd of the sheep destined to die: 'Become shepherd of the flock doomed to slaughter, for their lords and shepherds no longer watch over them but abandon them to death.' And man takes on the task of being the shepherd: 'I tended the sheep doomed to be slain, indeed, I tended the miserable ones among the sheep' (11:4–7B). Yet now man experiences the misfortune and end of the pastoral state even more. The shepherds' staffs break in his hand; images of the shepherds' death appear to him, as if he himself were guilty of inflicting death on them: 'I slew three shepherds in one month' (11:8B). Man is forced to give up to perdition what is about to become corrupt; to death what is dying; to mutual tearing to pieces what has singled itself out (11:9). The ego loses heaven and the community. While it does sense that it is finding itself, it does so as slayer and slain one.

Death is the destiny and prize of ego-attainment. At this point, man faces the temptation of deluding himself concerning the fact of inner death brought about by the development of earthly ego-consciousness. He believes he amounts to something in his very being and asks what he is worth. Weighed on the scale of the universe, he receives the reply: 'Thirty pieces of silver' (11:12B). What does that mean? Thirty is the number of the moon; it shows the number of days of one moon orbit. Silver is the metal of the moon. The reply therefore means to indicate: your ego is merely of lunar, not solar quality. It is semblance, not true being; it simulates light of its own but merely possesses borrowed, reflected light. You say 'I.' But in fact, insofar as you say that, you lie. All that you are you have merely received, even as the moon has all its light merely from the sun.

Man is confronted with a decision. Will he think that the thirty pieces of silver are a goodly sum of money? Will he think that he is sun, even though he is only moon? Will he remain caught up in the illusion of the mirror, in the silvery, cold, moonlike ego-consciousness of the earth? Or can he become unselfish in his'I'? Can he learn in true self-knowledge to say 'Not-I' to himself and thus find the path out of the shimmering death of the lower to the higher ego? Will he shape his moonlike nature to be the chalice into which a sunlike content can flow from above? The prophetic vision continues. A supportive voice resounds to man: 'Cast away the thirty pieces of silver so they will be given to the potter.' Discern how the splendid sum fools you! He who obeys this challenge at the right time passes the test and can say: 'So I took the thirty shekels of silver and cast them into the house of the Lord to be given to the potter' (11:13*B*).

Ordinary ego-consciousness lives predominantly in intellectual thoughts of the head. But these thoughts are connected with hidden processes of decomposition and death in human nature. They are a metamorphosed form of what otherwise pulses as living formative force through the human body and kneads and forms this body like a sculpturing potter. Something living always dies when etheric formative forces are coined into the thirty pieces of silver, the coins of mere head consciousness. Human beings who do not remain tied to the moon illusion and instead see through the semblance-character of mere head thoughts and ordinary ego-consciousness; who, loosening the inner paralysis, strive toward a universal attitude of receptivity in regard to things spiritual, return to the formative forces what they had withdrawn from them. The thirty pieces of silver once again benefit the temple of the human body. Once more, the invisible potter, the etheric body of man, can build up, shape and create based on these etheric forces. What died in the vain illusory ego can come alive again, if human beings open to the sun-force of a higher world in inner selflessness. It is necessary to say 'I' but, to begin with, it only leads to the lower ego. The inward move forward to the 'Not-I' frees the path to the higher, true I, the Christ-I — 'Not I but Christ in me.'

The imaginative vision of the prophet's scripture turned to history in the fate of Judas. With almost spectral clarity, the soul-images solidified to outward scenes. Archetypal pictures of the tragedy of egohood appeared visibly before humanity. Along with the thirty pieces of silver, which according to legendary traditions originated from age-old temple treasures and were brought by Alexander the Great to Jerusalem, Judas held in his hand a picture of his own being. His actions arose out of deeper roots than merely human, all-too-human motives such as avarice and perfidy. Humankind's destiny was being symbolized. An invisible producer presented a mystery play on the stage of history.

Illusion had power over the soul of Judas. When remorse filled him and he threw the pieces of silver back into the Temple, it was too late. The lower ego, the moon-like I of the thirty pieces of silver, had already delivered the higher ego, the I of the golden sun, into the hands of death. And insofar as the lower ego becomes the betrayer of the higher I, it destroys itself. Murder and suicide go hand in hand. The potter's field turns into the burial ground in which the vessels of the potter of humankind disintegrate and decompose. Instead of turning into a formative power, the thirty pieces of silver become a ferment of decomposition. Through Judas, the world becomes a grave. Only Christ, the victor over the grave, returns to the ego-endowed human being the living formative force and ability to live in community with others. He restores the pastoral office. He is the good shepherd. Once again, in him, there is present what had become lost on the path from Abraham to Judas.

6.5 The youth of Judas

The Judas legend is one of the documents that appear utterly worthless to prevailing historical research. Yet in actual fact they are of far greater importance, particularly for a comprehension of historical aspects, than purely mundane documentation can ever be. The mythical content of its images allows us to recognize that the legend originates from those factions of early Christendom that had access to hidden spiritual knowledge and believed they were supposed to bring out in imaginative form something which could contribute to the clarification of the Judas riddle. But this document reveals its full value to us only when we do not stop short at the point of viewing it merely as a pictorial representation of certain states of soul. The veil of imaginative depiction that interweaves it becomes transparent to us if we dwell for long enough on its shape. It then turns transparent even for important highlights in the external biographical course of Judas' life. A deeply moving tragedy in three acts begins to be unveiled to us and we will attempt to trace its outlines.

As in the traditions concerning the childhood of Moses and Joshua that we possess, so here, too, the image of the basket in which the little boy is abandoned indicates to us that a person of special significance has been born. A soul has made its entrance into a human body that brings along a rich resonance of initiations and destinies undergone in earlier lives.[73] Here, too, we quote one of Rudolf Steiner's clarifications that were studied when considering the childhood of Moses:

> In the manner of ancient descriptions, the enclosure of Moses in the basket soon after his birth symbolically indicates that, in the case of this individual, one deals with a soul that relied on eternal sources for the highest gifts it had to give. One who is familiar with such descriptions in religious evolution knows that, in this way, they always try to refer to something significant. We know from earlier descriptions ... that when a man wished to reach up to higher spiritual worlds with his perception, he had to undergo certain states of soul development. He did so by isolating himself completely from all his surroundings. Then he awakened the deepest forces of his soul. Now, when the intention is to describe that such an individual already brings those faculties along with him at birth, faculties that lead to the higher dimensions attainable by mankind, then this cannot be described any better than by stating: For this personality it was necessary ... to undergo an experience, even down to the physical level, whereby his or her senses, everything that he or she possessed of faculties of comprehension, was cut off, as it were, from the physical world ...[74]

The parents and those of the little child's immediate surroundings become aware of the unusual special destiny that enters into their midst. This comes about either through supersensory experiences of the mother, other signs that precede the birth or because, early on, the traits of a special providence are noted in the little boy's character. At the birth of Moses, auspicious signs completely dominated. Every effort was therefore made to save the child from the threatening Pharaonic danger. At the birth of Judas, as in the cases of Joshua and Oedipus, everything came together to frighten the parents. Not only extraordinary gifts were sensed but in addition great tragedy. Parental concern was filled by the troubled question: What can possibly be done to turn the menacing fate in a positive direction?

We can only dimly sense through the legend's pictorial veil what exactly was done by the parents to prepare the Judas boy for a propitious life and vocation despite the presentiments of catastrophe that arose at his birth. When we are told that Judas grew up on a distant island as the adopted son of the queen of the land, this may indicate an association with a faraway place of learning. We see young Judas approach a circle of people who were in possession of ancient traditions of wisdom. His unusually great talents gave him access. As a favoured pupil he was accepted into the precincts of the mystery location. Yet, surprisingly, it became evident that Judas basically faced the spiritual life nurtured around him as a stranger. To those who had high hopes for him, he caused bitter disappointment. Not only did he not adapt to the soul-spiritual nature of his environment but — worse — a strong aversion to it arose from the depths of his being. This aversion finally grew to hatred and produced uncontrollable rages. When the leaders of the school were forced to confront him and called to his attention that he, the stranger, owed his admission into the ranks of discipleship only to a special favour, Judas completely lost control of his easily aroused temper. He committed the first great misdeed of his tragic life. He inflicted a grave wrong on the mystery community that had been willing to accept him into its ranks, perhaps by betraying important secrets. The continuation of its spiritual life into the future became impossible for this community and it was thus doomed. Events such as these may be concealed behind what the legend relates when, conferring the Cain-motif on him, it says that in his rage Judas killed the queen's son.

Perhaps the tragic development of young Judas can be compared with the events that Augustine suffered a few centuries later. When, with fervent soul, Augustine struggled for truth in his youth, he also engaged in a relationship with a mystery community that would have liked to accept him into its ranks. For nine years, he was a disciple and novice at a school of the Manichees. But instead of more deeply penetrating the teachings that people tried to introduce to him, a feeling of rejection more clearly arose in him. Finally, he completely renounced his teachers and as a Christian theologian turned into one of the most outspoken and effective opponents of Manichaeism.

As with Augustine later on, in a sense it must have been the case with Judas. Due specifically to contact with a supersensory world conception, Judas was driven to an extremely intellectualistic way of thinking — a thinking to which he was predisposed because of his origin and lineage. Born of fear, opposition against the supersensory world was aroused in the Judean in whom the moonlike head forces were one-sidedly developed at the expense of sunlike activities. Judas lacked the sense organ for the higher worlds, for the spheres of true life. Pride of the intellectual ego-consciousness, on the other hand, prevented him from recognizing the limits of his perceptual faculties. Hatred against the unperceived erupted therefore all the more forcefully, particularly because it had been a longing, hidden deeply within his nature and destiny, that had led him to that foreign group of people in the first place. Moon element raged against sun nature, even though it owed all its light and life to it.

6.6 Judas and Pilate

The second act in the drama of the Judas biography is already set in Jerusalem. Legend shows us Judas in a certain relationship to the Roman procurator, Pilate. During this period, Judas' soul must have fallen completely under the spell of political ideas and impulses that culminated in fantastic utopias although their passionate intensity adhered merely to the physical plane. Perhaps the emotional rejection of the mystery school, assigned by legend to the mythical island of Scariot, contributed to the fierceness with which Judas now became involved in earthly-political endeavours. In contrast to those 'ideologists,' he now wanted to be a 'consistent realist.'

It goes without saying that the aim of his restless mind and will was the re-establishment of the Davidian-Jewish kingdom with extended powers and splendour. But the suggestive power of Rome that stirred deep within him played into his Jewish nationalism. The legend mirrors his subconscious bond to the admired and envied Rome by describing his unrestrained officiousness toward Pilate. It is quite probable that Judas really had an actively pursued connection to Pilate. As if the hope that Judas Maccabeus once entertained for the still democratic Romans lived on directly in him, Judas appears to have believed that he could realize his plans with the support of the Roman procurator himself, who in his nature still bore a reminiscence of pre-Caesarean Romanism.

When the legend tells us that Judas incurred the twofold curse of Oedipus, patricide and marriage to his mother, in the service of Pilate, this allows us, first of all, to recognize the extent to which his political ambition had not only eliminated all sensitivity for the supersensory world but moreover for intimate human relationships. Even if we were to remain within the images of the legend that no doubt do not try directly to convey external events, we would have to ask: How is it possible that a man is unable to recognize his father and mother, not even through any trace of intuition? A short circuit occurs between the abstract, earthbound thinking of the head and the passionately erupting will. The golden middle of the feeling heart is absent. Feeling, stunted and powerless, can neither dampen the coldness of thinking to wise presence of mind nor the hot fury of will to abiding strength of love. A man outdistances his own humaneness and unleashes disaster after disaster.

A covert wrong fraught with consequences must be concealed behind the horrible picture of the father's murder, a wrong that Judas inflicted on his own nation that he was trying to raise to unimagined prominence. This was the second great evil deed of his life. Merely as an indication of the direction in which historical reality would perhaps have to be sought — a reality that the legend points to in mythical imagery — an episode is mentioned that occurred in Jerusalem at that time. There were groups of fanatical Jewish nationalists who believed that through a general popular uprising similar to the one that had broken out against the Diadochi during the age of the Maccabees, they would be able to shake off alien Roman rule. They were just waiting for an opportune moment to unleash the revolt. At one point, they thought it had come. In order to pay for a huge aqueduct that was to supply water to the arid city of Jerusalem — to this day, one can see remnants of it — Pilate had misappropriated some of the Temple treasure. He felt he had a right to do so, for he was only acting in the interest of Jerusalem's inhabitants. The conspirators, on the other hand, saw in his action a desecration of the sanctuary and prepared to strike, certain that all the people would join them. But much as they tried to keep their plan secret, it was betrayed. During the Easter festival when the city was filled to overflowing with pilgrims, Pilate's legionaries at a given command took off their pilgrims' cloaks, under the guise of which they had entered the city. They embarked on a monstrous blood bath and nipped the revolt in the bud. Is it really so unthinkable that a man like Judas could have been the traitor who revealed the plans of the revolt to Pilate? For he belonged to the nationalists and yet condemned their intentions because he hoped to achieve more through compromise with the Romans. We need only think this through as a possibility and the historical realities we are trying to touch through the veil of the legend will appear before us a degree more clearly.

Caught up in the illusion of doing his nation a service by preventing the planned insurrection, Judas in reality brought a dreadful misfortune on his people. Perhaps his own father lost his life during a massacre to which Judas motivated the Romans without meaning to do so. But even if something like this was not the case, at one time Judas must have confronted dreadful and shocking consequences of his actions, not unlike Oedipus when he realized he had slain his own father.

Simultaneously, the legend pictures Judas as becoming aware of the incestuous relationship with his mother. It certainly must remain an open question whether any physically real incest actually took place, though carried out unknowingly. Perhaps here we deal with a theme of the legend that refers almost exclusively to inner soul facts. When Judas beheld the abysmal horror he had conjured up in such a frightening and sudden way, he may have realized, more than he had wanted to admit to himself, that personal ambition and selfish greed for power had played a part in his utopian ideas and actions. Had he himself not succumbed to the Caesarean seduction of Romanism when he had curried favour with Pilate? Under the pretense of wishing to attain new prominence for his people, had he not in fact thought only of himself?

6.7 *The disciple of Jesus*

At the end of the second part of his life, Judas appeared as one weighed down and crushed by remorse. Where was his glowing passionate will now? Inner anguish and desperation made him find his way to Jesus. Now it seemed as if, from all directions, invisible higher powers were making the effort to give the tragic fate a turn towards redemption. Maybe the legend contains a motif that should be viewed in a directly historical sense when it says that Judas became aware of Jesus through his devout mother. Again, we are reminded of the story of Augustine's youth where, through the prayers of his mother and after long unfulfilling paths that led him astray, he found access to Christianity.

The image is urged upon our mind how the infinite quiet benevolence emanating from the being of Christ lifted up the broken soul of Judas and filled it with confidence. The encounter with Jesus and the circle of the disciples, which by then had probably become partly established, in many ways must have meant an elating fulfilment of destiny for Judas. For in these simple men from Galilee, as different as they were from him, he found those again who in his last incarnation had been his brothers and had enthusiastically fought by his side. Without becoming fully conscious of it, it must have imbued the soul of Judas with newly dawning radiant hope that he found himself again in the circle of those who once had embodied the miracle of the age of the Maccabees. While the balsam of consolation had streamed over him from Jesus himself, now this occurred again in a more will-emphasized way when he had the experience that Novalis coined in the words: 'Long-lost brothers I rediscover in his disciples.' In the circle around Jesus, the fiery will of Judas became revitalized, now filled through and through with Messianic content.

It was not as if in Jesus of Nazareth he had recognized the Christ being. But the confident hope had awakened in him that eventually the all-triumphant might of the Messiah would radiantly blossom forth from this man. What he experienced in the way of miracles of humaneness and benevolence in the circle that had accepted him could only confirm the highly-strung expectations of the one great miracle: the world-transforming emergence of divine power. And for the third time, the disunity of his nature and the earthbound disposition of his thoughts became a temptation for Judas. The old political illusion, nurtured through Romanism, distorted for him the conception that he had formed of the Messiah's being and activity. The ray of divine kindness that emanated from Christ had struck deeply within his soul. But before long, the passionate unrest of his nature obscured this experience which could only have matured to clear perception in peaceful inwardness. With tense impatience, he waited for Jesus to rise to the occasion of the great political miracle of visibly establishing the kingdom of God on earth.

The third act of the tragedy unfolded. Storms of highly-strung hopes and crushing disappointments, of overly-enthusiastic certainties and almost demonic attacks of unrest and impatience, must have torn the soul of Judas hither and thither. Judas had no share in the quiet miracles in which the supersensory greatness of the Christ being became revealed to the receptive souls of the disciples — after the wondrous feeding of the multitudes, at the stilling of the storm on the Sea of Galilee, and later on the Mount of Transfiguration. For Judas, only the earthly senses were open. The earthly greatness of Christ which he so impetuously envisioned did not materialize.

Finally, a split became apparent more and more disturbingly in Judas' soul. Christ's inconspicuously great deeds of salvation provoked an obscurely rebellious feeling in him. He expected quite different actions from the Messiah. Why did he occupy himself for so long with matters that would not change the world anyhow? He delayed for too long what, so Judas believed, was the one necessary thing to do. In the end, the resurrection act of Christ at the grave of Lazarus must have plunged Judas into wild confusion of soul. Finally, when Mary Magdalene, Lazarus' sister, anointed the feet of Jesus with the costly nard, and the scent of the sacrificial gift and peaceful solemnity of devotion filled the whole house, he lost his patience.

Abrupt restlessness burst out sharply from him and his angry accusatory words cut discordantly through the sacramental still-ness. Judas acted as if his disruptive intervention was for the sake of a social idea: 'Would it not have been better to sell this costly ointment for three hundred denarii in order, with the proceeds, to alleviate the suffering of the poor?' Here speaks a man who has lost himself completely to the idea that something visible and tangible has to occur if the world is to progress. The purely earthly conception of the kingdom of God caused him to shake his head in incomprehension, indeed to become angry over all expressions of a piety quietly flowering in the human heart. He was the religious and social activist and did not realize that his high-sounding demands and programmes were based on inner untruthfulness.

A social-minded will is only genuine and true when it springs from a heart capable of love. True love of humanity only flour-ishes on the maternally nurturing ground of an inwardly secure soul at peace with itself. Inner unrest and impatience is the death of any love. A social activism as represented by Judas and as can be encountered everywhere among contemporary humanity is untrue, because it is without heart and love. In the end, it is merely an expression of a person's own inner disquiet. Judas believed he was being practical with regard to life as opposed to those unworldly pious ones who wasted time and even angered him. In reality, Mary Magdalene chose to do the right thing even in the social sense. In her pious soul, capable of worship and solemnity, grew the self-composed power out of which alone can flow a genuine social attitude and true love of humanity.

In cutting words, the Gospel of John unveils the inner untruth of the objection raised by Judas against the anointing in Bethany: 'This he said, not that he cared for the poor but because he was a thief' (12:6). Here we are shown that the mental dissonance in Judas' nature had led to confusion in his moral behaviour. Where the heart, the golden middle of human nature, fails in its soul function, the short circuit between thinking and willing cannot but lead finally to pathologically distorted conceptions. The intel-lectuality of the head pours into the will region of the limbs; as moral dysfunction, a tendency arises in the will that is only healthy and justified within the activity of thinking and the senses, namely, the tendency to accumulate as much as possible from out of one's surroundings and make it one's own.* More frequently than one would think, when provoked by one-sided intellectualism, stinginess and greed spring from a half-pathological imbalance between thinking, feeling and willing, even though morally this does not excuse such tendencies. In Judas, too, the selfish tension of will that he cloaked in the guise of social ideas was a result of the soulless spirit he had allowed to invade him.

6.8 Nocturnal darkness

In the final decisive chapter of the drama, the mental disruption in Judas increasingly reached a clearly pathological degree. Hallucinatory pictures concerning the Messianic future as envisioned by him and the possibilities of how to actualize such a future must have appeared before his soul. Much here suggests that once again he believed he could come closer to his goal with Pilate's help; that he used his personal connection to the Roman procurator in order to make any number of fantastic plans. From the words and demeanour of Pilate when Jesus stood before him as a prisoner, one could almost conclude that Judas had to a large extent been successful in winning the Roman for his plans. Perhaps Pilate's readiness to proclaim Jesus King of the Jews does in fact refer to the driving endeavours of feverishly impatient Judas.

For one who knows how to read the language of the New Testament, the Gospel of John gives a clear-cut description of the last decisive outbreak of Judas' pathology. It describes him in the end alienated from his own nature, under the influence one after the other of Luciferic and Ahrimanic beings. The Gospel allows us to view the plan of the betrayal as a Luciferic suggestion, a betrayal that tied in with the fantastic desperate thought of forcing Christ to do at last what he had all too long been hesitant to do: 'Diabolos [Lucifer] had already put it into the heart of Judas Iscariot ... to betray him' (13:2*B*). Judas was no longer in control of his actions and thoughts. Images and

---

* In a course he gave for teachers of curative education, Rudolf Steiner once spoke in a most instructive way about the pathological causes of kleptomania in children. There we find described for a specific pathological case what is here indicated in a more general form as a moral danger.

plans that were no longer under the control of his ego stole into his divided soul.

When, at the solemn gathering on Maundy Thursday, Christ had handed Judas the morsel, the ego-coherence of his being finally tore apart. 'Then, after the morsel, Satan [Ahriman] entered into him' (13:27*B*). In the one who now went out into the night, received the thirty pieces of silver and led the soldiers to Gethsemane, the actual human ego no longer prevailed. It had separated from Judas, even as the I separates from a human being who passes through death. Now it only appeared as if a human being were the subject in the drama of the thirty pieces of silver. The sacrament with its peace-bestowing blessing that would have been the remedy whereby Judas could have received healing, made his illness and schizoid mental state complete. Because he was too troubled to allow peace to be given to him, he now succumbed to the tragic condition that nowadays is customarily designated as a 'mental illness.'

Nevertheless, Judas followed the events with feverish tension. Neither at the Sanhedrin nor in front of the Roman procurator did matters take the direction he had counted on so certainly. Remorse shook him when, in the distance, he saw the Cross erected on Golgotha, a remorse that was like the first genuine reflex of his higher self. But since the link with the I had already torn apart, this remorse could only bear fruit in a later life. Then the seed would germinate which, through the encounter with Christ and life with him as a disciple, fell into the buried depths of the Judas nature. Now the Judas tragedy ended with the horrible scene of suicide, as would the life of Pilate a few years later. Judas went away and hanged himself in a gorge on the path that led from Jerusalem to Bethlehem.

Two deaths stand closely side by side. One was light-filled and radiant, although the sun turned dark during those hours. The other is like the shadow of this light. He who died on the Cross on Golgotha lived through the example of death for humanity, a death which at the same time was the victory over death. He who hanged himself in the gorge was the human being who knew not the art of dying, because he gave death too much power over himself.

In Christ and Judas, the pictures of the higher and lower I stand before us. In him who died on the Cross, the human being had completely turned into the vessel and bearer for the divine content. The human chalice of the earthly ego-form was filled to overflowing by the sun of the higher I. Death was utterly infused by the forces of life. What could death retain of its terrors? Christ's death was the free, redeeming outpouring of divine life into the kingdom of death. Judas, by contrast, was the human being who is unable to open up to a higher content; who turns rigid in the earthly ego-form. Did death not have to be victor over him who hardened and closed himself off against the forces of life? Judas lived and represented the tragedy of ego-endowed human beings who believe they are able to survive based only on earthly and human nature. Because he failed to recognize the one who was victorious over death, Judas was vanquished by death, a death that had been victorious in him even before he died.

Judas is the only one among the disciples of Christ who, in that incarnation, no longer shared in the events of Easter. He only attained to the view of the Crucified One whom he confronted with the sense of ultimately crushing guilt. Only one who learns to still the inner unrest through the divine power of sacramental devotion will penetrate through the Good Friday darkness of Judas to the light of Easter morning. Even Christianity will only cast aside the spell of Judas and thus become truly mindful of Easter when, instead of constantly turning its vision to the Crucified One in the awareness of human sinfulness and guilt, it builds the temple of the Sacrament which bestows peace and mercy.

7. The Easter Experience of the Disciples

7.1 Mount Zion and Mount Moriah

Experienced even in antiquity as the centre of the world, what was Jerusalem like when, though quietly and imperceptibly, it truly became the stage for events that are the central turning point of humanity's whole history?

Everywhere interspersed with and eclipsed by the ostentatious Herodian white marble structures, the jumble of houses covering Jerusalem's slopes at first glance showed no trace of the ancient archetypal character of the high-lying city. The colourful noisy din of nations and languages, of people speaking Aramaic or Greek, of Jewish priests and merchants, Roman legionaries and officials, Greek, Arabian and Egyptian travellers, probably distracted attention away from the inconspicuous figure at the heart of events. The indistinguishable sea of houses above the labyrinth of the many narrow and steep alleys and roads covered the city's two hills which, in their cosmic polarity, were really a picture of world duality.

If one looked from the Mount of Olives over the Kidron Valley to the city, one's glance was attracted in particular to the pompous Temple structures at the right, erected on the ancient sacred Mount of Moriah by Herod. One had to be sensitive to quiet unobtrusive things in order to become aware of the less built-up, overgrown part of Mount Zion, in the background at the left rising slightly above the city, so that it could be seen as holding the balance against the marble complex on the Temple Mount. Two thousand years earlier, the cosmic archetypes of the twin hills was still visible in clear outline. Then, Jerusalem was hardly a city. It was a quiet mystery centre containing only a few humble dwellings such as formed the surroundings of locations like these for teaching and worship. Separated by the deep cleft of the steep Tyropoeon Valley that ran from north to south,[75] Mount Zion, the hill of peace which, enveloped by cosmic benevolence, gave the city its name, rose in the west and the stern peak of the rock of Moriah, the 'site of justice,' rose up in the east.

The sharp contrast of the two hills repeated and mirrored the same polarity that manifested in the adjoining locations of Galilee and Judea, symbolizing and summarizing the history of our planet Earth. The paradisal sun element which, in Galilee, retained a larger — and in Jerusalem's Mount Zion a more concentrated — form, seemed like a memory of the celestial origin of earth and humanity, a memory transformed into an object of nature. Judea's rigid, lifeless lunar landscape, spread out in the stony Judean Desert and summed up symbolically once more in Jerusalem in the rocky plateau of Moriah, was an admonishing image of creation's cosmic descent into rigidity and the Fall.

In Abraham's days, the mystery site of the enigmatic priest-king Melchizedek* was imbedded in the miracle of Mount Zion. The centre of this quiet sanctuary on the southern part of Mount Zion was formed by the holy stone pillar, the menhir. The name 'Zion' *(tziyun* means 'erected stone monument,' from *tzawah,* to erect) is reminiscent of its placement there and the uplifting force it symbolized.[76] This may have been the very place where the underground temple grottoes were located that harboured the actual mystery centre. From them, the exalted priest-sage emerged with the sacred sun-offering of bread and wine to welcome Abraham who had returned from battle (Gen.14:18).

The rocky plateau of Moriah was the exoteric place of sacrifice that belonged with the esoteric sanctuary of Zion. There, on the ancient rock-altar, still visible today in the Arab Dome of the Rock on the Temple site, the burnt offerings were made to which even uninitiated people had access. There, anybody who wished to be admitted to the inner sanctuary of Zion and its community first had to undergo difficult trials. In the story of the sacrifice of Isaac which occurred on the rock of Moriah, a

---

* In earlier descriptions, it was explained that this mystery site was called the 'School of Noah and Shem,' because it was believed that, through the figures of both Melchizedek and the biblical Noah, the 'great Manu' could be discerned, the teacher of primal wisdom who had saved and brought the future-bearing part of humanity from submerging Atlantis across to the new world. See *Genesis:* 'Melchizedek.'

pictorial reflection of such trials can be recognized within the scriptures of the Old Testament.

A thousand years after Abraham in the Davidian age, Jerusalem presented a completely changed appearance. By then, it had turned into a real city. But the archetypes of the two hills on both sides of the gorge were still clearly recognizable. After David had gained possession of the city — the rest of the land had long since belonged to the Israelites — and after the Jebusite king had solemnly transferred to him the sacrificial rock of Moriah, the 'threshing-floor of Araunah,'[77] David built his royal castle on Mount Zion at the site of the ancient sanctuary of Melchizedek. In the western wing, he added a consecrated chamber designed to house the ark of the Covenant, the sacred altar of Israel. Taking the place of the tabernacle, it became a new one.

If we consider that in the ancient world people always adhered to the principle of erecting a sanctuary at the very location of an earlier one, we can assume that the chapel of David's castle, the humble predecessor of what represented the Holiest of Holies in the Solomonic Temple, stood at the site of Zion's sacred stone. Under David, silence prevailed around the stern rock of Moriah. Due to the fact that Mount Zion was the stage for that part of the ritual* which was conducted in Jerusalem, the mystery origin of Israelite culture with its proximity to the gods became evident once more. Having performed the preparatory washings at the Pool of Siloam where the Tyropoeon Valley merged into the Kidron Valley, lines of pious pilgrims, solemnly chanting psalms, ascended the steps that led them to the longed-for goal of their pilgrimage, the peace-bestowing sanctuary on Mount Zion.

You need only listen to the sound the name Zion makes in the psalms to become immersed in a whole sphere of grace and divine peace. Those who directed their glance and steps up to Mount Zion yearned for and were sure to encounter a loving, kind deity who related quite differently to humanity than did the sternly judging god of Moriah. Finally, however, in connection with an affliction visited upon the people in the form of a plague, the aging David received from an archangel who appeared to him

---

* At that time, the tabernacle with the altar of the burnt offering was still located on the ancient sacred hill of Gibeon, a few hours north of Jerusalem.

the inescapable spiritual command to transfer the sanctuary to the rocky bluff of Moriah and erect the Temple there. Full of deep, questioning sadness, David set out to obey the new expulsion from paradise and bid farewell to the beloved hill of divine peace.

Solomon actually implemented the construction of the Temple on the eastern hill of Jerusalem. For him, it was not hard to part from Zion. He sensed the dawn of a completely new age of free cultural development that would move outward. To him, the spiritual life of the past seemed even then to have become darkly superstitious and useless. He changed Jerusalem's appearance completely by filling in the ancient mysterious gorge that ran between the two hills. The archetypal character of the city became obscured. The accent of history moved from the esoteric hill of the sun to the exoteric hill of the moon. Overgrown by vegetation, it turned quiet on Mount Zion. David was buried in one of the ancient grottoes under the spot where he had once placed the ark of the Covenant. In time, the graves of the next ten kings of Judah were added. Like a silent memorial of the formerly mystery-imbued life, tranquil Mount Zion towered over the now dramatically expanding city. Increasingly, the number of those diminished who felt a sense of loss when they looked up to Mount Zion; who longed for the hour when the divine life lying dormant there would reawaken and David would emerge from seclusion within the mount and reveal the sun of Zion anew.

Severe storms of destiny passed over Jerusalem, as they did over Palestine generally. When the troops of Nebuchadnezzar destroyed the city, it so happened — as was the case during later destructions of Jerusalem — that the southern part of Mount Zion, the site of the ancient sanctuary, by and large was spared because the bulk of Jerusalem's houses had not extended in that direction. In the days of the Babylonian exile, on the other hand, along with the whole city, Mount Zion also became desolate. The tombs of the kings, from David to Hezekiah, in the Melchizedek-grottoes, succumbed to oblivion below the covering of green shrubs that grew there. And they escaped notice even when Jerusalem was rebuilt in the age of Ezra and Nehemiah. The city's focal point increasingly moved eastward.

After the battles of the Maccabean age, those in power

remembered David's tomb more frequently. But the reason was not that these rulers wished to restore Mount Zion to its former prominence. On the contrary, they had designs on the gold treasures that were presumed to be in the subterranean vaults. It was above all John Hyrcanus, son of Simon Maccabeus, who, led on by the Sadducees, secretly broke in, opened the tombs of the kings and seized the treasures. A few decades before the turning point of time, Herod the Great was the last to violate David's tomb. But instead of finding gold, he was frightened by fiery phenomena that blazed forth from the earth's depths toward him. When, moreover, the anger of Jerusalem's inhabitants was directed against him, the desecrator of the sanctuary, he had a splendid monument with four portals erected at the ancient holy spot over David's tomb so as to give proof of his veneration for David and Israel's past. When this structure collapsed some time later, many people may have viewed this as a sign whereby Herod's hypocrisy was made evident. We shall see that a pious community then took charge of the desecrated holy place and constructed one of the houses of its Order over David's resting place.

7.2 The location of Golgotha

We have reached the point in time when the archetypal character of the city became extinguished. More splendid than its predecessors, the Temple, newly erected by Herod, stood on the rocky hill of Moriah. The city covered everything with its noisy uniformity, even Mount Zion. Only on its southern part could a little of the old peaceful atmosphere still be felt.

Then, through a quiet, almost unnoticed event, yet decisively important for humanity's future, a place was newly inscribed in the spiritual map of Jerusalem: Golgotha. This location mysteriously emerged from obscurity. It was the place of execution where the gallows and crosses were erected. But, directly adjacent to it, a noble councillor owned a garden. In it, despite the sinister neighbourhood, he had the rocky tomb prepared wherein one day he wished to be buried.

Doubts have often been voiced whether the Church of the Holy Sepulchre, supposed to be harbouring the hill of Golgotha and Christ's grave under its two cupolas, really stands at the right spot. It is in fact hard to imagine that this site, nowadays hidden deeply within the labyrinth of alleys in the Old City, was then outside the city's gates and walls. Yet the place of execution could not have been located within the city. People therefore searched for Christ's actual grave further to the north in areas situated outside the present city walls — walls that were built later on. Yet proof that the Church of the Holy Sepulchre really stands on the actual rock of Golgotha can be ascertained in the immediate neighbourhood in an old turner's workshop filled with rubbish. It is truly incomprehensible why historians have not paid more attention to this evidence. There, in a wall, one can see a piece of the Herodian city wall and even the stones of the edge of a city gate. There can be no doubt that Golgotha, the place of execution, was in fact located about eighty to a hundred metres in front of this gate when the city as yet did not extend so far north. And we even know the name of this gate. From the descriptions given by Josephus, we learn that it was called the 'Garden Gate.'[78] Obviously, it led to an area that contained gardens among which belonged the garden of Joseph of Arimathea as well.

It is of the greatest spiritual-historical significance to recognize that, within the archetypal character of Jerusalem, Golgotha occupies a quite definite place. The long deep canyon, the primal gorge that divided the city into the two utterly different elevated areas in pre-Solomonic days, must have passed through the area of Golgotha. Hence, the ground between the rocks of cross and grave had not naturally developed but had come about through the building activities of Solomon. Proof of this can be found in pilgrims' reports, such as as the one by Antonius Placentus, that show how, far into the first Christian centuries, an open crack was visible in the ground next to the holy grave. It led down into a far-extending system of deep gaping clefts and subterranean gorges. It says that when one put one's ear to the crack, the rushing of streams of water in the depths could be heard and if an apple or another floating object was thrown down, it could be fished out later on from the water that emerged at the spring of Siloam. The actual wording of the report by a travelling companion of the martyr, Antonius Placentus (middle of the sixth century), is as follows:

> It is eighty steps from the sepulchre to Golgotha. On one side, you walk up the steps that our Lord went up for the Crucifixion. For even the spot where he was crucified can be seen with the traces of blood in the rock. Nearby is Abraham's altar; the one to which he came to sacrifice Isaac. There, Melchizedek likewise offered up sacrifice.* Directly by the altar is a crack in the earth. You put your ear to it and hear the rushing of streams of water. And if you throw an apple into it or something else that can float, and then go to the spring of Siloam, you will find it there. The distance between Golgotha and Siloam is about one mile, I believe ...[79]

Siloam is located where the Tyropoeon Valley once joined the bed of the Kidron brook below the southern edge of the city. Golgotha, on the other hand, was located high up outside the city's northern edge. One therefore had to walk down a long and steep path in order to follow the subterranean waters that flowed deep below Golgotha, finally emerging into the light of day at the spring of Siloam. Particularly around Golgotha and the tomb of Christ, the earthquake at Easter could rend the layers of rock and cause the earth's depths to gape open because here, barely concealed by human hands, the deep, primal gorge rent the city's features. Through the events of Good Friday and Easter, the midpoint between the ancient polarity of Zion and Moriah compellingly emerged. The cosmic signs, by which the otherwise quiet events were accompanied, evoked the approach of a force that, even topographically, transcends differences and can therefore unite the world duality and heal torn creation.

If one walked from the Garden Gate northwards out of the city, one stood at a primal, mythological spot. According to ancient legends, the tomb of Adam, the first human being, was located there deep within the earth. And there must have been

---

* It cannot be taken in the literal sense in this text that the sacrifice of Isaac and Melchizedek's offering are placed on Golgotha. What was divided onto the polar heights of the Temple Mount and Mount Zion, is here drawn together in the middle.

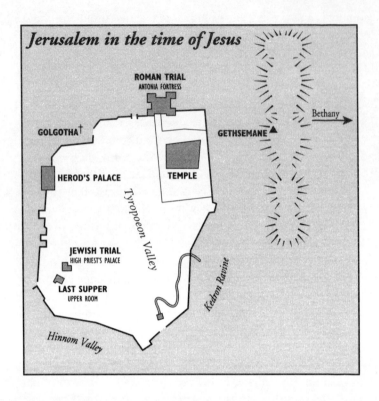

Jerusalem in the time of Jesus

people in Jerusalem who had an awareness of the special significance of this place. This is the only explanation for why Joseph of Arimathea constructed his garden and grave so close to the gruesome hill of the gallows. From the Garden Gate, one could glimpse two rocks. To the right, in the shape of a skull, rose the dark hill of Golgotha, the 'place of the skull.' It was the furthest outpost which the lifeless, lunar, stony world of the Temple Mount extended to the midpoint of the gorge. To the left, the rock into which the tomb of Joseph of Arimathea had been hewn represented the border of a green domain of gardens that possessed a particularly life-supporting element. Thus, they were actually designated as 'the paradises.'[80] Because of them, the sun-filled life sphere of Mount Zion extended to the middle of the gorge. The Cross on which Jesus died stood on the side of death; the grave that was rent open by the Easter force of Resurrection designated the shore of life even in Jerusalem's archetypal nature.

7.3 The house of the Last Supper

The events before and after the hour of Golgotha must be considered over and again from new aspects if they are to reveal even a little of the secret depths concealed within them. This is why the attempt ought to be made to follow them on the spiritual map of archetypal Jerusalem.

Burning with the fiery will of final, unrelenting determination, Christ had entered Jerusalem on the first day of that last week. His whole being was one of readiness and challenge for battle. He therefore went up to the Mount of Moriah and entered the precincts of the Temple. People were frightened by the flashing anger and noble sternness of his countenance. It was as if the forbidding deity of judgment who dwelt there was himself entering in human form. The tables of the money changers turned over; the money rolled over the tiles of the marble floor. In panic, men and animals took flight.

This scene is called the 'Cleansing of the Temple.' But it was not as if, cleansed of rubbish, the Temple could now be restored to its holy and solemn purpose. The essential effect that had emanated there from the Christ-figure signified more than a cleansing; it was a sentence of death. Henceforth, despite its Herodian splendour, the Temple stood there like a marked tree ready for felling. Along with the Temple, a whole world was doomed. Then came Maundy Thursday, the day of preparation for the Passover festival. And now the opposite event to the act of judgment — the cleansing of the Temple — took place in quiet fulfilment. Unnoticed by the world, the foundation for a new temple was laid.

The celebration of the Last Supper, held by Jesus among the circle of his disciples, established the sacramental environs that was to replace the cult of the Moriah Temple. And something of the patterns of providence and the guidance of history seemed to become visible which normally remain obscure. For, once again, the stage of events moved from the mount of stern judgment, where the old Temple still stood, to the height of peace, the ancient summit of Mount Zion. The expulsion from paradise, proclaimed by David and fulfilled by Solomon, was reversed. In the quiet room of the Last Supper's circle, which thereafter turned into the cradle of Easter-like life until Whitsun* and beyond, the miracle of Zion was renewed on a higher level.

According to the report by the Gospels, when Jesus sent two of his disciples ahead of him to Jerusalem and charged them to prepare the Passover meal, he indicated in a strange manner the house they were to find. In the Gospel of Matthew, when the disciples ask him, 'Where do you want us to prepare the Passover meal?' Jesus says to them, 'Go into the town, you know to whom' (26:18B). We sense that a secret is involved that is not expressed in words. Yet it deals with a connection to a person or group of people, a connection familiar to the two disciples. In the Gospels of Mark and Luke, the description of the house, of whose hospitality they are to avail themselves, is more pictorial but also more mysterious: 'Go into the town. There a man carrying a jar of water will meet you. Follow him, and where he enters, say to the head of the house ... And he will show you a large upper room which is furnished with cushions' (Mark 14:13f). At first glance, this indication sounds quite strange. Is there a prior secret agreement between Jesus and the host in the city or do we deal with the miracle of supernatural precognition and prophecy? Both would have to impress us strangely. We would either have to raise the question: Why such secretive behaviour? Or: What induced Jesus to resort to means that are reminiscent of magic?

In reality, the description of the house of the Last Supper must be understood quite differently. It is made in such a way that a specific secret is both revealed and veiled at the same time. In his interesting book, *In the Steps of the Master,* the British traveller of Palestine, H.V. Morton, makes us realize how he almost got

---

* From the reports in Acts, also affirmed by early Christian traditions, it becomes obvious that the experiences of the disciples between Easter, Ascension and the morning of Whitsun had as their stage the same room in which the Washing of the Feet and the Last Supper took place.

on the track of the secret. The passage about the man with the water jug had always puzzled him. He had been bothered by the question of how such an everyday, commonplace sight could have served the disciples as a sign. For it could have been possible that the disciples might encounter several men carrying water jugs at the same time. Then they would not have known at which house to call.

When Morton arrived in Palestine, he made an experiment. For days, he sat by a well to count the men who might come to fetch water with jugs. He wanted to see how frequently the image appears to which the disciples had been referred. Now, anybody familiar with the Orient will know beforehand the result of H.V. Morton's experiment. Nowhere will you see men fetching water in jugs in the Orient! While there are professional water carriers who fetch water in goat skins, only women are seen carrying water home in jugs from a well. After H.V. Morton had waited in vain for a man with a water jug, the question was settled for him. At least the image outlined to the disciples was not such a frequent sight that confusion would have resulted.

We have to go a step further in our conclusions. The image to which Jesus referred the disciples was by no means part of the daily bustle that reached a particular culmination on this day when Passover pilgrims flocked together in Jerusalem from all over the country. Rather, it clearly represented a part of the practices of a certain religious community, well known to anybody in that age, namely the Order of the Essenes. In fact, day after day before sundown at the southern rim of the city, an unusual sight could be observed. Carrying a water jug, a man in a white robe emerged from the city gate. In Old Testament times, this gate had been called 'Fountain Gate' or 'Water Gate' (Neh.2:14 and 12:37), but according to the testimony of Josephus,[81] it was then called 'Essene Gate.' Anybody who wished to fetch water had had to go out of the city here in order to descend to the Kidron Valley and reach the only flowing spring Jerusalem possessed. The gate was located in the immediate vicinity of the ancient holy site on Mount Zion where once the altar of Melchizedek had stood and later, under David, the ark of the Covenant. Now, a house of the Essene Order had been erected above David's tomb. Evidently, the proximity of the Essene house was the reason that the old Fountain Gate was now called the Essene Gate.*

For Essenes, the fetching of water was more than an outward chore. True to the order's rule, fresh spring water was needed for the solemn ablution of hands and feet, a cleansing conducted daily prior to the sacred communal meal in remembrance of the baptism. Since the Essenes disdained not just the status of the slave but also that of a servant in their communities,[82] the fetching of water as well as serving at table was handled in person by high-ranking members of the Order. Particularly on that Maundy Thursday, when it was a matter of fetching water for the holiest meal of the year, the Passover meal, the man with the water jug who emerged from the Essene Gate, went down into the valley and then, balancing the full jug on his head, returned through the same gate to the house of the Order where the brothers were even then gathering, may well have been one of the leaders among the Essenes in Jerusalem. We might also keep in mind that the water in the jug, carried by the man whom the two disciples followed, later on actually served for the Washing of the Feet carried out by Christ on his disciples.

The hieroglyphic picture of the man with the water jug thus conceals an important aspect of religious history. By recognizing it, we acquire a key for all the events within the apostolic circle, a circle out of which the first Christian life was born between Easter and Pentecost. The Essenes of Jerusalem, among whom may well have belonged personalities like Joseph of Arimathea, had recognized in Jesus of Nazareth the fulfilment of their Messianic longing and expectation to such an extent that they made the cenacle — the sacred hall of the meal in the house of their Order — available to him and his disciples for the important celebration of the Passover meal. So it happened that on the very spot of the ancient Melchizedek sanctuary above David's tomb on Mount Zion, Christ washed the feet of his disciples and offered them bread and wine along with the pregnant words: 'This is my body; this is my blood.'

---

* Today, the southern city wall demarcates the city further to the north; the southern-most part of Mount Zion with David's tomb and the Cenacle is therefore located outside the walls, not far from today's Zion's Gate.

236

The room of the Last Supper, the cenacle, enlarged during the time of the Crusades into a lovely, quiet, Gothic hall, is the one spot in Jerusalem to which the oldest, most uninterrupted and reliable traditions are linked. Even though the Arabs had turned the cenacle into a mosque, you could believe that here you were still encountering the soul traces of the sacred event which, continuing the streams of Melchizedek and Essenism in changed form, transpired in this room between Maundy Thursday and Whitsun. Under the cenacle, constructed as an upper room like all similar halls in Essene houses, the Muslims jealously guarded the rooms containing the entrance to the tomb of David and the other royal tombs. The mosque of David's tomb, located below, is considered especially holy and appeared to be used exclusively by certain Arabian secret organizations. For almost four hundred years, neither Christian nor Jew has been allowed in there.*

7.4 Maundy Thursday

Imagine that we were in the streets and alleyways of Jerusalem on the afternoon of Maundy Thursday. Every place overflows with the many thousands of pilgrims who have come here from all over the world. The crowding and clamour could be no greater. Then, shortly before six o'clock, as the sun is nearing the horizon, the clear trumpeting from the balustrade of the Temple sounds out far and wide above the din. It proclaims the start of Passover night and the eve of the day preceding Passover Sabbath. Within a few minutes the city has become silent. The streets and alleyways are suddenly empty. Everything appears to be enchanted. The people have all obeyed the strict rule of the festival and quietly gather in their homes around the tables for the solemn celebration of the Passover meal. Night falls, a night in which the angel of death and destruction goes about as he once did in Egypt prior to the people's exodus. He only passes by those houses where the door frames have been marked with the blood of an immaculate lamb. During this night, none would

---

* I am unable to say anything about the current state of affairs because I have not been back there since 1934. [Both the upper room and the Tomb of David have open to all since 1948. Editor].

dare venture out of the house. For they would helplessly be exposed to the angel of destruction. And so, in ghostly silence as in a cemetery, the city, fields and hills are bathed in the glistening, silver light of the nearly full Easter moon. In the homes, when the meal is finished, the father reads the ancient stories and tales from the Haggadah. Only when the light of day dawns once more does the spell lift. A reflection of the freedom and relief once experienced by the Israelites during their liberation from the Egyptian yoke passes through their souls.

In the cenacle of the Essene house, the spell of this night must have prevailed in even more intense oppressiveness. In actual fact, the disciples should have felt completely overwhelmed by all the gifts of grace. Did Christ not kneel before them in overflowing love and kindness to wash their feet? Did he not give up his very soul to them when he handed them bread and wine? But a dark pressure weighed down their minds. This was not only due to the presentiment of impending events. They had lived through such unimaginable events, events which in all their outward humbleness were so grand that their mental capacities were as if extinguished. What took hold of them was like a deep depression. And when, as family patriarchs were wont to do in other homes, Christ began to speak to them; when, as he had done earlier with the bread and wine, he now allowed his being to stream out overwhelmingly to them in the speech of the Johannine words of farewell, their hearts and minds appeared dazed. Only an occasional word of this holiest Last Supper instruction actually reached their ears as if from far away. A horror had penetrated them when, like a sleepwalker, Judas Iscariot had gone out into the night.

They were shocked when suddenly Jesus, too, rose, left the house and bid them follow him. Breaking the strict, ancient Passover rule, was he not straightaway going to meet the angel of destruction? In the glare of bright moonlight, in a world where, far and wide, no living person seemed to be about, they walked with him down through the broad white expanses of graves of the Valley of Josaphat, across the Kidron Brook to the slope of the Mount of Olives into the Garden of Gethsemane. Under these very olive trees, he had often gathered them together for special, intimate council. It was particularly frosty that night;

something of approaching storms was in the atmosphere. The disciples were no longer able to maintain consciousness. Even the three closest disciples, whom Jesus took with him further into the silent olive grove, succumbed to the strange overpowering faintness of the Gethsemane sleep. 'They had fallen asleep for sorrow' says the Gospel of Luke (22:45). They were unaware of Christ's superhuman struggle with death. Not fully in command of their senses, they fled when Judas appeared with the band of soldiers and Jesus was bound and led away.

In the cenacle of the Essene house on Mount Zion, from where they had departed earlier, most of the disciples came together again when midnight was past. At some distance, on the same path but somewhat more slowly, the group of soldiers followed. The palace of Caiaphas where the prisoner was taken was in the direct neighbourhood north of the house on David's tomb.

The place where the seat of the high priests was reputedly located is shown today inside a large garden which, together with its little church, is cared for by Armenian Christians. Here, the atmosphere that prevails in the quiet streets of the southern part of Mount Zion has remained particularly palpable. Many debates have taken place as to whether this is really the authentic location of Caiaphas' palace. The Roman Catholics especially have frequently contested the Armenians' claim to authenticity of the site because they in turn contend to be in possession of the dwelling of the high priests. This is where they built a pompous church to St Peter atop the remains of the tiny early Christian church, St Peter in Gallicantu (Peter at the Crowing of the Cock).

The arguments that were advanced against the Armenian garden appear plausible at first. The point was made that it seems odd that on Maundy Thursday, when his persecution was already under way, Jesus would have chosen a house for the celebration of the Passover meal that was located in the immediate vicinity of the main quarters of his antagonists. And it must seem even more incomprehensible that the disciples are supposed to have returned to the cenacle after their flight from Gethsemane. Would they not have run straight into those whom they were fleeing? If it then says that the disciples remained hidden for forty days in the room of the Passover meal, 'the doors being shut ... for fear of the Jews,' why did they not select a hiding place that was much further away from the house of Caiaphas? Why, of all places, did they proceed to the cenacle where their pursuers could look in on them through the windows? Lastly, it is hard to imagine how the events of Whitsun morn that reached far beyond the apostolic circle — events placed by both Acts and early traditions in the cenacle — could possibly have occurred without a disturbance in the direct neighbourhood of the high priest's palace.

Apart from the fact that these arguments would remain valid even if the house of Caiaphas was located where the Roman Christians would like to place it — that location being only two hundred metres further to the east — there is a sound reason for the authenticity of the Armenian garden. When, at the very site of the later cenacle, David erected the consecrated room for the ark of the Covenant on the western side of his castle, directly adjoining it on the northern side, and based on the original resolutions recorded in the Book of Ezekiel, the house of Zadok, the high priest charged with the ministry of the ark,* was built. As the ancestral house of their family Order, this structure was evidently held to be sacred by the Sadducees who were such proponents of the principle of tradition. It became the seat of the Sadducean council. It is exactly this spot where the house of Zadok stood in Davidian days which is shown in the Armenian garden as the location of the palace of Caiaphas. The monastic houses of the Essenes and Sadducees did not stand next door to each other by coincidence. The proximity of the cenacle and Caiaphas' house was due to a certain connection of cultural history. In the first house, Jesus had celebrated the holy meal with the disciples. In the adjoining one, a few hours later, he was brought before the Sadducean family council, presided over by the aged miser Annas, and subsequently the Sanhedrin.

Why of all places did Jesus and the disciples select the house located next door to the enemy's very centre as refuge from their pursuers? They certainly were not concealed there. But they were under the dual protection of a sanctuary and the Essene Order. They enjoyed the right of asylum available in antiquity to any

---

* Ezek.40:46: 'And the chamber which faces north is for the priests who have charge of the altar; these are the sons of Zadok, who alone among the sons of Levi may come near to the Lord to minister to him.'

persecuted person who stopped at a tomb or cultic room. David's tomb prohibited the soldiers from laying a hand on Jesus. Jesus could be betrayed by Judas only after he had left the house. At the time of the Caesarean persecutions, the catacombs in Rome likewise did not serve the first Christians as hiding places. The pursuers were well aware of the kind of gatherings that took place there below ground. But the catacombs were tombs. In their walls rested the bodies of the dead. The living were therefore under the protection of the dead. In the subterranean hallways and rooms, the Christians were safe from harm.

Picture once more the solemn circle at the table on Maundy Thursday evening. Peace and security by no means prevailed around it. Impatient hatred surged round the walls of the house. Their fanatical opponents may have even cast a watchful eye on them, all the while pondering destruction. Had the classic and dramatic greatness of the psalmist's words (Ps.23:5) not become reality here: 'Thou preparest a table before me in the presence of my enemies'?

7.5 Good Friday

The Gethsemane night, whose spectral cold air caused people to shiver so that even Peter pushed his way nearer the coal fire along with Caiaphas' servants, was replaced by a stifling sultry day. Even as the sun rose, its pale green light appeared as if through an atmosphere of death. When it turned dark around the noon hour, the atmospheric horror reached a high point. Obviously, this could not have been an astronomical eclipse of the sun which caused the light of day to dim for three hours. A total eclipse never lasts longer than a few minutes. But above all, it is only possible at the time of the new moon, for it occurs when the moon moves between earth and sun and stands directly in front of the sun. And it was full moon on that Good Friday.

The darkness at noon must have been caused by an extraordinary intensification of the hot sirocco-like desert storm called khamsin by the Arabs. This is a phenomenon that occurs regularly with unusual force in springtime. The storm carries along huge clouds of sand from the desert. They are not driven along the surface of the ground but high up through the sky. Finally, they can completely obscure the bright light of the sun. Then, even at noontime, it can become dark. Furthermore, the clouds of sand and dust high up in the sky cut off any breeze so that all living creatures struggle for breath. Merezhkovsky gives a vivid description of this unusual natural phenomenon:

> The cunning yellow devil of the khamsin is worse than the black storm devil. Sweeping high across the earth and hardly touching the ground, the wind from the Arabian desert whirls almost imperceptible dust clouds high up into the sky. One only senses them crunching between one's teeth; they weigh down the breath and inflame the eyes ... Over sky and earth like smoke from a fire, dirty yellow clouds swirl round and the red rayless sun hangs in their midst like a bloody sphere. Suddenly, nocturnal coolness is replaced by oppressive heat that feels as if it were streaming out of a glowing oven. An indeterminable odour of sulphur, asphalt and tar draws the air across from the Dead Sea ... Grass and flowers in the fields droop. Sheep bleat and cows moo woefully. Dogs wander around with hanging tongues; people are gripped by a feeling that is like a presentiment of impending, inescapable disaster. It is as if the threatening shadow of primal chaos and the coming world's end were moving across earth and heaven.[83]

Even though humanity paid little heed to the Golgotha Event, the cosmos gave it powerful attention. No coincidence but a most profound world necessity ordained that all creatures truly broke out in sighs and cries of pain when Christ hung on the Cross. As they had over the death of Baldur, so, too, over this death did all the beings of creation lament. A shriek tore through the whole configuration of earthly nature and made manifest the cosmic significance of what took place on the northern edge of Jerusalem. But it was not enough that horror up in the sky filled the atmosphere. As the women watched the gruesome heartbreaking course of the Crucifixion from the Garden Gate, and just when it then seemed that nature was trying to draw a protective veil before the horrible image, even though one woven out of ominous darkness, they were beset by yet another horror. The earth's depths responded to the atmosphere's lamenting cry: 'The earth shook and the rocks split, and the tombs opened' (Matt. 27:51f). So powerful was the turbulence of the elements that the Roman centurion who stood under the Cross recognized it to be a sign of the Crucified One's divine greatness (27:54). And everywhere in the city the most amazing supersensory experiences were evoked in people's souls: the dead moved about and appeared to frightened minds.

The earthquake was not caused by distant volcanic activity of the earth's interior. Its centre must have been right around the Place of the Skull itself. The titanic subterranean forces under the Tyropoeon Valley — forces that had once torn ancient Jerusalem into two parts and then, dormant, had been shackled by the filling in of the gorge — became active. In fact, to the great dismay of the people around Golgotha, the abyss opened as if to expose once more the ancient gorge.

The aftershocks continued even after the darkness had made way again to oppressive greenish-yellow brightness and the corpse of the Crucified One had been laid in Joseph of Arimathea's rocky tomb when night fell. On the following day as well, the heated rumbling dialogue between heaven and earth persisted. Finally, all the aroused activity of the elements culminated and concentrated in an unseen event, yet one that was the most exalted cosmic manifestation of the mystery that was taking place. Based on his spiritual research, Rudolf Steiner tells us that the earth opened up even under the rock-hewn grave on Golgotha and received into herself the already decaying and disintegrating corpse which had been taken down from the Cross.[84]

The author must admit that for a long time he felt that this disclosure by spiritual research was hard to comprehend. But when he made the discovery of the Tyropoeon Valley and its significance for the primal history and archetypes of Jerusalem (see *Kings and Prophets),* the idea that the ground under Christ's grave was torn asunder by the earthquake suddenly became much more graphic and plausible. In the end, it was in fact an outward confirmation of the description by Rudolf Steiner, a description attained by purely spiritual means, to chance upon the fact that, on Golgotha, deep cracks and splits in the rocky ground were traceable for many centuries.

People may easily be inclined to see in such a description a tasteless and forced explanation for the riddle of the empty tomb. They will go on thinking this way until a feeling is developed that, more than all other earthly happenings, the facts and events on Golgotha are matters that go beyond any sort of coincidence. In them, spiritual image and physical process are completely identical; even apparently insignificant details turn into evincing runes of destiny. Through the thunder and roaring of the elements, the earth, which is not merely an accumulation of matter but a soul-bearing entity, shared in a cosmic-divine dispensation. She received the body of Christ, even as she had received the blood of Christ that flowed from the wounds of the Crucified One onto the rock of Golgotha. The human being receives the body and blood of Christ in the form of bread and wine. The earth received bread and wine in the form of the body and blood of Christ. This most direct tellurian communion was the cosmic continuation of the internment begun by men. The deepest chasms of the earth were blessed and took in the seed of a new life.

7.6 Easter morning

We like to picture the early morning of Easter Sunday as the most beautiful hour of spring's miracle. We think of sceneries over which the fragrant breath of new blossoming life and the enchanting beauty of flowers are poured, landscapes covered by a million dew drops that glisten like precious gems in the rays of the rising sun. The first Easter morning, on the other hand, had nothing of this beautifying loveliness. When, before sunrise, the women were on their way to the tomb to anoint and lament over the body of Christ, they were surprised and frightened once more by a strong aftershock. The ground shook under their feet and boulders tumbled down around them. They even observed that the large stone that sealed the tomb in the garden of Joseph of Arimathea was moving. And at this moment — was it due to the shock or to the sun which just then rose and finally brought the three-day-long khamsin to an end — the light of a visionary experience was enkindled in their souls.

They beheld the otherwise invisible spiritual being active in the furore of the elements. The angel of the earthquake appeared to be moving the stone back from the tomb. 'When the Sabbath was over, in the early morning light of the first day of the week, Mary Magdalene and the other Mary came to see to the tomb. And see, there was a great earthquake, the angel of the Lord descended from heaven, came and rolled the stone away and sat upon it. His appearance was like lightning, and his garment was shining white like snow' (Matt.28:1–3). The great force of the event caused the guards at the tomb to fall to the ground as if dead. But to the women, fear changed to a comforting presentiment. If such powerful signs flashed forth at the tomb, then the death which had been suffered here was special and enfolded by an auspicious secret. And so it seemed as if the angel who appeared in the lightning and earthquake were confiding to their hearts the Easter-like intimation of resurrection.

When, in great consternation and excitement, the women were on their way home, one among them — Mary Magdalene — was granted yet another spiritual encounter. She had taken the peace-bestowing Easter premonition to heart most deeply. Thus, the growing presentiment was strengthened in her to joyful certainty. A figure appeared before her that she first believed to be the gardener. But when she felt herself addressed by him, she recognized in him the Christ.

Ordinarily, one thinks that Mary Magdalene's experience was the first encounter with the Resurrected One. It is important, however, to realize that, as yet, we are dealing with the preparatory act of the Easter drama, a drama that took its course outside, in the sphere of the aroused elements. Resurrection is more than immortality. It is a corporeal mystery. To begin with, Christ revealed himself to Mary Magdalene only in his immortal spirit-form. He still concealed from her the mystery of the resurrection body. With the stern words, *Noli me tangere,* (do not touch me!) he warned her off, though later he actually encouraged the disciples and Thomas to behold him physically by touching him.* What was experienced more than once in those days in Jerusalem in a frightening manner, namely, that the immortal being of one

---

* Paul, too, does not count Mary Magdalene's experience among the actual Easter encounters which he lists in precise order in 1Cor.15:5–8.

who had passed through death appeared to the living, was experienced here by Mary Magdalene in a stern yet also consoling and hopeful way when she met up with the spirit-form of Christ.

When the women brought the message of their unheard-of experiences to the disciples who were gathered together in the cenacle, Peter and John immediately proceeded to Golgotha. They did not walk, they ran hastily, for the question of what had happened burned in their minds. And then they stood before the tomb and looked in. They were not granted a supersensory experience as were the women. At this decisive moment, dependent on their earthly senses, they were confronted by a shocking riddle. The tomb was empty; the linen cloths in which the corpse had been wrapped were lying at the edge of the rock chamber as if flung there by whirlwinds. And then the disciples became aware of an unthinkable secret. Regardless of whether the fissure under the tomb was still gaping open or had closed again, Peter and John felt that they stood before the cosmic abyss, the dark depths of the earth's interior, which had just received the seed for a new world. In a physical image, the secret of Christ's descent into hell stood before their souls. But as yet these were only open questions that flashed through their hearts and minds. Would something now occur that would bring them the solution to the great riddle?

In the first act of the Easter drama, which took place outside in the landscape of Golgotha, the people who were involved were guided through one archetypal situation after the other. As yet, the joyous, beautific, redemptive content of the Easter event remained veiled. The experiences were trials of soul more than bestowals of gifts. The women walked over ground that shook under their feet. The two disciples stood at the abyss of existence with questioning minds. In our time, the number of people who feel the ground of their destiny shaking under their feet is growing; who face their life as if standing before an abyss. We might ask whether the first signs of a new Christ-presence may not be recognizable in this, as was the case then when the miracle of Christ's Resurrection was first proclaimed through such soul trials.

7.7 Easter in the Cenacle

The Easter drama leads to the actual encounters with the Resurrected One only by making the important turn from without to within. The scene changes between the first preparatory act and the one of fulfilment. In order to continue being spectators and witnesses, we have to leave behind the nature encompassing Golgotha — a nature in upheaval from above and below — and, though it too is surrounded by violence, enter the quiet, sacred, inner space of the cenacle.

As the atmosphere gradually calmed and settled back into its normal rhythm, the transition from outside to inside, from the elements' realm into the realm of devotion, occurred. This transition had a prelude in what befell two disciples who belonged to the larger circle of followers on the afternoon of Easter Sunday. They were walking through the countryside that was just beginning to breathe again after three days of being under the spell of storms and earthquakes. Their hearts burned with shock and agitation. The more they let the memory of everything they had experienced pass through their souls, the more urgent became the great puzzling question in their minds as to the being of Christ and the meaning of what had occurred.

Finally, the ardour of their question and memory drew forth the answer. They felt as if a third person were joining them who spoke to them and shed light on what was unclear. Intimations upon intimations were communicated to their amazed souls. When, from the hills they had traversed, they watched the sun sink in splendid radiance into the Mediterranean Sea, they had reached their destination. They entered their house and sat down to eat in an inward frame of mind. Then, along with the simple gesture of the breaking of bread, yet one carried out in pious remembrance, a bright light suddenly shone forth in the dusk. For an instant, the mysterious stranger who had joined them on the way revealed his countenance, a countenance that appeared woven out of glistening rays. And they recognized Christ in new, spiritual-corporeal form. Outside, they had merely received hints concerning him through the words they believed they were hearing. Inside, they encountered him himself and in the quiet everyday sacrament of breaking bread received the effects of his being.

When, in haste, they returned to Jerusalem and told the Apostles in the cenacle of the encounter they had been granted, it seemed as if that here, too, the fire of the actual Easter experience was being enkindled. The disciples had been sitting together until late in the evening in searching, questioning states of mind. Painful memories of an incomprehensible loss had passed through their hearts again and again. A dire spell that weighed them down would not be dispelled. The message from the women in the early morning and the report by the two who had run to the tomb had only served to make the riddles more impenetrable and heightened the agonizing tension. No ray of light had entered their struggling souls. Then, they darkly sensed a way. Only now, the frightening bewitchment of the elements seemed to cease for them. Earth's life, the gaping abyss, finally let go of them.

The room which they had occupied for days began to speak in its subdued inner language. Was not everything around them still filled by the memory of what had taken place there on Maundy Thursday? The images of the Washing of the Feet and the Last Supper once more stood before them so vividly that it seemed they did not belong to the past at all. With something like a faint shock, the disciples became aware only now of what they had experienced. When the Lord had given them bread and wine, had that moment not been the fulfilment of all that had been celebrated in the sacred meals of the Essenes? Was it not the fulfilment of the longing and presentiment which had always imbued their own pious breaking of bread? The secret of the table circle seemed to descend on them anew. And lo, the breath of sacramental devotion, which thus stirred their as yet spell-bound souls, evoked a figure whose fiery, radiant luminescence initially shocked them to the core.*

Was their circle now being invaded by one of the spectral apparitions that had risen from the graves of late during the earthquake and had suddenly upset the mood of the Passover celebration? Despite the august light in which it shone, the figure

---

* We follow the description of the Gospel of Luke (24:36–49).

had an indescribably merciful, comforting attitude about it. It appeared to be at pains to erase even the last vestige of fright from the disciples' souls. Like a living greeting of peace, a blessing went out to them from this figure. The radiant guest drew quite close to them as if he wished to prove through his love-enfilled presence that he was not a spectral ghost but a being arrayed in spiritual corporeality. And on his hands and feet at the spot of the Crucifixion wounds, they beheld a glow that shone with special warmth. They could not help but realize that they beheld this radiance not just with the organs of their half-ecstatic souls but truly with their earthly eyes. Although they themselves had not seen the Cross on Golgotha when the blood flowed from the now radiantly shining wounds, they began to sense who was standing before them. Yet their whole being still trembled with questioning anxiety. Only when Christ sat down with them at the table and when the mystery of the table circle was truly present again among them in the sacred breaking of bread, did peace and certainty fill their souls and they began to comprehend the miracle of the Resurrection.

7.8 The forty days

From then on, for forty days, the disciples were privileged to associate with the Resurrected One. With ever greater generous benevolence, the act of the simple sacrament of breaking bread and prayer called into their midst the one whom they had lost at the moment when they truly began to recognize his being. They felt as if they were in a dream. They could not grasp what was happening to them day after day. In a sense never before anticipated, the cenacle became for them a heavenly home on earth, a dwelling of God among men.

Often, when death deprives us of one who was dear to us, we are overcome by remorse concerning all that we failed to do with the departed one. Only now, his being appears clearly before us and likewise an image of the considerations we could have extended to him. But we stand at his grave, incapable of making up any omission, of undoing the wrong. The disciples experienced the unbelievable favour of destiny to have in their midst once more the one with whom they had moved about for three years, although they had not recognized him nor remotely done him justice. Their dream-encompassed remorse was not in vain. All that emerged in their recollection, the value and significance of which they began to appreciate only now, was newly bestowed on them as something of the present in the light of Easter.

The spirit-body mystery of Christ's presence is what distinguished the quiet events of the forty days in the cenacle from anything else that has ever occurred on earth. Prior to Golgotha, during special moments of revelation, a few of the disciples had been allowed to behold the spirit-form of the one who was united with them in earthly bodily incarnation: both on the Mount of Transfiguration and in the night of the Walking on the Water. The experiences of the Apostles who were gathered together now round the table in the cenacle were both an intensification and a reversal of those other experiences. Then they had beheld a physically incarnated being light up spiritually; now they encountered a spiritual being who, through his death-vanquishing, fiery intensity, made himself known to their earthly sense perception. He who over and again entered into their midst had vanquished death in such a way that he could remain on earth and continue in his activity even though he had passed through death. The sovereignty of spirit over matter attained by one who conquers death was his in all perfection. What took place during the forty days, therefore, signified the actual sowing of new seeds of spirit and life into the dying ground of earth existence.

The eating by the Resurrected One, described in the Gospel of Luke and difficult to comprehend for modern thinking, allows us to recognize that the miracle of Christ's spiritual corporeality was at the same time a sacramental mystery. It would be wrong if we were to imagine that the Resurrected One ate and drank in the same manner as incarnated human beings are want to do. The body in which he appeared to the disciples was not woven out of perishable substance as is ours, nor was it furnished with material organs. It was a spiritual eating and drinking, yet one that did intervene in the world of earthly substance.

Perhaps we can find a way to come closer to this mystery when we pay heed to a quiet soul process that should play a role in all human eating and drinking. The human element in eating and drinking depends on whether the meal receives something, albeit in an imperceptible yet genuine attitude of soul, from human beings before they receive it. Even if only a hint of wonder and thankfulness passes through our hearts and minds concerning the fact that although we, too, are merely creatures, we are allowed to receive the ministering service of our brothers and sisters of creation from the other kingdoms of nature, then the gifts on the dining table acquire a reflection of the human soul element. The more joyfully and naturally grace is said, the more it is a blessing that is received by the offerings of the meal before a human being receives them.

The highest intensification of this quiet secret of life takes place in the sacrament at the altar. There, the communion in which a person receives bread and wine is preceded by the transubstantiation in which bread and wine are the recipients, inasmuch as they become bearers of a divine force. This process of the blessing and transubstantiation which precedes human eating and drinking could be described in the sacrament as an eating and drinking of Christ. Bread and wine become the body and blood of Christ through this spiritual eating and drinking, even as food and drink become the body and blood of the human being through each earthly eating and drinking. And to spiritual vision, once it reawakens in humanity in the future, the process of transubstantiation at the altar will prove to be an actual incorporation of the earthly elements into the light-corporeality, present there, of the resurrected Christ.

A transubstantiation extending all the way to earthly sense perception, this was what the Apostles experienced day after day in the cenacle when the Resurrected One ate and drank with them. Once the secret and reality of transubstantiation is recognized and experienced again, a new comprehension for the Easter mystery will develop at the same time. It is only because the mystery of transubstantiation has for centuries been beset by theological discussions and disappeared from humanity's field of vision, along with the abolition of sacramentalism in much of modern Christianity, that the message of Easter has no more potency and the Gospels' Easter stories sound like fairy tales. A living and abiding in the sacrament, in the miracle of transubstantiation — this is what the disciples were privileged to experience for forty days in the cenacle. Their encounters and association

251

with the Resurrected One were a constantly renewed insight into the sphere of transubstantiation, made possible through a special dispensation of destiny. They watched the spiritual sun power in its very first cosmic spring activity, an activity that eventually is meant to transform the whole earth into a sun.

As he had done during the Last Supper on Maundy Thursday, conducted still on the earthly-human level, so now also, during the forty days of Easter when he was close to the disciples during the sacred meal, Christ spoke to them. In Acts Luke relates that 'for forty days he ... spoke to them of the mysteries of the Kingdom of God' (1:3*B*). The early periods of Christendom saw the source of all Christian wisdom in the wondrous teachings by the Resurrected One. In the gnostic circles, a whole body of literature existed in which the attempt had been made to record something of what the Resurrected Christ had said during those forty days to the disciples.*

One important theme of the Easter instruction — an instruction equal to an inspiration from heaven reaching human ears — certainly must have been that everything experienced in the past three years by the disciples was shown to them in a bright new light. Their memory, illumined as it was by the light of Easter, was akin to a sense organ that enabled them to accept the teachings of the Resurrected One.

In the four Gospels, we have before us the fruit of retrospection inspired by the Resurrected One himself. It is wrong to assume that the Gospels originated from ordinary earthly memory of eyewitnesses as a sort of report. They issued from the elevated Easter-imbued memory, hence from the speech of the Resurrected One himself. The more we are able to recognize this, the more will modern humanity acquire genuine access to the inspired character of the New Testament scriptures.

As a part of the divine teachings conveyed to the disciples in those forty days, the Gospel, too, was born out of the sacramental mystery of the Easter encounter. Our intellectualistic age merely

---

* The *Pistis Sophia,* a text written in Coptic, is one of the few fragments that has come down to us from this gnostic literature. [This comment was made before the *Nag Hammadi* discoveries. Editor].

wished to acknowledge the sacrament to the extent that it is possible to derive it from the Gospel. In reality, the Gospel arises out of the ritual, not the ritual out of the Gospel. Eventually, when Christian sacramental life will have reattained enough luminous power so that a continuing flow of what originated in the cenacle during the forty days between Easter and Ascension can be experienced in it, then, as was true in early Christianity, the hearing and reading of the Gospel will once more be a continuous communion and encounter with the Resurrected One.

The forty days in the cenacle were the fountainhead for the future out of which flowed the whole abundant stream of Christian life. At the same time, they caused the spell to lift from all the sacred contents of the past which were linked with this quiet spot on Mount Zion. From here, Melchizedek had brought forth bread and wine to the 'father of the nations.' In the same locality, extending beyond the time of his earthly death, Christ portioned out bread and wine to his disciples so that ultimately they were able to pass on this sun-gift to all humanity. Having ripened, what once had germinated only furtively now entered the world in open abundance. In ancient times, Mount Zion had been experienced as the height where the ark had always landed whenever a deluge inundated humanity and from which emerged the bearers of the future who had survived the perils of the age. It was believed that in this very place Noah himself had instructed a new branch of humanity after the end of the ancient world.[85]

The disciples must have experienced this Easter time in the cenacle as if it were once again the forty days which Noah had spent on the summit of the holy mountain, waiting for the Flood to recede, before he proceeded to till the ground of the new world. The cenacle was the new 'Noah's Ark.' And the miraculous effects of a peace-bestowing, divine-earthly power which the Apostles were allowed to experience must have seemed to them like a fulfilment of the presentiments which the dove with the olive branch had borne long ago to the ark. They themselves were now the bearers of the future; having been brought through all the storms and dangers by an especially merciful fate, they were supposed to begin the guidance of a new humanity, Ancient sacred Mount Zion was redeemed from its enchantment. Although as yet unnoticed by the world, there was the new temple and altar. The psalmist's longing for Zion once again had its fulfilment: 'Oh send thy light and thy truth, that they may lead me to thy holy hill and to the tabernacle of thy sanctuary' (Ps.43:3*B*).

7.9 Ascension

Forty days after Easter something happened that at first caused the disciples joyous amazement but then left them perplexed. Obviously, a number of contributing circumstances came together. The abatement of the persecutors' hatred and the arrival of a large group of friends from their wider circle induced the disciples to leave the confines of the cenacle for the first time in a long while. Even as Noah and his kin had left the ark after the great Flood had receded, so they now emerged from the house that not only had given them shelter and protection but also their lives' fulfilment. Breathing a sigh of relief, and as if they were wishing to see the world with new eyes, they climbed up to the Mount of Olives. Shudders of memory may have moved their minds when they passed through the Garden of Gethsemane. Once they had arrived on the summit where the large number of brothers joined them, they looked down on Jerusalem.

How many remarkable, deeply painful and elating events had recently taken place in this city! And when they again confronted the inconceivable abundance and depth of their experiences with questioning soul, lo, the Resurrected One was suddenly among them even as he had been among them in the cenacle, but in a much more luminous, mighty form. Had his presence, possible until then only in the quiet, sacred, protected inner space, grown so mature and strong that it could become reality even outdoors on the windblown, cloud-enveloped hilltop? Following the transition from outside to inside that had occurred at the end of the Easter upheavals, a transition from within to without appeared to follow. What did it signify? The presentiment of yet another manifestation, of something completely novel and unheard-of, shone from the figure of Christ towards the disciples. A promise and prediction seemed to light up before them and they sensed that they would have to be prepared for its fulfilment.

But they had barely caught sight of the glory that appeared before them when it disappeared once again as if a cloud were moving in front of it. An inexplicable feeling of loss and abandonment gripped their souls. And when, after their return home to the cenacle, they became aware that the Resurrected One no longer stepped into their midst as had been the case for forty days, their anxiety and confusion became still greater and plunged the disciples — who were in any case moving about like sleepwalkers — into a profoundly dark mood of dullness.

Actually, through their experience of what was later called Christ's Ascension to heaven, they had become witnesses of how the Christ being had taken the next step on the path that has as its goal humanity's salvation. Christ does not change the world from without through magic miracles. Instead, he moves from one transformation to the next with his own being and thereby brings the power and possibility of transformation into the world. After the Baptism in the Jordan during the forty days of the Temptation, he fought his way out of the unique condition through which he could have turned into a magician and miracle worker. He thus completed the process of becoming human, a brother to all humanity.

Similarly now, after the forty-day-long Easter period, he moved forward beyond the exceptional state he had attained by having gained victory over death. In a spiritual-corporeal form that still closely resembled the earthly human image due to the powerful after-effect of the formative force that had been acquired in physical-bodily life, Christ had appeared for a while to those who had been with him on earth and had opened their hearts to him. And he could have held on to this special spiritual-corporeality that was able to proclaim its presence to a select few, even to the point of sensory perception. But love for the whole of humanity drove him on. Once, he had sacrificed the special preponderance of the divine over the human element in his being so as to be fully man among men. Now, he relinquished the special predominance of his spirit over earthly substance. In order to be equally close to all human beings, he poured his spiritual-corporeal power out into the whole realm of the forces of earth existence.

As a rule, the form of the soul-spiritual entity of a human

being who has passed through death is dissolved after a period of time and expands into spheres remote from earth. He, over whom death, the great dissolver, had no more power, carried out his cosmic surrender to earth herself. The Ascension did not signify a separation from the earth in favour of a heaven beyond. The cloud did not lift him up to heights far beyond earth. It arose in front of him and was itself nothing else but the veil of earthly elements which, in the clouds, has its clearest symbol. The Christ being did not cease being present in earth's nature. But it had been so completely poured out into the whole of the earth's etheric realm that the light of its special perceptibility, with which the disciples had been allowed to associate, was at first extinguished. As with his Resurrection, so also Christ's Ascension retained the inner directional force that from the very beginning of creation had determined his being and his path: from heaven to the earth. Christ became 'the lord of the heavenly forces on earth'; through him, the earth turned into heaven. This is the meaning of the event of Ascension.

The mighty sacrificing self-transformation that the Resurrected One performed forty days after Easter was the transition from the unique spiritual-corporeal form to the state of spiritual-corporeal omnipresence. At first, the disciples could not follow him. They believed that now they had lost him completely. But then, after the fortieth day, quiet revelations did occur of which we presently have to speak. Through them, a first inkling of the miracle of Christ's omnipresent state penetrated the disciples' souls. They began to feel as if One who was poured out into all the earth's widths were beckoning them to follow him and cause his being to shine forth the world over. But, as yet, the beckoning call only reached their inner ear as if from a great distance. This continued until, on the morning of the fiftieth day, they were gripped by the roaring storm of a new inner certainty that came over them like a mighty sunrise.

7.10 *Pentecost*

It is very likely that the disciples, who were still guests in the house of the Essenes, celebrated the ancient holy festival of Pentecost together with the Essenes and in accordance with their custom. Since we have a description in Philo's *Concerning the Contemplative Life* that illustrates how the festival of Pentecost was celebrated in the circles of the Therapeutae and Essenes, we are able to form an approximate idea of how the circle of the disciples arrived at the significant moment when the miracle of Pentecost took hold of them.[86] The number fifty has always played an important role in religious Judaism. It designates the most significant stage that is attained in every case in a larger or smaller rhythm of time when seven times seven rounds, be it days or years, have passed. Just as every fiftieth year was celebrated as a year of jubilee, a great extended Sabbath, so was the fiftieth day. Especially the festival of Pentecost,* the fiftieth day after Passover, was solemnly observed. The evening before, following special ablutions and dressed in their white ceremonious garments, the members of the Therapeutic Order gathered in their cenacle at the table that also served as the altar of their ritual life. In four great phases, the preparation began for the dawn of the fiftieth day.

Those seated at the table were first served with the sustenance of the teaching. One of the wisest among the brethren read from the ancient sacred scriptures and continued the reading in quiet meditative instruction. Then, when night had fallen, the pious gathering caused an answer to arise from their hearts to the spiritual world, a reply to the word of God heard in human words. A sacred hymn was sung expressing their worship and surrender to the divine. Only then, did the actual meal follow. Now, the humblest offerings of food on the table were no longer of a merely earthly nature. The divine blessing was woven into them. Eating and drinking were sacraments. And then — midnight was long passed — began the part that in a special sense was designated as 'the holy night celebration.' Now, souls released their feelings of thanks; the divine enthusiasm of

---

*   The word, Pentecost, comes from the Greek word, *pentekoste* or 'fifty.'

communal contact with the spirit streamed through them all. Two choirs were formed, men on one side, women on the other. The ancient festival hymns resounded in solemn responses. Then came the moment when both choirs united in one and the harmony of men's and women's voices evoked the feeling of great human concord and communion. Drunk with divine intoxication — so Philo described it — the singing choirs began to move in a circle. And the ecstatic enthusiasm reached its culmination when the whole celebrating community came together in front of the windows that looked out to the east at the moment when the first rays of the rising sun appeared over the horizon. The jubilant hymn to the sun greeted the holy fiftieth day. It was Pentecost.

So, deeply moved, the disciples too may have been absorbed in the sight of the rising sun when the threefold pentecostal event came over them in the cenacle: the roaring of the wind, the flaming up of the fiery tongues and the miracle of speech.

Outwardly and inwardly, the first experience that had united them in the cenacle on Mount Zion had been immersed completely in the dusk of evening. On that Maundy Thursday, the night of Gethsemane broke in over the world and the souls of the disciples. The final experience in which the disciples took leave of the cenacle was outwardly and inwardly completely illumined by the radiant brightness of the sunrise. The portals of Pentecostal enthusiasm opened wide for the disciples and, through them, for the whole world. All that had come to pass between the eve of Maundy Thursday and the morning of Pentecost, protected as it had been by the room of the sacred meal, now appeared as the content of a momentous night rich in destinies and wonders.

A great awakening drove the disciples into a flood of light. The dreaminess that had enveloped their souls during the forty days and the dark dullness of the last ten days were illuminated and overcome by the triumphant sunrise. The events of the seven Easter weeks and, through them, those of the past three years could only now stand in full lucidity and distinctness before their awakened souls and loosen their tongues. Now, the spirited language of the first witnesses could cause the spark of the spirit to flash over to men and women of all nations and countries.

The transition from Maundy Thursday to the morning of Pentecost was strange indeed. Then, they still had in their midst him who, through his Incarnation, had been the fulfilment of the deepest longing of the previous millennia. Yet the heavy spell of sadness had burdened their souls. Now, they were left alone, orphaned, completely on their own, yet a jubilant joy broke forth from them that would enkindle a worldwide fire. How was this possible? He who, outwardly visible, had stayed among them as Lord and Guide, had returned to them as the inner guide. The flame-being, that for forty days had been in their midst in a spiritual-corporeal form and then seemed to disappear from them, blazed forth again in their souls. From within, they felt its power. It surged through their breath and they felt the wind of the spirit blowing through the world. It burned in their blood and they beheld the fiery tongues that descended upon them. It spoke in their speaking. The sound of enthusiasm lifted the division and confusion of languages among the nations of humanity.

The experience of inner guidance and the recovery of the Resurrected One in their own souls signified the ordination and apostolic mission of the disciples. Initiations and ordinations of priests in antiquity had all been based on the principle of rapture. In order to unite with the divine, the souls of human beings had been lifted out of their bodies and up to the deity. A new spiritual principle now took effect. Incorporation replaced rapture. Inasmuch as the divine descended to them, sank down into their being and took up its dwelling in them, the souls of the disciples were united with divine power and equipped with the shining force of the Holy Spirit. The ever-present state into which the being of the Resurrected One had passed on Ascension Day began to be realized in the disciples' souls through incorporation on Whitsun morning. Now a circle of men was capable of journeying out into the world. By proclaiming the Gospel and spreading the sacramental miracle of bread and wine, they were able to make the power and being of the ever-present Christ effective everywhere. The cenacle became the fountainhead of early Christian life; soon, its stream was to pour over all the lands and nations.

8. Simon Peter

8.1 The miracle of Galilee

The destiny of Judas, the Judean, only allowed him to participate in the Christ Event up until the hour of Golgotha. The sight of the Crucified One was the final moment for him. To him, the portals of the Easter mystery remained closed. Peter, who in this mystery stands as the representative of the majority of the other disciples and could therefore be described as *the* disciple, was led by his destiny in such a manner that he did not experience the sight of the Cross on Golgotha. Instead, it was possible for him with all his being to live in the Easter element and be gripped by the mighty wind of Pentecost. This corresponded to the nature of Galilee embodied in him.

The Galilean miracle is evident particularly at the Sea of Galilee. To this day, we encounter the soul of the lake most directly at the paradisal, beautiful spot on the northwestern shore that nowadays is called Tabgha or 'Seven Springs.' The city of Bethsaida, 'House of the Fishes,' Peter's birth and dwelling place and that of several others among the circle of the twelve disciples, was located there on the slope of the hill. The old tradition that Tabgha was the location of ancient Bethsaida has frequently been disputed. Yet, apart from the internal evidence, an observation by Gustaf Dalman, a scholar on Palestine, proves this.[87] Seven springs flow into the lake in Tabgha, something to which the modern-day Arabian name makes reference. The springs differ greatly from each other in temperature and mineral content. This area at the lake's shore is therefore unique, because the water attracts fish in a special way by 'its temperature and taste.' The name, 'House of the Fishes,' fits no other location better than this one.

Once a person has become aware of the cosmic polarity of the Palestinian landscapes of Galilee and Judea, it is incomprehensible why travellers and scholars have perceived so little of this contrasting nature and, above all, the wonder of Galilee that to this day becomes immediately evident. Such perceptions, moreover, have not been made fruitful for insight into early Christian life. The brilliant Frenchman, Ernest Renan (1823–92), saw the significant scenic contrast. But since he became immediately enchanted with Galilee's loveliness and henceforth looked only with antipathy and disdain upon harsh Judea, he lost sight of the important cosmic balance that prevails between the north and south of Palestine. He exclusively claimed Galilee for Christendom; saw the contrast between the New and Old Testament mirrored in the two landscapes; and did not notice that the true greatness of Christianity lies precisely in its synthesizing character that encompasses the opposites of Galilee and Judea. Nevertheless, we find passages in Renan's *Life of Jesus* that actually do approach the miracle of Galilee and, although in a quite rhetorical manner, throw light on the soul nature of Galileans:

> The complete lack of a feeling for nature, which caused a certain aridity, narrow-mindedness and roughness, gave Jerusalem's accomplishments a grandiose but at the same time dark, rigid and detestable character. With its pompous scholars, tasteless prebendaries, hypocritical and melancholic bigots, Jerusalem would never have conquered the world. The north, on the other hand, gave the world the naive Shulamite, the humble Canaanite woman, the passionate Magdalene, the good-hearted foster father Joseph, the Virgin Mary ... A charming nature helped create this attitude ... which gave all of Galilee's dreams their idyllic and attractive attributes. The saddest stretch of land in the world may well have been the surroundings of Jerusalem. By contrast, Galilee was a verdant, shady, cheerful region, a proper home of the Song of Songs and the odes by the beloved one. No other country in the world has mountains that exhibit a more harmonious shape and inspire loftier thoughts ... This easily contented life did not lead to a coarse materialism of its inhabitants, however. It gave rise to a sort of dreaming poetic mysticism that united heaven and earth.[88]

What H.V. Morton writes in connection with Tabgha-Bethsaida

can serve as an example of the more recent but rare travelogues which, even though they do not draw the correct conclusions from it, touch upon the difference of the two sceneries and the miracle of Galilee. While his other descriptions, their liveliness notwithstanding, stick soberly to outer facts, he felt urged to seek for a poetic, almost hymnlike expression to describe the metaphysical element arising from prenatal realms which he encountered on the shore of the Lake of Galilee, even though he stopped there only briefly. He compares it with the presentient faculty, so near to nature, that we still possess in childhood, a faculty akin to a memory of the celestial worlds from which we originate:

There is a state of mind for which there is, so far as I know, no name. It is not happiness, which is an active appreciation of things, neither is it contentment, which is placid and might be termed the evening of happiness. The only words I can think of are both so worn-out, debased and generally ill-used that they will probably make you smile. One is 'well-being' and the other is our old friend, 'love.'

Everybody can, I hope, remember a time in childhood when this state of mind lasted not for seconds but for days and weeks on end. Sometimes by an effort of the imagination one attempts to project oneself back into those shining moments of life when the mind, untarnished by sin and undaunted by Eternity, lived as the butterfly lives, searching for, and finding, only sweetness everywhere.

In those days the earth and the flowers smelt more richly and the sun seemed brighter than it is today; the rain, the snow and the mist were enchantments, but we were unconsciously a part of the visible beauties which surrounded us. Life is to most of us a gradual growing-away from this enchantment. But amid the million trials and difficulties of life that can harden and embitter it is possible now and again to recapture fractional seconds of this earlier world: so momentary are they that one is left wondering whether they ever happened, or whether they may be a stray memory of some other existence.

> When I awakened in Tabgha on the first morning and looked at the Sea of Galilee, I felt such an unutterable sense of peace and so great a detachment from the world that I might have been Adam gazing with wonder at the Garden of Eden.[89]

In Morton's book, the polarity between Galilee and Judea is referred to several times (for instance, on pp.175–78). Mainly, however, he cannot do enough to describe the miracle that surrounds the Sea of Galilee: 'In its solitude, the Sea of Galilee emits a special peace and beauty that surpass anything else in Palestine' (p.183). 'Peace hovers over the lake like a blessing; the peace of silence, of solitude, of memory' (p.186). 'Of all the locations I know, the Sea of Galilee is the one where Christ's spirit is still noticeably present' (p.230).

Not only in an emotional and poetic but in an exact etheric-geographical sense, it is correct to speak of traces of a paradisal-cosmic element that has survived in Galilee as if from pre-physical, sun-enfilled primal times of our planet Earth.[90] Primal, cosmic recollections of the times before the 'Fall' prevail here and address in human beings the delicate echoes of the prenatal heavenly sphere that make up the magic of genuine childhood.

8.2 Peter the Galilean

Men like Peter and the other disciples from the Sea of Galilee, who were thus imbued with the nature of their Galilean home-land, are clearly distinguished from Judea's inhabitants. Nothing was more alien to their minds than the abstract intellectual consciousness of a typical Judean — a consciousness estranged from nature. Still partially encircled by the dream of humanity's childhood, their souls lived intimately enveloped in the realm of the elements and nature. Particularly in Peter, the Sea of Galilee in its cosmically peaceful surrender as well as its dynamically upsurging force appeared to have taken on human form. And the name 'rock,' given him by Christ, points to an essential connec-tion of human nature with the life realm of elemental forces, similar to the name 'Sons of Thunder' that Christ ascribed to the two brothers James and John, the sons of Zebedee.[91] Due to his closeness to nature, Peter was really more pagan than Jewish and may well have viewed Jerusalem and the official religious life cultivated there with a certain reservation.

In Peter, the fisherman from Bethsaida, the primal beginnings of humanity resounded as they did in the shepherds of Bethlehem. As wind and clouds moved over the lake, so cosmic intimations of supersensory elements passed through his soul. It nourished his heart and mind to be living together, intimately and humbly, with the realm of etheric forces in nature, with twilight, night and dawn that reveal their essence particularly at the Sea of Galilee. In regard to his consciousness, Peter was not a modern man. He still had a share in the ancient spirituality in which an earlier humanity had dwelt. What Renan calls '... a sort of dreaming poetic mysticism that united heaven and earth,' was actually an essential aspect of Peter's consciousness. As a Galilean, Peter harboured vestiges of the old natural clairvoyance in his being.

Peter represents the archetype of a strong, natural piety within the events that surrounded Christ. Accompanied by dreamy clairvoyant vision, religion as an inborn soul force was the last remaining metamorphosed form of sustaining union with the spirit, a union in which humanity lived and moved during their childlike beginnings devoid of egohood. Once, every human soul was intimately united with the divine, sheltered in the womb of the gods. A distant memory of this lives on in us, and along with it the longing to restore and reestablish the bond that has long since been cut for the sake of human egohood and freedom. Akin to homesickness, this yearning memory is basically the nature of religion. And in the literal sense of the word, *re-ligio* means nothing else but 'reunion.' In Peter, the soul legacy of ancient union with the spirit was still strong. This was what caused him to be the bearer of a quite elemental piety. Yet it also drove him to the great fluctuations of his inner destiny, fluctuations through which he penetrated to full ego wakefulness late in life. While Judas, having already forfeited his closeness to the spirit, was driven on from one tragic betrayal to the next, Peter had to progress from one conversion and awakening to another.

Nevertheless, the lives of Peter and the other Galilean disciples were by no means determined merely by the quiet humbleness of a fisherman's existence. As its name affirms, Galilee was 'the land of nations.' Unlike Judea, it had never been the base of a uniformly concentrated Judaism. At all times, it was suffused by a lively mixture of nations and cultures. And the idyllic quiet of this fishing village notwithstanding, Bethsaida was a lively transit point for travellers, pilgrims, caravans and armies. It was here that the ancient roadway that connected Babylonia, Assyria and Syria with Egypt, the *Via maris,* touched the shore of the Sea of Galilee. Even today, when you sit at the beach of Tabgha in the evening or at night under eucalyptus trees and dreamily gaze out across the lake, you can watch how camel caravans from far away pass silently by. It is as if the old 'path of the sea,' some sections of which no longer coincide with any streets of today, had been deeply ingrained in the instinct of the animals and their drovers. In former days, a worldwide current passed through the two adjacent towns of Capernaum and Bethsaida.

Peter, Andrew, Philip, as well as the other pious fishermen of Bethsaida did not share in their era's scholarly erudition. Nevertheless, apart from their bilingualism conditioned by Hellenism (they used both Aramaic and Greek as their spoken language), a quite definite, farsighted erudition must have been cultivated in their circle. We probably have to imagine that, either because of their own ancient traditions or because they had been instructed by travelling brothers of the Essene Order, these fishermen formed fraternal groups in which they were devoted to a form of Messianic piety. The colourful traffic that pulsed through their little town may frequently have brought brothers and friends, who shared in their Messiah expectation, to their gatherings from countries all over the world. And perhaps it frequently happened that, driven by his innermost impulse of heart, Peter in particular began to speak when such a group of 'quiet ones in the land' were together in one of the fishermen's huts of Bethsaida.

8.3 Peter and John the Baptist

The first great change entered Peter's life when news of the appearance of John the Baptist spread like wildfire throughout the land. The Messianic spark of the Baptist's teachings powerfully aroused the circle of devout fishermen at the Sea of Galilee.

Although Judea normally did not attract them and they often may have stayed home even at Passover time, when the large crowds of pilgrims streamed towards Jerusalem from everywhere, this time they were driven southward with irresistible force. Most likely along with a whole group of like-minded brothers, Peter, who was then in the prime of life, left behind the fishing vessels of Bethsaida and departed for an encounter with John the Baptist.

The scenery where Peter finally joined up with the flock of John's disciples formed a sharp contrast to his native land. Even the external surroundings in which he now found himself had to awaken and jolt him out of Galilee's paradisal dream enchantment. An infernal world of death had taken the place of the ethereal life sphere of home. A sobering that equalled an expulsion from paradise would have overcome Peter's soul if the words and baptism by John had not given the inner awakening occurring in him a spiritual direction. The Messianic tension emanating from John carried the fishermen from Galilee along, particularly as they met this tension with their inborn clairvoyant faculty. When they submitted to the effects of John's word and received the baptism in the Jordan, visions filled with presentiments of the Christ being's approach and the mighty turning point faced by humanity must have lit up in the souls of the 'men from Galilee' like flashes of lightning.

Eventually, the Baptist referred them again and again to the Other who was present so inconspicuously at all the events and yet was obviously surrounded by a mystery. The boundless love and prayerful reverence that John showed the Other passed over to Peter and those who had come with him. Again it was their clairvoyant ability that interpreted for them the puzzling indications given by the Baptist. Nevertheless, they were far from actual recognition of what lived in Jesus of Nazareth. A questioning and at the same time prophetic wonder filled their hearts and bound them together in a quite novel way. Even to those who had been close before, it seemed as if they were only now rediscovering each other as 'long-lost brothers.' The Galileans came together in Judea, not merely because of the influences of their commonly shared home but because of the dimly sensed spiritual destiny hovering over them. And so a group formed among John's disciples that in the majority consisted of Galileans, though it also included men from Judea. The great difference in consciousness was bridged by a unifying destiny secret.

8.4 The disciple of Jesus in Galilee

Events brought it about later on that Peter and his friends returned to their Galilean home. Once again, they pursued their fishermen's trade. But could they still be content in this work as they had been before? The overwhelming experiences occupied their minds even more because they felt confronted by the greatest riddles. Every time they went out on the lake in their boats, their souls, too, left the shores of the purely physical realm and they found themselves gliding on the sea of reminiscences. The hope that the nets they had cast might yield a good catch became instinctively linked with the yearning to be allowed a relevant catch with regard to images that would bestow clarification.

Now that they merged into the world of Galilee with transformed souls, earthly thought-images combined with heavenly archetypes in a novel way in their minds. Belonging simultaneously to two worlds, the visionary aspect of the Galilean miracle was now realized in them in such a way that they became as if enveloped in a spiritual surge of images. And so, Peter and his companions believed they were beholding a vision that approached them directly out of spiritual worlds when one day — they were sitting in their fishing boats on the beach or near the shore — Jesus of Nazareth walked along by the lake and bid them follow him. This may have been at Whitsuntide of that year. If they now left behind their fishing trade for good and obeyed his call, they did outwardly in the physical realm what their souls had done long ago.

Galilee found its fulfilment in the inconspicuous journeys that now began. Through them, the circle of Apostles formed more clearly around Christ. As if they were travellers of two worlds, the fishermen-turned-disciples went their way. It was a great gift of providence for them that the divine being who had become man, whose closest witnesses they were allowed to be without clearly recognizing this fact, also began his earthly journey in Galilee. Within this scenery, where reminiscences of earth existence's primal sun-beginnings seemed to be preserved, the Christ started out on his mission as if, one more time, he wished to recapitulate humanity's whole evolution. And round him he gathered those in whose souls also lived a resonance of the primal beginning in the form of a fully matured ancient spirituality. The Galilean disciples were privileged to receive Christ into their innermost core of soul and to walk with him.

The death of John the Baptist brought about an abrupt end to this blissful period. The disciples had to take a further step in their inner development. Yet, in so doing, they were still allowed to remain in the sphere of their native region. On their own, they moved in pairs through the land and were astounded by the healing, soul-transforming effects they were allowed to carry out through the forces that became available to them from another world. When Jesus finally called them together once more in Bethsaida and when the grail temple of the miraculous Feeding appeared in its universal greatness in their visionary souls, they began to sense the apostolic impulse and mission that was to blossom forth one day from their destiny as disciples.

Peter, along with Andrew, Philip and the other former fishermen and companions, must have recognized the most auspicious act of providence in the fact that Bethsaida became the scene of this prophetic spiritual event. Their homeland received a blessing that lifted the spell of the mystery slumbering in this region. In a new sense, Galilee became 'the land of nations' when future humanity appeared in the image of the Five Thousand. In Galilee, a fountain began to flow; from its stream, all nations would drink one day. And at the moment when, during the stormy night after the miraculous Feeding, Christ's spirit-form appeared to the disciples walking on the water, did the Sea of Galilee not receive the same blessing? Over the waters that are the purest earthly reflection of the prenatal world, did not a being enter earthly existence more clearly, a being whose world-historical, germinating power would be communicated from there to the whole of humanity?

When Christ began to travel about again with his followers, a new tension imbued the Galilean journeys. Again and again, Peter was carried aloft to blazing heights of enthusiasm by his elemental temperament, only to be cast down again into the vexation of disappointed expectations. He awaited the great Messianic miracle that he may well have pictured as an overwhelming outpouring of spiritual worlds. But just when he thought he could decipher indications of the beginning of God's kingdom from the marvels of living and working together with Christ, and was gripped by the stormy enthusiasm of acknowledgment, the reticent silence prevailed once again which he confronted each time with incomprehension. So, too, in the night of the Walking on the Waters, great depression and loss of momentum had come over him following a powerful surge of soul.

The most beautiful fulfilment of the Galilean miracle occurred on Mount Tabor, a hill that with its spheric shape appears as if heaven has become visible on earth. There, before Peter and the two other intimate disciples, Christ manifested in his spiritually transfigured corporeality, prophetically pointing to the Easter mystery. When they beheld him thus, the flower of Galilean vision opened in the hearts of the three disciples more wondrously and edifyingly than ever before. And when Peter referred in the Letters that are included in the New Testament to the hour when 'we were with him on the holy mountain' (2Pet.1:18), the unearthly grace and beauty of the experience resonates in these simple words.

When the images and words of the Tabor event still reverberated in Peter's soul, a quite unassuming scene took place, a simple conversation, in which Peter unintentionally became the spokesman for the apostolic circle and was assigned a leadership role among the Twelve that was fraught with consequences. Up in the northern Palestinian region at the foot of the majestic snow-covered mountain range of Hermon, Jesus and his disciples passed through the newly founded city of Caesarea Philippi. Perhaps they had just arrived in front of the portentous marble temple that Herod the Great had had erected in honour of the God-Emperor Augustus at the spring of the River Jordan. Over its portal an inscription in golden letters stated that Augustus was the Son of God. Jesus then asked the disciples who people considered him to be. He received a number of answers. Finally he asked, 'But who do you say that I am?' He had hardly posed the question when from Peter's soul the answer burst forth intuitively: 'You are the Christ, the Son of the living God.'

This was an inconspicuous yet world-historical moment. The temple inscription proclaimed the mighty Caesar in Rome to be the Messiah. And at the very same site, the fisherman from Bethsaida uttered the words by which the Nazarene, unnoticed as he was by the world, was for the first time designated as the divine being who had become man. The golden letters of Herod were in error; the confession of Peter expressed the great world-transforming truth. Peter's words had not sprung from human thought and perception. They were the most beautiful, ripest fruit of the clairvoyant consciousness which the nature of Galilee had bestowed on men. An intuitive illumination had flashed up in Peter. Out of it, he had uttered such words.

8.5 The disciple of Jesus in Judea

With the essential Christ perception which had found expression in Peter's confession, the mission of Galilee had been fulfilled. Farewell had to be bidden to the paradisal land of childhood. Without delay, Christ began to speak to the disciples about the direction he would have to take now, namely the one 'up to Jerusalem,' where he would have to pass through all the dark terrors of suffering and death. During the stern words of the first proclamation of his Passion, Peter's whole nature resisted and rebelled against this: 'Lord, do not allow this to happen to you' (Matt.16:22B). He had been lifted to the very epitome of blissful illumination of heart and soul. Suddenly he had been filled by the certainty that he belonged among the disciples of the divine Messiah who had been sent by God. He had believed that the powerful, redeeming spirit-outpouring was imminent which would cause the paradisal miracle of Galilee to pass on to all the world and humankind. What strange words was Jesus uttering now? It would cast him out of all the heavens if the shadow of Judea would be triumphant and, through the martyrdom and death of the life-bestowing One, would try to foil the start of God's radiant kingdom. The man from Galilee remonstrated against Judea with all his passionate nature. He who had just been described as the main support and rock-solid foundation for the Messianic humanity of the future had to experience the harshest rejection, for the spirit of deception spoke out of him: 'Get behind me, Satan!' And they proceeded on the gloomy way to Judea. Peter, too, had to take this path. There followed the second decisive journey to Jerusalem in Peter's life. Would he be up to the test? Would he even find his way now that he had been driven from the paradise of his Galilean homeland.

The path led from the blessed land of dreams to the tough land of wakefulness. Peter had to struggle to a completely new level of his consciousness in order, without losing all that he had experienced at the lake and on the mountain, to make the transition to the wasteland. As yet, he was not capable of the great ego-filled awakening expected of him. He did not pass the test. In Judea, he lacked the ego-strength to remain at the height of the Galilean experience. Instead of struggling through to greater alertness, his consciousness diminished. The same three disciples, who on Mount Tabor in Galilee had been alert witnesses of the Transfiguration, in Judea on the slope of Mount of Olives, succumbed to the darkness of the Gethsemane sleep. Peter, the one who in Galilee could profess: 'You are the Christ,' in Jerusalem spoke the words of denial: 'I do not know the man.'

Even as a fish cannot live when it is thrown out of its element onto dry land, so Peter's soul could not maintain its consciousness when the stage of events moved outwardly and inwardly so inexorably from Galilee to Judea. An overall diminution of consciousness now replaced the elevated experiences of Galilee. Peter still took a lively emotional interest in all that happened. But he resembled more and more a sleepwalker who in his actual being is absent. During the same decisive days when Judas Iscariot became caught up in the tragic crisis due to having become hardened in his merely earthly egohood, Simon Peter also had to pass through his most difficult trial, a trial due to the weakness of his ego's formative force as opposed to the powerful vacillations of his natural temperament.

During the spectral night of trials between Maundy Thursday and Good Friday when Judas had departed after he had partaken of the meal to carry out his betrayal, Peter's soul was once more shaken by a volcanic rebellion. It was expressed in his fierce avowal of faithfulness unto death and his militant intervention when he assaulted the soldiers with his sword. But this was followed by the fall into the soul-faintness and depression of the Gethsemane sleep. Even as Judas, the Judean, had become a traitor because of his tragic hardening of self, so Peter, the Galilean, became a renouncer through his tragic weakness of self.

He truly no longer knew what was happening around him; he no longer recognized the one through whom, a short while ago, he had beheld the radiant Christ-being shine forth. Not out of cowardly untruthfulness but because of a fateful failing of consciousness, Peter said: 'I do not know that man.' When the sun and atmosphere all around turned dark at noon on Good Friday, the outer sense world assumed the same condition to which Peter's soul had already succumbed. The night that held him under its spell was so dense and long that he slept through all that occurred on Golgotha. Peter never saw the devastating image of the crucified Christ dying on the Cross. The death of the One sent by God, a death against which he had rebelled because he had been unable to grasp such a thought, took its course without Peter being able consciously to share in it. Peter's consciousness, sustained as it was by ancient forces of devout exultation, also had to pass through a death when Christ died. It had to go through a final vanishing point so as to reawaken slowly in the light of Easter, finally to rearise with Christ.

8.6 The inner Galilee

In a mysterious way, the pendulum of Peter's destiny swings back from Judea to Galilee. But whereas Peter had outwardly returned to his Galilean homeland after his pilgrimage to John the Baptist, now the sphere of Galilee received the dream-enveloped one even though he never left Jerusalem. An inner Galilee arose for Peter and the other Apostles in the remarkable forty days they spent in the cenacle on Mount Zion. The summons of the Resurrected One that the women delivered to the disciples: 'Behold, I will go before you to Galilee; there you will see me, as I have told you,' was not meant in an outward sense but referred to the soul level. In order to comply with it, the disciples did not have to cover an outward distance. The designation, 'the little Galilee,' which has survived to this day in Jerusalem for the grove on the summit of the Mount of Olives where, according to the traditions of the Eastern Church, the Apostles beheld the Resurrected and Ascended One, can equally and with greater justification be applied to the cenacle. For it was most likely in the cenacle that the Easter encounter took place that is transposed by the imaginatively formulated epilogue of John's Gospel to the shore of the Lake of Galilee.

Inwardly, the miracle of Galilee, the life sphere of the lake, was present in the apostolic circle when the Resurrected One appeared in their midst and conducted the sacrament. A fountain of life sprang up right within Judea, the scenery of death. The great world contrast that was cosmically symbolized in the two Palestinian landscapes was joined together by the Easter events in a higher unity. When Peter and the other disciples beheld the spiritual-corporeal figure of the Resurrected One, what they had experienced in the blessed world of etheric forces on the Sea of Galilee during the night of the Walking on Water and on the mountain at the hour of Transfiguration was renewed and elevated to a higher stage amidst the lifeless world of Judea.

It had been a great good fortune for Peter that Christ had started on his earthly course in Galilee. It was a still greater gift of destiny that the Easter events, even though within Jerusalem's territory, a region alien to his nature, caused a sphere to come into being that was familiar and in accordance with Peter's nature and etheric soul faculty of perception. Although he had denied him, the Resurrected One tangibly came to meet him. In a profound dream, from which he woke only slowly, Peter was allowed in the cenacle to explore the inner Galilee and on a higher stage rediscover the secret of his homeland.

Moreover, the special relationship in which Peter confronted the sphere of the Easter encounters found expression in the fact that he was the first disciple who was privileged to receive an actual impression of Christ's Resurrection. When the two disciples from Emmaus arrived in Jerusalem on the eve of Easter Sunday, they were greeted by the Apostles gathered in the cenacle with the exclamation: 'The Lord really has risen and has appeared to Simon!' (Luke 24:34). Similarly, in listing the Easter encounters, the first that Paul mentions is the one which was experienced by Peter (1Cor.15:5). A dense veil of mysteries surrounds this first glimmer of the Easter light witnessed by

Peter. Nowhere in the Gospel are we told where, when and how it took place.

There does exist a tradition outside the Bible, recorded in the medieval *Legenda Aurea*.[92] It contains a most plausible element in its whole context of events and plays an important role in regard to Jerusalem's topography. We are once again led to the events of Maundy Thursday night. When, after the denial, Peter felt the stern, woeful glance of Christ resting on him, he was struck to the very core of his being. From the very depths of his soul, tears of remorse arose, the first sign of an initial awakening. Nevertheless, as if sleepwalking, he left the courtyard of the Sadducean dwelling and approached the edge of Mount Zion. There he hid in a grotto leading far into the mountain's interior, as if his angel had guided him. Because Peter heard the repeated cockcrows from there, that renewed the tiny spark of waking in him along with the abysmal sense of remorse and shame, the grotto was held to be sacred in early Christendom. A little church was built over it and named St Peter in Gallicantu, or 'Peter at the Crowing of the Cock.' It is the same location where today's Roman Catholics — being of the opinion that the palace of Caiaphas stood there — have erected their pompous Peter's Church. In reality, we are most likely dealing with the cave entrance to the ancient subterranean grottoes in which the mysteries of Melchizedek had their seat and where, later on, David and the succeeding kings of Judah were interred.

For three days — as long as Christ lay in the grave — Peter is supposed to have remained in this grotto in utter contrition until the Resurrected One appeared to him at sunrise on Easter. While the earth shook and rumbled, he dried his tears and filled his heart with consolation. Then, early in the morning, Peter supposedly went on his way to the other Apostles who were gathered in the cenacle above the grotto of his remorse. If this tradition is correct, the Easter events accomplished more than bring about a reopening of the most ancient mysteries of Zion. In his still sleep-enveloped soul, Peter experienced an Easter encounter in which the reverberations of the cosmic secret of 'Christ's descent to hell' were still contained. In the depths of the earth, in the space of the tombs, there appeared to him the One who, through his victory over death, had united with the whole

274

of earth existence. Peter himself first had to rise from a grave in order to enter the sphere of the inner Galilee.

8.7 Pentecostal awakening

At the end of the forty days, the Easter sphere relinquished the Apostles. Through the portal of the experience of Ascension, they returned to the prosaic earthly world. Their sudden state of abandonment, the extinction of the presence of Christ in his spiritual-corporeal form, inwardly and outwardly made them aware that they were in Judea, the land of dying earth existence. Once more but to a greater degree, Peter and the other 'men from Galilee' had to pass the trial that had been imposed on them. This was when, following his Transfiguration and the confession by Peter, Christ had proceeded on his way from Caesarea Philippi to Judea, 'up to Jerusalem.' Peter had not then possessed the inner strength in the darkness of Judea to hold on to the light of revelations which had been his share in Galilee's etheric radiance. Would he now be able to hold on to the miracles of light and power that had imbued him and the other disciples in the forty days and pass them on to a world that by then had everywhere assumed Judea's nature of death?

It was all a question of an ego-awakening in Peter's soul. During the last important transition to Judea, he had succumbed even more to dull faintness instead of wakefulness. Now that 'the cloud had taken Jesus away,' would Peter's bewilderment and consternation condense into a new and greater breakdown of consciousness or would his mind clear to a bright wakeful dawn owing to the ray of light he had received? The little spark of awakening, enkindled in him by Christ's glance in the courtyard of Caiaphas' palace and the remorse of his own heart, had glimmered and increased. The encounters and conversations with the Resurrected One that had passed like dreams through his soul — though they had not been dreams — nourished the glimmering spark of the awakening higher ego.

And thus, on the morning of the fiftieth day, in view of the Pentecostal sunrise, the brilliant fire could blaze forth out of Peter's as well as the other disciples' souls. The flame of Pentecost signified the great conversion and awakening of Peter's being. Now it was no longer just an outburst of his natural temperament that came over him and in turn would make way for that much greater inertia. Now, strengthened and heightened by the miracle of incorporation, there took place in him the breakthrough of the I, the awakening of the power that indwelt the core of his being. This power in turn generated inner balance and transformed the stormy mood swings into active inner peace.

Peter appeared before the people as spokesman for the group of disciples and the spirit of Pentecost. In him the fire of waking burned most strongly because earlier he had fallen asleep the most. In the course of waking up, all that had happened and touched his soul, even though without the light of insight, now rose into consciousness in overflowing abundance. Suddenly, no longer spellbound, brightly illuminated memory arose out of the depths of his soul and overcame him at the same time as directly present enlightenment and outpouring of spirit. Thus, his speaking was ensouled by an elemental impulse. It was as if the force that had enabled him to utter the name of the Christ at Caesarea Philippi was at this moment trying to turn into a wide rushing stream.

As was true of the Golgotha Event, so, too, the Pentecost event remained completely unobserved and unnoticed by the general public of that age, even though its universal importance could be felt in the miracle of languages. Nevertheless, it signified the victorious breakthrough of a principle that had emerged in Greece, Rome and Judea without truly being able to become effective, namely, the principle of mystery popularization. In Athens, Rome and Jerusalem, the new world had come to birth that no longer was to receive its being and stamp from the darkened magic of ancient divine forces but from the free human ego which in thinking was growing conscious of its own self. In the great withdrawal from the mysteries, in the publication and transformation, carried out on all levels of life, of ancient mystery practices into an intellectual and artistic culture equally accessible to all human beings, the proud young world of egohood revealed its will. But then ensued the great counterblow by the ancient world. The principle of mystery popularization had been confronted by that of power-hungry mystery abuse which had produced the magic of Caesareanism and the Caesarean cult. The delicate young world of the ego threatened to be smothered by the reawakening powers of the past. A Tiberius, a Caligula ruled the world. The daze of Caesarean madness tried to prevent the emergence of the bright light of the ego impulse.

Nonetheless, for three short years, a human being had quietly gone on his way whose humble self-effacement was the complete opposite of the arrogant Caesarean life style. In him dwelt the divine force that came to the aid of the endangered young human ego. Having gone through death and resurrection, this force and being surrendered in such a way to the whole of humanity that it could live in the ego of those human beings who were receptive and open to it. On Pentecost morning, in Peter and the other disciples, the miracle of incorporation by the Christ-I in the human I openly appeared for the first time. The path had been cleared for the free human I. The victory had been won for the world of true egohood.

Thus, from that hour of sunrise, a spirit-outpouring proceeded in which the mystery popularization, begun at the time of Phidias and Aeschylus, was elevated and fulfilled. The inconspicuous travels by the Apostles to all the nations of the world were like an Alexander-expedition of a higher kind. The fire of a spirit was borne out into the world in which all human beings can share equally because they are ego-endowed beings, a fire which therefore is the seed of true brotherhood. Through the Pentecostal impulse of apostolic early Christianity, true anti-Caesareanism thus appeared on the scene. In the form of the Apostles, the spirit of love that sees its brother or sister in every human being entered the arena of a world filled with the Caesarean armies' clash of arms and challenged the Caesarean spirit of power to battle. Caesarean Romanism soon recognized what kind of opponent had in all modesty arisen against it. The hatred and bloodshed of the centuries-long persecution of Christians are proof of this. Nevertheless, through the blood of the martyrs, the spirit of love and inner freedom only triumphed the more over the spirit of power and slavery. Similarly, in the future, it will always win the victory.

8.8 The falling away of the chains

The map of the apostolic journeys makes evident the world-encompassing power that awakened on Pentecost morning in the cenacle among that small circle of people. Thomas and Bartholomew moved eastward far into the interior of India, farther than Alexander the Great had gone on his expeditions. The older James made it westward as far as Spain. Andrew carried the spark of the spirit and the message of the Gospel to Greece and the regions around the Black Sea. Matthew reached the countries south of Egypt. The fishermen of Galilee had at last broken free from the magic but also from the limitation of their old homeland. They had made not only Judea but the whole world their new homeland. A spirit imbued them that allowed them in every country to surpass the scholars and initiates of the ancient world. The mighty resounding of the spiritual world within the earth's sensory sphere, something Peter had so ardently awaited, had become reality after all, although in a much more unassuming, liberating way than Peter had imagined before his soul awakened to ego awareness.

At first, Peter did not feel inclined to go out into the world. A benevolent fate granted him a reprieve so that the fruits acquired in the Pentecostal awakening could mature. Although he was around fifty years old at the time of the Pentecost festival, it took more than a decade before the apostolic impulse drove him beyond the Palestinian borders to foreign countries. In all that he did, he was slow and late to mature. The most momentous events fell like seeds into his soul. But it took a long time before the results came to full fruition. But because of this, he was also the one who far into old age — when in most cases people have long since completed their inner growth — remained capable of mental development and transformation. His strong-hearted piety that filled his whole being produced in him the miracle of never-ending childhood and youthfulness of soul.

And so, following his Pentecostal awakening, we see him maturing quietly but steadily. The fire of conversion did not burn out quickly as it had done earlier. An organic growth process and penetration of his nature with the holy spirit of wakefulness took place. His earlier, simply natural piety was reborn and, as it fought its way through to an ego-imbued state of consciousness, was blessed with light-filled wisdom. In Peter's Letters in the New Testament, we finally encounter the mature fruit of this long-lasting Pentecostal spiritualization of his being. Here, the inborn instinct of the fisherman from the Sea of Galilee is completely transformed into human and cosmic wisdom.

During the time following Pentecost, we see Peter again and again working with John. When they were sent to prepare the Passover meal in the cenacle; when, on Easter morning, they ran together to Golgotha to look into the empty Tomb, a bond must have been forged between them that could only become more intimate after Pentecost morning. Perhaps this bond was overshadowed by a reflection of the relationship that had prevailed between Jesus and the disciple 'whom he loved.' Together with John, we see Peter heal the lame person at the 'Beautiful Gate' of the Temple (Acts 3) and confront Simon, the magician, in Samaria (chapter 8). We find Peter and John together in the jail of their persecutors (chapter 4). Within the domain of Peter's destiny, this togetherness is a most beautiful expression for the patient benevolence that prevailed over him. It allowed him time and helped him finally to actively work on the basis of complete inner balance and peace of mind.

On occasion, the worldwide activity for which Peter was destined made itself felt. One time, for example, obeying a strange spiritual command, he appeared as the mediator of Christ's message in the house of the Roman officer, Cornelius. He accepted the whole group of people gathered there into the Christian sacramental community without having made the demand that, as a preparation, they had to fulfil the Old Testament Law.

Nevertheless, another event had to occur before the path which led out into the world could truly be cleared inwardly. This was an event that can appear to us like the lifting of a ban, a destiny-verdict of freedom (Acts 12). Eleven years after the events of Golgotha, under the reign of Caesar Claudius, several misfortunes befell the Christian congregation in Jerusalem in the days before Easter. The country had been suffering for some time from a scarcity of provisions. But now the famine grew worse and hit the Christians particularly hard, since nearly all belonged to the less privileged social groups. Worse, in the midst of the general uproar and tension, a persecution began.

A Herod ruled over the land who, like his predecessor, had succumbed to Caesarean madness. To divert the people's anger that otherwise would turn against him, he ordered James the Elder, who by then had returned from Spain, beheaded. This first martyr's death that struck the circle of the Twelve must have occurred precisely on Good Friday of the year 44. For the Christian congregation, an immediate present terror was added to the anguish of past memories. Herod saw that he had chosen the right means to appease the people and had Peter thrown into prison. As soon as the Passover Sabbath was over, on the Christians' Easter morning, Peter would be publicly pilloried.. Then the people were to decide whether he was to share the same fate as James. Trembling with fear, the congregation gathered in the house of the cenacle on Mount Zion, as had the circle of the Apostles eleven years earlier. The Essenes in Jerusalem had recognized that the mission of their Order was fulfilled. They had placed the house, located as it was on such an ancient holy place, at the disposal of the congregation of Christ, a congregation that most of them probably joined. Mary, the sister of Barnabas, the mother of young Mark, was retained as the housekeeper.

A living consolation was granted the community united together in prayer: Paul and Barnabas had just arrived as messengers from the congregations of Antioch. They brought gifts for the Easter festival which had been collected among the northern communities to alleviate the suffering in Jerusalem. Nevertheless, all their heartfelt, anxious concern was directed towards Peter's fate. Then the grey of morning appeared through the windows, the very windows through which the disciples had once greeted the rising sun of Pentecost. A knocking was heard at the gate. Was it the persecutors who would bring new disaster? It was as if the fate of the aroused age itself were knocking on the door. A maid went to the portal. Yet, without having opened it, she immediately rushed back in a strange state of shock, claiming that Peter was at the door and that she had heard his voice. None dared believe the maid's report. Perhaps it was his angel but not he in person. Again there was a knock and when the door was finally opened it really was Peter. Radiant light streamed out from him; all were rigid with fear and wonder. Only when Peter began to speak and related the miracle to which he owed his liberation, did the spell lift and joyful Easter jubilation fill their souls.

In prison, a strange experience had come over Peter. It seemed as if once more, but now with transformed soul, he was to pass through the dull depths of sleep in which he had been lost during the night of Gethsemane, due to which he had denied the Lord. Now, in the night before Easter, he saw how the nocturnal darkness was illuminated by the form of an angel who appeared before him. The chains fell away from his wrists. As if sleep-walking, he followed the light that moved ahead of him past the guards, out of the prison, down a long street. Finally, the state left him. He woke from the depth of his somnambulistic state of mind and, to his great surprise, found himself in front of the house of the cenacle. Had he not experienced this once before? Long ago, at the dawn of the first Easter morning, when he had climbed out of the grotto on Zion and, guided by an invisible hand, had stood in front of the same house where the other disciples were gathered. What kind of fate had led him again to the point of his departure and, at the dawn of another Easter, renewed in him the secret of that first Easter morning?

At last, Peter must have felt free of the guilt of denial and dullness of consciousness. Now, all was transformed in him. The outward falling away of the chains was at the same time a sign that the last inner fetter, too, had fallen away from him. Now the path was open into the whole world.

8.9 Peter in Rome

Peter went to Rome. An apocalyptic courage ensouled him. The fisherman from the Sea of Galilee dared venture into the metropolis, held to be the centre of the whole world, directly to the seat of the Caesarean cult. With all the vigour of his being he intended to carry the message of Christ to the dwelling place of the Antichrist.

When walking through the urban congestion of today's Rome in the vicinity of the central railway station, most people probably do not know that they are quite near an important site

of early Christian life. In one of the quieter streets by the slope
of the Esquilin Hill stands the church of S. Pudentiana. For a
long time it was not in use. Until it was renovated in the early
fifties, the walls of a house could be seen in the exposed floor in
which, according to ancient traditions, Peter had lived during his
mission in Rome. It had been the home of the wealthy senator
Pudens who had made rooms available there for the gatherings
of the Roman congregation of Christians. Moreover, he welcomed Peter to his house when the latter arrived in Rome.

In every respect, the congregation in Rome had a completely
different appearance from that in Jerusalem. Its ranks included
many noble, affluent Romans, a large number of whom had
suffered under the Caesarean cult. Since they favoured the
ancient Roman virtues, they readily found access to early
Christian life. Thus we might picture Peter, by now over sixty
years old, appearing in the small circle that was in the habit of
meeting in the home of Pudens. When he began to speak and
simply related the events that he had been allowed to witness, the
listeners felt as if they themselves were spectators of what had
come to pass; as if everything were occurring once more in the
immediate present and Christ himself were stepping into their
midst. And when Peter celebrated the sacrament there or in the
small chapels on the sides of the dark subterranean walkways of
the catacombs; when he distributed bread and wine, it was as if
the Easter-sphere of the inner Galilee had been poured all around
them and the Water of Life were rushing towards them from an
invisible Sea of Galilee. At that moment, the shrill pomp and
tyrannical violence of Caesareanism was far away. How could
that demanding world of illusion survive against the divine reality
which went out from the word and priestly acts of the Apostle!

For two decades, Peter joined in creating the quiet island of
peace within the clamour and Caesarean madness of the metropolis. Then it came to pass one summer night of the year 64 that
there was knocking on the gates of the house where Peter was
addressing the pious congregation. World history itself intervened. The wild hoards of Nero's soldiers demanded entry. The
whole congregation was dragged to the nearby pleasure gardens
at the golden house of Nero, the site of today's Colosseum.
There, with the wildest orgies already in progress, an especially

tantalizing spectacle was presented to the drunken guests. Before their eyes, the Christians were tortured to death; they were soaked in tar or naphthalene and burned as living torches on tall poles to illuminate the riotous scenes. The strength to bear all this came from the presence of the Resurrected Christ whose closeness they had experienced time and again in the sacrament. Tradition relates that when the guests of Nero's revelry had fallen into a deep sleep, the two daughters of Pudens, Pudentiana and Praxedis, who had escaped the blood bath as if by a miracle, carried the mutilated and charred corpses of their friends to the house of their father and there buried them in the cistern. Thus, all those were gathered together in death where, in life also, they had so often experienced the community of the life-bestowing Word and Sacrament.

Peter had not been dragged into the gardens of Nero. In order to set aside a unique spectacle, he was initially thrown into the historic rock prison on the old Forum, the Carcer Mamertinus, where many a renowned prisoner of Roman history had languished. Then he was led to the other side of the Tiber to the hill that today is called San Pietro in Montorio, a location from which one could have a splendid view of the seven hills of Rome. There, the eighty-year old man was nailed upside-down to the cross, as he himself had requested in order to be distinguished from his Lord. The universal greatness that the fisherman from the Sea of Galilee had struggled to attain could not be more grandly symbolized than through the death that he was made to suffer. With the Rome that ruled the world below him, Peter breathed out his soul. Seemingly the victim of tyrannical illusion, in reality he was the victor over the whole Caesarean world.

9. James, the Brother of the Lord

9.1 The riddle of James

Even the closest surroundings of the Christ Event, as classically simple as they seem to be presented in the circle of the twelve disciples, confront us over and again with the most difficult personal and biographical riddles. We become aware that a number of other personalities of great spiritual and historical significance are involved who are concealed behind the circle of the Twelve. Then, at a certain moment, they emerge and are immediately recognized.

An important example is James, the brother of the Lord. He can neither be equated with James the Elder, the Apostle of Spain, who suffered a martyr's death in the year 44 in Jerusalem, nor with James the Younger — although he has often been confused with him — that quiet, never particularly prominent member of the circle of Twelve denoted as the son of Alphaeus.* Soon after the events of Easter and Pentecost, this brother of Jesus not only steps into the foreground, but quite properly into the centre of the congregation in Jerusalem and with this into the whole of the growing Christian community. For more than three decades, he exercised uncontested leadership over the original congregation. When Paul came to Jerusalem after his Damascus experience so as to make contact with the original Apostles, he had to come to an understanding first of all with this James whose authority was even acknowledged by Peter.

How was it possible that such influence was suddenly conferred on a man who had not belonged to the Twelve at all; who must even be the one mainly referred to when the Gospels tell us of the almost hostile incomprehension towards Jesus on the part

---

* The confusion appears even to have penetrated into the Gospel, for there too (Mark 15:40), James, the brother of the Lord, is designated as James the Younger. Concerning the inner reasons for making these two into one person, see chapter 10.2, 'The disciple whom Jesus loved.'

284

of his brothers? One reason given by early Christian tradition for the great esteem and reverence accorded to James is that in a remarkable way he resembled the Lord in form and appearance. It is said that pilgrims came to Jerusalem from distant lands just to see James because, through him, they believed they could receive a reflection of what those had experienced who had still encountered Christ in his earthly-human form. Yet it is easy to recognize that all that we are told about James is but a groping for a secret that cannot be so readily unveiled.

In his list of the fundamental Easter encounters, Paul offers us the decisive indication, upon which one should be able to solve the riddle of James and his position of leadership. Indicating the stages of transformation that the Resurrected One underwent, Paul mentions the Easter encounters and how they occurred one after the other: to Peter, the Twelve, the large crowd of five hundred brethren, to James, then to all the Apostles, last of all, as to one 'untimely born,' to himself (1Cor.15:5–8). As if he were speaking of a generally known fact, he fits James' experience, about which not one word is contained anywhere else in the whole New Testament, into this sequence at a quite definite moment. He thereby attributes to it the significance of a developmental stage undergone by the Christ being himself.

Peter's encounter, mentioned at the beginning and placed by tradition into the ancient subterranean grotto on Zion, points to the mystery of the descent 'into the depths of the earth,' an event from which the Easter event is born in the first place. The experience of the Twelve indicates the forty days during which the spiritual-corporeal form of the Resurrected One was revealed to the disciples. The vision of the five hundred is the experience of Ascension, one in which the Christ being crossed over into the condition of universal presence on earth. With the appearance of the Resurrected One among 'all the Apostles,' Paul refers to the event of Pentecost; in it, the indwelling of Christ was experienced for the first time. And when Paul finally states that Christ had appeared to him, too, this refers to his Damascus event, an event through which he became the first to experience the Resurrected One's visibility in the earth's etheric surroundings, the 'Second Coming of Christ.'

The Easter experience of James therefore occurred in the ten days between Ascension and Pentecost when the disciples in profound grief and consternation believed they had lost Christ for the second time. Yet this was also the period when a new, more inward manner of sensing his presence was beginning to develop among them. In those ten days, James must have been privileged to have a Christ revelation that transformed his nature through and through and finally even assigned to him the leadership position within the apostolic circle, a position we subsequently find him in for several decades.

The descriptions that early Christian literature gives us of James' encounter with the Resurrected One all make it clear that this experience played a special role in the history of the holy meal, the Christian sacrament. But before we turn our attention in more detail to this important event that followed after Easter, let us try to outline what James, the brother of the Lord, had gone through until then.

9.2 James the Nazirite

In many ways, the figure of James has been obscured by the veils that spread over the secret of the childhood of Jesus. As we know from the spiritual scientific revelations of Rudolf Steiner — but also clearly outlined through the duality of the genealogies in the Gospels of Matthew and Luke — two different families existed at the beginning of our Christian era. One lived in Bethlehem, the other in Nazareth. Each brought forth a boy who was given the name Jesus.* Several other children were born to the couple from Bethlehem after their firstborn son, Jesus. The Gospel mentions four sons: James, Joses, Judas, Simon and, in addition, several sisters (Mark 6:3). The Mary referred to in the first chapters of the Gospel of Luke, on the other hand, who in her unearthly delicacy and virginal nature became the object of later Madonna-worship, gave birth only to one, the Jesus boy who was surrounded by the secret of a celestial childlikeness, as she was herself. The Jesus of the Matthew Gospel died when the Jesus of

---

* The secret of the two Jesus boys is dealt with in detail in the description of the life of Jesus. For this, see the volume, *The Childhood of Jesus,* which in its entirety is devoted to the unfolding of this mystery.

the Luke Gospel was twelve years old; he had given his being so completely to the somewhat younger companion that his mature 'I' henceforth lived on in the delicate soul of the other. Then, after Luke's Mary and the aged Joseph of the Gospel of Matthew had both died, the two families that now lived in Nazareth became one. Jesus thus spent the subsequent events of his youth together with James and the other step-siblings from the Bethlehemite family.

The birth of the Matthew Gospel's Jesus boy attracted the attention of the influential Sadducees and Pharisees of Jerusalem, for at that time he was heir to the Davidian royal rank. His genealogy is that of the generations of the kings of Judah.* From David to Jechoniah, they actually wore the crown publicly. Then, at the time of the Babylonian exile and afterwards, they were viewed as royal pretenders, as 'sons of David,' attired with invisible royal dignity by all who hoped for a Messianic reconstitution of the Davidian kingdom.

The politically coloured, genealogically calculated Messiah-expectation of Jerusalem's official circles rested on the firstborn son of the Bethlehemite parents. When Jesus was born, not only the three priest kings from the distant Orient paid homage to him. When his parents fled with him to Egypt, he was not only withdrawn from the hostile grasp of a Herod, but from the well-meaning demands of the high priests as well. The move by the parents to Nazareth after the three-year stay in Egypt continued to shield the boy from those who would have heaped honours upon him. Finally, his early death brought an end to all the hope placed on him in Jerusalem.

James, who was born a short time after his brother, perhaps in Egypt, became heir to the honour paid to the current firstborn 'son of David.' Like John, the son of the priest Zechariah, James had been dedicated at birth to Naziritism and grew up under the sternly ascetic rule of this Order. Hegesippus (around 180) says concerning him: 'He was holy from infancy. He indulged in

---

* The genealogy at the beginning of the Gospel of Matthew does in fact contain the names of all the fifteen kings of Judah, from David to the Babylonian deportation. This alone should make it appear foolish to speak of superficial confusion and errors between the two genealogies in order simply to dismiss the duality of the ancestral lineages.

neither wine nor intoxicating drink. Moreover, he allowed no barber's knife to touch his hair.'[93] It is quite probable that he was not friendly with his stepbrother, the Jesus of the Luke Gospel. The quiet, withdrawn youngster may often have been a puzzle to James. Moreover, because of his august background and strict Nazirite conduct of life, James may well have adopted a disdainful, arrogant attitude towards Jesus.

Early on, James enjoyed special privileges on the part of the guardians of the Temple in Jerusalem. He owed these to the particularly ascetic severity and holiness that people credited him with, but also surely to the esteem in which he was held as the noblest descendent of the royal family. It says that he was accorded the right, not conferred on any other layman, to enter the inner sanctuary of the Temple at any time for prayer. Hegesippus reported:

> He therefore always went into the Temple alone. Here,
> one saw him constantly kneeling and praying for the
> redemption of his people. He did this so unceasingly that
> his knees became calloused like those of a camel.

We have to assume that as a result of his ascetic and meditative exercises, carried on with such intensity, the light of Nazirite vision arose in James. His visionary state increased the holiness that one experienced in him. When people had questions, they may well have turned to him for advice.

What he experienced in a supersensory manner did not inculcate a more positive attitude towards his stepbrother. On the other hand, he appears to have looked up with the greatest reverence and expectation to John, the other Nazirite. And when the Baptist appeared before the world as the herald of the closely approaching spiritual world, James placed all his hopes in John. There even exists an ancient tradition, a segment of the otherwise lost Ebionite Gospel, from which we have to conclude that James directed his stepbrother Jesus to the Baptist and tried to persuade him to ask for baptism there.*

What was it that stood between the two stepbrothers after the

---

* The fragment, quoted by Jerome in his text against the Pelagians (III:2), states: 'The mother of the Lord and his brothers said to him: "John the Baptist baptizes for the forgiveness of sins; let us go and be baptized by him"!' It further states that Jesus objected to this idea.

Baptism of Jesus? The attitude that the Baptist assumed to the One he had baptized could not remain without an impression and effect on James. Perhaps it bothered the stern ascetic that Jesus did not participate in the fasting exercises and the like. The supersensory experiences to which James advanced through his ascetic efforts led him to distant spiritual regions estranged from the earth. In order to recognize the Christ in Jesus, he would have needed visions that could have shown him the spiritual in the earthly element.

Nevertheless, his brother's riddle must have occupied him increasingly. In many respects he was not satisfied with his brother. But something in his nature bothered James. He therefore may have crossed his paths more and more often and made contact with the circle of the disciples. The last act of the drama appears to have made a deep impression on James. Perhaps he perceived the superhuman fiery will that emerged from Jesus beginning with the resurrection of Lazarus, a will that was felt in an elemental way by people when Jesus entered Jerusalem and went into the Temple. In addition, when the Crucifixion on Golgotha, an act James felt to be unjust, was accompanied by such tremendous cosmic signs and disturbances, the great transformation must have begun in his soul. Jerome reports to us in *De Viris Illustribus* that, at that very moment, James made the resolve to fast for as long as it would take for the solution of the riddle to be revealed to him out of the spirit.

9.3 The Easter experience of James

As John the Baptist had done earlier, James must have associated with circles of the Essene Order. His Nazirite holiness gave him access to the Essenes, even though he himself did not belong to the Order. For that reason he, too, may have stayed at the house on Mount Zion at the time when the disciples were together in the cenacle and lived in the quiet confines of the Easter encounters. A powerful inner urge kept him in the vicinity of those who had always been around the One who had died on the Cross, persons in whom one could recognize that they now experienced quite special, unheard-of events. In the cenacle, the disciples maintained contact with the Resurrected One in the holy meal.

Somewhere near them, James gave himself up with greater intensity and ardour than ever before to his ascetic exercises and struggled for an answer to the puzzling question concerning the nature of Jesus. At the end of the forty days, after the experience on the Mount of Olives, having until then been surrounded by such consoling light, the disciples yielded to the darkness of abandonment and consternation. Where had the Resurrected One disappeared to?

It was then that James' prayer found its hearing. The portals of the spiritual world, on which he had knocked so urgently, opened to him at last. And lo, the Resurrected One, who had disappeared to the vision of the disciples, appeared in radiant light to him who until now had stood aside in alienation and had closed his heart to him. James experienced his Damascus.

The Easter encounter of James contains a paradox. Through stern fasting he had prepared his soul. Now the Resurrected One invited him to a meal and in a special way became manifest to him in eating and drinking. Jerome relates:

> The Lord said: 'Fetch a table and bread.' And he took the bread, gave thanks, broke it and gave it to James the Just and said to him: 'My brother, eat your bread, for the Son of Man has risen from those who sleep.'[94]

Other traditions add that, following Christ's direction, James called together the disciples and offered them the sacred meal, as the Resurrected One himself had done in their circle earlier. James therefore was the first to have celebrated Holy Mass. The Easter experience of James is described in this manner over and over again in the Middle Ages, for example in the *Legenda Aurea*.

We can only feel our way towards the spiritual occurrence that became manifest to the disciples through James between Ascension and Pentecost. For forty days, the Christ being had shown himself in his spiritual-corporeal form to the privileged circle during the act of the sacred meal. Then it had poured itself out into the earth so as to be equally present to all humanity. The secret began to be realized which subsequently was called by Christian theology the omnipresence of Christ. At first, the sacred meal appeared to the disciples as if emptied of its Easter-radiance since the Resurrected One no longer sat at the table with them.

It required the experience of another man who had not participated in the miracles of the forty days in the same way as they
had. But Christ after his new transformation of being was
revealed to James so that the disciples would be drawn out of
their darkness and shown the way which they would be able to
follow henceforth in order to serve the Resurrected One.

The new insight given the Apostles through the Easter
experience of James was that the holy meal, which they had
taken until then only as recipients of the Resurrection mystery,
was at the same time the means that made it possible for them to
become bearers of Christ's power and blessing for all the people
of the world. They understood that the sacrament of bread and
wine possessed the power to realize the omnipresence of the
Resurrected One; that, celebrated at the same time in many
different places, it would cause the presence of Christ in the
etheric circumference of the earth to shine forth and be experienced. Everywhere, they would merely have to carry out the
same act before the people that James was now carrying out in
their circle, following the direction received through his spiritual
encounter. They would simply have to take bread and wine, the
offerings of the sacred meal, bless them and pass them out, and
the promise would be fulfilled that Christ had made to them:
'Where two or three are gathered in my name, there I am in the
midst of them.' As James handed out the offerings of the meal to
them — a man from whom, until then, they had experienced only
rejection and doubt — did it not seem as if, in him and through
him, the Resurrected One himself were breaking bread anew?
This is how it would be for each one of them, were he to have
the courage to pass out the holy meal in the name of Christ.
Christ himself would be active in human action. It was this
certainty that dawned with new insight in the souls of the
disciples when James communicated to them what he had
received in his Easter experience.

The Christ revelation James was privileged to have, and the
experiences of the disciples that followed this, signified the actual
establishment and birth of the Christian ritual. After his Resurrection, Christ charged the Apostles to carry the sacrament out into
all the world. Rudolf Steiner repeatedly pointed out that the

installation of the Christian ritual did not precede the Easter event but occurred through the Resurrected One. For instance:

> The Christ who had passed through death ... taught his disciples. In the first four Christian centuries, this knowledge was still alive to a certain degree. Then it ossified in the Roman Catholic Church for, while retaining the Mass, the Church no longer has an interpretation for it. Pictured as the continuation of the Last Supper as the Bible describes it, the Mass naturally makes no sense ... The installation of the Mass with its wonderful ritual, its imitation of the four mystery stages, is something that definitely goes back to the fact that the resurrected Christ was also the teacher of those who could receive these teachings in a higher esoteric sense.[95]

In the past few centuries, during the era of Protestantism, the scene of the Last Supper on Maundy Thursday was generally considered to be the inauguration of the Christian sacrament. But this was the same period in which the understanding for the great, sustaining, more-than-personal significance of sacramentalism began to disappear; when the mystery of transubstantiation fell victim to theological debate. It could not be avoided that, in Protestantism, through the link to the pre-Easter Passion element in the evening hour of Maundy Thursday, the sacrament of bread and wine itself assumed an excessively stern, gloomy character and thus lost the radiance of Easter and the Resurrection which actually imbued it.*

Easter and the sacrament belong intimately and inseparably together. From the Easter encounters that the disciples shared in during the act of the sacramental meal, the sacrament was born as the means of the apostolic activity. The Resurrected One founded the sacrament so that, in it, he could establish his presence in devoutly celebrating human beings. The secret of Easter and the secret of the sacrament mutually enlighten and

---

* The Eastern Churches of Christendom consistently and unequivocally teach that the Resurrected One established the sacrament between Easter and Pentecost. Alfred Heidenreich confirmed that the Thomas-Christians of India share this view, having heard about it in a conversation with a bishop of this sect which has survived from the time of early Christianity.[96]

illuminate each other. If a clear and living comprehension of the facts of Easter is attained again in the future, then love and comprehension for the sacrament will grow. And to the extent that the secret of the transubstantiation is understood and experienced, the Easter character of Christendom will emerge again clearly and discernibly over against the merely Passion-related element.

9.4 The growing stages of the Sacrament

The Christian ritual, the fundamental sacrament of bread and wine, did not simply come into being externally following some sort of command. It was born like a living being. And even as the birth of a human being is preceded by conception and the quiet maturing in the mother's womb, so, too, a hidden development and maturing preceded the emergence of the Christian sacrament into the open. What occurred on Maundy Thursday evening was not yet the birth. That still belonged to the preparatory stages of growth. The inconspicuous Easter association of the forty days between the disciples and the Resurrected One allows us to have an idea of the mysterious development of the being that was to be born. The cenacle on Mount Zion was something like the outward indication of a spiritual womb. Early Christianity emerged from it together with the sacrament and the priestly impulse of the Apostles.

From its structure, modernized for the present time in the Act of Consecration of Man, it is clearly discernible that the basic Christian sacrament gives birth to itself anew each time it is celebrated, inasmuch as it passes through the four stages of the Reading of the Gospel, the Offering, Transubstantiation and Communion. The Christian ritual went through a similar extensive sequence of developmental stages when it entered historical reality for the first time in the mighty Christ Event. Around Easter of the year 32, one year prior to the Golgotha Event, the disciples gathered round Christ again after a fairly long separation. At the shore of the Sea of Galilee, in the experience of the extraordinary Feeding, they received the first presentiment of their priestly apostolic mission. It was then that the Christian sacrament went through its stage of the 'Reading of the Gospel.'

The disciples beheld themselves in a lofty vision where in the midst of future humanity they dispensed the nourishing gift of Christ. What took place was not an outward, earthly, tangible event. A wondrously grace-bestowing spiritual event enfolded them; a page of the eternal Gospel was opened to them. An invisible hand moved aside the curtain of the future and in a prophetic picture allowed them to see the stream of sacramental power that one day would pour forth from their apostolic activity.*

The sacrament reached the second stage of its development, the stage of the Offering, on Maundy Thursday evening. When, threatened all around by approaching darkness and yet in infinite benevolence, Christ administered bread and wine to his disciples, the greatest and most serious trial of souls took place. One betrayed him, another denied him immediately afterwards. It will always help in the purifying self-examination that is part of the preparation for receiving the sacrament and is undergone during the course of the second part of the sacrament, the Offering, to ponder the images of this scene. Each one should feel their share in the denial of Peter when the words are spoken so that the right attitude towards the Offering may arise.

The evolving sacrament entered the stage of Transubstantiation during the forty days when the Resurrected One was present in spiritual-corporeal form in the circle of the disciples. The sacrament then became more fully manifest. When, as if with earthly senses, the disciples beheld the resurrection-body of Christ, they were witnesses of the beginning of the phenomenon of transubstantiation. Earthly corporeality stood before them in spiritually transformed shape. The Easter-element that hovered round them and instilled in them a hint of a new earth and a new heaven was none other than the sacramental miracle of transubstantiation spread out around them.

Yet the last stage was still needed. The sacrament had to emerge from the confines of the mystery to its community-building activity. This was the stage of Communion that be-

---

* The most sublime interpretation of the Feeding of the Five Thousand does not come from a theologian, but from a poet. In his poem, *Alle,* Conrad Ferdinand Meyer lyrically expressed the visionary nature of this event.

stowed on the sacrament its humanness. Its origin lay in the hidden events between Ascension and Pentecost when James' Easter experience played such an important role; events that only then actually signified the inauguration of the sacrament. The full realization of the stage of Communion, hence the 'coming-into-the-world' of the whole sacrament, took place on Pentecost morning during that sunrise which brought about the miracle of the descent of the Holy Spirit. The fiery flames of Christ's incorporation sealed the disciples' ordination and apostolic mission. Now they were charged with carrying the sacrament out into the world as the Easter message that is saturated with earthly reality. And the remarkable audibility of the primal language in the speech of the disciples, a language common to all nations the world over, was experienced as the prophetic beginning of a great universal Communion.

If the disciples celebrated the festival of Pentecost in the manner of the Essenes and Therapeutae, as was probably the case, they went through the four stages of a ceremony during the night before the Pentecostal sunrise. It was a ceremony that in all simplicity repeated the sacrament's four archetypal stages of evolution. In the evening, the reading of the scriptures and the teaching of those gathered round the table once more echoed the stage of the Gospel Reading. The soul-loosening, heart-uplifting choral singing evoked the mood of the Offering. The meal itself was overshadowed by the breath of Transubstantiation. And the nocturnal celebration, lasting until sunrise, with its hymns and dances that elicited enthusiasm and fraternity, caused the miracle of Communion to blossom.

When the cenacle lit up in the light of the Pentecostal sun, the sacrament, too, changed completely from the sombreness of the dusk of evening, in which it had remained on Maundy Thursday, to the jubilation of early morning. 'Out of evening and morning,' the day of the sacrament was born. Since then, the evening's Last Supper has become the morning's break-fast. In those currents of Christianity that can attribute to the sacrament its true significance, the sacred celebration of bread and wine is therefore conducted together with the rising sun so that its Easter and Pentecost-imbued character can be experienced at all times in a living way. In every genuine Christian sacrament, the stream of forces flows on which, beginning at Easter, gathered in Jerusalem in the cenacle and then, on Pentecost morning, poured out into the world, engendering life.

9.5 Jewish Christendom and the Ebionites

The more we become familiar with the events that took place in the circle of the disciples after Christ's death on the Cross, the more clearly we recognize what an inaugurating force indwelt all the details of this event. James' emergence into the foreground is an important example of that. From his Christ-encounter and the transformation of soul that resulted, there must have issued forth such a convincing influence that the disciples, who from the very first had been witnesses and supporters of the Christ Event, could acknowledge the one who only now had found access to the mysteries of the Christ being. Perhaps the inner authority of James was established because the disciples experienced how Christ, who no longer appeared to them in his own spiritual-corporeal form, spoke to them for a while longer through James, thus continuing his Easterly instruction. Perhaps the exoteric tradition goes back to experiences such as these, namely, that James resembled the Lord so much that when people faced him they believed they were seeing and hearing the Lord himself. The episcopal leadership of the congregation in Jerusalem henceforth was in the hands of James until, three decades after the event of Pentecost, at the same time when Peter was crucified and Paul was beheaded in Rome, he was stoned by infuriated Jews in Jerusalem. Underlining the long duration of his leadership activity, Josephus even reports that it was not until the year 70, during the destruction of Jerusalem, that James was slain by the Romans.

It was of a quite specific significance for the whole inner development of Christendom that it was James, the brother of the Lord, who was chosen to play such an important part during the birth of the Christian ritual. As a stern and ascetic Nazirite, he was actually predestined to an attitude of soul alien to all ritual. His whole spiritual effort was turned inward and received its energy and motivation again and again through conscious negation of all that ties the soul to the outer physical world. All cultic elements, on the other hand, the sacrament of bread and wine, go in the opposite direction, inasmuch as they aim for the incarnating of spirit, the blessing-bestowing spiritualization of matter.

The fact that, through his Easter encounter, James had to arrive at a radical reversal and realignment of his religious efforts hitherto, is indicated in the paradox inherent in his manner of finding the way to the sacred meal through strict fasting. But it is obvious that, in the end, he included his zealous striving in all he did as leader of the Christian congregation. He stood within the first Christian community like an early incarnation of the impulse that, in recent times, has emerged in Protestantism. To this extent, he represented a living barrier against too broad an infusion of pre-Christian elements, elements of culture and ritual that aimed for external development.

The role that James, the stern Nazirite, had to play as priestly innovator of the Christian ritual can be well understood by those today who come from a Protestantism devoid of ritual and have struggled to arrive once more at a perception and cultivation of Christian sacramentalism, in order to be proponents of a religious renewal. Bearing in their being the egohood and inner freedom attained in Protestantism as a possession that cannot be lost, they will always know how to protect themselves from the Egyptianizing externalizations to which the ritual of the Roman Catholic Church fell victim early on. Destiny thus placed a personality at the beginnings of the Christian practice of ritual who, through his whole being, was fated to be the guardian of sincerity and simplicity.

James, the brother of the Lord, became the leader of the Jewish-Christian wing in early Christianity. He saw to it that those who wished to be accepted into the congregation at the same time pledged themselves to observe the rules of the Jewish Law. It was not long, however, before the one-sidedness inherent in this attitude became obvious, namely when, in larger numbers, Greeks and other non-Jewish people found their way to Christianity. Paul then made himself the powerfully effective advocate of a Christianity free of the Law. He thus became the leader of the gentile Christian wing within the first congregation. Peter had initially been more inclined towards James' standpoint. But just at the time when, his inner destinies having matured, he had found his way to Rome, Peter had struggled through to his own form of a Christian attitude of life. Between the two extreme wings of James and Paul, he thus established the middle way that increasingly emerged into the foreground.

When the first generation of Apostles had passed away, James' attitude played a certain role once again but now in exaggerated form. From early on, all kinds of sects split away from the main stream of Christian congregations. The reason for the establishment of a sect was always a particularly emphasized element of pre-Christian spiritual life, one from which some people were unable to part in their transition to the Christian congregations. Such an element was then carried over unchanged into the Christian context. A number of sects were therefore in existence that were based on adherence to certain Nazirite or Essene customs. Most likely, the Essene Order disappeared soon after the establishment of Christendom. A good number of its members found access to the Christian congregations. The essential forms of Essene communal life were maintained in them, although filled with a new content. Other Essenes heroically perished when, breaking the laws of their order, they engaged in battle when the Roman troops stormed Jerusalem.* After the destruction of Jerusalem, under the name of Nazirites and Nazarenes, only small fanatical groups remained who still followed certain aspects of Essene tradition. They either were actual surviving remnants of Essene settlements or had separated as sects from the Christian congregations.

One of Christendom's most eminent early sects was that of the Ebionites. They were the ones who traced themselves back to the brother of the Lord, James. They placed obedience to the Law, partly preserved from Nazirite, partly from Pharisaic Judaism, so much in the foreground that the new Christian impulse became quite insignificant and suffocated. Above all, they emerged within

---

* The extinction of the Order around AD 70 is the simply reason why Essenism is not mentioned in Talmudic literature, for it only came into being much later. Based on the absence of any reference in the Talmud, historians and theologians felt quite unnecessarily obliged to doubt the very existence of the Essene Order until, due to the discoveries of the scrolls and the subsequent excavations at Qumran by the Dead Sea, it almost became the fashion to write about the Essenes.

early Christendom as opponents of sacramentalism. Thus, they could be called the first iconoclasts. Lastly, their aversion to ritual determined their name. *Ebion* means 'poor.' But they were concerned with a principle of poverty in the ritual sphere more than with one in social life.

The paradox of the inner James-destiny appeared once more in acute one-sidedness on the stage of history. In the name of the one who had played such a decisive role in establishing Christian sacramentalism, a struggle for its abolition ensued. The Ebionites experienced a considerable increase in members when, during Jerusalem's destruction, the Jewish-Christian congregation, which had had its centre in this city, became homeless. Living in a remote region east of the Jordan in Ebionite settlements, these Christians increasingly went to extremes. The fanatically pursued Ebionite influence finally became so strong that, according to documents of that time, it almost seems as if all of early Christendom had been of Ebionite persuasion. And many descriptions by historians and theologians concerning early Christendom and particularly early Christian ritual are one-sidedly derived from the sect of the Ebionites and therefore misleading. Only through a more intimate acquaintance with the Apostle-destinies themselves, above all with what was experienced between Easter and Pentecost within the circle of the disciples, can we hope to arrive at true and realistic views of early Christianity.

10. John the Evangelist

10.1 The Ancient One of Ephesus

When we celebrate St John's Tide during the days of the summer solstice, the figure of John the Baptist appears to us first of all as an embodiment of life's fullness at the height of summer. The earth's soul, breathed out into the world's widths, together with the etheric radiance of sunlight, lingers at this time around the greatest unfolding of earthly nature. So, too, we behold the body-free soul of the Baptist, irradiated with flashes of the spirit's fire, as he affects the world around him with the greatest intensity. Yet St John's Tide is not just a festival of unfolding. We sense this in earth's nature and also in the figure of the Baptist. From here on, the days grow short again and John speaks of sacrifice: 'He must increase but I must decrease.'

In some regions of central Europe, the more serious side of the summer's solstice is brought to expression in that St John's festival is at the same time observed as the Day of the Dead. People go to cemeteries to decorate the graves. There is a summer's fullness of life to which we have access naturally through our birth. It is subject to the constant alternation of blossoming and wilting. Likewise, there is a summer of the soul, a sphere of deathless life. We find our way to it only through the sacrifices we make, and finally through death.

The Christian calendar affirms the inner duality of the St John festival through one of its most important secrets: June 24 has always been considered the birthday of John the Baptist and the anniversary of the death of John the Evangelist.* John the Baptist is the last who, through his birth and his very nature, bore within himself the abundance of the soul's summer. The Evangelist John

---

* The birthday of John the Evangelist is celebrated together with the Christmas festival in the days of the winter solstice, on December 27.

is the first who, through his unique relationship to and overcoming of death, advanced to the abundance of deathless life.

We encounter one of the most venerable, remarkable and at the same time mysterious figures of early Christianity when, a hundred years after the turning point of time, we imagine ourselves in the former mystery city of Ephesus on the Greek coast of Asia Minor. A man lived there who was so old that he had long since survived all his life's companions. Nobody knew any more where he had come from. He was like a living myth, without father, without mother, a picture and herald of eternity. The luminously august disposition and transfigured kindness of his being brought it about that all who knew him felt unbounded reverence for him. They saw in him the very image of priestliness; he reminded them of the lofty priest-king before whom even Abraham had once knelt; one of whom it was said that he was 'without father, without mother ... without beginning of days or end of life' (Heb.7:3).

A few decades later, a man who could boast that he had had pupils of the Ancient One of Ephesus as his teachers[97] said of him:

> Under Trajan, a man lived in Ephesus who was so old
> that not only his contemporaries but even his children and
> grandchildren had long since died and the great-
> grandchildren no longer knew who he was. They simply
> called him 'John' or 'Presbyter.'* Neither did they know
> how to honour him; they dressed him in precious
> vestments and hung on his forehead the mysterious
> emblem of the king and high priest, Melchizedek, a star
> of gold plate, the *petalon,* with the unutterable name of
> God.

In every word that has come down to us from those who had still seen him in person, the deeply moving reaction and reverent shyness reverberate that were evoked when he appeared before men. It says that he was no longer in a condition to walk across the street and so spent his days in quiet meditative contemplation. Only on Sundays was he carried to the place where

---

* 'Presbyter' means 'the eldest one.' It is moreover the Greek word from which our word, 'priest,' is directly derived.

the congregation of Christians gathered together. Subsequently, when he sat on the bishop's chair dressed in priestly vestments, emitting the transfigured glory of the Christ-permeated heart and a spiritually awakened mind, he did not give a long sermon. Yet, through the same words he uttered to the congregation on each occasion, 'Little children, love one another,' infinitely more was evoked in the listeners' souls than even a most inspired sermon could achieve.

Then, as we can discern from the traditions, precisely in AD 100 — the Ancient One of Ephesus was then ninety-nine years old[98] — a scene took place that both crowned and concluded all the wondrous moments of his appearance. Once again, 'the Presbyter' had himself carried to the church where the congregation had gathered. It was on John the Baptist day at the time of the summer solstice. On this occasion, to everybody's great surprise, the old man left the chair on which his friends had carried him. Erect and with firm steps, emitting an even brighter radiance than normal, the tall figure moved silently through the ranks with a gesture of blessing. The Ancient One stepped up to an open grave next to the altar. No words were suitable for what he had to proclaim today, not even the simple but meaningful command of love always uttered at other times. Today he spoke to those present by means of a silent deed that made all their hearts skip a beat. He laid down in the grave and breathed his last in full view of the astounded and startled congregation. It says that a wondrous cloud of light enveloped the grave when he died; that an indescribably sweet fragrance as of heavenly Manna filled the whole room.

Here, a man concluded his earthly journey who stood in a different relationship to death than other human beings. Even when, Sunday after Sunday, he spoke his words of love, he had appeared like a being whom death could not harm. Now it became evident that he commanded death, not death him. A free passage through a portal, behind which is no darkness, only overabundance of light — this was his death. In face of this soul, death had lost its sting and terror.

Who was this mysterious Presbyter John, the Ancient One of Ephesus? One thing becomes immediately clear from the early traditions and testimonies of the apostolic Fathers who, like

Irenaeus, set great value on having been pupils of the Presbyter's disciples. The Ancient One of Ephesus was the Evangelist John, writer of the Gospel that bears his name. At the same time, the early Christian scriptures make it obvious that John, the Presbyter, is not identical with the disciple John, the son of Zebedee, whom the Gospels mention in listing the twelve Apostles. To cite just one example, the same Bishop Papias, to whom we owe most of the reports of the Ancient One of Ephesus, clearly distinguishes the Presbyter from the Apostle John, inasmuch as he refers to them side by side:

> Therefore it came to pass that as soon as I encountered one of those who had still enjoyed the teachings of the oldest ones, I questioned him in the greatest detail about their words: What Andrew had said, what Peter, Philip, Thomas, James, John or Matthew or another of the disciples of the Lord had said; likewise what Aristion had proclaimed and the Presbyter John, both of them disciples of the Lord.[99]

Another tradition emerges in the theology of the early Middle Ages from different sources that quotes the same Bishop Papias as the authority and states that, like his brother James the Zebedee, John was slain early on by the Jews.*

From this observation, Protestant theology of the past century has deduced the right to deny the Gospel of John its value as a historical account of the Christ Event. The rash conclusion was drawn that if it was not the disciple John from among the Twelve who wrote this Gospel, then it derived from a man who may have been a great religious personality but did not have the close relationship of an eyewitness to the actual events. Consequently, the fourth Gospel is discounted; we must stay with the first three Gospels when we look for reliable historical reports. To no avail, the more dogmatic theologians tried to defend the Gospel of John by claiming that the Presbyter had to be identical with the Apostle after all.

Rudolf Steiner shed light even on the apparently hopeless darkness of this riddle. Early on, in his book *Christianity as*

---

* For example in the Syrian Calendar of Martyrs; in the texts by Philippus Sidetes and in the *Chronicle* by Georgios Hamartolos.

Mystical Fact, published in 1902, he showed that the Evangelist John is concealed behind the figure of Lazarus whose resurrection is reported by the Gospel. The fourth Gospel, therefore, issues from a much more intimate closeness to the events that are depicted than would be the case even if it had been written by one of the Apostles listed in the 'Apostle Catalogues.' Athough the Evangelist John, the Ancient One of Ephesus, cannot be equated with the son of Zebedee, he was identical with Lazarus who arose from death. And Lazarus in turn is the same whom the Gospel of John describes as the disciple 'whom Jesus loved.' Nowhere in the fourth Gospel is this disciple called John. Yet the fact is alluded to that he is none other than Lazarus, for he is mentioned only after the resurrection of Lazarus, and the important characterization, 'whom the Lord loved' is first applied to Lazarus, then to him (John 11:3). Again, a personality emerges in Christ's closest environment who did not belong among the enumerated Twelve, yet surpassed the Twelve in significance and nearness to Christ.

We grope our way to the secret that among the disciples of Christ there were two who were called John. One had this name from the beginning; through it, nothing special came to be expressed. The other was not called John in the Gospel. But later on, as the Evangelist and Ancient One of Ephesus, he is called by this name because evidently a special mystery of his being was to be indicated in this way. Moreover, we begin to sense what gave the ancient Presbyter John his sovereign freedom in regard to death. He had already passed through death once in this life. When the call, 'Lazarus, come forth!' resounded in Bethany, he who returned to life on earth brought along the right of dwelling in the sphere of deathless life he had acquired beyond the portal of death.

10.2   The disciple whom Jesus loved

Not one word is told us in the Gospels concerning the fortunes and developments undergone by Lazarus prior to the drama of death and revival. And the fragments of legends that exist are themselves so obscure that they hardly help us penetrate the secrets that surround the figure of Lazarus. We must try and take what the Gospel allows us to discern in regard to the Evangelist's inner nature and utilize it as the key to the hidden dimensions of his life. Then an image can arise that will at least show us how it might have been.

Without belonging to his immediate circle of pupils, a man may have appeared now and then in the environs of the Baptist who, despite his youth — he was half a year younger than John — had something quite special about him. He was of a completely different makeup than the fishermen of Galilee. It must have been possible at first glance to recognize that, as far as background and education were concerned, he brought with him a destiny completely different from theirs. Nevertheless, his inner deportment equally differed from the purely intellectual education of a Judas Iscariot. The bright light of a throughly Greek consciousness in which beauty and truth were joined shone forth from him. Perhaps he was originally from Greece or at least from a region where, at that time, Greek philosophy and art were still cultivated in a pure and vital form.

Later it was said of him that he had been a king's or lord's son who had great wealth at his disposal. It may be that he was of noble background even outwardly. In any case, such a characterization points pictorially to his soul's inner riches and noble maturity. What he had brought into his present existence by way of the fruits and effects from earlier lives on earth was more important than what he could avail himself of through birthright and legacy. Had he attained an advanced age in his last life so that he was now imbued with a wisdom that actually is acquired only in a very long life? Or did he bring along as a direct reminiscence what he had once attained and received in lofty initiation?

A quite special relationship to all elements of word and sound must have been characteristic for his inner life. As if a grand universal musical element and the murmurs of an exalted divine poetry were finding direct entry into his being, his speech seemed to be ensouled by the echo of the harmonies of spheres and the Word of Worlds itself, even if he was of reticent nature. In a different way from the great prophets of the Old Covenant, he was able to hear the Godhead speak and be an interpreter of the divine Word. Anybody who came into closer contact with him had to think: Here, a great friend and servant of the Logos is preparing himself for the consummating task of his life. If those who spoke of him later on could not do enough in praising his chaste nature, a memory of the profound impressionability and sensitivity of his nature may have been retained in such descriptions. Everything made a powerful impact on him and, because all the people recognized and acknowledged his soul's all-surpassing nobility of spirit, they understood why he only showed himself from time to time and then disappeared again into seclusion.

After John's imprisonment and beheading, Lazarus continued to behave in a similar fashion around Jesus as he had with the Baptist. In the transition from John to Jesus, he must have played a particularly important role, not least of all for Jesus himself. Lazarus may have been the one who had most keenly heard all the words with which John the Baptist had tried to point the men around him to Jesus of Nazareth. For himself, he would perhaps not have required these indications at all. As was true of the Baptist's soul, something may have arisen in him as if out of depths of destiny that attracted him to Jesus. Before the actual apostolic circle became more clearly aware that they were to follow not John but Jesus, Lazarus was able to detect what kind of power and being it was that had made its entry into the human state of Jesus. Woven of profound intimations of heart and mind, mental images and words of the spirit that flashed up in them, an intimate harmonious understanding lived between the three, John, Jesus and Lazarus. Regardless of whether they did or did not have conversations in the external sense in the brief span of time allotted to them by fate, a spiritual exchange united their souls.

After the death of the Baptist, these spiritual conversations continued. During the time when Jesus sent the disciples in groups of two out into the villages and towns of the land, he may often have been together with Lazarus. And when Jesus and Lazarus then spoke with each other, the genius of John was always present as well. The wondrous faculty for inspired knowledge through which Lazarus could hear the Word resounding out of the spirit may now have led to the beginning of a quite special relationship between his soul and the genius of the

Baptist. More than through the circle of the remaining disciples, John, even after his death on earth, found the possibility to be close to Christ in an earthly human sense through Lazarus. In the quiet talks between Jesus and Lazarus, Jesus and John conversed with each other at the same time.

From the beginning, the remaining disciples, particularly the Twelve, must have met Lazarus and his special position in their circle with unquestioning agreement and acknowledgment. Nobody felt that it was unjust partiality or merely personal preference that Lazarus was Jesus' favorite disciple. They themselves may have experienced and recognized the fact that Lazarus shared to a special degree in the miracle that overshadowed and ensouled their circle, namely, the miracle of the spiritual proximity and support of John the Baptist. When they were in the habit of designating Lazarus as the disciple whom 'the Lord loved,' they were aware that with this name — a name coined in reminiscence of ancient mystery terms — they brought to expression an obvious, objective, spiritual fact. This name was so exalted beyond the level of merely personal sympathy that Lazarus could even apply it to himself when, in old age, he wrote down the Gospel of John. The disciples must have experienced Lazarus, who appeared from time to time among them, as if he were a visitor from other worlds.

Novalis may have caught something of the feelings which then imbued their souls when, in the fifth *Hymn to the Night,* without any outward evidence, purely based on poetic visionary intuition, he relates that a Greek bard once mingled with the disciples. In wonderful poetic words, this bard praised the new relationship of man to death that had come into this world through Christ's overcoming of death:

Soon even the most childlike minds and hearts
gathered around him, wondrously gripped by intimate
love. Like flowers, a strange new life grew in his
domain. Unfathomable words and the most gladdening
messages fell like sparks of a divine spirit from his
kindly lips.

From a distant coast, born under Hellas' cloudless sky,
a bard came to Palestine and surrendered his whole heart
to the miracle child:

Thou art the youth who, since long ago,
Stands deep in thought on our graves;
A sign of comfort in the darkness here —
A higher mankind's joyful first beginning.
What cast us down into the deepest sadness
Now draws us on away in longing sweet.
In death was everlasting life proclaimed,
Thou art the death that maketh whole us mortals.

When Jesus had called the disciples back from their missions and they were once again united as witnesses of his words and deeds, it happened more frequently that Jesus took the Twelve or three of them aside for special intimate instruction. Here, a mystery begins that the Gospels conceal carefully, yet one that we must try to tease out if we wish to follow the paths taken by Lazarus as a disciple. We find that when a certain grouping formed around the figure of Christ through the choice of witnesses during special events and instruction, Lazarus was one of the Twelve or the three, even though he was not among the Twelve whose names are listed in the first Gospels. For example, when Jesus allowed the three closest disciples, Peter, James and John, to be present in the house of Jairus; when he took them along to the Hill of Transfiguration and finally the Garden of Gethsemane, Lazarus was among the three. The name John then refers to him, not to the son of Zebedee even though he is mentioned instead of him. How is this possible?

Perhaps this is how it was: one of the Twelve, precisely this John, son of Zebedee, willingly relinquished his place within the circle of disciples to the one whom he acknowledged as the bearer of his own stellar name, who eclipsed him by far. Somehow the disciples must have known that the number twelve had to be understood as a universal number, as the representation of the twelve starry possibilities of man, and that it therefore was not simply tied to their own personalities. Each disciple had to anticipate that another might come forth who would be better qualified than he to fill his place within the grouping of the Twelve. In this direction, we may find an answer to the question of how two persons could occasionally be merged into one in the Gospels, personalities who in reality must be distinguished from each other. And it may be that this not only applies to Lazarus and John, the son of Zebedee, but also to James, the brother of Jesus, and the younger James mentioned among the Twelve. This would explain why the Gospel of Mark (15:40) once speaks of James the Younger, when it is obvious that the brother of Jesus is referred to.*

10.3   The raising of Lazarus

The soul of Lazarus, a soul receptive and impressionable through and through, reached a state of crisis when he was increasingly drawn into the circle of the intimate witnesses. More powerfully and deeply than the other disciples, who lived and experienced it all in a dreamlike state, he was gripped by Christ's every word, deed and manifestation of being. The very issue the others did not comprehend because they were awaiting more external actions, namely, the ever more strongly inwardly-directed burning of the Christ-fire in the human entity of Jesus, took his breath away and almost threatened to overwhelm him. And finally, when the last decisive Passover festival was approaching, it came to pass that Lazarus' inner faculty of comprehension reached an end. He fell victim to a mysterious illness that could not be identified through any special symptoms. It caused him quickly to waste away.

Legend offers us descriptions that apparently relate to other more external processes but which most likely are an imaginative recapitulation of the soul process that led to Lazarus' illness. It says that Lazarus, the wealthy king's son, was present at the raising of the young man at Nain, as he had been at other deeds wrought by Jesus. What he had experienced disturbed and moved him so much that he forthwith gave away all his riches in order to follow Jesus. It was not external wealth that Lazarus sacrificed under the impression of Christ's deeds and his being. His own rich soul was gripped so powerfully and drawn into such boundless self-surrender that it finally separated from its own body. A mighty inner sacrifice is concealed behind the illness and death of Lazarus, a sacrifice that in its way was also an avowal of Christ.

* See footnote on p.284.

Down in the Jordan plain, where he had once received the Baptism from John the Baptist and where he probably met Lazarus as well for the first time, Jesus received the message: 'Lord, he whom you love is ill.' To the astonishment of the disciples, Jesus did not immediately make ready to go and help his ailing friend. He waited for two whole days until he revealed to the disciples that Lazarus had at last passed away. Only then did he make his way up through the Judean Desert to Bethany. Finally, he stood in front of Lazarus' rock-hewn tomb. The fiery will of his soul penetrated far beyond the earthly dimension into the sphere where the soul-spiritual being of Lazarus now was. And when, on earth, the call resounded, 'Lazarus, come out!' the soul of Lazarus obeyed the blazing spirit-flame appearing before it and followed it back to the realm of earthly corporeality. As if given wings, a completely new, never-before imagined, buoyant power was bestowed on this soul. Pointing to the secret of the Evangelist John who has always been depicted with the symbol of the eagle, the apocryphal Gospel of Nicodemus and the 'Easter Drama of Redentin,'* deriving from the latter, state that Lazarus soared up like an eagle, thus leaving behind the sphere where he had been subjected to the duress of death's power.

The innumerable depictions of the raising of Lazarus[100] in the early Christian art of the catacombs points in its austere gravity to a solution of the riddle that Rudolf Steiner first outlined in his book, *Christianity as Mystical Fact,*[101]0 and later in a number of lectures. In the catacomb representations,[102]0 we always see how the majestically erect figure of Christ with a commanding gesture stretches out the hierophant's staff towards the tomb of Lazarus. The process that everywhere took place in ancient times in concealed recesses of mystery and initiation centres was repeated one more time, but now openly before all the world. Then, the disciple who was about to go through initiation was purposely guided by his teachers through trials of soul. These were of a kind that caused him in the end to fall into the three-day-long deathlike temple sleep while he lay in a grave until, finally, the

---

* Note by translator: The *Redentiner Osterspiel,* a religious play from the Mecklenburg area of northern Germany, dates back to 1464.

hierophant called the transformed, reborn soul back into the body. Here in Bethany, the first act of the initiation drama was brought about by destiny itself. To be a witness of Christ's life and deeds evoked greater effects in the soul of Lazarus than what the most unheard-of trials imposed in a mystery temple could have produced. The second act of the initiation, on the other hand, the raising and guiding back of the initiated soul, was carried out by Christ himself who assumed the role of the hierophant.

In the description of the prophets of Israel, our attention was drawn repeatedly to how, at significant turning points of their inner development, these great spiritual leader-personalities went through fateful events fully reminiscent of the mysteries of death and resurrection, events that could not but appear like recalled memories and repetitions of initiation experiences from earlier lives on earth. We are told of Elijah that he 'raised the son of the widow.'[102] In the myth of Jonah, we see how the prophet was swallowed by a whale and was released again after three days.[103] We hear of the puzzling, three-day-long illness of King Hezekiah.[104] In all these events, we witness how the karmic echo of a once experienced initiation is elicited in a man through certain inner developments and thereby the prophetic genius is awakened. What Lazarus went through in Bethany was the highest and purest intensification of those experiences of the prophets. His Christ-discipleship generated a crisis in him in which the reminiscences of initiations undergone in former lives came together. Christ himself led him through these and carried out an initiation of a completely new kind on him. As one transformed and reborn through and through, guided by Christ, Lazarus emerged from the crisis of death.

One of the changes that became evident in Lazarus afterwards must have been that the genius of John the Baptist, with whom he had previously had an intimate connection, was now united with his ego in a way that fully imbued his being and constantly overshadowed him. From then on it may have been customary that Lazarus was called 'John' as well. Through the miracle of Bethany, he had become 'John.'

Having passed in such a wondrous way through death and resurrection, and filled with a power which, having been wrested from death, was capable of triumphing over death, Lazarus was now permitted to be a witness to the death and resurrection of Christ.

But it would be wrong to think that Lazarus-John henceforth passed without new inner tribulations through the events which, for the other disciples, signified the most severe trials. It has never been sufficiently considered that all the occurrences of Passion Week had to affect Lazarus with special impact and intensity because his soul was actually like a 'newborn soul.' Recast in the fire of the spiritual world, it had to find its way again into earthly corporeality with as yet delicate, impressionable organs. Only very slowly could it struggle for and attain earthly certainty. It must have been a powerful inner test of strength for Lazarus to witness how Christ with his fiery will of determination went on to challenge the continuing course of destiny. A few days after Lazarus had emerged from the tomb, the crowds of people sensed the spiritual majesty of him who was entering Jerusalem and they broke out into enthusiastic praise. Then, following the scene in the Temple, where the tables were overturned, popular excitement shifted more and more clearly to antagonism and hatred. Persecution surged forth and certainly targeted Lazarus, too, whose life the Sadducees sought as much as that of the one who had raised him (John 12:10).

It was a great relief for Lazarus to submerge himself in the sphere of the sacrament on the eve of Maundy Thursday. A heavy, mysterious pressure weighed on the souls of the other disciples and they did not comprehend what was happening. Lazarus, on the other hand, for the first time could calmly direct the heightened faculty of perception, a faculty he had brought along from beyond the portal of death, upon the being of Christ. With special kindness, Christ took him who had recovered from death under his protection. And so it says in the Gospel: 'Now one of his disciples was at the table, lying close to the breast of Jesus, the disciple whom Jesus loved.' (John 13:23).

In that hour, Lazarus experienced the most remarkable fulfilment of his higher sense of word and sound: he heard unspoken words resound from the heart of Christ. An inner hearing allowed him to listen to a hidden speaking in Christ's speech and silence. In inner listening, he found his way into the Being of the Logos, the Word of Worlds itself. Augustine once said: 'In secret, John drank from the heart of the Lord.'[105] And when the Gospel of John reveals the infinite wealth of the 'Farewell Discourses' all the way to the 'High Priestly Prayer' of Christ within the report of the Washing of the Feet and the Last Supper, we are given the opportunity to share in that 'Johannine hearing.'

In Gethsemane, Lazarus-John with his still unprotected vulnerability was exposed once again to the roaring tempests of destiny. Did not the sight of Christ contending with death almost wrench his soul back to those spheres into which the overwhelming force of experience had carried him off once before? Peter had succumbed to a deep depression's dullness of sleep. John was in danger of being drawn upward to supersensory alertness of a body-free spirit. A reoccurrence of the sickness that had gripped him only a short while ago in Bethany threatened him again. But he stood the test. When all the other disciples had fled, he finally could stand under the Cross and listen once more to the inner speech of Christ's heart. One more time his soul faced a great shock when, on Easter morning, he looked down into the empty grave with Peter. Consternation must have filled him when he stood again before a rocky tomb similar to the one in which he had been laid in Bethany. But then the shock may well have slowly faded because of a first distant presentiment of Easter. In Bethany, too, there had been an 'empty' grave. What had taken place here had to be a divine intensification of what he had undergone in his own dying and rearising.

For Lazarus-John's soul, the miracle of the forty days in the cenacle signified the final, full recovery and moreover the highest fulfilment and bliss. He, the awakened one among the awakening ones, must have often been an interpreter for the other disciples of the secret essence of words alive in the Resurrected One's teachings. Clement of Alexandria, the famous theologian of early Christianity, states: 'After his Resurrection, the Lord conveyed the secret knowledge (the Gnosis) to James the Just, John and Peter; they communicated it to the other Apostles.'[106] Here we see that Lazarus, as well as James, the brother of the Lord, had fully moved into the circle of the Twelve. We can perhaps gain a faint idea of the significance that John in particular had for the fulfilment of that period of special Easter encounters through his Logos-faculty.

10.4   Patmos and Ephesus

Following the event of Pentecost, we come across Lazarus-John only a few more times as Peter's silent companion and assistant before the latter departs for Rome. Then he disappears to our view for more than half a century. Silence surrounds him, but a silence that, for him, must have contained a rich fullness. Even before the dark hour of Golgotha, he had been able to have those conversations with Christ that needed no physically spoken words. Now, in these decades, he must have remained a witness to 'the word of Christ.' The very basis of his inconspicuous activity must have been a living and moving about in the element of inspiration, a listening to Christ's spirit word.

A number of years after that Pentecostal morning, John appears to have gone to the Greek towns on the coast of Asia Minor in order, like a sower of the Word, to pass through the small Christian congregations that were forming everywhere. On the foundation of ancient Greek life where the oldest mysteries of the new world had blossomed and where the blind bard, Homer, had coined the gods' wisdom in poetic human words; where the first Greek philosophers had proclaimed the secrets of the Logos, the disciple whom Jesus had loved sowed the spirit seed of the Logos who had become human: 'The Word became flesh and lived among us.' One can understand how the saying concerning John spread: 'this disciple would not die' (John 21:23), as stated by the epilogue of the fourth Gospel. When all the other disciples of Jesus had long since died; when three decades had passed following the martyrdom of Peter and Paul, the Presbyter John was still active in the congregations of Asia Minor. Death seemed to have no power over him who had gone through death once before. In the three Letters of John in the New Testament, we have the most beautiful document of this long, quiet, Johannine activity. The Presbyter John's speech of the heart, richly saturated with starry harmonies, resounds to us there:

It was from the Beginning. We have heard it, we have
seen it with our eyes, we have beheld it and touched it
with our hands: the divine Word which bears all life
within itself (1John 1:1).

Finally, however, the harsh dissonances of the age invaded the
seemingly ageless harmony of the Johannine pattern of life. In
the year 95 or 96, the fury of Domitian's persecutions of
Christians afflicted the region of John's congregations in Asia
Minor. In the rebuilt temple of Artemis at Ephesus, which had
gone up in flames on the day of Alexander the Great's birth, the
aged Presbyter, too, was to be forced to make an offering, one
that would have represented a confession to Caesarean worship.
Because he refused to do so, even as old Eleazar* in Jerusalem
had once refused to pay homage to the Seleucid Antiochus
Epiphanes, he was put in chains and eventually taken to Rome.
Fate now led him westward but the West did not receive him.
The historic course of events appeared to turn into a symbol for
the fact that Europe's ongoing culture was as yet not ready for
the Johannine element. Nevertheless, outside the gates of Rome,
the attempt was made to break the will of the steadfast man or
make him suffer a painful death by immersing him in boiling oil.
But lo, to the shocked consternation of the tormentors, the boiling
liquid could do no harm to the old man. Today, the round little
church, San Giovanni in Oleo, constructed by Bramante at the
Porta Latina, designates the location where this occurred.

John was returned to Asia Minor and exiled to the rocky white
island of Patmos located near the coast. On Patmos, having done
battle with the antichristian powers of his time, John wrote down
the mystery book of early Christendom, the Apocalypse. In this
book of the seven seals, the trumpets and the vials of wrath, the
veil is drawn aside from the spiritual battles whose shadows had
so dramatically fallen over the age of early Christianity.

We should not assume that John's Revelation originated then.
Such a text had always been present spiritually for those who
were capable of deciphering the supersensory script. Earlier, the
great prophets Isaiah, Hezekiah and Daniel had brought portions
of it down from the heavens.[107] Rays of the eternal apocalypse,

---

* 'Lazarus' is the Grecianized version of the Hebrew name 'Eleazar.' See p.66

like those that had found expression in the books of Enoch or Job, were reflected in the early wisdom traditions.[108] Moreover, we probably have to imagine that John had orally presented the mighty apocalyptic pictorial visions repeatedly and for a long time to certain specially prepared groups within his congregations. At the behest of the spirit, he now turned the misfortune that the persecutors tried to visit upon him in a positive direction. He translated the whole of the apocalyptic book with its divinely powerful composition into human words and put it in writing as a spiritual sustenance for the future centuries of Christian evolution.

In the year 96, Domitian was killed and a time of undisturbed peaceful growth ensued for the Christian congregations. John returned to Ephesus. And just as he had made use of the time of mounting Caesarean fury to write the Apocalypse, so now he bestowed on humanity the greatest document of peace, the Gospel of John. In a hermitage located within the confines of the Ephesian mysteries that once had been so close to the deity, at a spot that, according to tradition, was unusually safe from the hazards of the elements, he recorded the Gospel. Again we should not presume that it was only then that the Gospel of John originated. In oral tradition, it may have lived wholly or in part in the Johannine congregations for some time. Now the aged Presbyter himself gave it its final form and composition. He was able to harvest the ripest fruit of his Logos-thinking and contemplation. Thus, he captured and brought to life a sound which, even in the distant future, will play its part in transforming the earth and kindle the sun element of heaven in all that is of the earth.

A number of events are told us from this very last part of John's life — events that, from different viewpoints, allow us to recognize the superior triumphant relationship the aged Evangelist had in regard to death. We see how he tried to liberate people from clinging to earthly wealth and how he managed this through the other-worldly impact of the Lazarus-allegory, which recalled his own sojourn in the realm beyond the portal of death. Once he even presented the same allegory in an actual deed to the people. He called a young man back to life whose soul had just departed the earth. He then made him speak of what he had beheld in the soul realm. And before those who were entangled in earthly matters, the recovered man bore witness saying that he had seen their angels weep. Once, when John was about to be forced again to pay homage to the Caesarean cult in the temple of Diana, he chose to drink the cup of poison he was handed. But as with the boiling oil before the gates of Rome, so here, too, the poison could not harm him. He was even able to call back to life those who had also drunk from the cup. After that, John was often depicted with a goblet from which a serpent's slithering form arose.

Everything that is told of the Ancient One of Ephesus ends with praise of the living divine love that shone from his heart like sunlight. Once he inquired about a young man in a congregation who had been his pupil and had learned to control his pride and unruliness in John's presence. When John was told that the old unrest had surfaced again in the man and that he roamed the mountains as leader of a band of robbers, he himself, his age notwithstanding, did not rest until he had confronted the man he had looked for in the desolate mountains. Like a good shepherd, he sought the lost. And the young man's violent attitude could not resist the old man's kindness.*

At last, the time arrived when the physical strength of the Presbyter diminished. The hundred-year-old no longer addressed more than the words, 'Little children, love ye one another,' to his congregation. Supported by his death-overcoming benevolence and power of love, those who were allowed to experience the miracle of a community that was imbued with true brotherly love had a presentiment of humanity's Christian future. This continued until, at last, the Presbyter John settled down in the grave in full view of his congregation in Ephesus and radiantly bid farewell to the earth.

10.5 Judas, Peter and John

The three disciples whom Leonardo da Vinci placed together in a group in his painting of the Last Supper, Judas, Peter and John, represent three forms of Christianity. Judas only reached the point where he beheld the Cross on Golgotha, a sight he viewed with

* See the poem by Herder, *The saved youth.*

an abysmal sense of guilt and sin. His earthly destiny abruptly came to an end before the Easterly fulfilment of Christ's earthly life had even begun.

As Judas only experienced Good Friday, so Peter only experienced Easter. He avoided the sight of the Crucified One and rose slowly to self-awareness and his mission while he lived and moved about in the disciples' association with the Resurrected One.

The disciple whom Jesus loved stood under the Cross. He could look Christ's death in the eye, since Christ himself had guided him through death. He was moreover among those disciples who for forty days were allowed to receive the word and being of the Resurrected One in the cenacle. Early Christendom with all its miracles was but a continuation of Peter's destiny. As yet, the image of the Crucified One played no part. The Easter-element was so immediately present; the miracle of the forty days and the cenacle flowed on so powerfully in the catacombs of Rome and all the places where the sacrament was celebrated that the dark Golgotha-earnestness was outshone by it. When, following the first three centuries, ecclesiastical Christianity replaced early Christendom, the ongoing Peter-destiny was replaced unawares by a reemerging Judas-attitude. Even though the Western Church considered itself to be Petrine, it increasingly and inevitably assumed the image and attitude in which the life of Judas had culminated on Golgotha. In the end, along with abolishing sacramentalism during the last centuries, the Easterly stream of energy was completely pushed into obscurity in favour of a Good Friday theology.

John, who lived far beyond the first early Christian age, stands in history like an embodied promise for a new form of early Christianity which need not avoid the earnestness of Good Friday so as to experience the presence of the Resurrected One in the living stream of the sacrament. The dawn of a Johannine Christianity, a Christianity infused by a power that overcomes death, is beginning to emerge. Along with all the earnest freedom of egohood that Protestantism has acquired in looking up to the Cross, this comes to pass wherever the ever present cenacle, the sphere of the sacrament, imbued with the spirit of Easter and Pentecost, is reacquired.

Appendix

Philo of Alexandria:
On the Therapeutae and Essenes

The Contemplative Life (De Vita Contemplativa) by Philo, the most important source material about the Therapeutae, related as they are to the Essenes, has often been difficult to find in translation. Even though, in parts, the text is distorted and thus often obscure, particularly in the middle section that describes Roman and Greek banquets, it is here rendered in full without the addition of any critical textual analysis and explanations. Even the unusual depiction of the orgiastic banquets belongs to the whole. Philo purposely gives such gross descriptions in order, by contrast, to show the customs and attitudes of the Therapeutae in an even more favourable light.

Philo of Alexandria, the brilliant Hellenistic-Jewish philosopher and writer during the age of Jesus and the Apostles, was an admirer of Greek philosophy. But, as the text presented here clearly demonstrates, he encountered so much decadence in the Greek rituals and customs of his time that he could not really do justice to the spiritual content which had prevailed in them in earlier times. In the circles of the Essenes and Therapeutae, therefore, he saw the true heirs and propagators of philosophy.

On the Contemplative Life: De vita contemplativa

§1   Mention was already made of the Essenes insofar as they devote great diligence and much care to the structure of practical life and, in so doing, excel in all or at least in most instances. Here, I shall continue in my studies and speak of them insofar as they embrace the life of contemplation. In so doing I shall only say what is proper for me to say and not add anything of my own in the way of embellishment, even

319

though all poets and writers are in the habit of doing this where suitable material is lacking. I shall quite simply hold to the truth, in the proclaiming of which even the best fail. This is the goal of all my efforts and quest for knowledge. For one who deems it right that nothing good should be kept quiet, he ought not to be induced to silence by these men's fullness of virtue.

[2]The intention of this school is quite apparent from their name. For they are in fact called *Therapeutae* and *Therapeutrides,* male and female healers. On the one hand, they are called this because they consider their art of healing to be superior to the one practised in the cities. The latter supposedly serves only to heal the bodies, whereas theirs cures the soul as well from severe and incurable illnesses caused by desires and passions, sorrows and fears, selfishness, folly and the uncountable other weaknesses and afflictions. On the other hand, they bear this name because nature and the sacred laws have taught them, through holy service, to worship the True Being that is higher than the Good, holier than the One and more ancient than the World Soul itself.

[3]Which spiritual direction among all those we have heard of would be worthy of comparison with that of the Therapeutae in regard to its worship of the deity? Perhaps the devotees of the elements, earth, water, air and fire, which they sometimes name one way, sometimes another? They call fire *Hephaestus* after the activity of kindling it; the air *Hera* after the process of rising up and soaring in the heights; the water *Poseidon,* perhaps after the image of drink; the earth *Demeter* because she appears like the mother of all that grows and all living creatures.

[4]Yet, these names are inventions of the sophists. The elements are nothing but inanimate matter, incapable of moving of their own volition. They are subjugated to the hand of one who forms them, one capable of turning them in any number of ways into an expression of his ideas.

[5]Or should we think of those who worship the perfect bodies, the sun, the moon and the other stars, planets and fixed stars, the all-encompassing heaven and the universe? Yet these too have not originated on their own but through a creator and his perfect thoughts.

[6]Or should we maybe think of the admirers of demigods? This would in fact make us worthy of ridicule. How can one and the same being be immortal and mortal at the same time? Moreover, a defect clings to them due to their origin and conception. For they are tainted by their youthful abandonment which, in ill manner, one dares attribute to the blessed divine powers as if, driven by frenzy, they, who are free of any passion, had consorted with mortal women.

[7]Or would those by chance come into consideration who pray to

carved images and pictures of deities? These consist of stone and wood, having been completely formless a short while ago. Stone masons and wood carvers have cut them out of the remainder of the material. From the other related parts of this material, jugs for the bath, wash bowels for the feet and other such lowly objects were made and serve better for what occurs in the dark than in light.

[8]When we look at the ritual of the Egyptians, there too we encounter nothing that would really be of any account. They have elevated animals that lack the power of thought, and not only tame ones but even the wildest among them, to divine honours. Of all the species that exist under the moon, they have chosen one; of the land animals, the lion; of the creatures in the water, the crocodile that is native there; of the creatures of the air, the vulture and the Egyptian ibis.

[9]And even though they see that these animals are born and in need of nourishment, insatiable in eating and filled with filth; that they poison and consume human beings and succumb not only to natural death but frequently are violently destroyed, nevertheless the noble beings worship the wild and unruly ones; those gifted with reason, the ones void of reason; the godlike ones those that cannot even be compared with the animals of prey; the leaders and rulers those beings that are subjugated under nature and serve.

§2 [10]Inasmuch as all these men affect not only beings who are of the same kind as they are but the others that surround them with their torrent of words, they remain in a condition far from salvation, deprived of seeing, the most necessary sense. I do not speak of the eye of the body but the eye of the soul which alone is in a position to distinguish truth from error.

[11]The community of the Therapeutae unceasingly advances on the path of vision and aspires to perception of True Being. It tries to transcend beyond the visible sun and never strays from this well-ordered path that leads to perfect blessedness.

[12]Those who aim for the goal of salvation receive their incentive neither through tradition nor the advice or admonition of a human being. They are carried away by heavenly love and are filled with zeal like the Bacchants and Corybants. They do not cease until they behold what they long for.

[13]Since they believe that, through the longing for that deathless and blessed life, they have brought mortal life to its culmination, they leave their possessions to their sons and daughters or even other relatives, voluntarily appointing them their heirs ahead of time. And if they have no relatives, they bequeath their assets to companions and friends. For

those who have attained the riches of vision must leave blind wealth to those who themselves are blind in spirit.

[14]The Greeks praise Anaxagoras and Democritus because, due to their longing and love of wisdom, they allowed their land to become a pasture for sheep. I admire these men, for they have risen beyond all attachment to earthly goods. Yet, those who have not released their land to herds as grazing fields but have alleviated the needs of men, be they relatives or friends, thus turning poor persons into those of means, do they not stand on a much higher level? I would have to call the other manner of action in men who have the admiration of Greece thoughtless, yes, perhaps even eccentric. This, on the other hand, has been thought through with sober mind and mature reason.

[15]What do enemies do other than lay waste to the region of their opponents and destroy all the trees therein, so that the latter are forced to surrender due to the scarcity of the most necessary things? The men around Democritus acted in exactly this manner in regard to their own nation, inasmuch as they brought privation and suffering upon their people by their actions. Even though perhaps not intentionally, still they have done so because of their lack of foresight and consideration of the welfare of others.

[16]How much higher those others stand, how much more admirable they are! They by no means place less value on the joint quest after wisdom. But they prefer generosity to indifference and give away their property instead of ruining it and thus benefit others and themselves; the others through the generous abundance of belongings, themselves through the cultivation of wisdom. Care for earthly goods and possessions consumes time. But time must be put to good use since, according to the physician Hippocrates, life is short but art lasts a long time.

[17]It seems to me that Homer too points this out in the *Iliad,* at the beginning of the thirteenth song, in the following words:

> The Mysian, courageous in hand-to-hand fighting;
> And dwellers on the Scythian lands,
> They live on milk, are poor and yet
> Are the most just of men.

So it appears that anxiety concerning outer life and earthly possessions creates injustice due to the inequality that arises from it, whereas the opposite attitude establishes justice through the equality that arises from it, in which the wealth inherent in man by nature is acquired, a wealth that surpasses all empty fame in happiness.

[18]Now, when they have disposed of their earthly goods, they unequivocally escape. Tempted no more by anything, they leave brothers, children, wives, parents, their numerous relatives, affectionate

friendships, their native land where they were born and raised, for habit poses a powerful bond and strong temptation.

[19]But they do not merely settle in another town, as do shipwrecked people and bad slaves who beg their masters to sell them, only intent on a change of masters instead of freedom. For any town, even the most well-ordered, is full of noise, misfortune and unspeakable confusion, which none who has once been gripped by love for wisdom can readily tolerate.

[20]Rather, they take up their abode outside the walls in gardens and remote fields, submitting to seclusion, not because of outright aversion to people but to avoid mixing with different customs, concerning which they know that these would be detrimental and harmful to them.

§3 [21]This community can be encountered at many locations in the world, for it was fitting that both Greece and the country of the barbarians should partake of whatever is perfectly good. They live in Egypt in large numbers, in every one of the provinces, which are called *nomi,* and are most numerous in the surroundings of Alexandria.

[22]From everywhere, the most outstanding people are sent as into a common homeland to the site of the Therapeutae, a particularly suitable location, as far as safety as well as the balmy warmth of the air are concerned, by the shore of the Mariotic Sea, lying in a somewhat level plain a little raised above the rest.

[23]Safety is assured by the farms and villages which surround them. The pleasant temperature of the air is due to the lake that pours into the ocean and to constant winds that blow from the nearby open sea. The lighter air comes from the sea, the denser air from the lake ending in the sea. And the mixture of both brings about the healthiest climate.

[24]The dwellings of those who have come together there are as simple as can be and offer protection only against two things, the heat of the sun and the cold of the air. They do not stand closely together as do houses in the cities, for neighbourhoods are oppressive and not very attractive to those who seek and cultivate seclusion. But they are not too far apart either, for the Therapeutae do love and nurture community; also, so that they can help each other in case of an attack by robbers.

[25]In each house is a sacred room, called the sanctuary or *monasterium,* in which they retire by themselves and celebrate the mysteries of holy life. They carry nothing inside, neither drink, food nor anything else that serves the gratification of bodily needs. They take along only the commandments and words of truth proclaimed by men of prophecy; the hymns and all else whereby insight and piety are advanced and perfected.

[26]They never allow awareness of the divine world to slip from their minds. Even in their dreams they are imbued by no other conceptions save the beauty of divine virtues and powers. Even in their sleep, many utter the solemn sentences of the sacred philosophy while dreaming.

[27]They are in the habit of praying twice a day, early in the morning and in the evening. When the sun comes up, they pray for a good day, but a good day in the true sense of the word, a day on which the heavenly light fills their thoughts. At sundown, they ask that their soul, quite free of the burden of the senses and sense perceptions, may enter its own consistory and council-chamber so as to find the traces and the path of truth.

[28]The whole span of time between morning and evening is for them the time of meditation and the practice of virtue. When they take up the holy scriptures, they submit to philosophy and interpret allegorically the paternal wisdom by assuming the presence of a hidden higher nature behind the sounds and meaning of the actual words, a higher nature revealed in these indications.

[29]In their circle, the writings of the ancients are preserved, men who as leaders in such spiritual quests have left behind many monuments of this allegorical system of writing and explanation. The Therapeutae employ these as examples and imitate the manner of the older school. Thus, they not only devote themselves to inner vision; they compose songs and hymns of praise to God in any number of metres and melodies to which they give a special loftier form through solemn rhythms.

[30]They spend six days exclusively, each in solitude, in their monasteries, dedicated to philosophy without crossing the threshold or even taking a look around outside. On the seventh day, they gather together as if joining in council and sit down in order according to their age, in the prescribed position, the hands inside their garments, the right between chest and chin, the left down on the side close to their flank.

[31]Then the oldest and most experienced in the teaching comes forward and begins to speak, restrained in his expression, restrained in his voice, with clarity of thought and intelligent presence of mind, not in impressive words like rhetoricians of old and today's sophists, who show off with their lectures, but searching for and explaining the exact meaning of thoughts, a meaning not accessible to superficial ears but one that penetrates and remains in the soul only through inner open-mindedness. In silent repose, all the others listen, demonstrating their acclaim only through the eager look of the eyes or nods of their heads.

[32]The communal sanctuary where one meets on the seventh day consists of two partitioned rooms, one for the men, one for the women's group. For the custom prevails that women too are among the listeners,

insofar as they are imbued by the same aspirations and belong to the same spiritual direction.

[33]Between the two sections is a wall that rises three or four cubits from the floor, not unlike a battlement. The intermediate space up to the ceiling is left open. One arranges it like this for two reasons; first, to maintain the modesty befitting the female, but then also to make comfortable seating possible for them without anything being in the way of the speaker's voice.

§4 [34]They have made abstinence in their soul the foundation on which the structure of all other virtues can be erected. Hardly any one of them will partake of food and drink before sundown, for they only consider the cultivation of philosophy as worthy of light; bodily requirements, on the other hand, so they believe, are suitable only to darkness. This is why they dedicate the days to philosophy; to the bodily needs, on the other hand, a small portion of the night.

[35]Some are mindful of food only every three days; they are the ones in whom the desire for knowledge predominates. Others in turn gain so much pleasure and enjoyment from the meals of philosophy which are granted them generously and liberally, that they can be without food for twice that time and have hardly any need for it after six days; they have become used to living on air, as is said of the grasshoppers for whom, so I do believe, song makes it easier to bear the deprivation.

[36]They consider the seventh day to be an especially holy and festive one and for that reason confer special honours on it. After having given care to the soul, they now oil the body, even as they make it a point to free the cattle from constant work.

[37]They do not consume expensive dishes but inexpensive bread and, as a seasoning, salt that the most spoiled among them mix with hyssop. Water recently fetched from the spring serves as their drink. Thus they pacify the two rulers installed by nature in mortal creatures, hunger and thirst. They partake of nothing that could serve to pamper them, only of what is necessary to survive. Thus they eat in order not to starve and they drink so as not to thirst; they avoid any gluttony as a conniving foe of soul and body.

[38]There are two kinds of covering, garments and shelter. Concerning housing, mention was made of it earlier, namely, that they are un-adorned and quite plain, only furnished for barest necessity. Clothing is likewise extremely simple and serves only to repel cold and heat. In winter, they wear a thick overcoat instead of the woollen fleece; in summer, a thin mantle or linen garment.

[39]In all regards they endeavour to be free of vanity, for they know

that vanity has its source in falsehood; that humility, on the other hand, has its source in truth, and that everything bears the nature of its origin. Out of falsehood arises all forms of evil; out of truth, on the other hand, flows the abundance of human and divine goods.

§5 [40]Now I shall also tell of the gatherings in which they practice their community, of the festive customs of their banquets and compare the banquets of others with them. For when the others indulge in the enjoyment of undiluted wine, it is as if they were not drinking wine but a stimulant that evokes madness and frenzy, or, what is worse, a means for completely relinquishing natural reason. They shower each other with insults and become angry like mad dogs. They fall upon one another and bite each other, injuring each others' noses, ears, fingers and other limbs, so that they prove the truth of the story of the Cyclops and companions of Odysseus, inasmuch as they consume raw human flesh, as the poet says, and thus perpetrate an even worse savagery than the Cyclops.

[41]Because of his suspicion, the Cyclops takes revenge on his enemies. But these drunkards assault their companions and friends, sometimes even their relatives, while having the salt and dinner-table before them, inasmuch as they do things contrary to peace similar to what happens in gymnastic competition where the weaker push aside the strong ones because money takes the place of proper exercise, and instead of athletes they become miserable men. Unfortunately, this must be said of them.

[42]For what those do soberly in the stadium in daytime, in that they run skillfully in the Olympic games in view of all the watching Greek people in order to gain victory and the wreath, this these do in devious actions during the banquets at night in the dark, drunken and full of wine, without spirit and skill; without honour and shamelessly, finally ending in complete immorality.

[43]And if an arbitrator would not step between them to keep them apart, they would wrestle each other to the ground with unlimited licence and in so doing murder and kill each other. Yet are their own sufferings no less than those they inflict on others. Without knowing it, they lose their reason through wine and thereby do damage, as the poet of comedy says, not only to other men but to themselves, since they have to bear the consequences of their drinking.

[44]For verily, those who a short while ago arrived safe and sound and as friends at the banquets, soon depart as enemies with mutilated bodies. And some among them are in need of advocates and judges, others of surgeons and physicians and the relief they receive from them.

[45]Others from among the drinking companions who appear to be more temperate drink unmixed wine like the sap of the mandrake root. They incline their upper body forward, support themselves with their lower left arm, turn their neck forward sideways, drink cup after cup and fall into a deep sleep. They no longer see nor hear anything. It is as if they had only one sense, the lowest, namely the sense of taste.

[46]I also know a few who, before they succumb to complete intoxication, prepare for the drinking bout of the following day, because they believe that part of the present enjoyment is looking forward to subsequent drunkenness.

[47]In this manner, they constantly live without home and hearth, alienated from their parents, wives and children, estranged from their country, even alienated from themselves. For such a debauched, dissolute life is harmful to all men.

§6 [48]Perhaps someone might now go for the new sort of banquets that are coming into vogue everywhere. They spring from the craving for Roman opulence and luxury, of which Greeks as well as barbarians are jealous. They are arranged to serve outer show more than actual pleasure.

[49]Dining sofas for three or more persons are set up which are made out of turtle leather, ivory or even more precious materials, frequently even decorated with gems. Purple covers interwoven with gold and silver are spread over these sofas. In addition, others are embroidered to feast the eyes with multicoloured floral patterns. A profusion of drinking-vessels are available, arranged according to their various forms: drinking horns and bowls and cups and many other containers, artistically decorated with hunting scenes engraved painstakingly by an expert hand.

[50]One encounters slaves serving there who are of the most exquisite beauty, as if they were actually not present to serve but merely to gladden the eye of the beholder by their appearance. Some, still the age of boys, pour wine; others, looking like adolescent shepherds, carry in the water. Properly washed and smooth, their faces are rubbed with cream and painted, their hair artfully curled and braided.

[51]For they wear their hair long and do not shave it at all, except for the hair over the forehead which they cut the same length in front so that a precise circular line is created. They wear their shining white tunics, made of the finest material, kilted up. In the front, the tunics reach to the knees, in the back a bit lower; the slaves draw all the parts together with woollen double ropes at the fastening of the undergarment so that they stick out on both sides of the abdomen. In this way, they manage to make the curves of the hips appear wider.

[52]Others have noble youths, who already have a first growth of beard, who are thoroughly prepared for more painful service. They are supposed to demonstrate the affluence of the hosts, but, as the guests know, actually show only their lack of really good manners.

[53]The greatest variety of sweetmeats and delicacies are served, dishes on which bakers and butchers have laboured. But the purpose is not the taste, which alone would be sensible, but the aromatic smell and splendour of mere appearance.

[54]Seven full tables are carried in, loaded with all that earth, sea, rivers and air produce, choice pieces of good meat from creatures of land, water and air, each prepared and served in a completely different way. So that nothing is lacking of nature's abundance, dishes loaded with fruit are finally carried in for those who are feasting as well as for those who, as we say, have had their fill.

[55]Then these dishes are carried out empty because of the insatiable greediness of those present. And now a sort of fried chicken is served that the guests wolf down in full view of everybody. Even crunching the bones, they deal with the chicken coarsely, tear them into pieces and swallow whole chunks. At last, when they are tired, their stomachs full to the gullet, yet feeling empty in their greed, they leave the dishes standing and turn their head around in a circle, searching through the room with their eyes and noses. The eyes seek the abundance of good meat, the noses the rising steam. When they have had their fill through looking and smelling, they begin to talk about the meal and give no mean praise to the preparation and the host in his wastefulness. This, according to custom, is done at length.

[56]However, why need I dwell with such prolixity on these matters, which are already condemned by the generality of more moderate men as inflaming the passions, the dimunition of which is desirable? For any one in his senses would pray for the most unfortunate of all states, hunger and thirst, rather than for a most unlimited abundance of meat and drink at banquets such as these.

§7 [57]Of the banquets in Greece, the two especially famous and significant are those in which Socrates participated: the one in the house of Callias on the occasion of awarding the wreath to Autolycus and the other in the house of Agathon. These two banquets were deemed worthy of remembrance by men who were true philosophers, namely Xenophon and Plato. They recorded these banquets as being memorable and thought that people of their age should take them as examples for generally conducting banquets harmoniously.

[58]But though many of our contemporaries who would like to dedicate

themselves to a contemplative life are of the same opinion, even these will appear ridiculous. Each has its own attractions but the banquet of Xenophon has greater human immediacy. Female flute players and male dancers, magicians and comedians are present who are proud of their appearance and graceful behaviour and whatever else is customarily offered at jovial events of recreation.

[59]The Platonic entertainment deals almost exclusively with love, not only with the one in which men are smitten with women or women with men, for this desire follows a natural law, but also with the love of men for one another differing only in respect of age. And even though the conversations concerning Eros and the heavenly Aphrodite appear to be artfully invented, they are introduced merely for the sake of making a neat speech.

[60]The greater part is occupied by the common, vulgar, promiscuous love which brings to naught the most useful virtue in war and peace, namely manhood. It is something that evokes an effeminate affliction in souls and turns men into male-females, men whom one should by all means possible train once again in the faculty of valour.

[61]After Eros has corrupted the age of youth and has produced the profession of lover, it also harms their lovers in regard to what they must prize the most, in body, soul and their possessions. For the fanciers of young boys are under the compulsion of inwardly focusing completely on their little lovers. They are alert and attentive only here, whereas in all other affairs of their ordinary life they are blind because of their passion. And when their love is unrequited, they usually pine away. They lose their possessions for two reasons, on the one hand due to carelessness, on the other because of the extravagant expenses for the beloved.

[62]Still another social evil arises from this. What they bring about is that the cities become depopulated; that there is an increasing lack of the noblest kind of men and that sterility and devastation ensue. In their actions they resemble those who ignorantly till their soil and instead of sowing seeds into fertile soil, sow it on fields below sea level, or on stony hard ground where nothing can grow and flourish and the sown seed must decay.

[63]I shall remain silent concerning the fabulous fictions as well as the stories of persons with two bodies who, through powers of love, are fundamentally grown together and yet are separated like two fused limbs and robbed of the harmony that unites them. I have let all this pass through my mind. By the attractive novelty of their imagination, it will allure our ears. But the friends of Moses, who from the time of their childhood have learned to love truth, will in the end hold all this

in low esteem. They will know how to stand their ground against all temptation and illusion.

§8 [64]Since these famous banquets are full of empty words and basically convict themselves, a judgment that cannot be a commendable one — I shall ignore the rumour that circulates about them, as if they were well ordered in every regard —'I shall now compare them with the meals of those who have dedicated their life and themselves to understanding and contemplating the higher nature according to the sacred instructions by Moses, the prophet.

[65]They always have their most important gathering after seven times seven days, inasmuch as they not only revere the simple number seven but the square of seven. They see in it a holy and eternally virginal number. And to them, this day is therefore an especially exalted and lofty festival because the secret of the number fifty (the secret of Pentecost) is contained in it, the most holy and natural number, taken from the square of the right-angled triangle wherein originates all creation and existence.

[66]Now, when they have come together in white garments, full of joy and in a most uplifted mood of celebration, one of the *Ephemereutae,* the guardians of the day, as they are in the habit of calling those who serve at this festival, gives a sign. While still standing, before they sit down at the table, in well-ordered sequence one after the other, they lift up their eyes and hands to heaven — the eyes because they have learned to contemplate things worthy of vision, the hands because they are free of any covetousness and unspoiled by any ambitions for gain. And so they pray to God that the meal may be pleasing to Him and its course follow the laws of His reason.

[67]After the prayer, the elders take their seats at the table, where age is reckoned by the time of their reception into the community. For they do not consider as elders those who have reached old age, those advanced in years; rather, they look upon them as young boys if love for their spiritual direction awoke in them only late in life. Those are considered elders who, from their earliest youth, have found access and developed mature strength in the meditative part of spiritual striving, which indeed is the most beautiful and godly part.

[68]Women likewise partake of the meal, women of whom most are virgins who have retained their innocence, not because of duress like some of the Greek priestesses, but voluntarily because of their own conviction, seeking ardently for wisdom to which they wish to be wed. They value bodily pleasures but little, and long not for mortal but immortal offspring whom only the soul that befriends God can give birth

to out of herself, when the Father of the Universe has sent His spirit's rays of light into her, whereby she can behold the teachings of wisdom.

§9 [69]The celebrants at the table are divided in two groups; the men sit separately on the right, the women on the left. If somebody is of the opinion that cushions, even if not valuable nevertheless softly woven ones, are spread out for these noble and sensitive nurturers of philosophy, he is mistaken. Rather, they are hard mats of common material, cheaply woven ones out of the native papyrus plant, which are simply laid on the floor and raised only in the area of the elbow so that a person can support himself on them. Those present remain free of laconic sternness, always exhibiting a liberal, cheerful frugality, thus protecting themselves from all lures of pleasure.

[70]They do not allow slaves to serve them, inasmuch as they consider the possession of servants and slaves to be unnatural. For nature has created all human beings to be free. Only the injustice and selfishness of some who are intent on bringing about inequality, the source of all evils, has placed power over the weak into the hands of the stronger.

[71]Therefore, as I have said, there are no slaves during this sacred meal. Only free men are the servants and perform their service neither under compulsion nor in obedience to orders, but of their own free will, quickly and helpfully anticipating any command.

[72]Moreover, not by chance are the free ones simply called upon for these services. Instead, youths are very carefully chosen from within the whole brotherhood according to their inner nobility. So one really encounters only capable, high-minded personalities among them who have risen to the summit of virtue. Like true sons, they minister in cheerful rivalry to their fathers and mothers and believe that these, their collective parents, are closer to them than those who are their blood parents. Indeed, for those of good will, nothing comes more naturally than all that is noble and good. Those who are serving enter ungirdled and in letdown garments, so nothing which bears any resemblance to a slavish appearance may be introduced into the community partaking of the meal.

[73]I know that some who hear this will laugh about it. Those will laugh whose actions are in themselves deplorable and lamentable. Wine is not served on such days, but sparkling clear spring water, cold for most of them, and hot water for the more sensitive ones among the old men. Likewise, the table remains free of bloody dishes. Bread is the food at this dinner, and salt serves as a supplement to which hyssop is added on occasion as a spice for the indulgent ones.

[74]Sobriety which is proper for priests who offer up sacrifice is

331

present in their mind as true behaviour throughout their whole life. For wine is the magic potion that causes want of reason and lavish food produces the insatiable creature, greed.

§10 [75]Now these are the preparations for the meal. When the guests of the dinner have taken their seats in prescribed order and those who serve stand orderly and ready for service, the drinking bout does not begin, as one might think. Instead, a greater stillness than before ensues, so that none dare move or even take a deep breath. One person then chooses a passage from the holy scriptures in order to interpret it, or he presents the solution to a question that another has raised without being in the least intent on making himself important. For he does not seek after the fame of eloquent speech. His wish is merely to attain better insight concerning some point of the teaching; and when he has attained this insight, he unselfishly passes it on to the others who may perhaps not possess such penetrating thinking and yet have just as much deep longing for knowledge.

[76]The one who speaks makes use of a detailed and slow manner of instruction; he dwells on one thing again and again and inserts repetitions in order to instill his thoughts deeply within the souls of his hearers. The comprehension of the listener cannot keep pace with an interpretation that proceeds in a hurried breathless tempo, for he misses the repetitions.

[77]The others, their heads turned to the speaker, remain in one and the same position listening attentively, and express their comprehension and understanding by nodding and in the way they look. If they wish to praise the speaker, they turn their face to him with a cheerful demeanour; a doubt they express through a slight shaking of the head and by moving the index finger of the right hand. No less attentively than those who sit at the table, the youths listen who stand nearby.

[78]The interpretation of the holy scriptures is based on the deeper meaning of the allegorically understood text. The whole book of the Law seems for these men to resemble a living being whose body consists of the direct wording of the commandments and whose soul consists of the thought-content indwelling the words invisibly in hidden form. In this thought-content, the thinking soul begins above all to behold and recognize her own being. In the mirror image of names, they see confronting them the archetypes of great beauty beyond all measure. They learn how to distinguish and unveil the symbols, to bring to light the uncovered inner substance for those who, from subtle indications, are able to decipher the hidden meaning of phenomena.

[79]When the one in the chair believes that he has presented a

332

sufficiently long discourse and if his feeling in this regard coincides with the gathering, meaning when he has brought the consideration of the subject to a proper conclusion and the audience is satisfied with what they have heard, then, as a sign of general pleasure, they all applaud by clapping their hands.

[80]Then the speaker rises up and begins to sing a hymn of praise to God, either a new one he himself has composed or one that is by a poet of the past. For they have left an abundance of verses and melodies, epics in three parts, songs for processions, hymns, songs accompanying offerings, altar songs and choruses in a variety of rhythms and metres. Following him, the others likewise sing one after the other in proper order, while the rest listen without making a sound, except when the concluding verse and the joint hymns are sung. For then, all raise their voice, the men and women.

[81]When each has finished his hymn, the youths carry in the above-mentioned table on which the most sacred food is placed, namely sour-dough bread and the salt to be eaten with it — to which is added hyssop — out of reverence for the table which stands in the holy ante-room of the Temple. For on it, loaves of bread and salt without another spice are placed.

[82]The breads are unleavened and the salt is not mixed, for it is proper that the simplest and purest is portioned out to the highest rank of the priesthood as a reward for conducting the ritual. The others are all supposed to seek for the same purity but must deny themselves the enjoyment of unspiced bread so that those of higher rank retain a privilege.

§11 [83]After the meal, they conduct the sacred ceremony during the night. This nocturnal ceremony takes the following course. All of them rise and, around the table in the middle, two choirs are formed, one of men, the other of women. On each side, one choir leader and precentor is chosen, namely the most respected and musical one.

[84]And then they sing hymns composed for the praise of God and in a variety of rhythms and melodies, sometimes all together, then again in antiphonies in which they accompany the rhythm with gestures to which they dance. Moreover, they break out in prophetic ecstasy and either sing as they stride solemnly or stand still, frequently creating on their own the verses and responsive verses required for this.

[85]Then, when each group, the men by themselves and the women by themselves, are satiated, even as the celebrants of the Bacchus festivals are by wine, they join, filled with divine love, so that, out of the two groups, one choir comes about. This is an emulation of the ancient

festival that was celebrated at the Red Sea, on account of the miracles that occurred there.

[86]For there, following the divine command, the sea became a source of delivery for one group, for the others a source of disaster. Surging upwards and subsiding, the sea formed itself on the two opposite sides like solid walls, and the space in between turned into a level, dry, wide country road through which the people passed over to the opposite land. When the sea ran together again and poured on both sides over solid land, the pursuing enemies were swallowed up by the waves and perished.

[87]When they saw and experienced this great miracle, an event beyond all description, beyond all imagination, beyond all hope, both men and women together under the influence of divine inspiration joined in one chorus and sang the hymns of the thanks-offering to the god of deliverance, Moses, the prophet, the leader of the men's choir, Miriam, the prophetess, the leader of the women.

[88]The celebration of the male and female Therapeutae is intended to be a replica of these events. When the deep voices of the men joins with the high voices of the women in concerted and contrasting sounds, it culminates in a harmonious and truly musical symphony. Beautiful are the thoughts, beautiful the words, holy the chorus-dancers. And the goal of thoughts, words and choral dance is piety.

[89]Intoxicated with this beautiful drunkenness, without heaviness of head and tiredness of limbs, instead more awake than before they came to the meal, they await the dawn. They stand, with their eyes and their whole body turned towards the rosy first light and when they behold the sun rising, they lift up their hands to heaven and pray for a blessed day and truth and clear vision of the spirit. After the prayer, everybody returns to the sanctuary of his own house, turning once more to their customary philosophical striving.

[90]So much of the Therapeutae, those admirers of the higher nature, living only in this and in the innermost soul. They are both citizens of heaven and of the world; recommended to God on account of their virtue through which they have attained His love as the most beautiful reward. The increase of virtue excels over all happiness; it leads to the summit of blissfulness.

From: Every Virtuous One is Free:
Quod omnis probus liber sit

In the preceding section examples of true virtuousness are listed: The seven sages of Greece, the magicians of Persia and the Gymnosophists. In the twelfth section, as an added example, the Essenes are described. In conclusion, the Essenes' nobility of soul is contrasted with the bestial insanity of Caesarism.

§12 Palestine and Syria, too, where a by no means small portion of the exceedingly populous Jewish nation lives, are not unfruitful in noble virtue. Among them are those who are called Essenes, over four thousand in numbers. I believe that their name, though not according to any accurate form of the Grecian dialect, is related to the Greek word for holiness, for they wish above all to be God's Therapeutae. They do not offer up animal sacrifices, but endeavour to shape their own thoughts and attitudes in such a manner that they are suitable for sacred service.

[76]They live predominantly in rural communities. They avoid towns on account of the appalling lawlessness of those who inhabit them. They know that even as polluted air causes disease, so, through association with wicked men, a moral disease would stamp an incurable evil on their souls. Some of them till the field, others are devoted to peaceful arts. Thus they benefit both themselves and their fellowmen. They do not accumulate treasures of gold and silver. Neither do they allow themselves, misled by the desire for property, to obtain larger parcels of land. Instead, they prefer to own precisely what they require for living.

[77]They are almost the only ones among men who live without goods and chattels, and they do this based on active intention more than due to lack of good fortune. And yet they consider themselves the richest of people, inasmuch as they view contentment and composure as the best of all riches, as in truth they are.

[78]Craftsmen who make arrows, spears or daggers, helmets, armour or shields, armourers, manufacturers of war materials or any objects used in battle are not found among them. Even those things that might lead to wrongdoing in peace are not produced among them. Not even in their dreams do they think about commercial dealings and maritime commerce, for they avoid any opportunity for avarice.

[79]Not a single slave exists among them; they are all free and help one another. They condemn all despotic men, not only as unjust because they violate equality but likewise as godless because they destroy the order of nature which like a mother has born and nurtured all human beings in the same way as if they were all legitimate brethren not in

name only, but in reality and truth. Cunning covetousness, which through its prosperity has become insolent, dissolved this kinship among all men inasmuch as it put alienation in place of affection, and enmity in place of friendship.

[80]Insofar as the logical part of philosophy is not needed to attain virtue, they leave that to the word hunters. To the extent that philosophy reaches beyond human nature, they leave the aspect dealing with physics to those who like to let their gaze wander up to the heights of heaven. Of this, they only exempt what philosophy has to say of the existence of God and the creation of the universe. On the other hand, they do devote great diligence and effort to the ethical part of philosophy. In so doing, they follow the laws of the fathers as if they were guidelines, laws that the human soul would have been incapable of inventing without higher spiritual inspiration.

[81]They instruct themselves on this at certain times, but most especially on the seventh day. For the seventh day is held by them to be sacred. Then, they refrain from any labour and gather at holy sites which they call synagogues. According to age, older and younger men take their seats in strict order and listen with eager attention.

[82]One man then takes the scrolls and reads from them and another, one of the most experienced, steps forward and speaks like a teacher concerning what is difficult to understand. For in most cases, their philosophy follows the ancient form of allegorical explanation.

[83]They are trained in piety, holiness, justice, in practical and social awareness, in true comprehension and perception of good and evil as well as in what is indifferent, namely in grasping what is necessary and in avoiding the opposite. In so doing, they apply a threefold rule and guideline: the love of God, the love of virtue and the love of humankind.

[84]As the mark of the love of God, many things are familiar to them: purity that dominates all of life and is always tried and true; avoidance of oaths and lies; faith that the divine is the source of all goodness, but not of evil. It is part of the love of virtue to be free of the craving for possession, fame and sensual enjoyment; to practice temperance and steadfastness, and furthermore frugality, simplicity, composure, modesty, reliability, determination and anything that lies in this direction. With love of humankind belong friendship; equal esteem for one and all, an attitude that is safe against all challenges; the cultivation of the community, concerning which it is not inappropriate to make a few remarks.

[85]First of all, nobody owns a home that does not belong likewise to them all. They not only live in the houses in certain groups but also open them to supporters of the same cause who arrive from elsewhere.

[86]Furthermore, they have communal storage rooms and their

expenditures are made jointly. Clothing is community property as are the foods among those who eat together. One will not readily find the communal element of dwelling, life style and eating repeated elsewhere in such vigorous manner. Can this indeed even be surpassed? They retain nothing of what they receive as compensation for labour during the day. Instead, they bring it into their circle as common goods for the use and benefit of whoever wants it.

[87]The sick therefore do not suffer neglect because they cannot earn anything. What they need for their care is available to them from the communal possessions. So they suffer no deprivation but can draw from their abundant means. Humility, respect and willingness to serve is felt towards the elders, even as is offered to parents by their real children. Into their old age, with advice and exertion in richest measure, one devotes to them all manner of care.

§13 [88]Such champions of virtue are in fact produced through a philosophy that remains unencumbered by the superfluous examining into Greek names and instead describes admirable deeds for the purpose of emulation and training, deeds, the fruit of which is a freedom that cannot be enslaved.

[89]This became evident when rulers emerged again and again in those countries who differed in character and disposition. Some endeavoured to surpass wild animals in unbridled violence; they missed no opportunity to unfold their savagery. They sacrificed their subjects in droves, slaughtering them alive limb by limb as the butchers are want to do with animals. And they did not desist from this until they were overtaken by the same fate through the justice that oversees all things human with an alert eye.

[90]Others again gave different expression to madness and folly and made themselves instruments of evil in a surreptitious manner. They exhibited unspeakable savagery. Although they indulged in peaceful speech, they betrayed the ferocity of their real disposition under the hypocrisy of a gentle voice. Like vicious dogs, they fawned and cajoled, but like such dogs caused irreparable harm. As monuments of their godlessness and hatred of men, they left behind in the towns unforgettable suffering. Yet, not one of them, neither the arrogantly bloodthirsty nor the cunningly vile ones, could undertake anything against the community of the Essenes of whom we have spoken. They were all disarmed by the noble virtue of these men and had to acknowledge them as independent persons free by nature. And they felt compelled to acclaim their meals and their community that is beyond all praise, a community which is proof of a perfect and truly blissful life.

Discoveries at the Dead Sea 1950–57

*Important discoveries in the desert**

In the years 1946 and 1947, two large collections of ancient manuscripts consisting of significant religious documents were found in the remote deserts of upper Egypt and Palestine. The scholars who are engaged in deciphering them are continually astounded by their exceptional importance. One set of texts, discovered in the region of the rocky shoreline by the Dead Sea and dated between 150 and 100 BC, belongs to the domain of the Old Testament and its apocryphal extensions. The other group from upper Egypt contains Gnostic books which, in a wider sense, can be counted among the apocrypha of the New Testament and date from the time when early Christendom was drawing to a close around the year 300.

The Egyptian find is more voluminous; the Palestinian find, on the other hand, is probably the more significant one. Up to now, a good deal of drama surrounds the manuscripts discovered by the Dead Sea, especially as fantastic sums are being offered for them in America. In the summer of 1947, a Bedouin shepherd was on his way from Jericho to Bethlehem or Hebron with his animals. The road first runs south to the Dead Sea and continues for a while along the rugged, rocky shoreline in that subterranean world of death (400 metres below sea level) until it turns westward along an ancient path that leads up into the mountains. One of the animals disappeared in a crevice. When the Arabs removed the rocks in order to rescue the animal, they found themselves in front of a cave. Its floor was covered by rubble and shards. When they looked more closely, they discovered a number of broken clay jars and — within them — leather scrolls in covers that were soaked in wax and tar. The content consisted of eight to twelve scrolls with text; a large part appeared to be well preserved.

The scrolls passed through many hands and were not even kept together. Finally, they arrived in localities where it was possible for scholars to examine them. The script was determined to be Hebrew and Syriac. In the end, the scholars believed they could determine with certainty that the scrolls originated from the last period of the Macca-

---

* *Die Christengemeinschaft*, 1950. 3/4.

bean age, the second half of the second pre-Christian century. To their amazement, the first scroll they were able to decipher contained the whole book of the prophet Isaiah. Up until then, only handwritten texts of the Old Testament scriptures from a much later time existed; none went back further than to the ninth century AD. The scholars continue to be occupied with the assessment of the other scrolls, many more of which the Bedouins may still retain because of greed. In part, these other scrolls contain hymnlike, partly legendary-imaginative texts in the style of mythological and apocalyptic apocrypha that are grouped around the Old Testament. Recently, in Washington, where some of these finds have ended up, it was a great surprise and sensation to discover that one scroll contains the *Book of Lamech,* a text sought for since Christian antiquity, whose title was frequently quoted by ancient Jewish and early Christian theologians. Perhaps people will be initially disappointed by its content. For one *only* discovered that Noah's birth, childhood and mission is reported in it.

I believe that the key for the actual significance of the Palestinian find results from the place of discovery. Not far from there, only slightly more to the south and coming from the more western, higher region of Hebron-Bethlehem, the valley of En Gedi runs into the Dead Sea. The main seat of the Essene Order was located in this valley, right up to Jesus' time. All around it stood the humble dwellings that belonged to the Essene brethren who either lived in smaller monastic communities or as ascetic hermits.

When, in 1934, I conducted a guided tour through Palestine for fifty friends of the Christian Community, I included a two-day excursion around the Dead Sea, a trip that was still unusual in those days. One of the main goals was a visit to En Gedi. The friends who were with us will clearly remember the hours that we spent at the shore of the Dead Sea. We know from Philo and Josephus that the Essenes' greatest, carefully guarded treasure was a collection of holy scriptures from which they read and sang during their ritual gatherings. I have no doubts that, in the case of the location of the find, we deal with one of the caves adjacent to the monasteries in which the Essenes stored their mystery treasure, or hid it during the threats of persecution in the Maccabean age. From the manuscripts, particularly those that contain the psalms and hymns, it appears that they served a community that called itself 'the New Covenant.' This designation is none other than the one we use to denote the holy scriptures of Christendom, 'the New Testament.' Here, this title appears in pre-Christian times, at the time of the Old Testament, and must therefore have alluded to a community that had an altogether Messianic attitude, full of expectation for what signifies the fulfilment of the Old Covenant and therefore establishes the 'New Covenant.' This is true in the exact sense of the Essene Order.

If one meticulously pursues this direction and seriously considers the ancient mystery knowledge in the way it was still cultivated by the Essenes, the true nature of the apocryphal books found there (in addition to the prophetic works by Isaiah and Habakkuk) — works that resemble legends — becomes discernible. Behind Noah stands the figure of the loftiest Atlantean initiate whom the Indian Orient calls 'the great Manu' and who in a later manifestation of his being in the Old Testament was called Melchizedek.* His biography and mission, namely to rescue the best of Atlantean life before the great Flood and, by so doing, prepare the birth of future civilizations, cannot be told even in legendary form without touching upon the most profound mysteries of earthly and human evolution.

Another text that has been discovered by the Dead Sea will be even more significant than the *Book of Lamech.* In it, once again in mythological pictures, the 'Struggle between the Sons of Light and the Sons of Darkness' is depicted. In the first Christian centuries, the Manichees concealed their most sacred secret knowledge concerning the mystery of humanity's destiny in a legend that described the same struggle. But this legend already looked back to the Deed of Christ who, as the highest 'son of light,' sacrificed himself to the world of the 'sons of darkness' in order to illuminate and transform this world from within. It now appears that the Essenes possessed and cultivated an earlier Messianic version of this Manichaean legend, a version steeped in the precognition of the coming of the greatest 'son of light.'

If the finds in the desert are to have more than a merely literary and academic value, they must be understood as a clarion call for today's humanity to rediscover and renew the forgotten and lost world of the mysteries in a form that befits the present.

The Hebrew manuscripts from the cave†

Two and a half years ago, I first reported on the exciting discoveries of manuscripts made by a Bedouin shepherd in 1947 in a cave of the desert near the Dead Sea. Quite apart from the literary significance of the previously unknown Hebrew texts, I immediately evaluated these finds as offering an insight into the world of the Essene Order. From

---

* See *Genesis,* chapters 5 and 7 concerning Noah and Melchizedek.

† *Die Christengemeinschaft,* 1952, August.

the writings of the older Pliny (a Roman contemporary of the Apostles), it had always been known that this Order had its central monastic settlements within the valley of En Gedi in the Judean Desert by the Dead Sea. For more than a century, the existence of the Essene Order was put in doubt by scientific reasoning. This is a particularly glaring example of how modern historical research has tried to ignore all the mystery streams of earlier times. It simply resulted from the fact that the mystery communities had always been at pains to maintain their secrecy and avoid any emergence of written documents, whereas today's descriptions of history, estranged as they are from mystery traditions, wish solely to rely on such written documents.

Now, step by step, there is verification of the fact that, through the accidental discovery by that Bedouin, we have actually come upon the world of the Essene Order. Suddenly, the existence of this movement is no longer in doubt or — what is worse — denied. As yet, the importance of the specific indications is not understood; they are registered as details. But people will eventually discover that, in one particular location, they have come in touch with the mystery practice that prepared Christianity. And they will find that the existing historical descriptions will be corroborated (see Chapter 4).

Thus, at the shore of the Dead Sea, not even one mile from the above-mentioned cave, the remains of a settlement that consisted of several dwellings were unearthed — Qumran. The leaders of the excavation (Father de Vaux, director of the Ecole Biblique in Jerusalem and G.L. Harding, director of the Department of Antiquities for Transjordan and Arab Palestine) confront nothing but riddles. Since there were no layouts of roads at all here, they thought they were dealing with a settlement that was abandoned soon after its establishment. In reality, the absence of any constructed streets is explained by the manner in which the Essenes built their monasteries in the desert. The two researchers do in fact propose that this has to do with Essene practices. The presence of special supply pipes through which water runs from a cistern into the main house, pipes that are remarkable under such primitive conditions, has to be explained by the important part that the washing of hands and feet played during the ritual gatherings of the Essenes.

Based on articles in the *Manchester Guardian,* a report in the *Jerusalem Post,* dated April 15, 1952, states that the main building had an upper floor. There, in the larger room, a bench ran along the walls round the table. The Essenes in fact always constructed the cenacle, the room of their 'sacred meal,' in an elevated position so as to protect it from the direct influences of the earth. Such cenacles played an

341

important part in several passages of Acts, since the first Christian congregations were in many instances continuations of such Essene communities. The site of the Last Supper in Jerusalem, shown to this day, is indeed such an 'upper room,' and the most famous example. In every place where the Latin Bible has the word, *coenaculum,* this is accurately translated in the Revised Standard Version as 'upper room' (Acts 9:37 and 20:8). It is obvious that the cave of the scroll-finds was probably not just a hiding place at special times of danger but was the place of safekeeping for the ritual texts of this Essene community that were considered to be secret writings.

In the Habakkuk commentary, one of the Hebrew documents discovered in the cave, a passage was found according to which the origin of the scrolls was fixed at the middle of the first pre-Christian century (previously, one had in mind a point in time one century earlier). This passage refers to a catastrophe that had recently overtaken the people on *Yom Kippur,* the autumn Jewish festival. It was experienced as God's punishment for the execution of the saint under whose leadership the Order, the Messianic community of the 'New Covenant,' had been formed. He is designated as the 'Master of Justice.'

Professor Dupont-Sommer raised the hypothesis that this refers to the autumn festival of the year 63 BC, because it was the moment in time when the Romans under Pompey invaded the country and brought to an end to the people's Maccabean self-rule. In the spring of 1951, publications by this scholar found an echo in the press under such titles as, "Did Christ have a predecessor? Martyr's death of the 'Master of Justice'." Since the descriptions in the Habakkuk commentary of this master sound more Christian than pre-Christian and could even fit Jesus of Nazareth himself, they provoked many discussions. Actually, here, too, historical research encountered mystery facts which, until now, historians believed they could ignore as legendary. In the case of this 'Master of Justice,' we deal with Jeshu ben Pandira, the great Messianic reformer and inaugurator of the Essene Order, who, not long before the invasion by Pompey, under Queen Alexandra (76–67 BC), was cruelly slain and nailed to a cross. It should be interesting to see whether historians will recognize the historical reality of such a figure at last.

Two mystery settings *

Four years ago, an initial report appeared in this magazine concerning the sensational discoveries of scrolls in the years 1946 and 1947 in the remote desert in Palestine by the Dead Sea and in upper Egypt near the River Nile. In both locations, a meticulous search quickly began in which the locals, enticed by the large sums offered for the finds, feverishly participated. The result has surpassed all expectations. The number of manuscripts unearthed is now so large that one can speak of whole libraries from antiquity.

At the Dead Sea, soon after the initial discovery and at a mere distance of 800 metres, a similar cave with even greater treasures was located. Seventy scrolls were found there. Meanwhile, having widened the search, more than forty such caves are known. About 250 scrolls are being mentioned. For the purpose of conservation, they were largely wrapped in tar-coated linen and kept in clay jars.

The revolutionary significance of the finds does not lie merely in the fact that the amount of ancient scriptures known to us has been significantly increased. It pays to focus attention on several fundamental reevaluations that result from these discoveries. They not only concern the canonic scriptures of the Old and New Testaments that have always been familiar to us. Early on, during the first find by the Dead Sea, scrolls with large segments of the Book of Isaiah were located. Meanwhile, at the same location, early manuscripts of approximately thirty books of the Old Testament were discovered. In addition to Hebrew, they are written in Phoenician, Aramaic and Greek.

The press frequently points out that the texts of all these biblical books exhibit interesting departures from the familiar versions. From an overall viewpoint, however, the newly appearing versions are not all that significant. The important point is that we are now in possession of authentic manuscripts of various parts of the Bible that are older by many centuries, some even by almost a thousand years, than those available until now. This in turn proves that the Bible text that has always been familiar to us retained its original form for far longer than theologians of the last hundred years were prepared to admit. An inordinate amount of time and effort has been expended by scholars in distinguishing and researching the sources, sorting the authentic from the fictitious in the Bible, and the original from later additions and edited versions. Whole libraries of works dealing with Bible criticism by prominent and even famous theologians suddenly prove to be out-

---

* *Die Christengemeinschaft,* 1954, February.

dated and immaterial. Up until now, theological circles have made no comment about this.

Immediately after the southern Palestinian finds became known, we pointed out that not only had scrolls of antiquity been uncovered but also an all-important setting of religious history, namely an obscure and remote centre of the Essene Order. In the meantime, general agreement has been reached concerning this aspect of the discovery. For it was not long before clues other than the scrolls surfaced. In the vicinity of the second cave, near Qumran, the remains of a foundation of a rectangular building (30 by 37 metres) were located. In its main room, rows of seats ran along the walls. Behind the building, a cemetery with more than a thousand graves was unearthed, where the dead had been buried without burial treasures of any kind. Decades ago, Dalman, the famous Palestinian explorer who possessed a remarkable faculty for tracking historical facts, had already come upon the ruin of the building. It was his belief that he dealt with the remains of a Roman stronghold.

Now, the generally held opinion is that one of the mother-houses of the Essene Order stood here. According to the reports by the elder Pliny (23–79), several more such mother-houses were located further south near En Gedi at a distance of twenty-five to thirty kilometres. We demonstrated (see p.341) that in the case of the main room we deal with the cenacle in which the Essene brothers, living as they did as ascetic hermits in the surrounding desert, celebrated the communal sacred meal, their regular hours of instruction and worship; that the cemetery with its large number of graves, an oddity for this desolate region, had been the burial site for the whole Order. Among the Essenes, only the Order was allowed to have property. For individuals, any personal possessions, especially money, were frowned upon. Discoveries of coins have now made it possible to ascertain several dates from the history of the Essene dwelling. Between AD 15 and 40, the house collapsed due to an earthquake. Was it perhaps the earthquake during the mighty days before Easter of the year 33? In the year 70, hence at the time of Jerusalem's destruction by the Romans, it was destroyed for good and abandoned.

The fact that no documents belonging to Essenism existed for the pre-Christian and first Christian decades — a fact that supported the scepticism and silence of established history — was explained from our perspective firstly by the esoteric character of the Order, secondly by the fact that after AD 70 most of the Essenes were assimilated into the Christian congregations, and finally by the gradual departure of the insignificant remnant who still existed after Jerusalem's destruction. One now reads in the reports concerning the finds: The history of the building of the house of Qumran is important because it can be determined that with the year 70 the history of the Essenes comes to an end.

Among the texts discovered in the first cave, there were *Rules for the congregations of the New Covenant.* They afforded a glimpse into the sphere of the Essene Order and its monastic life. Later, in addition to this quite complete text, generally designated as the *Scroll of the Sect,* supplementary scrolls were found, above all the *Damascus Document.* From this we learn a good deal of the rules of life and even the solemn monastic rule that the Essene brothers followed in their ascetic and meditative practice. It is now known that anyone who wished to be accepted into the Order first had to undergo a novitiate that lasted two years; that the novice passed through and attained 'grades' as he progressed on the inner path. Only males belonged to the Order. The oath of silence that bound them to the Order had to be the only one in their life. They renounced marriage, family life, and any personal possessions. They wore white garments. The communal sacred meal was their daily worship. Many dedicated themselves to the care and healing of the sick. For this reason, the Essenes were called *Therapeutae* in Egypt.

Access has also been gained to an important former monastic site in Egypt [Nag Hammadi]. The thirteen volumes (1000 pages) with forty-eight Gnostic texts that were discovered were part of a monastic library that offered the large numbers of hermits who lived there foundations for their contemplative life. The scholars who are at work on the find have indicated that the discoveries were made quite close to Tabenna, an island in the Nile on which St Pachomius established the 'first Christian monastery' around the year 340. It appears that they have not yet paid proper heed to the obvious inner connections. But they will eventually realize that the views prevalent in Church history concerning the origin of Christian monasticism are inappropriate. Christian monastic life arose directly out of the Essene element and is therefore considerably older than is commonly assumed. Nevertheless, its origins too were of an esoteric nature and therefore no documents exist that deal with them. Orthodox scholarship determined origin according to the first documentary records. In reality, however, that was merely the moment in time when decadence set in, at least insofar as the spell of secrecy was then broken.

Pachomius did not establish the first monastery. Rather, he stands at the beginning of a new, henceforth exoteric chapter in the history of Christian monasticism. Now that Christianity had been declared the state religion, it seemed obvious to turn formerly esoteric institutions into exoteric ones. Pachomius started the actual ecclesiastical, monastic stream subordinate to the Pope. And he did this at a location where,

345

previously, a flourishing esoteric spiritual life had existed in a monastic context.

The Essenes were a special Messianic spiritual stream within Judaism. Among them prevailed a view of the expected Messiah that differed completely from that of the Pharisees. The gnostic adherents in early Christendom, who mostly shared a communal monastic life, also represented a separate stream. But Essene deviation from customary Judaism signified at the same time a preparation and slow merging with Christianity whereas the deviation of the gnostics, who failed to find a relationship to the physical Incarnation of the Logos, produced a development away from Christendom.

For too long, historical research has had neither sensitivity for nor interest in the mystery element and the esoteric spiritual movements that ruled the world of antiquity. And they certainly survived up until the time of early Christendom and partly even beyond that period. The discoveries in Palestine and Egypt can help advance our views considerably if the mistake is not made to understand and evaluate them only in a literary historical sense. We have to refrain from picturing monastic and ascetic life in pre-Christian and early Christian contexts as having been utterly illiterate, lacking in thought content and only concerned with penitence. Moreover, we have to stop interpreting the biblical, apocryphal and gnostic scriptures as literary creations similar to those of a modern author. Even in the desert, the ancient monastic practices had as their setting centres of wisdom with a decidedly mystery character. And it was in settings such as these that the biblical scriptures with their apocryphal supplements, among which the mostly lost gnostic literature must be counted, were taken to be holy, 'secret books.' This meant they were seen as texts of wisdom gleaned from higher sources of cognition. When the scriptures of the New Testament were used in the growing Christian congregations, a mystery element and atmosphere of an Order thus imbued the latter.

It is clearly discernible that the Essenes in En Gedi and Qumran placed the books of the Old Testament alongside the specific scriptures and psalms of their Order. Doubtless, the gnostic circles near Tabenna, the island in the Nile River, also used and taught the Gospels and letters of Paul in this manner together with their particular literature. Not until the canonic development of both Old and New Testaments was the separate literature of esoteric schools and Orders, which were declared to be heretical, finally eliminated. This brought it about that Pharisaism was at pains to obliterate Essene writings and that growing Christian ecclesiasticism tried to destroy the gnostic texts.

The finds at the Dead Sea*

The discoveries of scrolls in the caves by the Dead Sea and the excavations that ensued in Qumran have become a public sensation to such an extent that one wonders: Is it possible that humanity today instinctively senses that they are here dealing with more than just an academic historical and philological discovery? A mystery is indeed involved here that is closely linked to the mysteries of the Christ Event at the beginning of the turning point of time. Nevertheless, clear insights that could end all speculation can hardly be attained if, in accordance with a knowledge of history that consists of a patchwork of single facts, we only ask what we can find out through these discoveries. For their significance lies in the fact that previously existing but ignored insights are recognized through them.

I shall clarify what is meant here with a personal report. During a guided tour of several weeks through Palestine that I undertook in the spring of 1934 with a group of about fifty friends, we included a two-day excursion around the Dead Sea. Among the sites to which we paid special attention were the surroundings of the spot where, later on in 1947, by coincidence, a Bedouin shepherd found the first scrolls in a cave. We remained where the valley of En Gedi ends in the brine of the Dead Sea, in order mentally to go back to the time when one of the main centres of the Essene Order flourished here on the hills. A curious group of Arabs surrounded us when we settled down to read passages from the lectures of Rudolf Steiner that deal with the Essenes and the contacts made with them by John the Baptist and the young Jesus. At that time, we had among us an Armenian student who assisted me during the journey with matters of organization. While he had guided tourists on a number of occasions in and around Jerusalem, on this journey he was definitely the one who learned something, a fact he willingly admitted. I could lead my friends to places where I knew that most significant things could be encountered for re-experiencing the environment of the Gospels. In a surprising way, he always followed up my leads so that together we made many discoveries. In En Gedi, he was amazed with what assurance we made contact with the history of the place.

Recently, friends sought him out in Jerusalem and found that he belonged among the best known Palestinian tourist guides. He must have been pleased to meet up once again with persons who were connected to our group of 1934. Based on the experiences he had made in our

---

* Slightly abridged from *Die Drei*, 1956, 2 (Summer).

circle, he had developed a quite novel and successful form of guiding tourists. Most recently, so he said, he had continually followed the European news in the press, for he was certain that one day he would come across my name under the sensational headlines. 'Now I constantly guide large bus loads of visitors to the discovery sites at the Dead Sea. But Licentiate Bock led us there as early as the year 1934. In truth, he is the actual discoverer!' Naturally, my part was a quite secondary one. I was familiar with the passage in Pliny who, at the beginning of the Christian era, had mentioned the significance of En Gedi for Essenism. However, I would not have directed our group there based on that alone. What motivated me were the detailed disclosures made by Rudolf Steiner concerning the Essene Order as the most important Messianic community in late Judaism. Historians were not really interested in the Essenes; they considered the data that was handed down concerning them to be inexact and legendary. But Essenism shared this fate with all the other esoteric communities of antiquity. Accurate historical insight into mystery practices and esoteric movements of the past can only exist once again when the official view of history no longer rejects the esoteric element but makes it a part of itself.

Through the finds at the Dead Sea, the life of the Essenes and Therapeutae has been moved from 'mystical darkness' into the bright light of history. And, paradoxical as it may seem, one has to say: anyone wishing to be informed in more detail about the conditions of life that gave rise to the newly discovered scrolls — scrolls that in a crucial sense had as their stage the inner and outer surroundings of the monastery of Qumran — should read the lecture cycles Rudolf Steiner gave in the years 1909–14. Based on the directions indicated by Rudolf Steiner, I have been able, in my books dealing with early Christendom, to describe some of the aspects of the great significance that life in the Essene communities had for the preparation and organization of life in the first Christian congregations. With regard to their form, for instance, the two main Christian sacraments, baptism and communion, certainly evolved from the customs of washings and the daily communal meals practised among the Essenes.

For today's way of thinking about history, a thinking that is unable to grasp the nature of esotericism and the actual essence of Christianity, a touchy problem results from the unexpected insights into Essenism that have been gained. One is forced to say: if, more than a hundred years earlier, the Essenes practised what subsequently became the content of Christian life, then Christianity is merely a secondary phenomenon that derives its origin from something else, hence it loses its value; it was nothing new when it appeared.

The problem comes to a head through a specific report found above all in the recently surfaced commentary of the Prophet Habakkuk. Reference is made to a great spiritual leader and reformer of the Essene Order, the 'Master of Justice,' who suffered a martyr's death about sixty or seventy years prior to the birth of Christ. It is thought that we are dealing with two Messiah figures who lived shortly one after the other and the question is being asked: who really was the greater of the two? Does it not suggest that the earlier one should be viewed as the more original, creative spirit? This question is raised in many reports and commentaries and almost gives the impression that in the end the sensational finds may actually result in a devaluation of Christianity and the figure of Jesus. The *Neue Züricher Zeitung* (May 1, 1956) reports that the Semitic scholar, Dupont-Sommer of Paris, 'has tried to establish a far-reaching correspondence in the life and teachings of both men; that priority could only be applied to the sect and that Christianity has merely grown out of the latter. Jesus diminishes to a "remarkable reincarnation" of the "Teacher of Justice".'

It is true that such relativizations of Christianity have certainly brought forth objections even from among the ranks of scholars specifically engaged in the investigations. Nevertheless, a compelling objection can only be raised if it is possible to penetrate to the actual spiritual solutions of the mysteries of history connected with Essenism. And these solutions, even with regard to the 'Master of Justice,' have been accessible for almost half a century through the results of Rudolf Steiner's spiritual research. The 'Master of Justice' would always have been historically evident had not a tragic error from the days of early Christendom continued on through the centuries. His name was Jeshu ben Pandira. Originally, he had emerged from the Pharisaic Order and, together with his teacher, had been forced to flee to Egypt. There he attained to an understanding of himself and his universal mission through mighty soul-transforming experiences. He became a final, powerful, inspiring herald to humanity of the imminent coming of the Messiah. But in so doing he refrained from any public activity and instead turned into a reformer and inaugurator of the Order of Essenes and Therapeutae. This was an Order whose whole inner nature was directed towards preparing the proper reception for Christ among humanity. Around the year 70 BC, he was killed by his adversaries in Lydda.

Even though Jeshu ben Pandira must be viewed as one of the greatest among men, conventional history and its documentation does not know him. In actual fact, it knows him quite well. But because he was confused early on with Jesus of Nazareth, it so happened that his image was extinguished and Jesus of Nazareth's image became distorted. Even

Celsus, prominent opponent of Christianity in the second century, against whom Origen wrote the great work, *Contra Celsum,* lumped the two Jesus figures into one. He then tried to denigrate Jesus of Nazareth with features of the Essene predecessor, saying, for example, that Jesus had been the illegitimate child of Mary, a harlot, and a Roman soldier named Panthera (ben Pandira = son of Pandira).

This mix-up played a role until the end of the nineteenth century. For example, it prevented the Indian-oriented Theosophical movement, established by Blavatsky, to find a positive attitude to Jesus of Nazareth and Christendom. In *Esoteric Christianity* by Annie Besant, one can still read that Jesus was not born around the turn of time but 105 years earlier. Although the figure of Jeshu ben Pandira was still revealed to those who tried in some way to look back into history with spiritual perception, nevertheless in this way the figure of Jesus of Nazareth and his Christ-destiny became obscured.

When, in the years 1910 and 1911, Rudolf Steiner began to speak of Jeshu ben Pandira, he did it in vigorous rejection of the fundamental Christological error by the Theosophists. The latter certainly were focusing on the personality of a great spiritual leader but this very personality became superimposed for them over the true origin of the Christian stream. Insofar as they did not recognize Jesus of Nazareth, they could direct their sight even less on the lofty divine Christ being, a being that incarnated in the body and soul of Jesus in his thirtieth year in sublime uniqueness, thus bringing about the turning point of humanity's history. When the Theosophists spoke of Christ, they had Jeshu ben Pandira in mind who was only a human being, even though one of the greatest. Only in this way could they claim that Christ had become man again in the present. In so doing, they pointed to the then young Indian boy, Krishnamurti. Rudolf Steiner had to take a decisive stand against this. With unequivocal clarity, he could speak of the unassuming role of Jesus of Nazareth and the divine greatness of the Christ being who had become man only once. In order to unveil the tragic ancient error, he spoke moreover of Jeshu ben Pandira and his role in the late history of the Essene Order. In so doing, he emphasized that not only did esoteric tradition and spiritual research know of this teacher of wisdom but also Talmudic literature.

The passages in the Talmudic texts that deal with 'Jesus' were thought to relate to Jesus of Nazareth — at least by Christian circles — and were then quite naturally viewed as distortions and defamations. If they are related to Jeshu ben Pandira and added together in a basic outline, the astonishing result is that they present a complete biography of this figure ...

For the tricky question dealing with the priority between Essenism and Christendom, between the 'Master of Justice,' Jeshu ben Pandira, and Jesus of Nazareth, it is not enough, however, to have views concerning the historical relationship in which the two Jesus figures stood to each other. This question is in fact seriously raised through the findings of the Dead Sea. Those who push the problem aside in favour of Christianity make it too easy on themselves. So long as one views the essence of Christianity in the 'teaching of Jesus' or generally in an element of a teaching, one has to admit that almost all of it already existed in the environs of the Essenes. What Jeshu ben Pandira was able to teach based on highest inspirations has basically not been surpassed on a Christian basis. But perhaps the questions that arise from the new discoveries will generate an impetus to think differently about the nature of Christianity.

Christianity is not a new teaching. It is based on a being's earthly manifestation, a being about whom instruction was offered by all true initiates and sages of pre-Christian times. Jeshu ben Pandira, too, spoke of Christ, as did John the Baptist. The Christian stream began when he — of whom all earlier wisdom had been able to teach — himself passed through the three years of human incarnation and the mystery of death and resurrection. Christians still find it difficult to understand the difference between Jesus and Christ. But they will have to arrive once more at the insight, still possessed by early Christianity, that, upon receiving the baptism by John the Baptist, the human being, Jesus, turned into *Christophorus,* meaning that from then on the Christ being, who belongs to the highest hierarchical levels of existence, was incarnated in him. Perhaps it will be helpful in this regard to understand the difference between Jeshu ben Pandira and Christ. Rudolf Steiner unequivocally spoke about this while he rejected the theosophical incomprehension.

He counted Jeshu ben Pandira among the lofty teachers of humanity whom the Orient indicates with the name 'Bodhisattva.' Twelve exalted beings of wisdom exist in the spiritual worlds. Each great epoch of humanity's evolution stands under the guidance of one of these beings. In each case, such a being links up with a human personality and inspires and accompanies that person from one life on earth to the next. The Bodhisattva of our time worked through Jeshu ben Pandira after the one who preceded him had reached the end of his activity in Gautama Buddha. According to Oriental wisdom, and graphically described by Rudolf Steiner, the twelve Bodhisattvas have been pictured in lofty spiritual spheres grouped in a circle around a sun-like centre. They bear in themselves and pass on to humanity the knowledge of light. On the other hand, the being in the middle is the light itself, the sun of the spirit: Christ.

Thus, the wisdom-teachings of Jeshu ben Pandira and the Essene Order stand in the same relationship to Christianity as do prophecy and fulfilment.

Since the discoveries of the Dead Sea Scrolls*

Since a shepherd found clay jars containing scrolls in a cave by the Dead Sea about ten years ago, a whole chapter of pre-Christian cultural life has been revealed to a surprised world from the darkness of a forgotten past. The discovery of the scrolls soon led to the conjecture that the documents in question were sacred texts of the Essene Order. Although any references to this Order had until then been generally met with the greatest scepticism, nevertheless there were indications by authors of the first century that a main centre of Essenism had existed in the vicinity of En Gedi on the western side of the Dead Sea. Now, sizeable foundations and remains of that central monastic settlement have been excavated in Qumran north of En Gedi. Thus, in this way images of Essene life arise even more directly than through the discoveries of the scrolls. In the last few years there was probably nothing more historically revealing than the final report concerning these excavations by Father de Vaux in the *Revue Biblique* (1956, Vol. 4), from which the daily *Neue Züricher Zeitung* of April 9, 1957 reports the most important excerpts.

A whole complex of buildings can definitely be reconstructed, structures that covered an area of approximately 100 metres in length and 75 metres in width. The main building contained two rather long halls. One of them commands our special attention. A low bench ran all around its walls. In the middle stood long, slender tables; their shape could clearly be fitted together from the surviving fragments of wood. Since large numbers of dishes were found in the other long narrow room — seventy jugs and pots, over two hundred plates, seven hundred bowls and seventy-five mugs — it is assumed that at least one room, if not both, were dining rooms. It is necessary, however, to leave aside all conceptions that originate from profane life. Since the communal meal was at the same time the 'daily service' (see Acts 6:1) among the Essenes, namely the regularly conducted sacramental ceremony, one of the two longish halls, the one in which stood the benches and tables,

* *Die Christengemeinschaft,* 1957, July.

could only be the cenacle, the hall of the sacred evening meal. It was the actual sanctuary, the temple room of the Order's community.

Directly by the foundations of the complex of buildings, a cemetery was unearthed with twelve hundred well arranged graves that contained only male skeletons without any burial treasures. At some distance from this was another field of graves, less well maintained and not laid out in such strict order. Here, women, too, were buried together with inexpensive jewelry. Even today, therefore, the coexistence, side by side, of a strict monastic settlement and a small village becomes evident, a village inhabited by ministering brothers who could marry. (I refer here to the descriptions of Nazareth that I gave in the book, *The Childhood of Jesus*. There, utilizing disclosures that Rudolf Steiner made, I explained that Nazareth arose as a colony of the Essene Order. It was originally inhabited by such lay-brothers who were allowed to start families so that, in accordance with the Order's spiritual directives, they could establish an exemplary community.)

The picture we can form of the environment of the whole settlement is decidedly enriched because vestiges of eleven cisterns, four larger and seven smaller ones, were unearthed. Since the place itself was situated within the desert where water was nonexistent, the wells had to be fed by a canal. Here too, this cannot simply be viewed in a profane manner by saying: after all, where so many people lived together in narrow confines, water was needed for drinking and washing. Particularly here, water had above all a sacred significance. This becomes obvious because in a settlement that otherwise must be pictured as having been extremely plain, drums and bases of columns were discovered and, probably in the case of a larger cistern, even remains of a colonnade that strikingly contrasts with the primitive form of construction of the houses. A kind of baptismal sacrament existed among the Essenes which, as an integral part of their whole life, imbued the year's and day's course. The sacred washings that followed a precise ceremonial sequence were equally as important as the sacred meals. A kind of prophetic primary stage of the main Christian sacraments, baptism and communion, represented the most important support for the religious life of the Essenes. The colonnade in Qumran, remains of which have now been uncovered, may have transformed one of those cistern-locations into the actual baptismal site, a site that possessed the nature of a temple.

Above all, the discoveries of coins must have excited the excatavors working in Qumran. Certain dates can most readily be established through numismatics. Coins from quite different periods were found that could be dated exactly. In addition, oddly enough, four hundred silver coins (Tyrian *tetradrachma* from the first pre-Christian century) were uncovered in two pots buried at the main entrance of the settlement's complex.

Thus, it becomes quite obvious that one should resort to a viewpoint that perceives everything from the Essene Order's sacred esotericism rather than the perspective of profane superficiality. For it becomes clear from the descriptions of the Essene Order given by the writers of antiquity that currency was disdained in the setting of the Order. The Order's monastic rule was generally oriented towards protecting the souls from too close an association with earthly affairs, leading them instead to a spirituality that turned away from the natural world. Thus, money in particular had to be avoided at all costs. For, in it, the dark demonic power of 'Mammon' or Ahriman was seen to be active. An individual was not allowed to have any private possessions; above all, he could not carry money on his person. Money and weapons did not exist for an Essene. Of course, the Order as a whole could not totally avoid the handling of currency. When somebody entered as a novice, for instance, and relinquished his former personal possessions to the Order, or when the Order received donations, for example, from those who had been healed of sickness, then money temporarily existed within the confines of the cloister.

The baffling pots with their silver coins can thus be explained by refernce to the Order's customs as indicated here. Due to symbolic and ritual reasons, they were buried at the portal. The intention was to perform a kind of exorcism, a banning of the demon. All things exoteric, money being the most extreme of these, had to remain outside; spiritually it had to be excluded from the protective domain of the cloister.

I must admit that, personally, the most exciting aspect of the excavation results in Qumran is the report that in a lower level underneath the remains of the Essene buildings from the Roman era, foundation walls of a significantly older settlement from the iron age were unearthed that date back approximately to the eighth or seventh pre-Christian century (the age of Elijah). Even here, at this place, our glance is directed back to ancient times of Israelite history. This necessitates that we speak of a second methodological principle that is lacking in conventional views of history. It is a principle that is indispensable if we wish to penetrate to the essential secret of the location that now has so conspicuously moved to the centre of historical interest. We have earlier spoken of the first key aspect that must be taken into consideration, namely the esotericism which pervaded everything, down to all the details, at such an ancient centre of the Order. The second aspect is linked with the symbolic nature or — to put it more precisely — with the etheric character of the Palestinian landscapes.

As far as En Gedi, located south of Qumran, is concerned, the Old Testament itself gives indications that a sizeable settlement existed there in the distant past. In its very first chapter, the Song of Solomon (from the tenth pre-Christian century) mentions this site. It says of Sulamith, the beloved, whose beauty is being praised that she is like 'a cluster of henna blossoms in the vineyards of En Gedi.' Blossoms and fruits of unique paradisal beauty and taste must have been available there. Moreover, along with a number of other cities in the region that had just been apportioned to the twelve tribes which had migrated there, the Book of Joshua also refers to En Gedi (15:62). Now, it is of decisive importance that the Essene centre was not established in En Gedi itself, even though En Gedi's vicinity was not without significance for this establishment. It is clear that the Essenes moved their site out 'into the desert.' As is said later of John the Baptist and even Jesus of Nazareth (after the Baptism in the Jordan) — 'He went into the wilderness,' — thus could it also have been said of the Essene Order when it established its Palestinian centre that 'it went out into the wilderness.' This expressed the fact that, for the purpose of an organized communal pursuit of meditative discipline, one withdrew from all outward relationships with nature and humankind and instead sought 'lonely seclusion.'

En Gedi was not a 'wasteland.' It was the exact opposite — an oasis of quite special beauty, vitality and fertility in the midst of the desert. But it was not possible for a sizeable Essene monastery to exist in a desolate arid site because of the importance that water had for the rituals of baptism and washing. The brine of the Dead Sea was not 'water' in this sense. By settling in Qumran, where water had to be piped into the cisterns from springs, the Essenes had both: desert and water.

Nevertheless, it would be wrong to assume that Qumran was chosen merely because of such utilitarian reasons. Conscious symbolizing was at the basis of the choice of this location. Earthly and human prehistory of the scenery must have played a part in this. We are drawn back again today to this prehistory because of the older strata that have now been excavated in Qumran. The final act in the drama of eruptive, natural catastrophes that shaped the countenance of the earth here must have been the mythical 'destruction of Sodom and Gomorrah,' set by the Bible as a sort of world-conflagration in the time of Abraham (around 2000 BC). Forces of fire that erupted out of the underworld created grandiose symbolic sites of destruction and rigidity. These fiery forces did not explode like volcanoes, spewing out molten lava that subsequently solidified. Rather, they were of the gaseous combustible kind. The salt rocks of Sodom at the southwestern corner of the Dead Sea are but crystallized products of the rigidity of death which in addition brought about the brine of the Dead Sea. Perhaps the earth most rigidified into columns of salt where, earlier, a life of particular sultriness and opulence had held sway. It is of the greatest significance that the catastrophes of the age of Abraham — reverberations of the most momentous primal cataclysms — did not exclusively produce a region of death. Areas of petrification existed adjacent to those that had been spared.

The pictorial style of the Old Testament narrations gives the impression that the destruction was a judgment pronounced on a degenerate humanity, namely the inhabitants of Sodom and Gomorrah; that the deliverance signified preferential divine protection for the good, particularly Abraham and his people. In reality, a previously existing polar difference of that region's nature must have been at the basis of this duality. Among people, contrasting mentalities lead to a choice of diverging sceneries as their settlements. For this reason, spiritual and moral factors brought it about that, apart from locations of destruction, there were also areas that were preserved. The latter remained in existence like islands of life within the wilderness of death. Above all, there was the 'grove of Mamre' in the Hebron region, the domicile of Abraham and his people and, north of that, the idyllic grasslands around Bethlehem that were overshadowed by such a mighty Messianic promise.

We cannot picture the dissimilarity of the two types of scenery strongly enough. Levelling everything, the same breath of aridity, of a deprivation of life, spread out across Judea from early on. Yet, doubtless, both before and after the turning point of time, the people who lived there still perceived this duality with an instinctive certainty of feeling. They experienced it as if Hades and paradise met up with one another here; in the midst of the scenery of the Fall marked by the depths of hell, a merciful providence of destiny had preserved islands on which pure and blessed life forces of paradise had not yet been drawn into the cosmic descent.

When I guided a group of friends through Palestine in 1934, we undertook a two-day voyage along the shores of the Dead Sea. Sailing northward from Sodom along the western shore, we finally disembarked in En Gedi in order, through reading and conversation, to turn our minds back to the life of the Essenes. At that time, a shepherd with his donkey passed us and moved up the valley of En Gedi to the westward hills. When, replying to my question, he told me that this path led to Hebron, I realized that the former oasis of En Gedi owed its paradisal, beautiful life to an emanation of a vein of life from the island of safety around the grove of Mamre. Further north, between En Gedi and Qumran, several more such paths run down the valleys to the depths of the Dead Sea. The most important one originates from Bethlehem and leads past the cone-shaped hill which to this day is named Jebel el-Furadis, 'Mountain of Paradise,' by the Arabs.* It is the same hill on the levelled plateau of which Herod the Great erected a huge complex of gardens and palaces shortly before the turning point of time in order to compel the increasingly disappearing powers of earth's paradisal state into his service.[91]

The excavations in Qumran were not the first attempt to force this location to relinquish its secrets. It was commonly thought that the remains of walls that rose out of the ground there were those of a Roman fortification. But a little more than a hundred years ago, the French explorer, F. de Saulcy, engaged in initial excavations. He susequently believed he had discovered the site of ancient Gomorrah. In that case, next to Sodom, this location would be the second focus of the former catastrophic destruction. Even if this hypothesis is not directly accurate — but why should it not contain a grain of truth, as there could even be a linguistic connection between the words Gomorrah and Qumran — it still has value as a lively stimulus. In any case, when the Essenes established their Palestinian centre there, they chose a location where the secret of Judea emerged with greatest visibility: the proximity of extreme desert and an oasis of life, of hell and paradise. Even though living on the ground of death and the Fall, at their sacred wells and baptismal sites they became immersed in water which came from paradise and prophetically pointed to the awaited Messiah who would bring paradise back to humankind.

---

* Nowadays called Herodion (Editor).

References

1   From A.W. Hunziger, *Das Christentum im Weltanschauungskampf der Gegenwart* [Christianity in the Ideological Struggle of Today], quoted in Steiner, *Building Stones for an Understanding of the Mystery of Golgotha*, Lecture Five (April 14, 1917) p.111f.

2   Report by Heraclides, as quoted by Eustratius.

3   Aristotle, *Nicomachean Ethics*, III, 2.

4   Clement of Alexandria, *Stromateis* II, par. 60.

5   Handed down by Plutarch (biography of *Alexander the Great*, ch. 7) and in the writings of Gellius (XX, 5).

6   Steiner, *Occult History*, Lecture Six (Jan 1, 1911) p. 105f.

7   Plutarch, *About the Deterioration of the Oracles*, ch. 17.

8   Josephus, *Antiquities of the Jews* XI, 8, 4f; Pseudo-Callisthenes II, 24.

9   Gorion, Josef bin, *Der Born Judas* III, 210f.

10   *Genesis*, 'Gilgamesh — Nimrod — Abraham.'

11   Polybius XXVI, 10.

12   *Kings and Prophets*, p. 341f.

13   *Moses*, 'Thutmose III and the Battle of Megiddo.'

14   *Moses*, 'Expectation of a Messiah.' The master-builder Hiram and the prophet Elijah as 'sons of the widow': *Kings and Prophets*, p. 162f and p. 206.

15   Steiner, *The Gospel of Mark*, Lecture Two (Sep 16, 1912) p. 33f.

16   The dramatic fragment *Marius und Sulla* by Chr. D. Grabbe conveys a realistic view of the two main figures.

17   Theodor Birt, *Römische Charakterköpfe*.

18   Oskar Wertheimer, *Kleopatra*.

19   *Moses*, 'Osiris, Yahweh, Christ'; *Kings and Prophets*, p. 192f.

20   Steiner, *Building Stones*, Lecture Five (April 14, 1917) p. 115f.

21   *Genesis*, 'Gilgamesh — Nimrod — Abraham'; *Moses*, 'Rameses II and the infanticide.'

22   Steiner, *Building Stones*, Lecture One (March 27, 1917) p. 20ff.

23   *Kings and Prophets*, p. 349f.

24   The ten degrees of holiness that had to be passed in the spiritual exercises of the Pharisees' order: *Kings and Prophets*, p. 350.

25   *Kings and Prophets*, p. 257.

26   *Kings and Prophets*, p. 351.

27   *Kings and Prophets*, p. 67f.

28   *Kings and Prophets*: 'Solomon, Favourite of Destiny.'

29   D. F. Strauss, *Ausgewählte Briefe;* See Emil Bock, *Boten des Geistes*.

30   Josephus, *The Jewish War*, VI, 5, 4.

31   Steiner, *Building Stones*, Lecture One (March 27, 1917) p. 23f.

32 *The Jewish War,* II, 5, 4.

33 Philo, *De vita contemplativa,* par. 3.

34 *Naturgeschichte* V, 16f. Instead of Jericho, the text has Jerusalem, which must be an error.

35 *Moses,* 'Samson.'

36 Steiner, *The Gospel of Matthew,* Lecture Four (Sep 4, 1910) p. 84.

37 Steiner, *The Fifth Gospel,* Lecture Six (Dec 17, 1913) p. 126.

38 Steiner, *The Gospel of Matthew,* Lecture Six (Sep 6, 1910) p. 108f.

39 Philo, *De vita contemplativa,* par. 9 and *Quod omnis probus liber,* par. 12.

40 *De vita contemplativa,* par. 2.

41 *The Jewish War,* II, 8, 10.

42 *The Jewish War,* II, 8, 12.

43 *The Jewish War,* II, 8, 11.

44 *The Jewish War,* II, 8, 7.

45 Steiner, *Deeper Secrets of Human History in the light of the Gospel of St. Matthew,* Lecture Three (Nov 23, 1909) p. 56.

46 *The Jewish War,* II, 8, 6.

47 *De vita contemplativa,* par. 1.

48 *The Jewish War,* II, 8, 2.

49 *The Jewish War,* II, 8, 13.

50 Emmerich, *Das Leben der Maria.*

51 *The Jewish War,* II, 8, 4.

52 Josephus, *Antiquities of the Jews,* XVIII, 1, 5; Philo, *Quod omnis probus liber,* par. 12.

53 *The Jewish War,* II, 8, 5.

54 *The Jewish War,* II, 8, 5.

55 *De vita contemplativa,* par. 3.

56 *De vita contemplativa,* par. 8–11; see also 'Pentecost', Ch. 7.10.

57 *Babylon. Shabbath* 104b; *Sanhedrin* 67a.

58 Steiner, *The Gospel of Matthew,* lectures of Sep 4–6, 1910) pp.85f, 89, 109f.

59 *Kings and Prophets,* pp.187, 203.

60 Josephus, *Antiquities of the Jews,* XVIII, 5, 2.

61 Josephus, *The Jewish War,* VII, 6:1–4.

62 *Kings and Prophets,* p. 208f.

63 See p. 268 and p. 290

64 Steiner, *The Gospel of Mark,* (Sep 20, 1912) p. 113.

65 Lectures from the year 1905.

66 Lecture from the year 1905.

67 Steiner, *The Gospel of Mark,* Lecture 3 (Sep 17, 1912).

68 See p. 77

69 Steiner, *The Gospel of St Mark,* Lecture Two (Sep 16, 1912)

70 *Moses,* 'The "Son of the Fish".'

71 Steiner, *The Gospel of John and Its Relation to the Other Gospels,* Lecture 11 (July 4, 1909).

72   *Genesis,* 'Joseph and his Brothers.'

73   *Moses,* 'Moses' basket of bulrushes' and 'The "Son of the Fish".'

74   Steiner, *Menschengeschichte im Lichte der Geistesforschung,* (March 9, 1911).

75   *Kings and Prophets,* 'Jerusalem and its History.'

76   *Kings and Prophets,* p. 96.

77   *Kings and Prophets,* p. 98.

78   Josephus, *The Jewish War,* V, 4, 2.

79   Paulus Geyer, *Itinera Hierosolymitana,* p. 175. *Kings and Prophets,* p. 101.

80   *Kings and Prophets,* p. 92.

81   *The Jewish War,* V, 4, 2.

82   Philo, *De vita contemplativa,* par. 9.

83   Merezhkovky, *Tod und Auferstehung.*

84   For instance, *Das esoterische Christentum und die geistige führung der Menschheit,* (Jan 9, 1912).

85   See footnote p. 226

86   *De vita contemplativa,* par. 8–11.

87   Dalman, *Orte und Wege Jesu.*

88   Renan, *The Life of Jesus.*

89   Morton, *In the Steps of the Master,* pp.205f.

90   *Genesis,* 'Adam — Paradise — The Fall.'

91   Steiner, *The Gospel of Mark,* Lecture 2 (Sep 16, 1912).

92   *Von der Auferstehung des Herrn,* ed. by R. Benz, p. 362.

93   Hegesippus, *Memoirs,* quoted by Eusebius in *The History of the Church.*

94   *De viris illustribus* II.

95   'Die Lehren des Auferstanden' (Lecture of April 13, 1922) in *Das Sonnenmysterium und das Mysterium von Tod und Auferstehung* (GA 211).

96   See report on the World Church Conference of August 1937 in Edinburgh, *The Christian Community,* 1937, 7.

97   Papias, Bishop of Hierapolis in Phrygia; quoted by Eusebius in *The History*

98   *Legenda Aurea* and *Acts of John.*

99   Papias in Eusebius III, 39.

100   Bock and R. Goebel, *Die Katakomben, Bilder aus der Welt des frühen Christentums.*

101   Steiner, *Christianity as Mystical Fact,* 'The Lazarus Miracle.'

102   *Kings and Prophets,* p. 205f.

103   *Kings and Prophets,* p. 242.

104   *Kings and Prophets,* p. 264.

105   Augustine, *Tractatus in Johannem* 36: Ex illo pectore in secreto bibebat.

106   Clement of Alexandria, quoted by Eusebius II, 1:4.

107   *Kings and Prophets,* p. 277, 326, 338.

108   *Genesis,* 'Cain — Seth — Enoch.' and 'Noah — Job.'

109   *The Childhood of Jesus,* 'Views of Bethlehem.'

Bibliography

Birt, Theodor, *Römische Charakterköpfe,* Quelle und Meyer, Leipzig 1913.

Bock, Emil, *Boten des Geistes,* Urachhaus, Stuttgart 1987.

—, *Genesis,* Floris Books Edinburgh 1978.

—, *Kings and Prophets,* Floris Books, Edinburgh 1989.

—, *Moses,* Floris Books, Edinburgh 1986.

—, and R. Goebel, *The Catacombs,* Christian Community, London 1962.

Dalman, Gustaf, *Orte und Wege Jesu,* Bertelsmann, Gutersloh 1919.

Edwards, Ormond, *The Time of Christ. A Chronology of the Incarnation,* Floris, Edinburgh 1986.

Gorion, Josef bin, *Der Born Judas,* Insel, Leipzig 1916–20

Merezhkovsky, Dmitri, *Tod und Auferstehung,* Huber, Frauenfeld 1935.

Morton, H.V. *In the Steps of the Master,* London 1934.

Renan, Ernest, *The Life of Jesus,* Trubner, London 1864.

Steiner, Rudolf, *Building Stones for an Understanding of the Mystery of Golgotha* Vol. 175 of the Complete Works (GA). Steiner Press, London 1972.

—, *Christianity as Mystical Fact* (GA 8). Anthroposophic Press, New York 1997.

—, *Deeper Secrets of Human History in the light of the Gospel of St Matthew* (GA 117). Steiner Press, London 1985.

—, *Das esoterische Christentum und die geistige führung der Menschheit,* (GA 130). Steiner Verlag, Dornach 1995.

—, *The Fifth Gospel* (GA 148). Steiner Press, London 1968.

—, *The Gospel of John and Its Relation to the Other Gospels* (GA 112). Anthroposophic Press, New York 1982.

—, *The Gospel of Mark* (GA 139). Steiner Press, London 1977.

—, *The Gospel of Matthew* (GA 123). Steiner Press, London 1965.

—, *Menschengeschichte im Lichte der Geistesforschung* (GA 61). Steiner Verlag, Dornach 1983.

—, *Occult History* (GA 126). Steiner Press, London 1982.

—, *Das Sonnenmysterium und das Mysterium von Tod und Auferstehung* (GA 211). Steiner Verlag, Dornach 1986.

Wertheimer, Oskar, *Kleopatra,* Amalthea, Zurich 1930.

Index